Slavery and the Supreme Court,
1825–1861

Slavery and the Supreme Court, 1825–1861

Earl M. Maltz

Foreword by Mark A. Graber

University Press of Kansas

© 2009 by the
University Press of
Kansas

All rights reserved

Published by the
University Press of
Kansas (Lawrence,
Kansas 66045),
which was organized
by the Kansas Board
of Regents and is
operated and funded
by Emporia State
University, Fort Hays
State University,
Kansas State
University, Pittsburg
State University, the
University of Kansas,
and Wichita State
University

Library of Congress Cataloging-in-Publication Data

Maltz, Earl M., 1950–
  Slavery and the Supreme Court, 1825–1861 / Earl M. Maltz ;
foreword by Mark A. Graber.
     p. cm.
  Includes bibliographical references and index.
  ISBN 978-0-7006-1666-4 (cloth : alk. paper)
  1. Slavery—Law and legislation—United States—History—
19th century. 2. United States. Supreme Court—History—
19th century. I. Title.
  KF4545.S5.M354 2009
  342.7308'7—dc22
                              2009024287

British Library Cataloguing-in-Publication Data is available.

Printed in the United States of America

10 9 8 7 6 5 4 3 2 1

For Peggy, David, Elizabeth, and Jonathan,
who put up with the nutty professor

Contents

Foreword
The Banality of Constitutional Evil
by Mark A. Graber

Adolf Eichmann's psychiatric evaluations did not yield the expected result. Doctors anticipated discovering various disorders. Instead, they confronted an apparently mentally healthy human being. Nothing proved notable about Eichmann's relationships with family members and neighbors. On no psychological dimension did he exhibit psychotic or sociopathic tendencies. Eichmann did not even demonstrate irrational feelings toward the persons he shipped to concentration camps. As Hannah Arendt detailed, he had no "insane hatred of Jews," no "fanatical anti-Semitism," and no "indoctrination of any kind." Six psychiatrists concluded Eichmann was normal or, as one declared, "more normal . . . than I am after having examined him." This finding disturbed his interlocutors, who had commonplace medical and legal assumptions about human evil. No one involved with the Eichmann trial was comfortable acknowledging "that an average, 'normal' person, neither feeble-minded nor indoctrinated, nor cynical, could be perfectly incapable of telling right from wrong."[1]

Readers of Earl Maltz's *Slavery and the Supreme Court, 1825–1861,* are likely to experience a similar disquiet. Popular understandings and much scholarship suggests that the justices who decided such cases as *Prigg v. Pennsylvania*[2] and *Dred Scott v. Sandford*[3] must have been vicious racists lacking in common decency, moral sense, and legal rectitude. The Taney Court, conventional wisdom suggests, was staffed largely by southern extremists and northern doughfaces who took every legal and extralegal opportunity to solidify the chains that bound enslaved Africans. Normal justices, standard commentaries imply, would no more sanction the south's "peculiar institution" than mentally competent civil servants would participate in the final solution. Far different judicial characters than this commonplace understanding suggests walk the pages that follow this foreword. Taney Court justices provided legal protections for human bondage, but for the most part they refrained from paeans to slavery or racial epithets. Rarely if ever did commitments to human bondage trump commitments to the rule of law. When presented with dramatic challenges to human freedom, the justices often responded with technical analyses concerning choice of law, federal jurisdiction, and federalism. Antebellum justices, more often than not, were more interested in avoiding constitutional questions about slavery than in having the last say on authoritative rules. They usually sanctioned human bondage, but they did so as normal judges and human beings.

Slavery and the Supreme Court provides a far more nuanced understanding about the extent to which the antebellum federal judiciary was proslavery. Professor Maltz cheerfully agrees that the justices were proslavery in the sense that few were committed to an antislavery interpretation of constitutional ambiguities. Taney Court decisions were not guided by the Lincolnian understanding that the framers had placed human bondage on a "course of ultimate extinction."[4] Justices Joseph Story, John McLean, and perhaps, Benjamin Curtis were the only antebellum Supreme Court justices who endorsed the principle of *Somersett's Case,* that the "state of slavery is of such a nature, that it is incapable of being introduced on any reasons, moral or political, but only by positive law."[5] Other justices either explicitly rejected that claim or did not mention the matter. Justice Robert Grier described Lord Mansfield's opinion as containing "rhetorical flourishes rather than legal dogmas."[6] Southern justices seemed utterly oblivious to the *Somersett* precedent. Still, with the controversial exception of Justice Daniel's concurring opinion in *Dred Scott,* the Taney Court was not proslavery in a Calhounian sense. Decisions upholding slaveholding rights did not proclaim slavery to be a positive good that ought to be maintained and expanded. What is notable about the opinions that follow is the judicial tendency not to use words of any affect when discussing human bondage. Slavery in the judicial eye seems a fact of life, a sectional irritant, but not something a justice should regard as either an evil practice to be discarded as soon as constitutionally possible or a practice whose extension should be legally encouraged. Rarely did the merits of slavery as a political or economic practice provide most Taney Court justices with a rule for decision or interpretation.

This surprising lack of concern with slavery as a public policy highlights some complexities about judicial behavior. Although Maltz is not a political scientist, his work constructs a marvelous test of that discipline's attitudinal, strategic, and legal models.[7] *Slavery and the Supreme Court* offers readers detailed accounts of each justice's beliefs about the morality of slavery and the judicial role in constitutional cases. The text also provides sufficient political background on each case so that the costs and benefits of different judicial decisions can be reasonably assessed. The result confirms the increasing consensus that justices act on a variety of motives, that persons on the Supreme Court are not single-minded pursuers of any particular good.[8] Taney Court justices were concerned with the political environment; they sought to make good policy, but they did so within the parameters constructed by legal texts and legal precedents. Even *Dred Scott,* often Exhibit A for claims that justices behave no differently than other political actors, illustrates the numerous factors that must be considered when explaining judicial behavior. The judicial votes in that case on whether slavery could be banned in American territories reflect underlying attitudes toward slavery fairly closely, although one may wonder why on an attitudinal account Justices John Campbell and John Catron bothered writing concurring opinions. The Taney Court opinions on whether slaves and their descendants could be American citizens cannot be classified as easily. As Maltz details, before reaching the merits of that issue, the justices had to consider whether John Sanford had waived the question of black citizenship in his pleadings before the federal district court. On that procedural matter, two bisectional coalitions formed. Taney (Maryland), Wayne (Georgia), Curtis (Massachusetts), and Daniel (Virginia) believed that the citizenship issue was properly before the Supreme Court. Catron (Tennessee), Campbell (Alabama), Grier (Pennsylvania), McLean (Ohio), and probably Nelson (New York) disagreed. This division does not appear to correspond with any known attitudes toward persons of color or any strategic logic. Whether the justices who decided *Dred Scott* believed the citizenship issue was properly before them seems better explained by beliefs about federal jurisdiction than by hostility to persons of color.

Remarkably from some political science perspectives, the sectional judicial division on the slavery issue in *Dred Scott* was the exception rather than the rule. Many judicial decisions on slavery were unanimous or were decided with only one dissenting vote. Judicial divisions in other cases were grounded in matters seemingly far removed from concerns about the constitutional status of human bondage. Consider *Prigg v. Pennsylvania.* As Maltz details, the primary issue that divided the justices in that case was whether federal power over fugitive slaves was exclusive or whether both state and federal governments could make rules governing the rendition process. Sectionalism, at most, only weakly explained the judicial lineup. Justices Story and Wayne were the leading proponents of federal exclusivity. Justice Smith Thompson of New York joined other southern justices who championed concurrent power. These divisions were rooted in the ongoing controversy over whether federal power over interstate commerce was exclusive.[9] Story and Wayne defended federal exclusivity in both commerce clause and fugitive slave cases. The justices who believed states had power to regulate interstate commerce, as long as state laws were not inconsistent with federal policy, applied the same principles when determining state power over fugitive slaves. Attitudes toward slavery may to some degree explain judicial votes on commerce clause issues. Nevertheless, a fair case can be made, particularly with respect to Justice Wayne and Justice Thompson, that their understanding of state power over the rendition of fugitive slaves was to a large degree determined by legal commitments they had made in cases concerning state power to regulate interstate commerce. Judicial votes in such commerce clause decisions as *Miln v. Mayor of New York* and *The Passenger Cases* may have been motivated by policy concerns. Still, that justices in fugitive slave cases were motivated more by concerns with state power over interstate commerce than by concerns about human freedom suggests both that justices may decide policy matters differently than other political actors and that justices bore a distinctive responsibility for constitutional evil in antebellum America.

That justices confronting fugitive slave cases may have been thinking more about the commerce clause than human freedom highlights the more important lesson *Slavery and the Supreme Court* teaches about the banality of constitutional evil. The antebellum judiciary Maltz depicts was not staffed by jurists eager to push proslavery policies to the limits of constitutional law and beyond. Rather, the immorality of the judicial system was rooted in its apparent amorality. The justices in *Prigg* seemed more committed to notions of federal power than human freedom. The rights of African Americans in *Dred Scott* were hostage to the rules of federal civil procedure. Which slaves were freed in *The Antelope* depended more on complex fact-findings and luck than on the universal condemnation of the international slave trade. Choice-of-law doctrine determined the status of slaves voluntarily taken to free states. Repeatedly, in short, Maltz's justices bear a greater resemblance to Arendt's Eichmann than Joseph Goebbels. Faced with the greatest injustice of their generation, their concerns are elsewhere, with the normal tools of constitutional law.

Two other, quite different, studies of American race law further illustrate the American judicial tendency to act as "good Germans." The first is Helen Tunnicliff Catterall's five-volume *Judicial Cases concerning American Slavery and the Negro*.[10] Catterall in that work presented excerpts from every legal case—constitutional, statutory, or common law—she could find that raised questions about the legal status of slavery or former slaves. In sharp contrast to Supreme Court justices, state court justices were far more inclined to use racist invective and celebrate the virtues of slavery. Nevertheless, the legal system presented in those volumes does not seem unduly biased in the sense that existing laws are construed in favor of slavery whenever interpretively plausible. Rather, justices for the most part seemed sincerely committed to enforcing the law of slavery as written and previously decided. When a reasonable observer might think a southern slave had a case for freedom under existing law, southern justices had some tendency to support the lawsuit. Faithful slaves defeated rapacious heirs when passages in their former master's will suggested an intention to manumit. Some justices worried whether freed slaves would be a burden to society, but most decided such cases on beliefs about probate law.

The second study, Julie Novkov's *Racial Union: Law, Intimacy, and the White State in Alabama, 1865–1954,*[11] provides a far more sophisticated conception of legal amorality in a racist regime. Her study of miscegenation cases in Alabama observed that, particularly when southern racial practices were not under outside pressures, the Supreme Court of Alabama was inclined to focus more on legal technicalities than substantive moral judgments when determining whether convictions for an interracial marriage would be sustained. Many appeals turned on whether the prosecution had presented hearsay evidence. In several instances, convictions were surprisingly overturned when appellate courts determined that the prosecutor had attempted to unduly inflame racial passions. These decisions, one should emphasize, did not reflect nascent views of racial equality that would later blossom during the Warren Court. Rather, what both Novkov and Maltz present are legal systems that, when not subject to undue political pressures, tended to try to resolve the controversies that arise under what we now regard as evil laws by rules external to the racist practices. Beliefs about the morality of slavery or Jim Crow, during normal times and for normal justices, neither warranted interpreting the underlying racist laws and precedents broadly or narrowly. Other, nonracial concerns provided the appropriate grounds for decision.

The banality of American constitutional evil differs from the moral-formal problem identified by Robert M. Cover in his seminal study, *Justice Accused: Antislavery and the Judicial Process.*[12] Cover wrote about northern justices who experienced conflicts between their moral duty to free slaves and their legal duty to decide cases according to legal principles. With important exceptions, the Supreme Court justices Maltz discusses do not exhibit that tension. We do not see Justices Catron or Grier agonizing over potential conflicts between their commitment to follow the law and their commitment to human flourishing. The Taney Court contained no Felix Frankfurter who repeatedly reminded readers that his judicial duty required him to sustain laws he found personally abhorrent.[13] The justices often sought sectional compromises because they disdained the persons they perceived as hotheads on both sides of the issue. Mentally healthy people, most federal justices in antebellum American thought, did not believe slavery worth fighting over.

Oliver Wendell Holmes may have been the legitimate heir to the Taney

Court tradition in most slavery cases. "To a remarkable degree," Yosal Rogat notes in his penetrating analysis of that justice's conception of the judicial role, "Holmes simply did not care."[14] Holmes cared only about solving legal problems, not about the human beings affected by those solutions. With the important exception of *Dred Scott,* Taney Court justices similarly did not see the human beings affected by the litigation before the bench. A certain kind of legal formalism often reigned because questions of slavery were treated as matters appropriately resolved by legal technicalities and political maneuvers, rather than as questions about human freedom under constitutional and moral law.

The routine cases that come before justices during the normal functioning of an evil regime facilitate this indifference. Justices (or bureaucrats) are rarely confronted directly with the great moral issues of the day. They do not decide whether Jews are to be slaughtered, whether African Americans are to be enslaved, or whether people are permitted to marry the loved ones of their choice. Instead, as Benjamin Cardozo pointed out, judgment takes place in the "interstices" of the law.[15] Justices (and bureaucrats) are asked whether existing rules mandate a particular person to be slaughtered, enslaved, or permitted to marry. As Maltz details at several points, the slavery controversies the justices decided typically existed at the peripheries of that practice. The precise status of the Africans who seized control of their slave ship may have raised fascinating questions worthy of an Academy Award–winning movie. Nevertheless, incidents of that sort were sufficiently rare as to give such decisions little practical precedential value. A reasonable case can be made that almost every other slavery case heard by the Supreme Court could have been decided differently without causing any noticeable increase or decrease in the number of enslaved persons. Even *Dred Scott,* at least for the immediate future, largely concerned "an imaginary negro in an impossible place,"[16] given that slaveowners were not eager to bring their human chattel into territories that Congress had not yet made open to human bondage. Slavery cases may have been decided for reasons of federalism or civil procedure, this analysis suggests, only because no good practical reason existed for deciding the issue on more fundamental constitutional or moral norms, unless the justices wanted to declare some principle far broader than necessary to resolve the case before them.

Many stories are packed into the following pages. Earl Maltz has penned an exceptionally accessible account of Supreme Court decisions on slavery, the justices who made those decisions, and the political background of those decisions. *Slavery and the Supreme Court* will be the first place citizens and scholars turn to for basic information on how the federal judiciary responded to the most pressing moral and constitutional concerns of antebellum Americans. Readers should not, however, ignore what may be the most important contemporary contribution of this book: legal systems, the American experience with slavery and racism suggests, contribute to human suffering more by routinizing evil practices than by affirming those practices as positive goods.

Preface

The Supreme Court's treatment of the issue of slavery has been scrutinized by many outstanding legal historians. The literature on *Dred Scott v. Sandford*[1] is particularly voluminous,[2] but *The Antelope*,[3] *United States v. The Amistad*,[4] and *Ableman v. Booth*[5] have all been the subjects of excellent monographs.[6] While still awaiting a book-length treatment, *Prigg v. Pennsylvania*[7] has also drawn extensive scholarly comment, and other important slavery cases have been studied in a variety of different contexts as well.[8] This book, however, is the first to essay a comprehensive study of all of the major cases in a single dedicated monograph.

In writing this book, I had three objectives. One major objective is to provide the reader with an understanding of the background of each of the important slavery-related cases that came before the Court and the nature of the forces that shaped the Court's disposition of each of those cases. While specialists in the field will be familiar with much if not all of this background information, this book is the first modern effort to provide detailed information on all of the important cases in a single volume.

The description of each case almost inevitably begins with an analysis of political context, which varied greatly depending on the precise nature of the issues presented to the Court. For example, the decisions in cases such as *The Antelope* and *The Amistad*, which dealt with the international slave trade, were less significant to the relationship between Northern and Southern states than *Dred Scott*, which focused on the explosive question of slavery in the territories, or *Prigg* and its progeny, which grappled with issues related to fugitive slaves. In the latter cases, the justices were clearly cognizant of the potential impact of their decisions on the sectional dynamic, and they often shaped their analysis accordingly. But at the same time, even in *Dred Scott* and the fugitive slave cases, it would be a mistake to characterize judicial decision making as a simple byproduct of the justices' personal opinions about the sectional conflict; as commentators such as Charles Warren and Robert G. McCloskey have suggested, other forces were at work in these cases as well.[9]

First, the justices of the pre–Civil War era did not see themselves as free to implement their own simple political judgments about issues related to slavery. Instead, all of the justices shared a commitment to the idea that (at least in theory) the issues before the Court should be resolved by reference to a complex set of distinctively legal, "neutral" principles.[10] The influence of these principles was clearly evident in *Dred Scott,* where a dispute over a technical issue of pleading both had a profound impact on the evolution of the Court's treatment of the case and ultimately determined the treatment of the citizenship issue by a number of the justices. Similarly, the import of the doctrine of *stare decisis* was apparent in the opinions of the justices, which were replete with references to cases that on their face had little if anything to do with the dispute over slavery per se.

In a number of cases, the idea of *stare decisis* interacted powerfully with judicial concerns about the structure of American federalism. In resolving many important questions related to slavery, the Court was called upon to explore the limits of the powers of Congress; to decide whether those powers were exclusive or could instead be exercised concurrently by the state governments; and to define the circumstances in which the federal courts were required to defer to the legal judgments of their state counterparts. A number of the relevant opinions suggest that many of the justices were acutely aware of the importance of such concerns and believed that the same principles of federalism that governed other issues should be applied in cases involving slavery as well.

Of course, one would have to be extremely naive to believe that the Court's decisions in the slavery cases were determined wholly or even primarily by the application of distinctively legal principles or considerations of federalism uninfluenced by the special political context of the slavery cases. Nonetheless, such principles clearly had an impact on the Court's resolution of at least some of these cases. Moreover, even in cases where an outside observer might view decisions as reflecting ordinary political judgments, justices on all sides of the controversy no doubt *believed* that their views were at least consistent with distinctively legal principles and preexisting concepts of federalism, and structured their opinions accordingly.

A final complicating factor is the reality that the Court's decisions were not the reflection of a single, unified worldview but rather were derived from a combination of the views of seven to nine justices who often differed sharply on the proper approach to controversial issues. To be sure, all of the justices shared certain basic premises—most notably, that each state was free to make its own decision on the purely domestic aspects of slavery. But on other issues, the dynamic of the decision-making process was more complicated—a point that was clearly evident in both *Prigg* and *Dred Scott,* which are generally seen as the two most important slavery cases decided by the Court. In *Prigg,* the justices produced six separate opinions suggesting six different views on the issues presented to the Court, while in *Dred Scott* each of the nine justices issued opinions, once again reflecting at least six distinctly different viewpoints. Thus, to understand the mechanism by which the "doctrine of the Court" was constructed, one must focus both on the process by which the diverse forces interacted to create the views of the individual justices and also on how the views of the individual justices combined to generate the positions attributed to the Court as an institutional entity.

In addition to giving detailed accounts of the slavery cases individually, this book is also designed to provide insights into the trajectory of the Court's slavery-related jurisprudence more generally. On this point, I take sharp issue with commentators who espouse the neoabolitionist perspective on the Court's performance. Scholars who take this view, including luminaries such as Don E. Fehrenbacher and Paul Finkelman, argue that the representatives of the "slave power" used their control of the federal government to stack the Court with Southerners and their doughface Northern allies. As a result, these commentators contend that, particularly during the Taney era, the justices consistently and unfairly elevated the interests of slaveowners over the rights of those who were held in bondage.[11]

The accuracy of such characterizations depends in large measure on the standard against which the decisions are to be evaluated. One might, for example, take the view embodied in the radical antislavery jurisprudential theories of men such as Salmon P. Chase of Ohio and William H. Seward of New York, who argued that, because slavery was such a great evil, the Court should have taken every opportunity to attack the institution as vigorously as possible. Measured against this standard, almost all of the Court's major slavery decisions could indeed be properly described as proslavery.

This perspective, however, vastly oversimplifies the complexities of the issues facing the Court in the slavery cases. As a matter of political and constitutional morality, radical antislavery theory ignored the fact that the Southern states had joined the Union on the implicit understanding that they would be equal partners with their Northern counterparts, and that Northerners would not work to undermine the basic institutions of Southern society. However distasteful one might find slavery in the abstract, these understandings, which were fundamental to the formation of the constitutional compact, gave rise to legitimate claims of right that the Court was obligated to honor. This view underlay the analysis of more moderate Northerners such as Justices Joseph Story and Benjamin Robbins Curtis of Massachusetts, both of whom sought to craft a constitutional jurisprudence that would provide the framework for a workable accommodation between North and South.[12]

Viewed from this perspective, the orientation of the Court's decisions changed substantially over time. The 1857 decision in *Dred Scott* is plausibly characterized as epitomizing proslavery constitutional analysis. However, the series of cases decided between 1840 and 1842 reflect a quite different perspective.

Prigg v. Pennsylvania, the seminal decision describing the import of the Fugitive Slave Clause, is typically the centerpiece of efforts to characterize the Court of the early 1840s as a strongly proslavery institution. But even if considered in isolation, *Prigg* was far less tilted in favor of Southern interests than many commentators claim. Contrary to the views of neoabolitionists, the decision did not deprive free blacks in the North of protection against kidnapping by Southern slavehunters. Moreover, the critics of *Prigg* generally understate the *Prigg* Court's recognition of the significance of the concessions made by Southerners to the antislavery position on fugitive slaves—concessions that ultimately played an important role in undermining the ability of slaveowners to recapture slaves who escaped northward. Thus, even if considered in isolation, *Prigg* does not provide strong support for the neoabolitionist thesis.

But in any event, the contemporaneous decisions in *The Amistad* and *Groves v. Slaughter* belie any effort to characterize the Court of the early 1840s as being committed to aggressively advancing the slave state agenda. In *The Amistad,* the Court delivered an unalloyed victory to the antislavery forces in a case which had divided the nation along sectional lines, and in *Groves* a large majority of the justices strove mightily to resolve a potentially explosive, slavery-related issue without unnecessarily inflaming the partisans on either side of the North-South conflict. Particularly when considered together with *Prigg, Groves* paints the picture of a Court dominated by justices who were concerned less with outright pursuit of sectional advantage than with the preservation of harmony between the free states and the slave states—a concern that cut across the political spectrum during the Jacksonian era.

However, beginning with the dispute over the annexation of Texas, the stability of the bisectional coalitions that comprised the dominant Whig and Democratic parties was shaken by a series of disputes over the status of slavery in the territories and the rendition of alleged fugitive slaves. For a brief period, the Compromise of 1850 seemed to have restored sectional peace. But in 1854, fueled by the passage of the Kansas-Nebraska Act and the furor over the rendition of Anthony Burns, sectional tensions boiled over, shattering the Whig Party and leading to the rise of the overtly anti-Southern Republican Party in the North.

The increasing acrimony in sectional relations was reflected in the tenor of the arguments that were made to the Court in the late 1840s and early 1850s, particularly in the presentations of antislavery advocates in *Jones v. Van Zandt*[13] and *Strader v. Graham*.[14] Nonetheless, as late as May 1856, most of the justices—both Northern and Southern—seemed determined to avoid any unnecessary intervention in the sectional crisis. After *Dred Scott* was initially argued in January of that year, a majority of the justices at first decided to resolve the case without addressing the explosive issue of slavery in the territories. The justices evinced much the same attitude toward *Ableman* in early 1856. Confronted with decisions from the Wisconsin Supreme Court that, in addition to attacking the Fugitive Slave Act of 1850, also challenged the established authority of the United States Supreme Court itself, the Court initially stayed its hand, giving the Wisconsin courts an opportunity to reconsider its position and perhaps defuse the situation.

However, by early 1857, the attitude of the Southern justices and their allies had changed in the wake of the strong showing of the Republican Party in the elections of 1856. After *Dred Scott* was reargued, they united around a proposal to use the case as a vehicle to enshrine proslavery orthodoxy in the fabric of constitutional law. Similarly, when the Wisconsin court reiterated its defiant stance in 1857, the justices had little choice but to aggressively assert their authority. In 1859, against the background of the continued deterioration in sectional relations, the *Ableman* Court issued an opinion that not only strongly affirmed the right of federal officials to perform their duties free from state interference but also vindicated the constitutionality of the Fugitive Slave Act of 1850. Thus, in both cases, the Court allied itself firmly with the proslavery political forces.

My final objective was to invite the reader to see the slavery decisions as a test of the Court's ability to decisively influence the resolution of political conflicts that have sharply divided the nation. *Dred Scott* was clearly intended to finally resolve the dispute over slavery in the territories, while *Prigg* was designed with an eye to at least dampen the controversy over fugitive slaves. The success or failure of the Court's efforts in this regard can teach us important lessons about what we can and cannot expect the Court to accomplish when confronted with other controversial political issues.

I am indebted to a number of people for their aid in the production of this book. The library staff at Rutgers was unfailingly efficient in helping me locate sources, and Debbie Carr provided her usual superb secretarial assistance. During her time at Rutgers, Beth Hillman had the misfortune to have an office next to mine and so was constantly subjected to interruptions whenever I needed a perceptive colleague to critique bizarre and half-formed ideas about the evolution of the Supreme Court's slavery jurisprudence.

The contributions of two people deserve special mention. Mark Graber spent an inordinate amount of time reviewing different iterations of the manuscript and patiently suggesting improvements to a sometimes obtuse author. And for twenty years, Fred Woodward at the University Press of Kansas has been a model editor for a less than model scholar. Without their invaluable guidance and support, this project would never have come to fruition.

The support that I receive from my family is of an entirely different character, but no less indispensable. Neither my wife nor my children provided much input about the development of the law of slavery. Indeed, I think that sometimes my wife wishes that I would stop fooling around with old books and get a real job. But without her and the children, I would be truly lost.

Part One

*The Jurisprudence
of the Marshall Court*

CHAPTER 1

Prelude to Conflict

The Marshall Court and *The Antelope*

In the thirty years following the ratification of the Constitution, slavery was not the central issue in national politics. To be sure, between 1796 and 1819, Congress periodically considered and intensely debated measures dealing with matters such as fugitive slaves, the international slave trade, and the future of slavery in the areas under the direct control of the federal government, including the territory acquired through the Louisiana Purchase.[1] Moreover, the two major political parties—the Federalists and the Jeffersonian Democratic-Republicans—were divided in substantial measure along sectional lines, with the Federalists being strongest in New England, while the Jeffersonians dominated the Southern states. But congressional and presidential elections were fought and either won or lost on issues that were not directly related to slavery. Indeed, the voting patterns on these measures often crossed both sectional and party lines, with conservative Northern Federalists at times aligning themselves with Southern Jeffersonians.[2]

The decisions of the Supreme Court during the chief justiceship of John Marshall reflected a similar reality. During this period, the Court routinely dealt with a variety of issues regarding the status of putative slaves. However, none of these slavery-related cases became important factors in the sectional conflict. Moreover, only the 1825 decision in *The Antelope*[3] was of lasting doctrinal significance.

In *The Antelope,* the Court was forced to consider the status of the international slave trade under both American and international law. Even as early as the late eighteenth century, many of those who supported slavery or tolerated it only as a necessary evil had often condemned the practice of transporting hitherto free Africans to the United States to be sold into bondage. Indeed, in an early draft of the Declaration of Independence, Thomas Jefferson excoriated King George for "wag[ing] a cruel war against human nature itself, violating its most sacred right of life and liberty in the persons of a distant people who have never offended him, captivating and carrying them into slavery in another hemisphere, or to incur miserable death in their transportation thither." However, in the face of opposition from the states of the Deep South, this language was dropped from the final version of the Declaration.[4]

At the Constitutional Convention itself, the dispute over the international slave trade led to the adoption of Article I, Section 9, paragraph 1, which prohibits congressional interference with that trade until the year 1808. The legislative history of this clause is relatively simple and straightforward. The original report of the Committee on Detail contained a provision forbidding federal regulation of the slave trade, as well as a requirement that navigation acts be adopted only with a two-thirds majority. On August 22, a number of delegates, led by George Mason of Virginia, launched a fierce attack on the Slave Trade Clause, while Charles C. Pinckney and John Rutledge of South Carolina declared that the prohibition was a sine qua non for the participation of the Deep South states in the Union. On this point, Pinckney and Rutledge were supported by Roger Sherman and Oliver Ellsworth of Connecticut. Gouverneur Morris of Pennsylvania suggested that the slave trade issue could be dealt with as part of a compromise package that included other commerce-related measures.

The issue was then recommitted to a committee, and a bargain was struck. The Deep South states—which had opposed federal power to adopt navigation acts—would agree to allow the passage of navigation acts by a simple majority, and in return Massachusetts and New Hampshire would support a temporary ban on federal prohibition of the slave trade. The agreement was consummated on August 25. Over the objections of Virginia, New Jersey, Pennsylvania, and Delaware, the convention adopted the current provision on the slave trade, which protected the right of states to allow the importation of slaves until 1808.[5]

Immediately after the constitutional bar expired, Congress acted to prohibit the slave trade. The terms of the statutory prohibition were strengthened in 1819 by the so-called Act in Addition. This statute not only made participation in the slave trade a capital offense but also provided that Africans found on ships illegally engaged in the slave trade would be returned to Africa.[6]

In taking these actions, the federal government allied itself with a growing number of European nations that had committed themselves against the trade in captured Africans. The British outlawed the trade in 1807, labeling it "contrary to the principles of justice and humanity," and in *The Amedie*, an English court declared that it would consider the trade prima facie illegal, even when carried on by nationals of other countries who came before the court. Similarly, at the conferences of Vienna in 1815, France pledged to use "all the means at her disposal" against the international slave trade, and two years later Spain agreed to outlaw the trade as well. But Portugal refused to immediately cease participation in the slave trade, and in *The Louis*, decided in 1817, the English High Court of Admiralty rejected the claim that such participation violated the law of nations.[7]

Moreover, in the United States itself, the importation of substantial numbers of slaves from Africa continued even after the adoption of the federal statutes. Smuggling human cargo was highly profitable, and enforcement of the legal sanctions was at times lax. The smugglers often used vessels that sailed under the flags of nations that continued to allow the slave trade. Disputes arising from the seizures of such vessels at times found their way to the federal courts.

The 1821 decision in *La Jeune Eugenie* arose from just such a dispute. The schooner that was the subject of that case had been built in the United States, but only two years later it had been placed under the jurisdiction of the French government. Subsequently, the ship was seized off the coast of Africa by the *Alligator,* an American naval vessel under the command of Lieutenant Stockton, on suspicion of being engaged in the slave trade. *La Jeune Eugenie* was then towed to Boston, where Stockton filed a claim against the ship in federal circuit court. Stockton's claim was opposed by the French consul, who appeared on behalf of the owners of the putative slave ship and also argued that, since both the ship and its owners were French and had been operating in international waters, only the French courts had jurisdiction over their alleged offenses.

The task of adjudicating these claims fell to Supreme Court Justice Joseph Story, who was sitting on circuit. Story began by reviewing the evidence and concluding that *La Jeune Eugenie* was in fact engaged in the slave trade at the time that it was seized. He also voiced the suspicion that the transfer of the vessel to the French flag was simply a subterfuge designed to take the ship outside the purview of the American prohibition on the trade. In addition, Story addressed a number of procedural issues surrounding the seizure of the French vessel by the *Alligator.* However, much of the opinion focused on the question of whether participation in the international slave trade was contrary to the law of nations as well as domestic law.[8]

Relying on *The Amedie* and rejecting the reasoning of *The Louis,* Story concluded that the slave trade was in fact prohibited by international law. Story carefully distinguished the slave trade from the institution of slavery itself, which he noted had "existed in all ages of the world, and has been tolerated by some, encouraged by others, and sanctioned by most, of the enlightened and civilized nations of the earth in former ages" and also "forms the foundation of large portions of property in a portion of [the United States]." He also firmly rejected the claim that the law of nations embodied only those principles that had found universal acceptance in domestic law, contending instead that international law derived from "general principles of right and justice" and the "customary observances of civilized nations," as well as "the . . . positive law that regulates the intercourse between states."[9]

Against this background, asserting that the slave trade was "repugnant to the great principles of Christian duty, the dictates of natural religion, the obligations, the obligations of good faith and morality, and the eternal maxims of social justice," as well as the domestic law of most nations, Story had no difficulty in concluding that participation in the slave trade violated the law of nations. Nonetheless, Story did not vindicate Stockton's claim; instead, *La Jeune Eugenie* was ordered to be delivered to the French authorities "to be dealt with according to [their] sense of duty and right."[10] Moreover, when *The Antelope* was decided three years later by the Supreme Court, Story sat silently as the Court rejected his analysis.

In *The Antelope,* the Court was called upon to adjudicate the status of over 250 Africans found on board the *Antelope,* a Spanish vessel that had been engaged in the slave trade off the coast of Africa. Together with three Portuguese vessels and an American ship similarly engaged, the *Antelope* had been captured by the *Columbia,* a privateer flying the flag of a short-lived Latin American revolutionary state. Under the control of a prize crew, the *Antelope,* with many African prisoners on board, sailed in tandem with the *Columbia* until the latter was wrecked off the coast of Brazil. At that time, a number of Africans who had been previously captured and were on board the *Columbia* were transferred to the *Antelope,* which was subsequently intercepted by an American revenue cutter off the coast of the United States and brought to the port of Savannah, Georgia.[11]

The case was initially tried before Justice William Johnson of South Carolina, who was sitting on circuit in Savannah. The captain of the *Columbia* and the master of the revenue cutter each claimed property rights in the Africans. In addition, officials of the Spanish and Portuguese governments intervened, each supporting the claims of their respective nationals for restitution of property that had been seized.

Like Lieutenant Stockton in *La Jeune Eugenie,* the captain of the *Columbia* argued that he had initially been justified in capturing the *Antelope* because the slave trade was illegal under the law of nations. However, unlike Story, Johnson rejected this contention, asserting that "the laws of any nation on the subject of the slave trade are nothing more in the eyes of any other nation than a class of trade laws in the nation that enacts them."[12] Johnson then proceeded to award most of the captured Africans to the representatives of Spain and Portugal.

This decision was appealed to the Supreme Court. There, speaking on behalf of the United States and the Africans themselves, were United States Attorney General William Wirt of Virginia and Francis Scott Key, a private citizen who

resided in Maryland. They were opposed by Sen. John Berrien of Georgia and
Charles Ingersoll, a private attorney from Philadelphia.

Key began his argument by declaring that "our national policy, perhaps our
safety, requires, that there should be no increase of [the number of slaves]
within our territory." He averred that the statutes of 1808 and 1819

gave fair warning to those engaged in the slave trade, that though we did not intend to
interfere with them on the high seas, yet, if their victims should come within the reach
of our laws, we should protect them. These acts constitute a solemn pledge to all nations
interested in the suppression of this inhuman traffic, and to Africa herself, that if the
objects of it should seek our protection, where they may lawfully receive it, within our
territorial jurisdiction, and at the feet of our tribunals of justice, they should be entitled
to that protection.[13]

Assuming for the sake of argument that the federal courts might in some circumstances be required to recognize the property rights of slave traders in their
human cargo, Key then turned to the question of what type of proof would be
sufficient to support such a claim. He first appealed to the principle that "by
the law of nature, all men are free" and contended that, therefore, "it would be
manifestly unjust, to [require the Africans] to prove their birthright." Instead,
Key argued, the captives should be deemed free men in the absence of an "overwhelming probability" that they had been lawfully acquired in Africa.[14]

Key dismissed the notion that possession per se was sufficient to satisfy this
burden of proof, observing that "if there be a permitted slave trade, there is
also a prohibited slave trade; and the prohibition is much more extensive than
the permission." Key also scoffed at the notion that the Spanish claimant could
simply interpose the legality of the acquisition under the laws of Spain, asserting
that "there is no reason of comity, or policy, or justice, which requires us to give
effect to a foreign law conflicting with our own law on the same subject. Besides,
the Spanish law is not only contrary to ours, but is inconsistent with the law of
nature, which is a sufficient reason for maintaining the supremacy of our own
code."[15]

In addition, Key argued that the claimants should not be allowed to rely on
the law of Spain because Spanish law was contrary to the law of nations. He
conceded that at one time the law of nations had sanctioned the slave trade.
But at the same time, noting the wide variety of recent treaties and other agreements that had denounced the trade, Key also asserted that "this trade is now
condemned by the general consent of nations, who have publicly and solemnly
declared it to be unjust, inhuman, and illegal." Further, Key observed that,
although Spain and Portugal still allowed their subjects to carry on the slave

trade south of the equator, those nations were signatories to agreements that branded the trade "inhumane and unlawful." Key insisted that these declarations were evidence that even Spain and Portugal considered the trade to be contrary to the law of nations.[16]

In their responses, both Berrien and Ingersol emphasized that, by their terms, the federal statutory prohibitions on the slave trade were directed only at American citizens and vessels. They also gave short shrift to the possibility that restitution should be denied under the laws of either Spain or Portugal, asserting that the representatives of the United States bore the burden of proof on this point, and that in any event the claimants had sufficient documentation to establish their right to restitution.[17]

The bulk of the claimants' argument was devoted to establishing the proposition that the slave trade was not prohibited by the law of nations. On this point, Berrien began by emphasizing what he saw as the centrality of the institution of slavery to the structure of American society and the incongruity of any attempt by the instrumentalities of the United States government to extend its statutory prohibition on the slave trade to the nationals and ships of other nations:

Would it become the United States to assume to themselves the character of censors of the morals of the world on this subject?—to realize the lofty conception of the adverse counsel, and consider themselves as the ministers of heaven, called to wipe out from among the nations the stain of this iniquity? Might not the foreign claimant thus rebuke them, in the strong language of truth? For more than thirty years you were slave traders; you are still extensively slave owners. If the slave trade be robbery, you were robbers, and are yet clinging to your plunder. For more than twenty years this traffic was protected by your constitution, exempted from the whole force of your legislative power; its fruits yet lay at the foundation of that compact. The principle by which you continue to enjoy them, is protected by that constitution, forms a basis for your representatives, is infused into your laws, and mingles itself with all the sources of authority. Relieve yourselves from these absurdities, before you assume the right of sitting in judgment on the morality of other nations. But this you cannot do. Paradoxical as it may appear, they constitute the very bond of your union. The shield of your constitution protects them from your touch.[18]

Against this background, Berrien took strong issue with Key's analysis, asserting that

the slave trade is not contrary to the natural law of nations, because, until recently, it was universally tolerated and encouraged. It is not contrary to the positive law of nations; because there is no general compact inhibiting it; and nothing is more certain, than that the usage, or compact, even of a majority of nations, cannot produce rights or obligations among others. To what other evidences of the law of nations can we resort, except those of usage and compact; the former interpreting the rules of natural reason, the latter stipulating those of positive institution?[19]

Rejecting the notion that the law of nations can be derived from widely accepted principles of general morality, Berrien also noted that, despite the strenuous efforts of Great Britain, a number of recent international conferences had refused to pass resolutions categorically denouncing the slave trade.

Ingersol emphasized the same point. After tracing the long history of slavery as an institution, he observed that

the slave trade was long the subject of negotiations, treaties, and wars, between different European States, all of which consider it as a lawful commerce. The very declarations in the recent European Congresses, and the negotiations between Great Britain and the United States, all show that the slave trade has not yet been prohibited by any thing like the unanimous consent of nations, so as to make it absolutely unlawful in the view of a Court of the law of nations.[20]

In his closing argument for the government, William Wirt focused primarily on the issue of the burden of proof. After noting that one who sought restitution of his property in an admiralty action normally bore the burden of proving his ownership, Wirt emphasized the significance of the Africans' interest in the controversy and the general principle that the law favored claims for freedom:

In the present case, the rule is peculiarly applicable, and the clearness and fulness of the proof ought to be in proportion to the importance of the matter in controversy. The case is one of human liberty. The Africans stand before the Court as if brought up before it upon a habeas corpus. Suppose them here, on such a process, asserting their freedom, and claiming your protection; what kind of proof would you exact from those who claim to hold them in slavery? Most certainly you would not demand inferior evidence to that which you require in a case of life or death. . . . Where any doubt is left, the decision should be in favorem libertatis.[21]

Wirt also reacted strongly to Berrien's claim that the United States was acting inconsistently in interfering with the slave trade carried on by the citizens of other countries while the institution of slavery was flourishing in this country:

The existence of slavery in the United States [does not] form any excuse or palliation, for perpetuating, and extending the guilt and misery of the slave trade. Slavery was introduced among us, during our colonial state, against the solemn remonstrances of our legislative assemblies. Free America did not introduce it. She led the way in measures for prohibiting the slave trade. The revolution which made us an independent nation, found slavery existing among us. It is a calamity entailed upon us, by the commercial policy of the parent country. There is no nation which has a right to reproach us with the supposed inconsistency of our endeavouring to extirpate the slave trade as carried on between Africa and America, whilst at the same time we are compelled to tolerate the existence of domestic slavery under our own municipal laws.[22]

But despite their best efforts, Key and Wirt were unable to persuade the Court to accept their views on the major doctrinal issues presented by *The Antelope*. Chief Justice John Marshall spoke for the Court in affirmatively rejecting the view that the international slave trade violated the law of nations. Marshall conceded that the slave trade was "contrary to the law of nature," but also noted that the trade was legal under "the usages [and] national acts" of the portions of the world in which the *Columbia* and the *Antelope* had acquired their cargo. Thus, emphasizing that he was acting as a "jurist" rather than a "moralist," Marshall concluded that he was compelled to hold that the slave trade did not violate the law of nations.[23]

However, this conclusion did not resolve the critical burden of proof issue. On this point, the justices were evenly divided. Thus, while this portion of the lower court judgment was affirmed, the Court did not discuss the principles that underlay this conclusion.[24] After further litigation, the Court ultimately freed most of the Africans. However, this decision was based narrowly on the idiosyncratic facts that underlay *The Antelope* rather than on principles that were of broader use to the opponents of the slave trade.[25]

While no important constitutional principles were at stake in *The Antelope*, in some respects the structure of the arguments foreshadowed the constitutional struggles which were to follow. In addition to relying on positive law, opponents of slavery often urged courts to take notice of the principle that slavery was inconsistent with natural law—a view that many Southerners shared with Northerners, particularly through the early part of the nineteenth century. The defenders of slavery, on the other hand, consistently pressed the courts to hew to the positive law established by the Constitution, even if judges and juries found that law to be distasteful.[26]

But in at least one crucial respect, *The Antelope* differed from many of the constitutional disputes over slavery that would later come to the Court. In the international slave trade cases, no one doubted that, subsequent to 1808, the Constitution vested the federal government with the authority to act against slave traders and that the states could also act against the international trade. By contrast, many of the important slavery-related cases that followed would raise delicate questions about the appropriate allocation of authority between the federal government and the states.

During the Marshall era, the Court grappled with a wide variety of issues dealing with issues of federal-state relations. None of those cases dealt specifically with slavery. However, an appreciation of the principles of federalism developed by the Marshall Court is indispensable to any effort to understand the Taney Court's efforts to come to grips with the legal status of slavery under the Constitution.

CHAPTER 2

The Marshall Court and Federalism

One of the most important features of the American constitutional system is that it provides for a division of authority between the federal government, which was established by the Constitution itself, and the state governments, many of which predated the Constitution. From the earliest days of the republic, Americans were deeply divided over the precise nature of this division. While some politicians and theorists aggrandized the role of the federal government, others emphasized the importance of maintaining the status and prerogatives of the states.

The debates ranged over a variety of related but analytically separable issues. The most fundamental theoretical questions involved the locus of sovereignty in the constitutional system. The Articles of Confederation, which established the terms of the relationship among the states prior to 1789, had clearly provided that "each state retains its sovereignty, freedom, and independence." By contrast, the Constitution makes no explicit reference to the issue of sovereignty.

Despite this omission, some continued to insist that states remained completely sovereign even after the ratification of the Constitution, which proponents of this position characterized as nothing more than a compact among the states that did not create a new sovereign entity. Others, no less committed to preserving the prerogatives of the state governments, adhered to a theory of divided sovereignty, conceding that the Constitution transferred a portion of the sovereignty of the state governments to the federal government but also arguing that the state and federal governments remained coequal in status. Those who were out of power in the federal government at times relied on some combination of these theories to argue that the state governments retained the authority to independently judge the constitutionality of federal actions. This position was embodied in the Virginia and Kentucky Resolutions that were adopted by the Jeffersonians in response to the passage of the Alien and Sedition Acts under the administration of John Adams, as well as the resolutions of the Hartford Convention of 1814, a meeting of New England Federalists who opposed the policies of the administration of James Madison.[1]

In 1816, the Marshall Court confronted analogous issues in *Martin v. Hunter's Lessee*.[2] *Martin* arose from Virginia state court proceedings that revolved around a dispute over title to a parcel of land that was located in that state. One group of litigants, which included Chief Justice John Marshall, based their claim on a provision of the 1783 Treaty of Paris that protected the land claims of British subjects in the United States. Their opponents relied on a 1779 Virginia statute that decreed that the property of hostile British subjects should be escheated to the state.

After a state trial court initially found in favor of the Marshall group, in 1810 the Virginia Supreme Court of Appeals reversed, concluding that the case was controlled by the provisions of the 1779 statute. This judgment was brought before the United States Supreme Court on a writ of error, and the Court disagreed with the state supreme court, agreeing with the trial court that the claim of the Marshall group should prevail. The case was then remanded to the Virginia supreme court for the entrance of an order effectuating the judgment of the Supreme Court.[3]

At this point, events took a dramatic turn. In 1815, the state court refused to honor the mandate of the Supreme Court, arguing that the Court could not constitutionally exercise appellate jurisdiction over the decisions issued by state courts. Chief Judge Spencer Roane and Judges William H. Cabell, Francis T. Brooke, and William Fleming each issued separate opinions in the case, all drawing on the principle of concurrent sovereignty. Thus, for example, Cabell declared that the state and federal governments "possess[ed], each, its portion of the divided sovereignty"; were "separate from and independent of each other"; and that "each government must act by *its own* organs [and] from no other can it expect, command, or enforce obedience, even as to objects coming within the range of its powers." Similarly, Brooke, explicitly embracing the arguments of the Virginia and Kentucky Resolutions, declared that "I have not been able to perceive in [the Constitution] any ground for the position that the state authorities can be controlled by the national authority."[4]

Not surprisingly, the Virginia court was quickly faced with another writ of error that "commanded" that the state court send the record of the case to the Supreme Court. Roane and his compatriots did not even officially acknowledge the writ. However, the attorneys for the Marshall group sent a certified record of the earlier state court decision to the Court, and the justices chose to proceed on the basis of this document.

Against this background, in 1816 the Court voted to reverse the decision of the Virginia court. Speaking for the majority, Justice Joseph Story conceded that "it is perfectly clear that the sovereign powers vested in the State governments by their respective Constitutions remained unaltered and unimpaired except so far as they were granted to the Government of the United States." Nonetheless, he firmly rejected the underlying premises of the proponents of the view that states retained exclusive sovereignty even after the ratification of the

Constitution, declaring that "the Constitution of the United States was or-
dained and established not by the States in their sovereign capacities, but emphatically, as the preamble of the Constitution declares, by 'the people of the
United States.'"[5]

Story also denied that the exercise of appellate jurisdiction by the Supreme
Court over state court judgments was inconsistent with the dignity of the state
governments in the federal system. After recounting the numerous restrictions
and obligations imposed on the states by the Constitution, he contended that
"when . . . the States are stripped of some of the highest attributes of sovereignty,
and the same are given to the United States; when the legislatures of the States
are, in some respects, under the control of Congress, and in every case are,
under the Constitution, bound by the paramount authority of the United
States, it is certainly difficult to support the argument that the appellate power
over the decisions of State courts is contrary to the genius of our institutions."[6]

Martin firmly established the position of the Supreme Court as the ultimate
arbiter of federal law in the American constitutional system. In addition, Story
observed that the powers of Congress "are expressed in general terms, leaving
to the legislature from time to time to adopt its own means to effectuate legitimate objects and to mould [*sic*] and model the exercise of its powers as its own
wisdom and the public interests, should require." The same philosophy would
guide the Marshall Court in cases where the scope of federal legislative power
was the central issue.

Like the question of sovereignty, the issue of the scope of congressional power
was the subject of intense debate in late-eighteenth- and early-nineteenth-
century America. All agreed, at least in theory, that the federal government was
one of enumerated powers—that Congress had only those powers granted to
it either explicitly or implicitly by the text of the Constitution itself. The most
prolific source of those powers is Article I, Section 8, which includes seventeen
clauses granting specific powers to Congress, and, in addition, the Necessary
and Proper Clause, which provides that Congress shall have the power "to make
all Laws which shall be necessary and proper for carrying into Execution" the
powers described in Article I, Section 8, as well as all other powers vested in the
federal government by the Constitution.

The struggle over the establishment of a national bank during the administration of George Washington provoked some of the sharpest debates over
the scope of federal power. Treasury Secretary Alexander Hamilton pressed for
the creation of such a bank in order to help strengthen the economy. Hamilton
relied on the Necessary and Proper Clause as the source of the requisite authority for the establishment of a bank.

Thomas Jefferson and his allies not only opposed the creation of the bank on policy grounds but also contended that the Constitution did not grant the federal government the power to charter a bank. In a 1791 letter to Washington, after noting that the Constitution nowhere specifically authorized the creation of a national bank, Jefferson asserted that "to take a single step beyond the boundaries thus specially drawn around the powers of Congress is to take possession of a boundless field of power, no longer susceptible of any definition." Turning specifically to the Necessary and Proper Clause, he contended that "the Constitution allows only the means which are 'necessary,' not those which are merely 'convenient' for effecting the enumerated powers. If such a latitude of construction [as would allow the creation of a national bank] be allowed to this phrase as to give any nonenumerated power, it will go to every one, for there is not one which ingenuity may not torture into a convenience in some instance or other, to some one of so long a list of enumerated powers."[7]

In his response, by contrast, Hamilton argued that "necessary often means no more than needful, requisite, incidental, useful, or conducive to. It is a common mode of expression to say, that it is necessary for a government or a person to do this or that thing, when nothing more is intended or understood, than that the interests of the government or person require, or will be promoted by, the doing of this or that thing."[8] Hamilton was victorious in the political struggle, and in 1791 Congress passed legislation authorizing the creation of the First Bank of the United States and providing that it be chartered to operate for a period of twenty years.

Jefferson was subsequently elected president in 1800, and his Democratic-Republican Party controlled the federal government for the next twenty-four years. In theory, Jeffersonians remained committed to a constitutional regime of limited federal power. However, as the decision to purchase the Louisiana Territory from France demonstrates, they were willing to take a more expansive view of the powers of the federal government when they believed that circumstances warranted it. Thus, after allowing the charter of the First Bank to lapse in 1811, the Jeffersonian-controlled Congress authorized the creation of the Second Bank of the United States in 1816. The state of Maryland responded by imposing a tax on all bank notes issued by banks that were not chartered by the state itself. It was a dispute over the constitutionality of the application of this tax to the Second Bank that gave rise to *McCulloch v. Maryland.*[9]

In *McCulloch,* the Supreme Court unanimously found that the state could not constitutionally impose a tax on an instrumentality of the federal government. Speaking for the Court, John Marshall's Supreme Court first examined the question of whether the Constitution vested Congress with the authority to charter a bank. Adopting the same basic position as Hamilton on this point, Marshall took a broad view of the Necessary and Proper Clause, declaring that "if the end be legitimate, and within the scope of the Constitution, all the means which are appropriate, which are plainly adapted to that end, and which are not prohibited, may constitutionally be employed to carry it into effect." Against this background, observing that "the power to tax involves the power to destroy," Marshall concluded that Maryland could not constitutionally impose a state tax on the bank.[10]

Martin and *McCulloch* clearly established the principle that the powers of Congress would be interpreted broadly, and by extension that Congress could, if it wished, override state laws that were inconsistent with its exercise of those powers. These cases did not, however, address the question of whether states retained concurrent authority to act in a manner that was not inconsistent with federal statutes on matters that Congress could (in theory) have regulated. Almost simultaneously with the decision in *McCulloch,* the Court addressed this question in *Sturges v. Crowninshield*[11] and *Houston v. Moore.*[12]

In *Sturges,* the Court took an equivocal view of the impact of the Constitution on state prerogatives in situations where Congress was empowered to act but had remained totally silent. The case arose from a challenge to a New York statute that allowed insolvent debtors to list their assets, assign their property, and discharge their debts. Among other things, those challenging the law relied on Article I, Section 8, paragraph 4, which vests Congress with the authority to "establish . . . uniform Laws on the subject of Bankruptcy throughout the United States." They argued that this provision granted Congress exclusive power to regulate bankruptcy, and that, even in the absence of a federal bankruptcy statute, this provision divested the states of all authority to pass local bankruptcy statutes.

Although holding the New York statute unconstitutional on other grounds, the Court rejected this argument. But at the same time, Chief Justice Marshall observed that "whenever the terms in which a power is granted to congress, or the nature of the power, require that it should be exercised exclusively by congress, the subject is as completely taken from the state legislatures, as if they had been expressly forbidden to act on it."[13] Thus, Marshall implied that, in other cases, a grant of power to Congress might be held to be exclusive.

In *Houston,* Justice Bushrod Washington was less equivocal in dealing with the impact of the Constitution on state laws that supplemented but did not conflict with federal statutes operating on the same basic subject matter. *Houston* was a challenge to a Pennsylvania statute that vested state courts with the authority to try and punish violators of a federal law which prescribed penalties for those who refused to serve in the militia—a statute that in turn was passed under the constitutionally granted authority to create and organize the militia. Apparently speaking for a majority of the justices, Washington ultimately rejected the constitutional challenge to a conviction obtained under the state statute. But at the same time, he indicated that, where Congress had acted in pursuance of its enumerated powers, states were not allowed to enact additional legislation on the same subject, even when the state legislation did not conflict with congressional mandates. The opinion averred that

if in a specified case the people have thought proper to bestow certain powers on Congress as the safest depositary of them, and Congress has legislated within the scope of them, the people have reason to complain that the same powers should be exercised at the same time by the state legislatures. To subject them to the operation of two laws upon the same subject, dictated by distinct wills, particularly in a case inflicting pains and penalties, is, to my apprehension, something very much like oppression, if not worse.[14]

While cases such as *Sturges* and *Houston* were important milestones in the evolution of the Marshall Court's jurisprudence, beginning with the 1824 decision in *Gibbons v. Ogden,*[15] disputes arising from the Commerce Clause took an increasingly prominent role in the struggle over the shape of American federalism. In *Gibbons,* the state of New York had granted Robert Fulton the exclusive right to operate steamboats in New York waters. The monopoly was challenged by Aaron Ogden, who was licensed by a federal statute to engage in the coastal trade and wished to provide ferry service between Elizabethtown, New Jersey, and points in New York. Ogden argued that, under these circumstances, the state could not constitutionally prevent him from operating the ferry service.

Ogden's challenge presented three questions. First, was the portion of the ferry service that took place entirely within New York "Commerce . . . among the states [interstate commerce]" as defined by the Commerce Clause? Second, if this portion of the ferry service was in fact interstate commerce, was congressional power to regulate exclusive, or did the states retain concurrent authority in the absence of contrary congressional action? Finally, assuming that states retained concurrent authority in the absence of congressional action, was Ogden nonetheless exempted from the New York regulation by virtue of his compliance with the licensing statute?

Against this background, the Court held that Ogden could not be prevented from operating the ferry service. Speaking for the majority, Chief Justice Marshall first determined that Ogden's claim did in fact fall within the purview of the Commerce Clause. Operating from this premise Marshall ultimately rested his decision on the ground that the licensing statute granted Ogden a right to operate his ferry that superseded state law. But Marshall also addressed the claim that the Constitution implicitly deprived states of concurrent authority to regulate interstate commerce generally, observing that the argument had "great force" and that "the Court is not satisfied that it has been refuted."[16]

In 1827, Marshall sounded a similar note in *Brown v. Maryland. Brown* was a challenge to a Maryland statute that required importers of dry goods to pay $50 for a license. Among other things, the challengers argued that the statute was inconsistent with the Commerce Clause. Although the case was ultimately decided on other grounds, Marshall also observed that "the power claimed by the State is, in its nature in conflict with that given to Congress, and the greater or lesser extent to which it may be exercised does not enter into the inquiry concerning its existence."[17]

But despite the language of the *Gibbons* and *Brown* opinions, the Marshall Court was not uniformly hostile to the exercise of state power on issues related to interstate and foreign commerce. First, in *Gibbons* itself, Marshall was careful to distinguish state laws that directly regulated interstate commerce from measures such as "inspection laws, quarantine laws [and] health laws," which, although perhaps having a "remote and considerable influence on commerce," he nonetheless described as "form[ing] a portion of that immense mass of legislation, which embraces everything within the territory of a State, not surrendered to the federal government."[18] Moreover, two years after the *Brown* decision, the Court *explicitly* countenanced at least some degree of concurrent authority in *Willson v. Black-Bird Creek Marsh Co.*[19]

In *Willson,* the Delaware state legislature had chartered a corporation and explicitly authorized it to build a dam across a small navigable creek. The dam prevented a sloop from using the creek. Notwithstanding the fact that the vessel was licensed under the same federal statute that had formed the basis for the decision in *Gibbons,* the Court unanimously rejected the contention that the Delaware statute was unconstitutional. Once more speaking for the Court, Marshall began by noting that Congress could have, if it had so chosen, affirmatively required that the creek remain open to navigation. Nonetheless, with little discussion, he concluded that "under all the circumstances of the case, [the statute cannot] be considered as repugnant to the power to regulate commerce in its dormant State [that is, without affirmative congressional action]."[20]

Obviously, none of the decisions from *Martin* through *Willson* had a direct impact on issues related to slavery. Nonetheless, the principles underlying those decisions provided critical jurisprudential background for the Court's consideration of a variety of issues that were central to the sectional conflict—issues that first came before the Court in the early 1840s. In the interim, however, the political context in which those issues and other slavery related issues were considered had changed dramatically.

Part Two

The Age of Accommodation

CHAPTER 3

Sectionalism and the Rise of the Second-Party System

The structure of American politics changed profoundly in the 1820s and 1830s. The collapse of the Federalist Party in 1816 left the Democratic-Republicans, the organization that had originally been founded by Thomas Jefferson and his allies, without major opposition as a national political party. Thus, in 1820, James Monroe became the only president other than George Washington to be elected without significant opposition.

But despite the unanimity of support for Monroe, the Jeffersonians themselves were riven with internal rivalries. Some of the disputes revolved around disagreements over economic policies and the proper role of the state and national governments, respectively, in the federal system. In addition, some Northerners resented what they viewed as the undue influence of Southerners—particularly Virginians—in party affairs.[1]

Sectional tensions boiled over in Congress in 1819, when the Missouri territorial legislature sought permission to draft a constitution that would provide the basis for admission to statehood. On February 13, Rep. James Tallmadge Jr. of New York moved to require that Missouri adopt a scheme of gradual emancipation as a condition for statehood.[2] Northerners of all political stripes united around the Tallmadge amendment, while representatives of the slave states were equally adamant in their opposition.

With Northerners in firm control of the House of Representatives and Southerners in effective control of the Senate, a deadlock ensued, punctuated by bitter denunciations of slavery and the structure of Southern society from Tallmadge's supporters on one hand and threats of secession from slave state representatives on the other. The deadlock was broken in 1820, when a small majority of Southerners and a handful of Northerners agreed to accept a compromise brokered by Henry Clay. Under the terms of this compromise, Missouri was authorized to draft a state constitution without restriction; Maine was admitted as a free state to maintain the balance of power between the sections; and slavery was banned from all other parts of the Louisiana Purchase north of 36 degrees, 30 minutes—the southern border of Missouri. Northern representatives made a further effort to block the admission of Missouri when the state constitution was presented to Congress for approval the following year, but once again Clay was able to forge a compromise that garnered enough votes to secure statehood for Missouri and end the crisis.[3]

The settlement of the Missouri controversy at least temporarily averted the permanent realignment of national politics along sectional lines that had been the goal of some restrictionists. Nonetheless, by the mid-1820s, it was clear that the Democratic-Republican Party was dividing into different factions. For a time, however, the shape of the future configuration of the American political landscape remained unclear.

Although all of the major candidates in the presidential election of 1824 ran under the Democratic-Republican banner and expressed support for the Missouri Compromise, the dynamic of the election in substantial measure reflected the lingering bitterness over the controversy. After the withdrawal of John C. Calhoun of South Carolina, who had run as a nationalist, four candidates remained viable possibilities. The appeal of three of the four was primarily sectional. Nationalist John Quincy Adams—an erstwhile Federalist—found most of his support in New England, while the equally nationalist Henry Clay was the candidate of the West. By contrast, the base of William Crawford of Georgia, a strong proponent of states' rights, was in the Southeast. The only candidate who demonstrated a strong national appeal was General Andrew Jackson, a hero of the War of 1812 and the Indian wars, who in 1823 had been elected to the Senate from the state of Tennessee.

By 1824, most states selected their presidential electors by popular vote, and Jackson was by far the most popular candidate in those states. Moreover, he also accumulated a plurality of electoral votes. Nonetheless, he failed to gain an absolute majority of the electoral votes, and the House of Representatives was called upon to choose among Jackson, Adams, and Crawford, the three candidates who had accumulated the most votes from the electoral college. In the House, Clay, who detested Jackson, engineered the election of Adams. When Clay was subsequently named secretary of state, the Jackson forces decried what they described as a "corrupt bargain"—a charge that would haunt Clay throughout the remainder of his political career.[4]

In the wake of the election, Martin Van Buren of New York pursued a project that would soon result in the reconfiguration of American politics. Van Buren's goal was to create a more ideologically cohesive Democratic Party, purged of nationalists and returning to its pure Jeffersonian roots. He also clearly anticipated the rise of a competing party that would champion the nationalistic policies that had been associated with the Federalists in the early nineteenth century.

Van Buren envisioned the backbone of the states' rights party as an alliance between his Albany Regency and like-minded politicians from the state of Virginia. Accordingly, he reached out to influential Virginians such as Thomas Ritchie of Richmond, a newspaper editor and spokesman for the states' rights forces in that state. In a well-known 1827 letter to Ritchie, Van Buren argued that the invigoration of the two-party system was necessary in order to suppress "prejudices between the free and slave holding states," which, beginning with the controversy over Missouri, had produced "clamour agt. [against] Southern Influence and African Slavery." Such rhetoric was aptly designed to appeal to men such as Ritchie, who had been harshly critical of Southern acquiescence in the Missouri Compromise. However, as Sean Wilentz has observed, Van Buren's objective was not to create a party that was in any meaningful sense either proslavery or even pro-Southern. Instead, the goal was to create a truly national party, united by ideology, whose members would share a partisan interest in dampening sectional controversy generally.[5] In the election of 1824, Van Buren had unsuccessfully sought to rally the supporters of states' rights around the candidacy of William Crawford. In preparation for the election of 1828, he formed an alliance with Andrew Jackson to create a new party and oppose the nationalist policies of the Adams administration.

Jackson was in many ways an ideal candidate to appeal to a broad national constituency. Southerners had a natural affinity with a Tennessee slaveowner. At the same time, Jackson's image as a war hero and the champion of the common man allowed him to attract many Northern voters as well. By the late 1820s, Jackson's personal appeal had combined with Van Buren's political acumen and organizing skills to create a combination that was initially unbeatable. In the elections of 1826, Jackson's allies took control of Congress. Two years later, sweeping the South and the lower North, Jackson easily defeated Adams, who ran as a National Republican, and succeeded to the presidency. Building on these successes, the Jacksonian Democrats—the political party that was formed by Van Buren and Jackson—would remain a dominant force in American politics until the Civil War.[6]

From the time that the Jacksonians came to power, they were opposed by nationalists such as Adams and Clay. Nonetheless, it soon became clear that the National Republicans alone were no match for the reconstituted Democrats. However, organized opposition to Jackson soon came from other quarters as well. In the North, the burgeoning Anti-Masonic Party disdained both the Democrats and the National Republicans.[7] In the South, the actions of the Jackson administration itself split the Democratic Party and raised the specter of the resectionalization of American politics.

The sequence of events that led to the rupture actually began before the election of 1828, with the passage of the protectionist "Tariff of Abominations."

Engineered by Van Buren and other Northern Jacksonians, the new tariff schedule was designed to benefit manufacturing and agricultural interests in the states of the West and lower North, thereby shoring up Jackson's support in those states in the upcoming presidential election. While the tariffs were opposed almost unanimously by Southern members in the Senate and the House of Representatives, Van Buren and his allies accurately calculated that Southern distaste for Adams, himself a protectionist, would nonetheless lead Southerners to support Jackson and his chosen vice presidential running mate, John C. Calhoun of South Carolina (who, ironically, had served in the same capacity during the Adams administration).[8] Seeking to mollify Southerners, in July 1832 the Jacksonian-controlled Congress lowered the 1828 rates somewhat, but the political leaders of the slave states remained dissatisfied.

The intellectual leader of the anti-tariff forces was none other than Calhoun himself. For most of the early nineteenth century, Calhoun had been associated with the nationalist elements of the Southern polity. However, soon after the election of 1828, Calhoun broke with Jackson. Seeing in the tariff controversy an issue that might rally Southerners behind a purely sectional party with himself at its head, Calhoun anonymously authored the *South Carolina Exposition and Protest,* which not only denounced the 1828 tariff as unconstitutional but also insisted that each individual state had the right to nullify within its borders any federal law that the state government deemed unconstitutional. Only such a right, Calhoun argued, could protect Southern minorities from what he viewed as the potential tyranny of Northern majorities.[9] While Calhoun's missive did not immediately move the South Carolina legislature to attempt to nullify the tariff, it reflected a fundamental difference in philosophy between Calhoun and Jackson. Though Jackson generally took a relatively limited view of the scope of federal power, he was also passionately attached to the Union and the idea that the federal government was supreme within its sphere of influence.

Jackson suspected that Calhoun was the author of the *Exposition and Protest.* Still, during the early years of the Jackson presidency, Calhoun contended with Van Buren for influence within the administration and designation as Jackson's anointed successor. But a dispute over the proper treatment of Peggy Eaton, the wife of Jackson's secretary of war, created further animosity between Jackson and Calhoun, and by the middle of 1830 their estrangement was complete. The rift between the two men was clearly reflected in the respective toasts that they offered at a Jefferson Day dinner on April 13, 1830. Jackson's toast was to "Our Federal Union: It Must be Preserved," while Calhoun responded, "The Union, Next to our Liberties the Most Dear."[10]

Following his break with Jackson, Calhoun maneuvered to create a more distinctively Southern party with himself as its standard-bearer.[11] This effort was entirely unsuccessful. Calhoun was replaced on the Jacksonian ticket by Van Buren, and Jackson won an overwhelming electoral victory over both Henry Clay, who carried the National Republican banner, and William Wirt, the candidate of the Anti-Masonic Party. Jackson was the choice of an amazing 88 percent of the voters in the states south of Maryland and Kentucky. Outside of New England, he lost only three states.

One of those states was South Carolina, whose electors, selected by the state legislature, cast their votes for John Floyd of Maryland. In November 1832, after South Carolina had conducted its election, a convention called by the legislature declared it unlawful after February 1, 1833 "to enforce the collection of duties within the state" and threatened secession if the federal government sought to override this resolution. On December 10, 1832, Jackson responded with his Nullification Proclamation, which not only condemned nullification itself but also, against Van Buren's advice, condemned secession as "a revolutionary act" to "be morally justified [only] by the extremity of oppression."[12] In addition, Jackson began making preparations to use force if necessary against the nullifiers, and requested Congress to adopt legislation specifically authorizing military action.

Faced with Jackson's resolute stand and politically isolated on the issue of nullification, South Carolina's leaders stepped back from the brink. Calhoun—who had resigned the vice presidency and was representing South Carolina in the Senate—agreed to accept a Compromise Tariff Bill that provided marginal relief from the rigors of the tariff itself. Nonetheless, Jackson insisted on the passage of his Force Bill. With many Southerners absenting themselves from the critical vote, the Senate passed the bill on a vote of 32–1. The House of Representatives also adopted the measure on a vote of 149–48. Several hours later, the passage of the Compromise Tariff of 1833 ended the immediate crisis.[13]

Although Jackson and his allies emerged victorious from the nullification crisis, the dispute weakened the Democratic Party in the South. While most Southern advocates of states' rights rejected the concept of nullification, many were disturbed by Jackson's attack on the idea of secession and found the Force Bill objectionable. The position of the Democrats in the South was further weakened by Jackson's decision to withdraw federal deposits from the Second Bank of the United States in late 1833.

During the election campaign of 1832, Jackson had made effective use of his decision to veto a bill rechartering the bank, which he characterized as a tool of the wealthy and powerful and whose creation, he argued, exceeded the authority granted to Congress by the Constitution. However, the original charter for the bank, which did not expire until 1834, allowed removal of the deposits only if Congress found that they were not secure. Yet as late as March 1833, the House of Representatives had overwhelmingly approved a report from the Ways and Means Committee that found that the deposits were in fact secure.

Nonetheless, acting through Secretary of the Treasury Roger Brooke Taney, Jackson effected the transfer of federal funds from the Second Bank to a number of state banks—but not before Jackson had first removed two previous treasury secretaries who had refused to do his bidding.[14] To some erstwhile Southern Jacksonians, the removal of the deposits was an unforgivable act of executive usurpation. For example, Sen. Willie P. Mangum of North Carolina asserted that the issue was not the future of the Second Bank but rather "law or no law, constitution or no constitution."[15]

The fear of the rise of an imperial executive was one that was shared by all anti-Jacksonians in the mid-1830s. However, it was still far from clear whether this common thread was sufficiently strong to bind together a unified national party. Oppositionists ranged from nationalists such as Daniel Webster of Massachusetts and Henry Clay to staunch defenders of states' rights such as John Tyler of Virginia. Moreover, any national political organization would have to somehow find a means to accommodate both antislavery Northerners and proslavery Southerners.

The problem was complicated by the rise of the radical abolitionist movement in the North in the 1820s. Even in the North, abolitionists remained a small, despised minority who lacked any real influence in the conventional halls of political power. However, the verbal assaults of men such as David Walker and William Lloyd Garrison rekindled Southern fears of a Northern assault on slavery. The 1830 slave insurrection led by Nat Turner in Virginia fueled Southern anxiety still further.[16]

The potential of abolitionist agitation to disrupt national coalitions emerged clearly in the mid-1830s, after the American Anti-Slavery Society deluged Congress with thousands of petitions to abolish slavery in the District of Columbia. Prior to December 1835, both houses of Congress had dealt with such petitions by either receiving them and tabling them immediately or consigning them to the netherworld of committee consideration. But on December 18, Calhounite Rep. James Henry Hammond of South Carolina, declaring that such petitions must receive "a more decided seal of reprobation," moved that the House of Representatives refuse to receive such petitions. On January 7, 1836, Calhoun himself made a similar motion in the Senate.[17]

In practical terms, the change in procedure would have been of no significance whatsoever. No mainstream politician took seriously the possibility that Congress would actually outlaw slavery in the District. In political terms, by contrast, the debate over the "gag rule" had potentially explosive implications. Any Southern politician who accepted something less than the Hammond-Calhoun formulation might be branded as soft on abolitionism and the protection of slavery. Conversely, Northerners who acceded to a gag rule in any form would risk being characterized as tools of the "slave power" that some saw as dominating Southern politics.

Against this background, Martin Van Buren and his allies worked furiously in the House of Representatives to craft a compromise that would satisfy both wings of the bisectional Democratic party. Ultimately they were able to devise a formulation that allowed antislavery petitions to be received but required such petitions to be submitted immediately to a select committee with instructions to report that slavery should not be abolished in the District of Columbia. This proposal passed by a vote of 117–68, gaining the support of almost 90 percent of the Southerners who voted and almost 80 percent of Northern Democrats. By contrast, the compromise was opposed almost unanimously by Northern Oppositionists, who refused to vote for any gag rule, and also by some Southern Oppositionists, who considered the compromise too weak.[18]

While the dispute over the gag rule per se was not a major issue in the run-up to the presidential election of 1836, the divisions in the House of Representatives illustrated the difficulties faced by the anti-Jacksonians as they sought to create a unified opposition party. As a result, the Whigs, as they were now becoming known, failed to agree on a single presidential candidate to oppose Martin Van Buren, who was selected as the Democratic nominee in March 1835. Instead, three different candidates carried the Whig banner: Sen. Hugh Lawson White of Tennessee in the South, William Henry Harrison of Indiana in most of the North, and Daniel Webster in Massachusetts.

The pattern of results was much like that of 1824, when Jackson, the only national candidate, had faced three candidates whose appeal was primarily regional. The major difference was that, unlike Jackson, Van Buren carried his home state of New York and also made major inroads in New England, which had been swept by John Quincy Adams in 1824. While in the South Van Buren lost Tennessee to White and South Carolina to Calhounite candidate Willie P. Mangum, Van Buren compensated by carrying Virginia, which had not supported Jackson in 1824. As a result, Van Buren gained a narrow majority of electoral votes and avoided having the election decided by the House of Representatives.[19]

Van Buren's victory left the future of the anti-Jacksonian coalition in doubt. More generally, the possibility that the political process would become dominated by sectional interests remained very real. In his farewell address, Jackson decried "systematic efforts publicly made to sow the seeds of discord between different parts of the United States, and to place party divisions directly upon geographical distinctions; to excite the South against the North, and the North against the South, and to force into the controversy the most delicate and exciting topics upon which it is impossible that a large portion of the Union can ever speak without strong emotions."[20]

Jackson's fears seemed justified as sectional considerations continued to play a large role in the run-up to the presidential election of 1840. Against the background of Southern agitation for the annexation of Texas, Daniel Webster unsuccessfully sought to unify Northern Whigs behind his candidacy by emphasizing his opposition to "anything that shall extend the slavery of the African race on this continent." By contrast, Southern Whigs of all stripes united around the candidacy of Henry Clay. But the Whig Convention that convened on December 4, 1839 bypassed both Webster and Clay in favor of William Henry Harrison of Indiana. The delegates then sought to broaden Harrison's appeal to slave-state voters by choosing as his running mate John Tyler of Virginia. Seeking to further cement the party's reputation in the South, in January 1840 Whig Rep. William Cost Johnson of Maryland successfully pressed the House of Representatives to adopt a more extreme version of the gag rule.[21]

Whigs continued their sectional appeals to voters throughout the campaign. In the South, noting that Harrison was a native Virginian and former slave-owner who had harshly condemned abolitionists, Whigs argued that he was a far more reliable protector of Southern rights than the Yankee Van Buren. In the North, Whigs pilloried Van Buren for his support of the modified gag rule.[22] Moreover, the radical antislavery forces in the North organized the Liberty Party, the first national political party explicitly based on antislavery principles, and nominated abolitionist James G. Birney for president.

However, the vote for Birney was minuscule, exceeding 1 percent only in Massachusetts. Moreover, despite the sectional appeals in the campaign, the election of 1840 was ultimately dominated by two nonsectional factors— national issues that transcended the divide between North and South and discussions of the personal qualities of the two major party candidates. In the wake of the Panic of 1837 and the ensuing economic depression, both Whigs and Democrats developed bisectional identities founded on differing conceptions of the role that government should play in the economy. Whigs generally favored a more activist government, while Democrats (with Calhoun having returned to the fold) advocated a more laissez-faire approach. In addition, Democrats emphasized that Andrew Jackson had chosen Van Buren as his rightful successor and portrayed Harrison as an aged, unqualified nonentity, while Whigs hailed Harrison as the champion of the common man and, in the words of Sean Wilentz, charged that Van Buren was "a depraved executive autocrat who oppressed the people by day and who, by night, violated the sanctity of the [White House] with extravagant debaucheries."[23] Ultimately, the appeal of the Whigs proved much stronger in both the North and the South. Harrison won a convincing triumph, carrying 53 percent of the popular vote and winning in the electoral college by a margin of 234 to 60.

The election of 1840 was in a very real sense the high-water mark of the two-party system that had been envisioned by Van Buren in the late 1820s. While sectionalism remained a powerful force in American politics, the election was contested between two bisectional parties that were content to focus largely on nonsectional issues in the presidential campaign and shared a commitment to the preservation of peace between North and South. This shared commitment provided the backdrop for the Supreme Court's consideration of three major slavery-related cases in the early 1840s.

CHAPTER 4

The Supreme Court in the Early 1840s

The Supreme Court of the early 1840s was dominated by Jacksonian Democrats. Seven of the justices had been chosen by either Jackson himself or Martin Van Buren. In addition, one member of the Court had been chosen by President James Madison and one by President James Monroe.

Despite their shared formal political allegiances, the justices were far from united in their respective attitudes toward many of the issues that came before the Court. Jackson drew his support from a broad-based coalition whose members held a variety of different views on important public policy questions. Many of these divergent views were represented on the Court as well. Each of the justices brought to bear a unique perspective based upon his individual background and experience. They differed not only in their views on the institution of slavery itself but also in their attitudes to the issues of federal-state relations that were often raised by the slavery cases that came before the Court.[1]

The leader of the Court during this period was Chief Justice Roger Brooke Taney.[2] Taney was born on a large plantation in Calvert County, on the eastern shore of Maryland, on March 17, 1777. He received his early education from local schools and private tutors before entering Dickinson College in Carlisle, Pennsylvania, in 1792. Taney graduated from Dickinson in 1795 and was selected by his fellow students to give the valedictory address at the graduation ceremonies.

In 1796, Taney moved to Annapolis, Maryland. After reading law under the tutelage of local judge Jeremiah Townley Chase, Taney was admitted to the bar in 1799. He returned to Calvert County in that year and was elected to the state House of Delegates as a Federalist at the age of twenty-two, serving one term before being defeated in his bid for reelection in 1801. Taney was defeated in his bid to return to the House of Delegates in 1803, but in 1816 he was selected to serve a five-year term in the state Senate. He left the legislature in 1821 and spent much of the 1820s establishing himself in Baltimore as a leading figure in the Maryland bar. His selection to become the attorney general of the state of Maryland in 1827 reflected this prominence.

After the collapse of the Federalist Party, Taney aligned himself politically with Andrew Jackson in the early 1820s. He supported Jackson's unsuccessful presidential bid in 1824, and in 1828 he played a leading role in the organization of the Jackson forces in the state of Maryland. In 1831, Jackson appointed Taney to be attorney general of the United States.

Taney's service in the cabinet was marked by his militant opposition to the Bank of the United States. Unlike a number of other cabinet members, he successfully urged Jackson to veto the renewal of the bank's charter that was adopted by Congress in 1832. After Secretary of the Treasury William J. Dunne refused to withdraw federal funds from the bank in September 1833, Jackson removed Dunne and appointed Taney to replace him. However, knowing that the supporters of the bank would oppose the nomination, Jackson did not send it to the Senate for confirmation until June 1834. Thus, although the Senate ultimately rejected Taney's nomination on June 24, in the interim Taney succeeded in removing the funds and transferring them to state banks.[3]

In January 1835, after Gabriel Duvall of Maryland resigned from the Supreme Court, Jackson immediately chose Taney to be Duvall's replacement. Taney's enemies worked indirectly against the nomination by proposing a plan that would have merged the states of Maryland and Delaware into the Third Circuit and created a new circuit in the West. By custom, each circuit was represented on the Court by one of its residents. Thus, if adopted, the plan would have effectively eliminated Taney from consideration. Although the measure was not adopted, it served the purpose of delaying action on the nomination until Congress had adjourned, thereby effectively killing the appointment.[4]

Taney's enemies had good reason to regret this success after Chief Justice Marshall died on July 6, 1835. On December 28, 1835, Jackson nominated Taney to succeed Marshall. By this time, the political winds had shifted, and the administration had enough support in the Senate to assure confirmation. Thus, on March 15, 1836, Roger Brooke Taney succeeded to Marshall's position on the Court.

Taney's perspective on federalism was that of an orthodox Jacksonian. For example, unlike some of his more nationalist colleagues, he consistently took the view that the Commerce Clause by its terms did not deprive states of the power to regulate interstate commerce in the absence of a contrary federal statute. At the same time, the views of the newly appointed chief justice on issues related to slavery seem to have hardened considerably as he aged. Taney apparently showed some sympathy for the plight of slaves and free blacks during his tenure in the Maryland state legislature.[5] Moreover, in 1818, he vigorously and successfully defended the free speech rights of a Methodist minister charged with attempting to incite slaves by delivering an abolitionist sermon in Hagerstown, Maryland. However, in his capacity as attorney general of the United States in 1832, Taney prepared a strongly worded opinion defending the legality of the Negro Seamen's Acts of South Carolina, denying that free blacks were citizens of the United States at the time of the drafting of the Constitution and describing African Americans generally as "separate and degraded people to whom the sovereignty of each state might accord or withhold such privileges as they deemed proper."[6] Although the opinion was never published, it reflected a powerful commitment to Southern ideology on constitutional issues related to slavery more generally—a commitment that was often reflected in Taney's approach to the slavery-related issues that came before the Supreme Court during his tenure as chief justice.

Joseph Story, the senior associate justice during this period, was cut from quite different cloth.[7] Story was born on September 18, 1779, in Marblehead, Massachusetts, the oldest of the eleven children produced by a physician and his second wife. Story received his early education at a local academy before entering Harvard in 1794. After graduating from Harvard in 1798, he read law first in the offices of Samuel Sewall, a member of Congress from Marblehead, and later under the tutelage of Samuel Putnam of Salem.

After being admitted to the bar of Essex County in 1801, Story quickly established himself both as a leading light of the practicing bar and a prolific legal scholar, writing or coauthoring five treatises in the period from 1801 to 1820. He also vigorously engaged in political combat as one of the few prominent Republican lawyers in the state, serving in the state legislature from 1805 to 1812 and rising to the speakership in 1811. In addition, he served briefly in Congress in 1808, filling the unexpired term of Jacob Crowninshield after Crowninshield's death.

Story was something of a maverick among Massachusetts Republicans, pursuing an independent course on a variety of issues. For example, as part of a committee appointed to adjudicate the disputed gubernatorial election of 1806, he favored the Federalist candidate, and during his short tenure in Congress, Story was a leading opponent of the embargo of 1807. The latter position gained for Story the lasting enmity of President Thomas Jefferson, who derided the future justice as a "pseudo-republican."[8]

Against this background, it should not be surprising that, despite Story's growing reputation as a legal scholar, he was not President James Madison's first choice to succeed William Cushing on the Supreme Court after Cushing's death in 1810. Instead, the offer first went to the able Republican lawyer Levi Lincoln of Massachusetts, who refused the nomination because of failing eyesight. Madison next turned to Alexander Wolcott, a party stalwart whose nomination was rejected by the Senate. The post was then proffered to John Quincy Adams, who declined in order to pursue higher office. Finally, Madison turned to Story, who eagerly accepted the nomination and was confirmed without incident by the Senate. Story joined the Court on November 18, 1811 and served until his death on September 10, 1845.

Story is generally portrayed as John Marshall's chief lieutenant during Marshall's tenure as chief justice. However, Story's brilliance as a legal theorist has also earned him a reputation as a great justice in his own right. Story's approach to constitutional law was outlined in his multivolume *Commentaries on the Constitution of the United States,* which first appeared in 1833.[9] Designed to counter the state-centered view of constitutional law propounded by Southern theorists such as John Taylor, St. George Tucker, and John C. Calhoun, the *Commentaries* propounded a strongly nationalistic vision of the constitutional order based on the view that the Constitution should not be viewed as a compact among the states but rather as a product of the will of the people of the United States as a whole. The same nationalistic themes generally resonated through Story's judicial decisions as well. Beginning with his treatment of *Martin v. Hunter's Lessee,*[10] Story issued a long series of opinions emphasizing the power of both Congress and the federal courts, at times exceeding even John Marshall himself in his zeal to expand federal power.

As one might expect from his opinion in *La Jeune Eugenie,* Story was also an outspoken opponent of slavery. Earlier he had clearly expressed his views on the institution in general in an 1819 charge to the jury in another case involving the slave trade. There, Story asserted that "the existence of slavery under any shape is so repugnant to the natural rights of man and the dictates of justice that it seems difficult to find for it any natural justification." He subsequently lamented that

our constitutions of government have declared, that all men are born free and equal, and have certain unalienable rights, among which are the right of enjoying lives, liberties and properties and of seeking and obtaining their own safety and happiness. May not the miserable African ask, "Am I not a man and a brother?" We boast of our noble struggle against the encroachments of tyranny . . . and yet there are men among us who think it no wrong to condemn the shivering negro to perpetual slavery.[11]

Story took analogous positions in other contexts as well. He publicly condemned the Missouri Compromise and strongly opposed any extension of slavery into the territories. In addition, he privately applauded the views expressed by the Supreme Judicial Court of Massachusetts in *Commonwealth v. Aves,* where the court concluded that slaves brought voluntarily into Massachusetts became free under state law. Subsequently, he would oppose the annexation of Texas on the grounds that it would "give the South a mischievous, if not a ruinous preponderance in the Union."[12]

However, unlike some opponents of slavery, Story's willingness to act on such sentiments was circumscribed by a deep suspicion of threats to the established order. Although nominally a Republican at the time of his appointment, Story's political worldview was basically that of a conservative Northern Whig. Thus, while deploring the expansion of slavery and what he saw as aggressive behavior by the South, Story also vigorously attacked abolitionists, whom he publicly described in 1842 as "those mad men, who . . . are ready to stand up in public assemblies, and in the name of conscience, liberty, or the rights of man, to boast that they are willing and ready to bid farewell to [the] Constitution."[13]

These sentiments clearly reflected Story's reverence for the Constitution and the idea of the Union itself. A similar attitude was embodied in the treatment of slavery in the *Commentaries on the Constitution.* There, while asserting that Northern delegates to the Constitutional Convention had made a number of compromises in the face of Southern "prejudices," Story also remonstrated that

he who wished well to his country will adhere steadily to [these compromises] as a fundamental policy which extinguishes some of the most mischievous sources of all political divisions,—those founded on geographical positions and domestic institutions. The wishes of every patriot ought now to be, *requiscat in pace.*[14]

Story's approach to legal issues related to slavery was further constrained by his commitment to the concept of law as an autonomous discipline. Thus, in 1843, he wrote privately that

I shall never hesitate to do my duty as a Judge, under the Constitution and laws of the United States, be the consequences what they may. The Constitution I have sworn to support, and I cannot forget or repudiate my solemn obligations at pleasure. [Although] I have ever been opposed to slavery . . . I take my standard of duty *as a Judge* from the Constitution.[15]

These competing concerns would shape Story's approach to the slavery-related issues that came before the Court in the early 1840s.

In 1840, Smith Thompson was the only other appointee from the pre-Jacksonian period who remained on the Court.[16] Born into a wealthy, politically prominent family in Amenia, New York on January 17, 1768, Thompson graduated from the College of New Jersey in 1788 and then briefly worked as a schoolteacher before beginning his legal training under James Kent in Poughkeepsie, New York. Kent was at the time in partnership with Gilbert Livingston, and when Kent left the firm in 1793, Thompson entered into a partnership with Livingston and married Livingston's daughter the following year.

Like Thompson's father, Livingston was influential in local Antifederalist circles. Thus it should not be surprising that Thompson himself quickly became prominent in the New York Republican party, securing election to the New York state legislature in 1800 before being named to the New York Supreme Court two years later. He remained on that court for sixteen years, succeeding to the chief justiceship after Kent left the court in 1814. In 1818, Thompson resigned this position to accept an appointment as secretary of the navy in the Monroe administration.

When Brockhulst Livingston died on March 18, 1823, leaving the Second Circuit seat on the Supreme Court vacant, the process of finding a successor became entangled in the maneuvering for the upcoming presidential election of 1824. Monroe offered the seat to Thompson on March 24, but Thompson, who was at the time engaged in gathering support for a presidential bid, initially refused the appointment, citing health considerations. However, on July 20, after it had become clear that his presidential ambitions had no realistic prospects for success, Thompson accepted Monroe's offer of a position on the Court. After an unsuccessful campaign for governor of New York in 1828, Thompson remained on the Court until his death.

Although in 1819 he described the slave trade as "inhuman and disgraceful,"[17] Thompson does not seem to have had strong feelings about the issue of slavery more generally. He is perhaps best known for his long-running battle with Chief Justice John Marshall and Justice Joseph Story over the issue of federal exclusivity. In sharp contrast to Marshall and Story, Thompson consistently argued that a simple grant of power to Congress did not, by its terms, divest states of concurrent authority to legislate on the same subject.[18] This view of federalism was the most prominent feature of Thompson's constitutional jurisprudence.

John McLean was the most senior of the associate justices appointed by Andrew Jackson.[19] McLean was born in northern New Jersey on May 8, 1787. During his early years, McLean's family moved steadily westward, journeying first to Morgantown, Virginia, and later to the vicinity of Lexington, Kentucky, before finally settling in Warren County, Ohio, in 1798. There McLean received his first formal education in a neighborhood school. Later, he also attended school in Cincinnati.

Beginning in 1804, McLean served two years as an apprentice to the clerk of the local court of common pleas. During this period he also studied law with Arthur St. Clair Jr., the son of the territorial governor. McLean purchased a printing office in 1806 and, in 1807, began publishing the Lebanon *Western Star*. The same year, he married Rebecca Edwards. In 1810, McLean disposed of the newspaper and turned to the practice of law as his profession.

McLean was first elected to Congress in 1812. As a member of the House of Representatives, McLean generally supported the Madison administration, and he was particularly aggressive in advocating vigorous prosecution of the War of 1812. He was reelected in 1814 and played an important role in securing congressional support for the presidential candidacy of James Monroe before resigning on May 16, 1816 to accept a position on the Ohio Supreme Court.

McLean's active involvement in politics continued after his appointment to the court. In 1822, he made an unsuccessful bid for the United States Senate, and became an early advocate for the presidential ambitions of Sen. John C. Calhoun of South Carolina—at that point in his career a strong nationalist. Later that year, Calhoun repaid this support by persuading Monroe to choose McLean for the position of commissioner of the public land office. The following year, Monroe appointed McLean to the office of postmaster general of the United States. After it became clear that Calhoun could not be elected president in 1824, McLean supported John Quincy Adams in his struggle with Andrew Jackson for the position. McLean was thus retained as postmaster general after Adams's victory in the election.

Although he was an able administrator of his department, McLean proved to be far from a loyal supporter of the Adams administration. While continuing to profess his support to the president himself, McLean also began to actively participate in the effort to pave the way for a Jackson victory in the upcoming election of 1828. In large measure, McLean's activities seemed to be a byproduct of a maturing ambition to eventually succeed to the presidency himself. Calhoun's turn toward Southern sectionalism had begun to alienate him politically from Jackson, and Henry Clay's prospects had been weakened somewhat by his behavior as secretary of state. Against this background, McLean reasoned that if Jackson was elected in 1828 but chose not to seek a second term in 1832, McLean himself might be well positioned to succeed him.

After Jackson's victory in 1828, McLean was considered for a number of posts in the new administration. His first choice was apparently to be named secretary of war. Other possibilities included continuing as postmaster general and becoming head of the Department of the Navy. Ultimately, however, McLean became Jackson's first appointment to the Court, succeeding Robert Trimble as the representative of the circuit that included Ohio. McLean was confirmed without incident almost immediately after Jackson's inauguration.

McLean was one of the strongest judicial nationalists on the Taney Court. In addition, he was a committed opponent of slavery. For example, while sitting on the Ohio Supreme Court in 1817, he declared in dictum that "viewing the question abstractly I could not hesitate to declare that a slave in any state or country, according to the immutable principles of natural justice, is entitled to his freedom; that, that which had its origin in usurpation and fraud can never be sanctified into a right." Pronouncements such as these led Senator Thomas Hart Benton of Missouri to declare that McLean was "abolitionist enough for anybody outside of a mad house—& his wife is abolitionist enough for all those who ought to be in one."[20]

This assessment was something of an overstatement. Like Story, McLean did not believe that his personal views on slavery were dispositive of all constitutional cases in which the rights of slaves and slaveowners were implicated. Instead, unlike the strongest opponents of slavery, he would at times subordinate his antislavery sentiments to other considerations. In particular, McLean rejected the view that judges could invoke the "higher law" to avoid the mandates of federal statutes and the Constitution:

It is known to every man that Judges are sworn to support the Constitution and laws. They cannot consider slavery in the abstract. If they disregard what they conscientiously believe to be the written law in any case, they act corruptly and are traitors to their country.... How is it expected or desired that a Judge shall substitute his own notions for positive law? While this [shall] become the rule of judicial action, there will be no security for character, property or life.[21]

In short, despite Benton's description, McLean did not truly subscribe to the tenets of the more radical elements of the antislavery movement. Nonetheless, throughout his tenure on the Supreme Court, McLean would prove to be the strongest antislavery voice on the Court.

Henry Baldwin's views were quite different from those of his fellow Northern justices. Baldwin was born into a prominent family in New Haven, Connecticut, on January 14, 1779. After graduating from Yale College in 1797, Baldwin moved to Philadelphia, where he read law in the offices of Alexander J. Dallas, an attorney who is perhaps best known for being the first official reporter of the decisions of the Supreme Court. After completing his studies with Dallas, Baldwin briefly relocated to Meadville, Pennsylvania, before permanently settling in Pittsburgh.

Baldwin was elected to Congress in 1817, where he served until 1822, when financial reversals and health consideration forced him to abandon his seat.

This period left Baldwin deeply in debt. He was ultimately forced to declare bankruptcy and suffered from financial difficulties for the rest of his life.[22]

An early and active supporter of Andrew Jackson, Baldwin hoped and believed that he would be appointed secretary of the treasury when Jackson was elected president in 1828. Much to Baldwin's dismay, the post was instead given to a candidate supported by Vice President Calhoun. However, by the time of Justice Bushrod Washington's death in 1829, Calhoun was beginning to fall from favor in the administration. Jackson's choice of Baldwin to succeed Washington was apparently motivated in part by a desire to embarrass Calhoun, whose supporters attacked Baldwin, while the vice president himself openly pressed the candidacy of Chief Justice John B. Gibson of the Pennsylvania Supreme Court. Although leading anti-Jacksonian Daniel Webster was relieved by the appointment, some Jacksonians were apparently not pleased. Nonetheless, only the two senators from South Carolina ultimately voted against confirmation, and Baldwin took his seat on January 6, 1830.[23]

During his career on the bench, Baldwin was not only jurisprudentially erratic but personally unstable. Indeed, he apparently missed the 1833 term of the Court because of a bout with mental illness. However, two points emerge clearly from his actions and writings.

First, he had a profound distaste for Story's jurisprudence, viewing it as unduly influenced by the civil law tradition. Baldwin's general approach to constitutional interpretation was outlined in his *General View of the Origin and Nature of the Constitution and Government of the United States,* published in 1837. Unlike Story's *Commentaries on the Constitution,* to which it was at least in part designed to be a response, *General View* is generally viewed as something less than a landmark in the development of American constitutional law. For example indeed, T. Edward White has described it as a "bizarre performance," and asserted that Baldwin "had strung together such a rag-tag bunch of disparate sources, citing each of them as an authoritative proposition . . . that his position was virtually unintelligible."[24]

Unquestionably, *General View* is far from a model of pristine legal reasoning. Nonetheless, some aspects of Baldwin's concept of the structure of American federalism emerge relatively clearly. He argued that it was inappropriate to infer grants of unenumerated powers from the constitutional text. At the same time, he contended that whatever powers were in fact granted should be deemed exclusive, contending that "'the grant [of power] does not convey power, which might be beneficial to the grantor, if retained by himself . . . but is an *investment* of power for the general advantage, in the hands of *agents,* selected for that purpose, which power can never be exercised by the people themselves, but must be placed in the hands of *agents* or lie dormant."[25]

In addition, Baldwin was strongly pro-Southern in his approach to slavery-related issues. For example, in sharp contrast to Story, Baldwin was one of the few Northern congressmen to support the admission of Missouri as a slave state even before the issue was linked to the admission of Maine—a position that would have been unthinkable for a man such as McLean, who was truly opposed to slavery. Baldwin's sympathy for Southern positions was also evident in a number of the decisions that he rendered after his appointment to the bench.

Baldwin's attitude toward the Fugitive Slave Clause in particular was clearly reflected in 1833, when Baldwin was sitting on circuit in *Johnson v. Tompkins*.[26] *Johnson* was a tort action in which the plaintiff, a slaveowner, sought damages because the defendants had forcibly interfered with his efforts to recover a slave named Jack. The defense was based on the theory that the plaintiff had acted unlawfully in seizing Jack without first obtaining a warrant, and also by not bringing Jack immediately before a magistrate to prove that he was in fact a slave. In essence, the defendants claimed that they had simply been arresting a wrongdoer.

Justice Baldwin charged the jury that the plaintiff had not violated either Pennsylvania or federal law in reclaiming Jack, essentially guaranteeing that the defendants would be found liable. What is particularly striking about the *Tompkins* opinion, however, is its extraordinary rhetoric in defense of the slaveholder's rights. In part, Baldwin's argument emphasized the significance of property rights and the rule of law generally. Thus, while seemingly agreeing that the institution of slavery "is abhorrent to all our ideas of natural right and justice," Baldwin also admonished the jury that "it is not permitted to you or us to indulge our feelings of abstract right on these subjects; the law recognises [*sic*] the right of one man to hold another in bondage, and that right must be respected." He also said that

if this is unjust and oppressive, the sin is on the heads of the makers of laws which tolerate slavery . . . to visit it on those who have honestly acquired and lawfully hold property, under the guarantee of the laws, is the worst of all oppression, and the rankest injustice towards our fellow-men. It is indulgence of a spirit of persecution against our neighbors. . . . If this spirit pervades our country; if public opinion is suffered to prostrate the laws which protect one species of property, those who lead the crusade against slavery may, at no distant day, find a new one directed against their lands, their stores, and their debts. . . .

When the law ceases to be the test of right and remedy; when individuals undertake to be its administrators by rules of their own adoption, the bands of society are broken as effectually by the severance of one link from the chain of justice, which binds man to the laws, as if the whole was dissolved. The more specious and seductive the pretexts under which the law is violated, the greater ought to be the vigilance of courts and juries in their detection.[27]

Moreover, in Baldwin's eyes, slaves were not simply an ordinary type of property. They were instead "political property," deserving of an even higher level of protection. He based this conclusion on the three-fifths compromise, which enhanced the power of whites from slave states by partially counting slaves in the basis of representation for the House of Representatives. Baldwin reasoned that if fugitive slaves were not returned to their states of origin, the number of slaves in those states would be reduced, thereby also reducing the number of representatives to which white voters in those states would be entitled. Thus, he charged the jury that

in protecting the rights of a master in the property of a slave, the constitution guarantees the highest rights of the respective states, of which each has a right to avail itself, and which each enjoys in proportion to the number of slaves within its boundaries . . . you see that the foundations of the government are laid, and rest on the right of property in slaves—the whole structure must fall by disturbing the corner stones—if federal numbers cease to be respected or held sacred in questions of property or government, the rights of the states must disappear and the government and the union dissolve by the prostration of its laws before the usurped authority of individuals.[28]

Finally, bringing the themes of his charge together, Baldwin concluded that

if there are any rights of property which can be enforced, if our citizens have personal rights which are made inviolable under the protection of the supreme law of the state and union, they are those which have been set at naught by some of the defendants. As the owner of property, which he had a perfect right to possess, and take away; as a citizen of a sister state, entitled to all the privileges and immunities of citizens of any other states, [the plaintiff] stands before you on ground which no law can take from—it is the same ground [on] which the government is built.[29]

Baldwin's opinion in *Johnson* would no doubt have met with the approval of even the most radical defenders of slavery. Unlike men such as Story, Baldwin did not simply characterize the Fugitive Slave Clause as a compromise that was necessary to preserve sectional harmony; instead, he emphasized the centrality of slavery in the American political system. The same perspective would also be reflected in his approach to the cases that came before the Supreme Court during his tenure. At times, however, Baldwin would subordinate his proslavery sympathies to his more general theories of constitutional law.

After Taney himself, James Moore Wayne was the first of the Southern justices appointed by Jackson.[30] Wayne was born in 1790, the twelfth of thirteen children of a prominent Savannah, Georgia, planter, businessman, and slave trader. Wayne received his early education from a private tutor before attending the College of New Jersey (the forerunner of Princeton University), graduating with a Bachelor of Arts in 1808. From 1809 to 1810, he studied law with Judge Charles Chauncy in New Haven, Connecticut, and was admitted to the bar upon his return to Savannah in 1811.

A tall, graceful man with a ruddy complexion and strong, intelligent features, Wayne soon entered politics, and in 1815 was elected to the state legislature. Two years later, he became the mayor of Savannah. The state General Assembly chose Wayne to be a judge of the court of common pleas in 1819. In 1821, he achieved more exalted judicial office, becoming a judge for the Eastern Circuit of the state. Wayne served in that capacity until 1828, when he was elected to the United States House of Representatives.

Although early in his career Wayne had been a strong supporter of the presidential ambitions of William Crawford, by 1828 he was a committed Jacksonian. This allegiance hardly distinguished Wayne from his opponents in the campaign of 1828; if nothing else, Andrew Jackson's attitude toward the Cherokee Indians assured him of almost universal popularity in Georgia. At the same time, candidates vied for support by attacking the highly unpopular tariff of 1828. As early as 1824, Wayne had served on a committee that recommended "prompt and efficient measures of opposition" to existing tariffs. In summer of 1828, he played a major role in an Anti-Tariff Convention, drafting resolutions which condemned the most recent tariff as "unconstitutional in spirit" but rejecting nullification in favor of a strategy of remonstrance and appeal.[31]

In the crisis of 1832, many prominent Georgians supported South Carolina in its struggle with the federal government. Nonetheless, while continuing to vigorously denounce the tariff itself, at a local anti-tariff meeting Wayne also supported an unsuccessful attempt to brand nullification as "dangerous and ruinous." In the election of 1832, this position cost Wayne the support of his former allies in the Democratic-Republican Party. Nonetheless, his personal popularity remained strong, and he was easily reelected to Congress. Soon after the election, he voted in favor of the Force Bill, which authorized military action against the nullifiers of South Carolina. During the following session, Senator Thomas Hart Benton ranked Wayne among the ten "zealous, able and determined" members of the House who spearheaded the Jackson campaign against the Bank of the United States. In the congressional elections of October 1834,

Wayne was once again the leading vote-getter in the state. Soon thereafter, he was nominated as the Union Party candidate for governor of Georgia.[32]

However, Wayne was not destined to either return to the House of Representatives or to serve as governor of the state. In the summer of 1834, Justice William Johnson of South Carolina died, and Jackson was faced with the task of selecting a replacement to represent Johnson's circuit on the Court. The nullification crisis had eliminated most South Carolinians from consideration. Most of the prominent Democrats in the state were supporters of John C. Calhoun, who had spearheaded the nullification movement, and Calhoun was in a position to block the appointment of any South Carolina Whig by the invocation of senatorial courtesy. Turning to Georgia, on January 6, 1835, Jackson appointed Wayne, his loyal supporter who also stood high in the estimation of Martin Van Buren.[33] Although the Senate was dominated by Whigs, they no doubt understood that Jackson was unlikely to appoint any person whose views were more acceptable to them. Thus, Wayne was confirmed without great difficulty and sworn in on January 14, 1835—the first justice of the Supreme Court to have been born under the Constitution.

Although a slaveowner himself, Wayne was by no means a proslavery zealot. As late as 1854, he denounced slavery as fundamentally evil, expressed the hope that Southerners would gradually emancipate their bondsmen, and advocated action by the federal government to encourage the return of all African Americans to Africa through a program of colonization. On issues which came before the Court during Wayne's tenure, he often differed with fellow Southern Jacksonians such as Roger Brooke Taney, Peter V. Daniel, and John Catron. Unlike them, Wayne often took a strongly nationalistic approach to constitutional adjudication; indeed, a subsequent appointee to the Court would later rank Wayne with John McLean as the two "most high-toned Federalists on the [Court]."[34] Still, Wayne was generally committed to protecting the interests of the South on slavery-related issues. These at times conflicting imperatives would shape Wayne's analysis of the question with which he was faced during his time on the Court.

The remaining members of the Court—John Catron of Tennessee, John McKinley of Alabama, and Peter V. Daniel of Virginia—were all appointed by Martin Van Buren. While the details of Catron's early life are less well established than those of other members of the Taney Court,[35] he apparently was born into the Kettering family of western Pennsylvania in 1781. During his childhood, Catron's family moved first to western Virginia and then to Kentucky. In both areas, Catron lived on farms, acquiring his formal education in local common schools. Catron changed his name and moved to Tennessee, beginning to read law in April 1812 and being admitted to the bar in late 1815. After inheriting a practice from a local attorney who was elected to Congress, Catron was appointed by the legislature to be the local prosecutor.

In 1818, Catron moved to Nashville. There he became known for his expertise in issues involving title to real property. Such issues were particularly important and complex in Tennessee, and thus Catron was a logical choice to fill a seat on the state supreme court when the seat became open in 1824. He remained on that court until 1835, serving the last six years as chief justice.

Catron's 1834 opinion in *Fisher's Negroes v. Dobbs* clearly revealed his attitude toward slavery. In concluding that a manumission clause in a will was valid only if the freed slaves were sent to Liberia, Catron declared that "the slave, who receives the protection and care of a tolerable master, holds a condition here, superior to the negro who is freed from domestic slavery. . . . The freed black man lives amongst us without motive and without hope." He also declared that "nothing can be more untrue than that the free negro is more respectable as a member of society in the non-slaveholding than in the slaveholding States. In each, he is a degraded outcast, and his fancied freedom a delusion. . . . Generally, and almost universally, society suffers, and the negro suffers by manumission."[36]

Catron had served under Andrew Jackson in the army, and he was an early and ardent supporter of Jackson's presidential ambitions. Appointment to the state bench did nothing to dampen Catron's enthusiasm for the cause, and he continued to campaign actively for Jacksonian policies. Catron publicly attacked the Bank of the United States, and during the nullification crisis drafted a set of resolutions supporting the position of the president. Moreover, his 1835 opinion for the court in *State v. Foreman*[37] was drafted with an eye toward inviting the Supreme Court to reconsider or modify its position in *Worcester v. Georgia*,[38] a decision that was anathema to Jackson because it impeded the process of forcing Native American tribes to abandon their traditional homelands and move west.

Catron not only supported Jackson himself but also the aspirations of Martin Van Buren, Jackson's anointed successor. Catron's support of Van Buren put him at odds with a number of important state political leaders in Tennessee, and when the state supreme court was reconstituted in 1836, Catron lost his position. After leaving the bench, Catron campaigned vigorously for Van Buren in the election of 1836.

The passage of the Judiciary Act of 1837 provided Jackson and Van Buren with an opportunity to reward Catron for his loyalty. This statute was passed in response to years of complaints that the Western states were not included in any of the existing circuits, and that Westerners were thereby denied both equal access to the federal courts and appropriate representation on the Supreme Court. In response, Congress reorganized the federal court system, created two new circuits, and added two seats to the Supreme Court, with one justice to be drawn from each of the new circuits.[39]

Although the conflict over slavery does not appear to have been a significant factor in the drafting of the new Judiciary Act, the new alignment of the circuits substantially changed the balance of power on the Court. From 1830 to 1837, Northerners controlled a majority of seats on the Court, even with the chief justice having been appointed from a slave state. Under the scheme of the 1837 statute, by contrast, the circuits (and the justices drawn from them) were divided equally between North and South. Given Chief Justice Taney's origins in Maryland, Southerners were left with a 5–4 majority on the Court.

Catron became an immediate beneficiary of the new Judiciary Act. By virtue of the statute, Tennessee had been removed from the Sixth Circuit and placed in a new circuit with Kentucky and Missouri. Catron was immediately appointed by Jackson to fill the new seat, and Van Buren supported the appointment after his inauguration. The Senate quickly confirmed Catron, and he took his seat on March 8, 1837.

His appointment to the Court did not deter Catron from continuing to take an active interest in politics. He was a close and trusted advisor to both James K. Polk and James Buchanan, and he actively campaigned for the annexation of Texas. In his judicial capacity, Catron proved to be something of a moderate on many of the important issues that came before the Court. His position on issues of federal-state relations is typical. While clearly less committed to preservation of states' rights than Taney and Daniel, he was by no means as strong a nationalist as either Story or Wayne. A similar moderation would be reflected in his approach to the slavery-related issues that came before the Court in the early 1840s.

John McKinley came to the Court at almost the same time as Catron. McKinley was born in Culpepper County, Virginia, on May 1, 1780.[40] When McKinley was a young boy, his family moved to Lincoln County, Kentucky, where he grew to manhood. McKinley had little formal education, and initially he sought employment as a carpenter. However, in 1799 he began to study law under General Bodley in Frankfort and was admitted to the bar in 1801.

In 1818, McKinley moved to Huntsville, Alabama. He soon became active in local politics and was elected to the state legislature in 1820. Running as a supporter of Henry Clay, McKinley made a bid for the United States Senate in 1822, but he was narrowly defeated by William Kelly. McKinley became an enthusiastic convert to the Jacksonian cause in 1824, and in 1826 he was selected to fill an unexpired term in the Senate. After being defeated for reelection to the Senate in 1831, McKinley was elected to the House of Representatives in 1832. At the end of this term, he chose not to seek reelection; instead, he successfully campaigned for a seat in the state legislature in 1836. Late in that year, he once again won election to the Senate for a term that would have begun in March 1837. However, McKinley was destined never to take this seat.

One of the new circuits created by the Judiciary Act of 1837 included Alabama, and four members of the House of Representatives—two from Alabama and two from other states—immediately recommended McKinley for appointment to the Court. Nonetheless, William Smith of Alabama was appointed and confirmed to the post. But when Smith declined to serve, Van Buren gave McKinley a recess appointment in April 1837. McKinley was confirmed without incident in September of that year.[41]

McKinley has been described as a man who was "out of his depth" on the Court and "made no significant contribution to legal thinking in any form."[42] During his fifteen years of service on the Court he wrote only twenty-two opinions. His opinion on federalism-related issues appears to have been much like that of Henry Baldwin; while taking a narrow view of the scope of congressional power generally, McKinley also expressed the opinion that congressional power was exclusive in those areas where authority was granted by the Constitution. His views on slavery were those of a Southern moderate.

Peter Vivian Daniel played a quite different role on the Taney Court. Daniel was born on April 24, 1784 on a family farm in Stafford County, Virginia, an agricultural region located approximately fifty miles south of Washington, D.C., and sixty miles north of Richmond.[43] He received his early education from private tutors, and in 1802 he spent a few months at Princeton before returning to Stafford County. In 1805, Daniel moved to Richmond to study law in the offices of Edmund Randolph, one of the most prominent figures in Virginia politics and society. After being admitted to the bar in 1808, Daniel returned to Stafford County to practice. In 1809 he returned to Richmond as a representative to the state legislature, and in 1810 married Randolph's younger daughter, Lucy. Soon thereafter, Daniel permanently relocated to Richmond.

The Randolph connection did not translate into great financial prosperity for the Daniel family. Daniel was a committed Jeffersonian in a city whose business establishment was dominated by Federalists and later Whigs, who tended to give their business to those who shared their political views. Thus, throughout his life, Daniel's income was far less than many of those in the exalted company in which he found himself.

At the same time, the son-in-law and protege of Edmund Randolph had immediate access to the highest circles in Virginia Democratic politics. He quickly became a prominent member of the so-called Richmond Junto, a network of influential Democrats that dominated Virginia politics for much of the first part of the nineteenth century. Daniel's formal base of power was his membership on the Virginia Council of State, a unique institution that shared executive power with the governor of the state. Daniel served on the council almost continuously from 1812 to 1835, and for much of that period was its senior member and, as such, lieutenant governor of the state.

Beginning in the 1820s, Daniel also began to take an increasingly active role in national politics. In 1824, the Junto threw its support behind William H. Crawford of Georgia for president. By contrast, in 1828, like most former Crawford supporters, Daniel vigorously supported the ticket of Andrew Jackson and John C. Calhoun of South Carolina, and was rewarded as the Jackson-Calhoun forces carried Virginia and thwarted Adams's bid for reelection.

While Daniel had great admiration for Jackson, he had a much closer personal relationship with Martin Van Buren. From the time that Van Buren had established a political reliance between his Albany Regency and the Richmond Junto, Daniel maintained an active correspondence with the "Little Magician," strongly supporting his campaign for the vice presidency in 1832 and the presidency in 1836.

This personal relationship may very well have been an important factor in Daniel's thinking when Virginia Democrats split between Jackson and Calhoun during Jackson's first term. The key issue dividing the two factions was the protective tariff, which had been adopted with Jackson's support but was opposed by Calhoun. Daniel agreed with Calhoun on the substantive issue. Nonetheless, Daniel remained the titular leader of the Jackson Democrats in Virginia. Moreover, despite his lifelong commitment to states' rights, Daniel continued to support the administration in its firm opposition to South Carolina's claim that it had the right to nullify the tariff on constitutional grounds. At the same time, however, Daniel also consistently adhered to the view that a state had the right to secede from the Union in response to more severe provocation.

Daniel's position on the tariff itself must have left him somewhat ambivalent about his support for Jackson in his struggles with Calhoun and the state of South Carolina. However, Daniel had no compunctions about rallying behind the administration in its war with the Bank of the United States. Daniel considered the Bank an abomination; for example, when asked to evaluate the claims of an aspirant to political office, Daniel replied that "he has professed a belief in the *constitutionality* of a *national bank,* and that is an objection which with me would overrule any and every recommendation which could be urged for him or for any other person."[44] Thus, Daniel had no difficulty in enthusiastically supporting Jackson's decision to remove federal deposits and place them in state banks.

When Roger Brooke Taney left his position as attorney general to oversee the process as secretary of treasury, Daniel was Jackson's choice to be Taney's replacement. Daniel refused this appointment for financial reasons. By contrast, in March 1836, when Philip P. Barbour left the Federal District Court for the Eastern District of Virginia to become an associate justice of the Supreme Court, Daniel accepted an appointment to be his successor.

Five years later, on February 25, 1841, Barbour died in office. Martin Van Buren, having succeeded Jackson in 1836 but then been defeated for reelection by Whig William Henry Harrison in 1840, had eight days left until his term expired. Seeking to deprive the Whigs of the opportunity to choose a justice, Van Buren quickly appointed Daniel to succeed Barbour on the Court.

There followed a brief but intense political struggle over the nomination. Democrats in the Senate had enough votes for confirmation. Whigs, however, knew that if they could delay Senate action for only eight days, the nomination would automatically die and the seat would be filled by a nominee of the incoming Whig president. Daniel's opponents pursued a two-pronged strategy in seeking to achieve their objectives.[45]

The opposition first sought to take advantage of the fact that recently admitted Southwestern states were not yet part of any circuit and had no representation on the Supreme Court. The Whigs introduced a bill that would have remedied this situation by abolishing the existing fourth circuit, merging Virginia and North Carolina into other existing circuits, and creating a new Southwestern circuit in place of the fourth. They hoped thereby to entice some Southwestern Democrats to oppose Daniel in the hope of having a justice appointed from their own region to service the new circuit.

This part of the strategy was a partial success. The circuit reorganization bill passed the Senate, and some Southwestern Democrats abandoned the Daniel nomination. Nonetheless, after it became apparent that the Senate bill could not be acted upon in the House of Representatives, it also became clear that Daniel retained enough support to be confirmed if the matter came to a vote on the merits. The Whigs then attempted to deprive the Senate of a quorum by abandoning the chamber en masse. This attempt also failed by the narrowest of margins, but only after the Democratic leadership had scoured the city of Washington in a desperate effort to locate absent Democratic senators. Thus, shortly after midnight on March 2, 1841, Peter V. Daniel was confirmed as an associate justice of the Supreme Court.

Van Buren soon reported to Jackson that, in nominating Daniel, he had taken the opportunity "to put a man on the bench of the Supreme Court . . . who will I am sure stick to the true principles of the constitution, and being a Democrat *ab ovo* [literally, from the egg] is not in so much danger of a falling off [of] a true spirit." In many respects, the tall, spare, dark-complected Daniel met or even exceeded Van Buren's expectations. A true agrarian conservative, Daniel was deeply committed to the constitutional theories embodied in the Virginia and Kentucky Resolutions and the work of John Taylor. He viewed the defense of these principles and the advocates of the nationalist, probusiness policies associated with the Whig Party as an apocalyptic struggle between good and evil.

Daniel's public comments on politics were notable for their forcefulness; he was described by one political opponent as "one of the most violent partisan writers in the state." Daniel was no less emphatic in private; for example, in an 1832 letter to Van Buren, he described the forthcoming election as a "great struggle between democracy and the constitution on the one hand, and corruption and profligacy unexampled on the other" and declared that "the conflict we are now waging [is] against that worst of all influences; that which puts intelligence, probity, patriotism, falsehood, venality, vice in every form, all upon an equality, that is, values them merely as they can become means to be wielded to its purposes—*the influence of money.*" Similarly, after meeting Daniel Webster, Daniel reported on one occasion that "my hand was actually contaminated with his." In short, as John P. Frank has aptly observed, "the Daniel who came to the Court in 1841 . . . was a man of controversy, ferocious, unyielding, and utterly humorless in dispute."[46]

These attitudes and personal characteristics shaped Daniel's treatment of the constitutional issues that came before the Taney Court. Not surprisingly, the chief justice was Daniel's closest friend and ideological ally on the Court. However, Daniel was considerably more uncompromising than Taney in his positions on issues such as federalism, taking an extremely narrow view of the power of Congress and consistently maintaining that states retained concurrent authority in the absence of congressional legislation. Thus, he dissented alone more than twice as often as any other justice during his tenure, and more than three times as often as Taney, John Catron, and John A. Campbell combined.

Daniel was also a vigorous defender of slavery and Southern rights. At times, this perspective dovetailed well with his strong aversion to the expansion of federal power. However, when his ideological commitments came into conflict, Daniel often gave preference to the protection of Southern interests.

The confirmation of Peter Daniel completed the Court that would decide the important slavery-related cases of the early 1840s. On its face, the membership of the Court was not one that was calculated to fill the opponents of slavery with confidence. Five of the justices—a clear majority—represented slave states. In addition, Henry Baldwin of Pennsylvania was as militant in his defense of the rights of slaveholders as any Southerner. Nonetheless, when presented with three concrete cases in rapid succession, this group of justices produced a set of decisions that was entirely consistent with the Jacksonian emphasis on the avoidance of conflict over slavery, filtered through a shared commitment to the conventions of legal analysis. Two of those cases—*Groves v. Slaughter*[47] and *Prigg v. Pennsylvania*[48]—raised profoundly important doctrinal questions about the place of slavery in the federal system. But it was the dispute that gave rise to the *United States v. The Amistad*[49] that generated the greatest political controversy.

CHAPTER 5

United States v. The Amistad

Like *The Antelope, United States v. The Amistad*[1] was a case arising from the African slave trade. The facts of *The Amistad* were, however, much more dramatic.[2] *The Amistad* involved the fate of a number of blacks who were purchased by Portuguese slave traders in Lombocko, on the west coast of Africa, in April 1839. The Africans were transported to Cuba on the slave ship *Tecora.* Although slavery itself was legal in Cuba, the African slave trade was prohibited there by both Spanish domestic law and a treaty between Spain and England. Nonetheless, like many before them, the *Tecora* Africans were smuggled onto the island and sold openly in Havana under the pretense of being *ladinos*— persons who were already slaves and had lived in Cuba long enough to become Spanish subjects and learn to speak Spanish.

On June 26, 1839, two Spanish slave traders—Jose Ruiz and Pedro Montes— purchased forty-nine of the *Tecora* Africans at auction. At the same auction, Ruiz and Montes also purchased four other children who had not been on the *Tecora.* None of the Africans spoke Spanish, and the children were too young to have been imported to Cuba before the international slave trade was outlawed on the island. Nonetheless, for a "fee," the governor-general of Cuba issued a passport describing those purchased as "black Ladinos" and authorizing Ruiz and Montes to transport them for sale to Cuban plantations at Puerto Principe.

At midnight on June 28, Ruiz, Montes, and their human cargo set out for Puerto Principe on the *Amistad,* a schooner that had been built in Baltimore, Maryland, specifically for use in the domestic coastal slave trade. On July 2, under the leadership of one of their number, Cinque, the Africans revolted, killing the captain of the ship and taking control of the vessel. The Africans ordered Montes to sail the *Amistad* to Africa. However, for almost two months Montes deceived the Africans, and on August 25, the ship anchored off the coast of Long Island, New York.

Seeking provisions, a number of the Africans went ashore, where they sought the aid of a group of five seamen, including Henry Green. The following day, the activity attracted the attention of the crew of the *USS Washington,* a brig in the United States Navy under the command of Lieutenant Thomas R. Gedney. Gedney ordered his men to seize the *Amistad,* and the two ships sailed in tandem to New London, Connecticut, where Gedney informed the local United States marshal of the situation. The marshal then notified Andrew T.

Judson, the United States district judge for Connecticut, who immediately went to the *Washington* to conduct an inquiry.

During the inquiry, Montes and Ruiz asserted that the *Amistad* had been legally engaged in the Cuban domestic slave trade, and that the blacks on board were in fact their slaves who had mutinied and murdered the captain of the ship. The Spanish slave traders produced the passports in support of their account and requested that the *Amistad,* the Africans, and the nonhuman cargo of the ship be delivered to the Spanish consul in Boston. Judson, however, decided instead to hold the black adults, and to have the situation presented at the next session of the grand jury of the United States Circuit Court, which was to meet in Hartford, Connecticut in September 1839. He directed that all of the putative slaves be held in the New Haven jail until that time.

Gedney responded by filing a claim for salvage in the Federal District Court for the state of Connecticut. He claimed that the crew of the *Washington* should be compensated for saving the *Amistad* and its cargo. In addition, the complaint asserted that, in order to satisfy this claim, Gedney had the right to seize and sell the cargo of the *Amistad,* including Cinque and the other Africans.

New England abolitionists quickly took up the cause of Cinque and his compatriots. They obtained the services of Roger Baldwin, a prominent Connecticut attorney with strong antislavery sentiments who, ironically, was the grandson of Roger Sherman, the Connecticut delegate to the Constitutional Convention who had supported the Deep South states in the dispute over the slave trade. Seth Staples and Theodore Sedgwick also agreed to serve as attorneys for the Africans from the *Amistad* in their legal struggles.

At the same time, the Spanish government, seeking to have the Africans placed into its custody, began to apply intense diplomatic pressure on the Van Buren administration. On September 6, Angel Calderon de la Barca, the Spanish minister to the United States, formally demanded that the Africans be delivered into Spanish custody. Calderon argued that the United States had no jurisdiction over Spanish subjects or to adjudicate crimes allegedly committed by Spanish ships in Spanish waters. He also relied on three provisions of Pinckney's Treaty, a 1795 agreement between the United States and Spain.

Article 8 of the treaty provided that, if a ship from either nation entered a port of the other "through stress of weather, pursuit of pirates or enemies, or through other urgent necessity," the ship should receive good treatment, help, protection, and provisions "at reasonable rates," and that the ship "shall no ways be hindered from returning out of [the port]." Article 9 stated that "all ships and merchandise . . . which shall be rescued out of the hands of any pirates or robbers on the high seas" should be placed in the care of port officials "to be taken care of, and restored entire" to the owners. Finally, Article 10 required that any Spanish ship "wrecked, foundered, or otherwise damaged" on the coasts or in the territorial waters of the United States was entitled to "the same assistance which would be due to the inhabitants of [the United States] and shall pay the same charges as the said inhabitants would be subject to pay in a like case."[3]

With Van Buren himself temporarily away from Washington, D.C., Secretary of State John Forsyth of Georgia initially took the lead in formulating the administration's response to Calderon's missive. From the beginning, the Van Buren administration was sympathetic to the Spanish position. Van Buren and his aides understood that *The Amistad* had the potential to arouse sectional animosity over the issue of slavery, and also to create problems for his political campaign in the upcoming election of 1840. The administration's agenda, therefore, was to dispose of the matter as quickly and quietly as possible. Acceding to the Spanish demands was the best way to accomplish this goal.

On September 5—even before Calderon had officially requested the return of the blacks who had been on the *Amistad*—William Holabird, the United States attorney for the district of Connecticut, requested instructions from Forsyth. After initially suggesting that he believed that the blacks should be brought to trial if they were not remanded to Spanish custody, on September 9 Holabird expressed the opinion that the United States courts lacked jurisdiction over any criminal charges. On September 11, Forsyth directed Holabird to ensure that the *Amistad,* its cargo, and its involuntary passengers did not "go beyond the control of the Federal Executive." By contrast, on September 13, Sedgwick and Staples sent Van Buren a letter, urging him to allow all of the outstanding issues in the case to be resolved by the federal judiciary.[4]

The legal maneuvering began in earnest on September 18, as the attorneys retained by the abolitionists petitioned the Circuit Court for a writ of habeas corpus. The petition specifically named the four children who had been purchased in Havana, chosen no doubt because their cases were the most sympathetic of all the Africans. The United States marshal who had charge of the Africans responded that they were being held pursuant to the pending investigation of murder and piracy charges based on their seizure of the *Amistad.* He also interposed Gedney's claim and two other libels—Montes's assertion that he had legal title to the Africans as slaves, and the claim of the Spanish government, pressed on its behalf by the United States government through District Attorney Holabird. In the alternative, Holabird argued that, if the court found that Cinque and the other blacks were in fact victims of the illegal international slave trade, they should remain in the custody of the district court pending arrangements for their repatriation to Africa under the provisions of the Act in Addition. Simultaneously, the grand jury that had been empanelled began to consider the merits of the murder and piracy charges.

The hearings took place in a courtroom crowded with spectators who had paid an admission fee to attend. Beginning on September 20, arguments were heard by Judge Judson and Justice Smith Thompson, who was sitting on circuit. That morning, they disposed of the claim that Gedney's libel justified the continued detention of the Africans, observing that, since the District Court had no power to sell the putative slaves in any event, Cinque and his compatriots could not properly be made the subject of a salvage claim. The same afternoon, based on findings of fact by the grand jury, the criminal charges were dismissed. Thompson concluded that, since all of the alleged criminal acts had taken place on a vessel sailing under the Spanish flag, the American courts had no jurisdiction to try the case. He also indicated that, even if the American courts had had jurisdiction, the district of New York would have been the proper venue in which to try the case.[5]

The remainder of the argument for the Africans featured a detailed effort to show that they were not in fact *ladinos* but had in fact been the victims of the illegal African slave trade. Their opponents disputed this contention and argued that, in any event, the issue was one that should be resolved at trial, rather than in a habeas corpus proceeding. William Holabird also contended that, even assuming that the Africans were free men, under the Act in Addition, the United States government had the authority to keep them in custody pending arrangements to repatriate them to Africa.[6]

After three days of argument, the court rejected the claim that the Africans should be released from custody. Speaking for the court, Justice Thompson emphasized that "*the question to be decided now is not as to the ultimate rights of either party*" but only the issue of whether the district court had jurisdiction to determine the ultimate status of the putative slaves. While declaring that "my feelings are as personally as abhorrent to the system of slavery as those of any man here," he also argued that, under the principles established in *The Antelope*, the claimants could prevail if they demonstrated that the blacks on the *Amistad* were legally held as slaves under Spanish law. This issue, he concluded, could only be resolved at trial in the district court.[7] Judge Judson then convened the district court in the same room, but he adjourned the proceedings until November 19.

In the interim, the Africans and their abolitionist allies opened another front in the legal conflict. On October 17, acting in the name of two of the putative slaves—Cinque and Fuliwah—the abolitionist attorneys instituted two separate civil suits for assault and battery and false imprisonment against Ruiz and Montes in New York, where the two slave traders were staying during the pendency of the legal proceedings. Based on affidavits from Cinque and Fuliwah, the Spaniards were arrested and taken to city prison in lieu of $1,000 bond.[8]

The institution of the civil suit and imprisonment of Ruiz and Montes was widely condemned in both Northern and Southern newspapers. Predictably, the suit also brought a strong protest from Pedro Alcantara de Argaiz, who had succeeded Calderon as the Spanish minister to the United States. Argaiz contended that the New York courts lacked jurisdiction over the civil suit because the alleged wrongdoing had taken place in Spanish territorial waters. He urged the Van Buren administration to use the writ of habeas corpus to obtain the release of the two Spaniards. Forsyth responded that the president could not intervene in an ordinary civil suit. Van Buren did, however, inform Argaiz that he was instructing New York District Attorney Benjamin F. Butler to offer "advice" and "aid, if necessary" to the imprisoned Spaniards.[9]

During the week of October 22, Judge Inglis of the New York Court of Common Pleas held two preliminary hearings on the suits filed by Cinque. He observed that the suits could not be maintained if the plaintiffs were in fact legally enslaved at the time of the alleged wrongdoing. Nonetheless, he refused to dismiss the suits, concluding that the issue of the plaintiffs' status could not be resolved at a preliminary hearing. At the same time, Inglis reduced the bail of both defendants. Inglis found that only Ruiz had been the owner of Cinque at the time the alleged wrongdoing took place and that Montes had been only tangentially involved in the incident. Thus, Montes was essentially released on his own recognizance. By contrast, because of his putative ownership of Cinque, bail for Ruiz was set at $250. Judge Jones of the New York Supreme Court issued identical rulings in the case filed in the name of Fuliwah.[10]

Ruiz promptly appealed the Inglis ruling, seeking to have the case dismissed. However, the appellate court affirmed the ruling, while at the same time barring the initiation of any further lawsuits until the Ruiz case could be resolved by a jury. Despite this admonition, the abolitionist attorneys filed a third civil suit on behalf of Tonni, another of the Africans who had been on board the *Amistad*.[11]

The civil suits against Montes and Ruiz never came to trial. After being freed on bail, both Spaniards left the country. Nonetheless, from the perspective of the abolitionists, the suits had served their purpose, keeping the *Amistad* affair in the public eye pending the hearing on the primary lawsuit before Judge Judson.

In preparation for this hearing, at Forsyth's request, in November 1839, Attorney General Felix Grundy of Tennessee issued an official opinion supporting the view that the putative slaves should be delivered to the representatives of the Spanish government. Grundy began by invoking the principle of comity and arguing that the representatives of the United States government should accept the passports issued by the governor-general of Cuba at face value. He asserted that "in the intercourse and transactions between nations, it has been found indispensable that due faith and credit should be given by each to the official acts of the public functionaries of others." To hold otherwise in the case of the *Amistad*, he argued, would place the government of the United States "in the embarrassing condition of judging upon the Spanish laws, their force, their effect, and their application to the case under consideration." Grundy also observed that a judicial determination of the rights and responsibilities of the parties involved in the dispute would necessarily put the United States government in the position of construing the treaty between Spain and England, to which it was not a party.[12]

Grundy sought to bolster his argument by relying on *The Antelope.* He noted that the Court in that case had explicitly held that the African slave trade did not violate international law, and also that the opinion had stated

that the right of bringing in and adjudicating upon the case of a vessel charged with being engaged in the slave trade, even where the vessel belongs to a nation which has prohibited the trade, cannot exist. The courts of no country execute the penal laws of another, and the course of the American government on the subject of visitation and search would decide any case in which that right had been exercised by an American cruiser on the vessel of a foreign nation not violating our municipal laws, against the captors.

It follows, that a foreign vessel engaged in the African slave-trade, captured on the high seas in time of peace by an American cruiser, and brought in for adjudication, would be restored.[13]

Grundy contended that the case for the application of these principles to the *Amistad* was particularly strong because Montes and Ruiz were citizens of Spain—the nation that had sovereignty over Cuba, where all of the relevant events took place—and were not engaged in the international slave trade at the time of the mutiny but rather in the lawful, domestic coastal trade in Cuba.[14]

The opinion then turned to the question of whether the courts of the United States had jurisdiction to try Cinque and his compatriots for their actions taken during the mutiny. Grundy noted that none of those who had been on board the *Amistad* were American citizens, and that the mutiny had taken place in

Cuban coastal waters. Therefore, he contended, the only conceivable basis for American jurisdiction would be a contention that the mutiny amounted to piracy.

Grundy firmly rejected the idea that the mutiny could be construed as piracy. He noted that in *United States v. Smith,* the Supreme Court described "pirates as "freebooters upon the sea, not under the acknowledged authority, or deriving protection from the flag or commission of any government." Moreover, in *United States v. Palmer,* the Court had rejected the contention that robbery on the high seas constituted "piracy" within the meaning of the relevant federal statute. Since the *Amistad* was "a Spanish vessel, belonging exclusively to Spaniards, navigated by Spaniards, and sailing under Spanish papers and flag, from one Spanish port to another" at the time of the mutiny, in Grundy's view, only the Spanish courts had jurisdiction to adjudicate the criminal claims against the Africans.[15]

Finally, Grundy addressed the question of the proper disposition of the putative slaves and the other cargo of the *Amistad.* He reasoned that while, by its terms, section nine of Pinckney's Treaty applied only to property rescued on the high seas, in spirit the provision applied with even greater force to property rescued within American territorial waters. He also argued that the "property" should be delivered to the representatives of the Spanish government, rather than the private owners, for four reasons: (1) that all of the owners were not in the United States; (2) that the matter had already been a matter of discussion between the governments of the United States and Spain; (3) that the Spanish government had jurisdiction to adjudicate any criminal charges against the Africans; and (4) that, once delivered to the Spanish government, Cinque and his compatriots would have an opportunity to pursue their claims for freedom in the Spanish courts.[16]

The position of the executive branch was thus firmly established when Andrew Judson reconvened the district court in Hartford on November 19. At the hearing, Jirah Heath, the attorney for Gedney and the other claimants from the *Washington,* joined William Holabird in characterizing the case as a simple claim for salvage against the owners of the *Amistad* and its cargo and arguing that the Africans from the *Amistad* were not proper parties to the action.

Baldwin's answer was twofold. First, he contended that the Connecticut district court lacked jurisdiction over the salvage action. Baldwin asserted that the *Amistad* had been seized within the territorial waters of New York, rather than on the high seas, and that, therefore, only a court in New York could hear the salvage claim. In addition, he observed that the salvage action was based in part on the assumption that the Africans were in fact slaves, and that "if they are not found to be property, they must be immediately discharged, as it is not pretended that they are criminals. If we cannot show that they are not property, then their most sacred rights are violated."[17]

Initially, at the direction of Judge Judson, the evidence that was presented was aimed entirely at the jurisdictional question. The Africans themselves were at first scheduled to testify on November 20. However, on that day, their translator was too ill to come to the hearing. Thus, at Baldwin's request, Judson ruled that the hearing would be postponed, to be resumed on January 7, 1840, in New Haven.[18]

In the interim, Argaiz continued to press the Van Buren administration to arrange for the Africans to be placed in the custody of the Spanish government, now asserting that the Spanish "did not demand the delivery of slaves but of assassins." Van Buren was anxious to oblige. Continuing to fear possible damage to his campaign for reelection in 1840, he wanted to bring the diplomatic and domestic controversy over the *Amistad* affair to a quick end. Van Buren hoped for a favorable ruling after the January 7 hearing and wished to forestall any appeal. Accordingly, at the suggestion of the Spanish minister, Secretary of State John Forsyth ordered the navy to make the *USS Grampus* available to transport the Africans to Cuba immediately after Judge Judson ruled on their status.[19]

When the district court reconvened before a crowded gallery in New Haven, William Holabird announced that the Spanish government had merged the claims of Ruiz and Montes, and that he was representing the interests of all of these parties. After three days of testimony, Judson issued his decision on Monday, January 13. The decision dashed Van Buren's hope for a quick Spanish victory. Judson first held that he had jurisdiction over the case because the seizure of the *Amistad* had taken place on the high seas. He also concluded that Gedney was entitled to salvage rights, and that Antonio—one of the blacks who had been on board—had been legally enslaved to the late captain of the ship and should be returned to Cuba. But at the same time, purporting to apply Spanish law, Judson dismissed all claims that the remaining Africans were in fact property under Spanish law. Placing the burden of proof on Ruiz and Montes, Judson rejected the claim that the license to transport the Africans provided definitive evidence of their status. He concluded that the blacks were fact *bozales*—natives of Africa—rather than *ladinos*.

However, Judson did not immediately free the Africans, as their abolitionist supporters desired. Instead, giving a rather bizarre reading to the statute of 1819, he ruled that the captives stood in the same position as persons who had been brought into the United States with the intent of making them slaves, and ordered the Africans remanded to the executive branch for purposes of transporting them back to Africa.[20]

For obvious reasons, this holding was unacceptable to the Van Buren administration. On instructions from the White House, Holabird quickly filed an appeal to the Circuit Court. After hearing arguments on April 29, in early May the appellate court affirmed Judson's decision pro forma, clearing the way for an appeal to the Supreme Court.

In the interim between Judson's decision and the hearing before the Supreme Court, abolitionists and their allies made every effort to keep the controversy in the public eye. On May 15, the *Liberator* reprinted an article from the New Haven *Herald* that documented both the Van Buren administration's support for Ruiz and Montes in the New York lawsuits and the plans to use the *Grampus* to spirit the Africans away if the administration had prevailed before Judge Judson. On June 12, the New York *Express* revealed that, in a packet of documents sent to Congress, the term *ladinos* in the passport that had been issued to Montes and Ruiz had been mistranslated as "sound negroes"—a translation that might have vitiated claims that the passports were fraudulent or had been issued in bad faith by the governor-general of Cuba. On June 12, the *Express* publicly reported the mistranslation, asking, "who ever heard of such frauds in governmental documents, transmitted to Congress by a President of the United States" and declaring that "there was no accident in this matter—it was a cunningly devised fraud."[21]

Reports of this kind cannot have pleased Van Buren, whose Democratic coalition was constantly threatened by sectional disputes over slavery. Van Buren lost the presidential election to William Henry Harrison, the candidate of the Whig Party. The poor condition of the economy was the central issue in the election. However, some have suggested that dissatisfaction with Van Buren's handling of the *Amistad* affair may have contributed to his narrow defeat in a number of crucial Northern states.[22] Nonetheless, even after the election, the administration continued to press its appeal of the *Amistad* case to the Supreme Court.

In the interim, the abolitionists sought to bolster their legal team in preparation for the coming legal battle in the Court. They first approached Daniel Webster, the Massachusetts Whig leader who was also one of the most highly regarded legal advocates of his era. Webster, however, demurred, as did Rufus Choate of Boston, who cited other commitments and the shortness of notice.

The reluctance of Webster and Choate was hardly surprising. While both men were opposed to slavery, as conservative Whigs they had little love for the abolitionist cause. Moreover, throughout his political life, Webster pursued the presidency with unflagging zeal, and, as Howard Jones has observed, an association with the *Amistad* defense could only have alienated Southerners whose support he would need to be a credible candidate.[23]

Finally, in October, the abolitionists turned to John Quincy Adams, the former president and secretary of state who in 1840 represented Massachusetts in the House of Representatives. In some respects, Adams was an odd choice; he had not argued a case before the Court in over thirty years. But, stirred by the debate over the gag rule, his distaste for slavery and the "slave power" rivaled that of the abolitionists themselves. Indeed, in late 1839, one Virginian wrote that Adams had become so "diseased" on the subject of slavery that his name had become "odious" to the South. Moreover, Adams had already evinced some interest in the *Amistad* case itself; on March 23, he introduced a resolution that led to the production of all of the correspondence between the Spanish government and the Van Buren administration that related to the case, as well as the *Amistad*-related correspondence between the State Department and William Holabird.[24]

Soon after accepting the invitation to argue *The Amistad* in the Supreme Court, Adams became publicly embroiled in the dispute over the mistranslation of the passport. On December 9, 1840, Robert Greenhow, the official translator for the State Department, complained that he had been accused of deliberately altering the meaning of the passport and asked Adams to vindicate his innocence. On December 10, Adams rose in the House of Representatives and asked that a committee be appointed to determine "by whom the fraud had been perpetrated, if it be a fraud and not a blunder." By an 87–46 vote, the House agreed, and Adams was appointed to chair the committee.[25]

To Adams, the alteration at first seemed part of what he privately described as an "abominable conspiracy, Executive and Judicial, of this Government, against the lives of [the Africans from the *Amistad*]." However, during the course of the committee's investigation, John H. Trenholm, the proofreader for the establishment that had printed the document, took responsibility for the change, but claimed that it was an innocent mistake. Nonetheless, Adams continued to entertain suspicions that the White House had somehow been involved in the alteration.[26]

Against this background, the Supreme Court began consideration of *The Amistad* in a crowded courtroom on February 22, 1841. In narrow legal terms, the arguments revolved around the appropriate interpretation of Pinckney's Treaty and the technical requirements of proof of ownership. From a broader perspective, however, like *The Antelope*, the case implicated the attitude that the American legal system would take toward issues of slavery and freedom.

Henry D. Gilpin of Pennsylvania, who had succeeded Felix Grundy as attorney general on January 11, 1840, presented the case for the government. Gilpin's argument was simple and straightforward. Noting that slavery was legal under Spanish law, he began by asserting that slaves were to be treated the same as any other property under the terms of Pinckney's Treaty. Beginning with this premise, Gilpin relied heavily on the description of the Africans in the passport issued by the governor-general to demonstrate that they should in fact be considered slaves for purposes of the litigation. Declaring that "where property on board of a vessel is brought into a foreign port, the documentary evidence . . . accompanied by possession, is the best evidence of ownership, and that to which Courts of justice invariably look," he proclaimed that "here is the authentic certificate or record of the highest official known to the spanish [*sic*] law, declaring, in terms, that these negroes are the property of [Montes and Ruiz]. We have it countersigned by another of the principal officers. We have it executed and delivered, as the express evidence of property, to these persons."[27]

Gilpin argued that this evidence would be conclusive under the law of Cuba, and that only the Spanish courts were entitled to look behind a certificate issued by a Spanish official in this context. He further contended that, even if the passport created only a presumption of ownership, the evidence presented in the lower court was insufficient to rebut the presumption. Finally, Gilpin asserted that the government of the United States was the appropriate party to vindicate the interests of the government of Spain and those of Ruiz and Montes themselves.[28]

Roger Baldwin spoke first in response. Baldwin declared that he would "appeal to no sectional prejudices, and [would] assume no positions in which I shall not hope to be sustained by intelligent minds from the South as well as the North."[29] Nonetheless, many Southerners would no doubt have taken umbrage with much of Baldwin's argument.

Baldwin first sought to link *The Amistad* to the most fundamental principles underlying the American national identity. He asserted that the case

presents . . . the question whether that government, which was established for the promotion of JUSTICE, which was founded on the great principles of the Revolution, as proclaimed in the Declaration of Independence, can, consistently with the genius of our institutions, become a party to proceedings for the enslavement of human beings cast upon our shores, and found in the condition of freemen within the territorial limits of a FREE AND SOVEREIGN STATE?

The remainder of Baldwin's argument reflected a similar view of the place of slavery in the American constitutional system.

Baldwin began by arguing that only the claimants themselves had legal standing to appeal from the judgment below, decrying what he described as "an unauthorized interference of the Executive with the appropriate duties of the Judiciary." Even assuming that in some cases the federal government could represent the interests of foreigners seeking to recover property in the United States, Baldwin also contended that "it has no right to appear on their behalf to aid them in the recovery of *fugitive slaves,* even when domiciled in the country from which they escaped" and that the imposition of such a duty on the federal government "would be wholly inconsistent with the fundamental principles of our government, and the purposes for which it was established." He observed that the Constitution did not prevent New York from emancipating fugitive slaves from a foreign country (as opposed to another state), and that the Africans from the *Amistad* had become free under New York law when they reached New York soil. Under these circumstance, Baldwin contended that "the question of the surrender of fugitive slaves to a foreign claimant, if the right exists at all, is left to the *comity of the States* which tolerate slavery" and that Ruiz and Montez "had [no] right to call on any officer or Court of the United States to use the force of the government, or the process of the law for the purpose of again enslaving those who had escaped from foreign slavery, and sought an asylum here."[30]

Baldwin then confronted the claim that the interposition of federal authority was in fact mandated by section nine of Pinckney's Treaty, which required the return of "merchandise." Here his argument took on a particularly strong sectional caste, drawing heavily on the tenets of radical antislavery legal theory.[31] Emphasizing that the delegates to the Constitutional Convention had made a conscious decision not to refer to slaves per se in 1787, Baldwin declared that "the United States, *as a nation,* is to be regarded as a free state. And all men being presumptively free, when 'merchandise' is spoken of in the Treaty . . . it cannot be presumed that human beings are intended to be included as such." To hold otherwise, Baldwin contended, would be contrary to "the fundamental principles of the government and people of the United States, in their *collective capacity as a nation,* as set forth in their Declaration of Independence." Indeed, he suggested that a treaty that did require the return of slaves who revolted at sea might well be void because it would be inconsistent with the terms of the Declaration.[32]

Finally, Baldwin turned to the status of the Africans under the Spanish law applicable in Cuba. He first contended that Spanish law should be applied to this question only if the Africans had become domiciled in Cuba and that, under the undisputed facts of the case, the Africans could not be found to have had such a domicile. Baldwin further asserted that the passports alone did not provide sufficient evidence from which to infer that the Africans were in fact *ladinos* and had in any event been obtained by fraud. Finally, Baldwin argued that the case did not need to be sent to Spain for trial in Spanish courts because the American courts were perfectly competent to determine and apply Spanish law.[33]

Despite the prominence of antislavery rhetoric in his presentation, Baldwin also took care to skillfully couch his arguments in the language of conventional legal analysis, linking his arguments to traditional notions of standing, burdens of proof, and jurisdictional authority. Adams, who followed Baldwin, took a dramatically different tack. Speaking for a total of over seven hours over the course of two days, Adams delivered a performance that Joseph Story described privately as "extraordinary . . . extraordinary . . . for its power, for its bitter sarcasm, for its dealing with topics far beyond the record and points of discussion."[34]

Early in his argument, Adams specifically eschewed any claim to be relying on standard sources of positive law to support his position. He pointed to the likeness of the Declaration of Independence in the courtroom and declared

I know of no law, but one which I am not at liberty to argue before this Court, no law, statute, or constitution, no code, no treaty, applicable to the proceedings of the Executive or the Judiciary, except that law, two copies of which are ever before the eyes of your Honors. I know of no other law that reaches the case of my clients, but the law of Nature and of Nature's God on which our fathers placed our own national existence. The circumstances are so peculiar, that no code or treaty has provided for such a case. That law, in its application to my clients, I trust will be the law on which the case will be decided by this Court.[35]

But even direct references to natural law did not figure prominently in Adams's presentation. Instead, the argument was marked by a sustained, vitriolic attack on the actions of both the Spanish government and the Van Buren administration, designed to "arraign . . . before this Court and the civilized world, the course of the [Van Buren] Administration in this case." He characterized the Spanish demands as "most extraordinary, inadmissible and offensive," requesting that the president "should first turn himself into a jailer . . . and then a tipstaff to take [the Africans] away for trial among the slave-traders of the baracoons." Adams also charged that the secretary of state "has degraded the country, in the face of the whole civilized world, not only by allowing these demands to remain unanswered, but by proceeding . . . as if the Executive were earnestly desirous to comply with every one of these demands." Turning to Felix Grundy's opinion, Adams declared that "I am ashamed! I am ashamed such an opinion should ever have been delivered by any public official of this country."[36]

Whatever its value in purely political terms, Adams's extravagant rhetoric added little to the strength of the legal argument for the Africans. Certainly, Henry Gilpin did not seem greatly concerned by Adams's accusations. In his response to Baldwin and Adams, Gilpin focused almost entirely on Baldwin's claims. Gilpin contended that, far from being an inappropriate interference with the judicial process, the participation of the Van Buren administration in the litigation was nothing more than a vindication of its obligations under Pinckney's Treaty. He also reiterated his view that slaves constituted merchandise under the treaty, that possession of the Africans combined with the Cuban passports provided ample evidence that Ruiz and Montes were in fact the legal owners of the Africans, and that any effort to discredit the documents must take place in the Spanish courts.[37]

The Court that took *The Amistad* under advisement consisted of only seven members. John McKinley did not participate due to poor health, and Philip P. Barbour died during the course of the oral arguments, leaving four Northerners and three Southerners to reach a decision on the case. On March 9, 1841, the Court handed down its judgment. The justices held that the lower court had erred in ordering that Cinque and his compatriots be returned to Africa under the terms of the 1819 statute. However, with only Henry Baldwin dissenting without opinion, the Court also concluded that, with the exception of Antonio, the Africans were entitled to their freedom.

Joseph Story delivered the opinion of the Court. The opinion was totally devoid of the provocative rhetoric that had characterized the arguments of Roger Baldwin and John Quincy Adams. The ringing condemnation of the slave trade that had marked Story's own opinion in *La Jeune Eugenie* was also noticeably absent. Rather, the opinion in *The Amistad* was a carefully measured discussion of the narrow legal issues that were critical to the disposition of the case.

Story pointedly refused to be drawn into a discussion of the Van Buren administration's role in the case, or even the question of whether the federal government had standing to prosecute the appeal. He began his discussion of the merits by agreeing with Henry Gilpin about the general scope of Pinckney's Treaty, concluding that "if these negroes were, at the time, lawfully held as slaves under the laws of Spain, and recognised by those laws as property capable of being lawfully bought and sold; we see no reason why they may not justly be deemed within the intent of the treaty, to be included under the denomination of merchandise, and, as such ought to be restored to the claimants."

Story conceded that the passports constituted prima facie evidence of the status of the Africans held on the *Amistad*. However, he also asserted that "although public documents of the government, accompanying property found on board of the private ships of a foreign nation, certainly are to be deemed prima facie evidence of the facts which they purport to state, yet they are always open to be impugned for fraud" and that the evidence produced in the trial court established "beyond controversy" that the Africans held on the *Amistad* were not in fact lawfully held as slaves under Spanish law.[38] In addition, Story averred that

it is also a most important consideration in the present case, which ought not to be lost sight of, that, supposing these African negroes not to be slaves, but kidnapped, and free negroes, the treaty with Spain cannot be obligatory upon them; and the United States are bound to respect their rights as much as those of Spanish subjects. The conflict of rights between the parties under such circumstances, becomes positive and inevitable, and must be decided upon the eternal principles of justice and international law. If the contest were about any goods on board of this ship, to which American citizens asserted a title, which was denied by the Spanish claimants, there could be no doubt of the right of such American citizens to litigate their claims before any competent American tribunal, notwithstanding the treaty with Spain. A fortiori, the doctrine must apply where human life and human liberty are in issue; and constitute the very essence of the controversy.[39]

The overall tenor of this passage aptly reflects the basic structure of moderate antislavery thought more generally. Most Northerners recognized that they might have to recognize the property rights of slaveholders in some circumstances. But many nonetheless had a strong distaste for slavery and were prepared to mold legal doctrine in a manner that reflected this distaste.

The reaction to the Supreme Court's disposition of the *Amistad* broke down along predictable lines. The antislavery New York *Commercial Advertiser* described the decision as a victory for "life and liberty," "a great and glorious triumph for humanity." Not surprisingly, many Southerners saw the case differently. For example, the Mobile *Commercial Register & Patriot* characterized the judgment as an "insult" to Spain and "no small triumph" for abolitionists. The extent of Southern dissatisfaction with *The Amistad* became even more apparent in 1844, when, in the wake of continuing Spanish demands for reparations, the Southern-dominated Committee on Foreign Affairs of the House of Representatives not only recommended that the demands be honored but also excoriated the decision itself in the strongest possible terms.[40]

Against this background, the decision of the Supreme Court in *The Amistad* and the near-unanimity of the Court becomes all the more noteworthy. The decision was profoundly antisectionalist in character. In a case in which public opinion was deeply engaged, each of the three participating Southern justices—Roger Brooke Taney, James Moore Wayne, and John Catron, all Jacksonians—demonstrated a willingness to ignore not only the wishes of a Jacksonian administration but also the widely held views of the South on an issue involving slavery. Instead, the Southern justices followed their more general views on the dictates of justice and conventional legal analysis.

At the same time, it would be a mistake to overstate the significance of *The Amistad* to the sectional struggle. In theory, at least, even many Southerners found the international slave trade distasteful. Moreover, despite the heated debate that surrounded the litigation, none of the legal issues raised by the controversy either directly implicated the domestic institution of slavery or had an impact upon the balance of political power between the North and South.[41] Thus, in a sense, the dispute over the status of the captive Africans presented the Southern justices with an easy case.

Almost contemporaneously with *The Amistad,* the Court was also confronted with two cases that were of far greater direct import for the status of domestic slavery—*Groves v. Slaughter* and *Prigg v. Pennsylvania.* The jurisprudential issues presented by *Groves* and *Prigg* were also of more general significance than those which underlay *The Amistad.* In *The Amistad,* none of the parties questioned the power of the federal government to deal with the international slave trade. By contrast, in addition to dealing with politically explosive issues related to slavery, both *Groves* and *Prigg* raised important questions about the structure of American federalism.

CHAPTER 6

Slavery, the Commerce Power, and *Groves v. Slaughter*

The doctrinal significance of *The Antelope* and *The Amistad* were limited by the fact that neither of those cases presented any issues of constitutional magnitude. All of the parties in both cases conceded that Congress had the authority to regulate the international slave trade. The only question was whether the statutes adopted by Congress (or some other extraconstitutional source) mandated that the slaves found on board the captured vessels should be granted their freedom. However, contemporaneously with the decision in *The Amistad,* the Court also began to grapple with the important constitutional issues related to slavery in *Groves v. Slaughter.*[1]

Like *The Amistad, Groves* called on the Court to confront the status of the slave trade. There was, however, one crucial difference. While *The Amistad* dealt with the foreign slave trade, the issue in *Groves* was the constitutionality of a state regulation of the domestic, interstate slave trade.

The domestic slave trade arguably stood on a different constitutional footing than the international trade. To be sure, the Slave Trade Clause does not by its terms make a distinction between the international and the interstate slave trades. Instead, the clause refers simply to "the Migration and Importation of Such Persons as . . . the States . . . shall think proper to admit." However, in drafting this language, the delegates to the Constitutional Convention do not seem to have been considering its potential impact on the interstate trade. Instead, the discussions at the convention focused solely on the African slave trade, as did the spirited ratification debates over the Slave Trade Clause.[2]

Moreover, the nature of the interstate trade in slaves was conceptually quite different from the international trade. The importation of slaves from Africa involved the enslavement of people who had hitherto been free. By contrast, a domestic sale did not fundamentally change the legal status of the person being sold. Instead, such a sale simply transferred ownership of the slave from one master to another. Indeed, the right to make such a sale was one of the basic prerogatives of the master. Thus, any overt suggestion that the Constitution would arm Congress with the authority to restrict the interstate slave trade would almost certainly have doomed ratification efforts in the Southern states.

Notwithstanding these considerations, many Southern whites, particularly residents of the Deep South, viewed the interstate slave trade with considerable ambivalence. On one hand, they understood the significance of the role played by importation of slaves from the upper South in replenishing and expanding the supply of labor that was vital to the structure of the Southern economy. At the same time, Deep South whites were suspicious of the tactics of those who speculated in the slave trade and were concerned that slaves who were "sold South" might foment rebellion, spread disease, or simply be unmanageable.[3]

But whatever their personal views regarding the morality and desirability of a flourishing interstate slave trade, mainstream Southerners generally rejected the idea that the federal government should have authority to interfere with the trade. They feared that recognizing any such power would arm antislavery Northerners with a powerful weapon that could potentially be used to strike at the institution of slavery itself. The depth of Southern feeling on this issue was made clear as early as 1807, during the discussions of a proposal designed to prohibit the importation of slaves from other countries. At the instance of Rep. Peter Early of Georgia, the bill initially passed by the House of Representatives contained a provision that explicitly stated that nothing in the bill should be interpreted to prohibit the interstate transportation of slaves that had not been illegally imported. Some senators, however, believed that regulation of the interstate coastal trade was necessary to the interdiction of slaves illegally smuggled from Florida. The Senate thus adopted a bill that limited the coastal trade to larger ships (which were more easily detected) and required that ship captains certify that any slaves being transported had been imported prior to 1808—the date on which the bill was to become effective.[4]

The conference committee produced a bill with a provision that was very similar to the original Senate version. The committee report brought vehement condemnations from Reps. John Randolph of Virginia and David R. Williams of South Carolina, who feared any implication that Congress had authority to regulate the purely domestic aspects of the slave trade. Randolph declared that the bill would "blow up the Constitution in ruins" and complained that "at a future period, it might be made the pretext for universal emancipation." He further asserted that "he had rather lose the bill, lose all the bills of the session, he had rather lose every bill passed since the establishment of the government, than agree to the provision contained in this slave bill."[5]

These protests were of no avail; the bill passed on an almost entirely sectional vote, and it was signed into law by Virginian Thomas Jefferson. In practical terms, the regulations of the coastal trade did not work any great hardships on either slave traders or slaveholders more generally. Nonetheless, Randolph's reaction showed the potential divisiveness of even the most modest attempts to interject the federal government into the regulation of the interstate slave trade.

The issue lay fallow for a number of years after the dispute of 1807. The most radical elements of the antislavery movement argued that the federal government should act to interdict the interstate sales of slaves. Radicals argued that, since the buying and selling of slaves was unquestionably a commercial transaction, the Commerce Clause vested Congress with the authority necessary to take such action. Southerners such as John Randolph also feared that the more expansive theories of federal power more generally implied that Congress possessed the authority to limit or outlaw the trade in slaves.[6]

Nonetheless, proposals to regulate the domestic slave trade made no headway in Congress itself. Many Northerners no doubt found many aspects of the trade distasteful. However, since by its nature the domestic slave trade was confined entirely to the South, mainstream Northern politicians were generally content to leave the matter to state regulation. Conversely, mainstream Southerners of all stripes continued to react strongly against any intimation that federal action against the interstate slave trade would be either desirable or constitutional.

Southerners were further sensitized to this issue by the abolitionist petition campaign of the late 1830s and early 1840s. Most of the antislavery petitions that flooded Congress during this period focused their attention specifically on the slave trade in the District of Columbia, praying that both the slave trade and slavery itself be outlawed in the District. However, some of the petitions went further, exhorting Congress to act against the interstate slave trade more generally. In 1838, the state legislatures of both Vermont and Massachusetts passed resolutions making similar requests.[7] Against this background, some Southern politicians began to associate any effort to regulate the domestic slave trade with the radical abolitionist movement.

Despite the petitions, Congress made no serious effort to significantly limit the interstate slave trade. Instead, the judicial assessments of the constitutional powers of Congress came in the context of challenges to a *state* regulation of the interstate trade. Those making these arguments relied on the same doctrinal formulation that had been pressed on the Marshall Court in cases such as *Gibbons v. Ogden, Brown v. Maryland,* and *Willson v. Black-Bird Creek*—the theory that the federal constitution had armed Congress with the *exclusive* power to regulate interstate and foreign commerce and thereby implicitly divested the states of the authority to regulate such commerce.

In 1837, the Taney Court had entered the debate over the scope of the Commerce Clause in *New York v. Miln.*[8] *Miln* was a challenge to a New York statute that regulated the entrance of passengers from other states or foreign countries who arrived by ship in the port of New York. By its terms, the case dealt only with the constitutionality of a section of the statute that required the masters of ships carrying such passengers to submit detailed reports on the passengers. Nonetheless, the justices were also well aware that other sections of the statute required every master to post a bond for each foreigner on his ship and to remove at his own expense any foreigner whom the mayor of New York found was likely to become chargeable to the city.

Against this background, with only Justice Story dissenting, the Court rejected the argument that the New York statute ran afoul of the dormant Commerce Clause. The majority opinion was written by Justice Phillip P. Barbour, who would die before either *The Amistad* or *Groves* was decided. Barbour argued that "persons . . . are not the subject of commerce; and not being imported goods, cannot fall within a train of reasoning founded upon the construction of a power given to congress to regulate commerce." He also declared that "it [is] as competent and necessary for a state to provide precautionary measures against the moral pestilence of paupers, vagabonds, and possibly convicts, as it is to guard against physical pestilence." Therefore, Barbour concluded that the New York statute was "a regulation, not of commerce, but of police."[9]

While clearly relevant to the evaluation of state laws regulating the interstate slave trade, the New York statute differed from such laws in at least one critical respect. Barbour's opinion rested on the theory that the interstate and international movement of people per se did not constitute commerce. By contrast, whatever else one might say about the interstate traffic, the buying and selling of slaves was clearly a commercial activity. Thus, *Miln* did not definitively resolve the constitutional issues surrounding state regulation of the interstate slave trade.

Nonetheless, *Miln* joined the Marshall Court decisions on the dormant Commerce Clause in providing the legal context for the Court's consideration of *Groves*. The specific enactment at issue in the case was a section of the Mississippi constitution of 1832 that prohibited "the introduction of slaves into this state, as merchandize [*sic*] or for sale," while at the same time explicitly permitting Mississippi residents to import slaves for their own use until 1845. The evolution of this provision reflected the ambivalence with which many Southerners viewed the interstate slave trade. The Mississippi constitution of 1817 had explicitly armed the state legislature with the power to ban slave traders from doing business in the state. In 1819, the legislature adopted a statute imposing a tax of $20 on slaves imported by nonresidents for sale and banning the importation of slaves convicted of serious felonies. Six years later, state lawmakers imposed a 2.5 percent tax on those engaged in the interstate slave trade. While both of these provisions were soon repealed, sentiment against the trade remained strong among some segments of Mississippi society, and the state constitutional convention of 1832 inserted the prohibition that gave rise to *Groves.*[10]

The constitutional proviso was adopted at a time when the interstate slave trade was particularly vigorous in Mississippi. In 1830 and 1832, vast new lands in the state were opened to white settlers for the first time by the treaties of Dancing Rabbit and Pontotoc, respectively. Many new slaves were needed to work this land. Thus, between 1830 and 1840, the slave population of Mississippi almost tripled. The increased demand led to a boom in the market for slaves that was marked by a rapid increase in prices and rampant speculation. Although purchasers of slaves had formerly been required to pay cash, speculators began to accept promissory notes in payment instead.

Against this background, in 1833, the state legislature refused to pass legislation implementing the constitutionally mandated ban on the interstate slave trade. Instead, a 2.5 percent sales tax on slave traders was once again adopted. At the same time, the legislature proposed to amend the newly adopted constitution by removing the ban on importation and replacing the ban with a provision similar to that which had been in the 1817 constitution. This proposal was sent to the voters for a referendum. More than two-thirds of those participating in the referendum voted to remove the ban. Nonetheless, the proposed amendment failed to become law because it did not receive the votes of a majority of all the voters in the state as required by the state constitution.

The boom in the Mississippi slave trade proved to be short-lived, as the market became flooded and the increase in prices slowed dramatically. Purchasers defaulted on their notes, which were often secured by mortgages on the land owned by the purchasers. Faced with this reality, in 1837 the Mississippi legislature finally adopted a statute establishing penalties for importing slaves in violation of the constitutional prohibition. Nonetheless, the tax on slave traders remained in effect. Thus, the state was in the position of taxing a practice that was banned by both the state constitution and legislative action. Still, many wealthy Mississippians who had purchased slaves on credit in the period between 1833 and 1837 faced potential financial ruin.

For some, the solution was to challenge the enforceability of promissory notes given in payment for slaves imported during the period prior to the adoption of the statute. Suits for payment were often met by defenses citing the state constitutional prohibition on the slave trade as evidence that enforcement of the notes was against public policy. In 1841, the Mississippi High Court of Errors and Appeals was confronted with just such an argument in *Green v. Robinson*

(*Green II*).[11] However, the procedural posture in which the issue arose created additional complexities for the court.

A dispute over the same promissory note had come before the court two years earlier in *Green I*. *Green I* was a suit at law against a surety, who was allegedly liable because the principal on the note had defaulted. The surety interposed a number of defenses in the suit but did *not* claim that the note was unenforceable on the ground that the underlying transaction was voided by the state constitution. The trial court concluded that the defenses that *had* been asserted did not vitiate the obligation of the surety and awarded judgment to the plaintiff. On appeal, the High Court of Errors and Appeals affirmed.

The surety then took a different tack. He attacked the judgment of the Court of Errors and Appeals in a different venue, the Court of Chancery. In this second lawsuit, the surety for the first time cited the constitutional prohibition on the importation of slaves for sale and sought an injunction preventing the enforcement of the original judgment. In the trial court, Chancellor Robert C. Buckner denied the injunction. Buckner concluded that the prohibition on importation did not void a contract for *sale* and also that, in any event, the surety had in effect waived this defense by not raising it at trial. *Green II* was an appeal from Chancellor Buckner's decision.

The appeal was heard by only two judges—Justice James F. Trotter and Justice William Sharkey. In sharp contrast to Chancellor Buckner, Trotter and Sharkey agreed that the state constitutional provision, by its terms, required the courts to hold that the contract for the sale of the imported slaves was unenforceable because it was against public policy. Trotter, who had been a delegate to the constitutional convention, asserted that

it is competent for the people in convention to establish a rule of conduct for themselves, and to prohibit certain acts deemed inimical to their welfare . . . and such rule . . . will be as obligatory as if the same had been adopted by legislative enactment. . . . It is endowed with greater claims upon the approbation and respect of the country, by being solemnly and deliberately incorporated with the fundamental rules of the paramount law, and thus placed beyond the contingency of legislation.

Trotter further contended that "I conceive it to be immaterial . . . whether the constitution is considered as merely directory, or as containing within itself an absolute prohibition. In either case it fixes the policy of the state on this subject, and renders illegal the practice designed to be suppressed."[12] Unlike Chancellor Buckner, Trotter refused to make a distinction between the act of importing slaves from other states and the sale of the imported slaves, contending that the prohibition on the importation of slaves for sale necessarily implied a prohibition on the sale itself. Nonetheless, he concluded that the defendants in *Green I* could not interpose this defense in a collateral attack.

Justice Sharkey did not write a separate opinion in *Green II*. Instead, he simply noted his concurrence with Trotter's conclusion on the question of whether the constitutional provision was self-enforcing and his disagreement on the question of whether the issue could be raised in a collateral attack. Sharkey elaborated on these conclusions in the companion case of *Glidewell v. Hite*, which presented substantive issues similar to *Green II*. In *Glidewell*, Sharkey declared that "in [*Green II*], it was decided by this court that [a contract for sale] was void by virtue of the constitutional provision which prohibit the introduction of slaves into this state as merchandize [*sic*]."[13] In short, both justices agreed that the constitutional prohibition was self-enforcing, and that in *Green II* the court had so held.

These state court decisions provided the backdrop for the Supreme Court's consideration of *Groves v. Slaughter* in 1841. *Groves* came to the Court unencumbered by the procedural issues that had complicated the consideration of *Green II* and *Glidewell*. Instead, *Groves* began as a prosaic diversity action in the circuit court of Louisiana to recover on two promissory notes drawn by John Brown, payable to R. M. Roberts, and endorsed to Robert Slaughter by Roberts, Moses Groves, and James Graham, payable at the Commercial Bank of Natchez, Mississippi. The defendants responded by asserting that the notes had been given in payment for slaves imported into Mississippi from other states in 1835 and 1836 and were therefore made void by virtue of the Mississippi constitution. The case was appealed to the Court on a writ of error after the lower courts ruled in favor of the plaintiffs, who claimed, among other things, that the state constitutional prohibition on the slave trade violated the federal Constitution, and therefore, the state rule could not be made the basis for a holding that enforcement of the promissory note would be against the public policy of Mississippi.

All sides to the dispute recognized the possible significance of a decision in *Groves*. Even in purely economic terms, the ramifications of the case were extremely important. At stake was the disposition of thousands of slaves, worth millions of dollars. In addition, the case implicated fundamental questions of federalism with potentially explosive implications for the dispute over slavery.

Not surprisingly, the case attracted some of the best-known advocates of the day. The validity of the notes was assailed by Attorney General Henry D. Gilpin and Jacksonian Sen. Robert J. Walker of Mississippi, who himself had at one time accumulated hundreds of thousands of dollars in debts to slave traders. The noteholders, on the other hand, were represented by Walter Jones of Virginia, a well-respected advocate with great experience before the Court, and two of the most prominent leaders of the Whig party, whom Jones described as "the Ajax and Achilles of the bar"—Henry Clay of Kentucky and Daniel Webster of Massachusetts.

The first question before the Court was whether the promissory notes at issue were void under Mississippi state law. On this point, the arguments of Gilpin and Walker relied in part on the decisions in *Green II* and *Glidewell*, citing the general rule that the Supreme Court was bound by the authoritative interpretations of state statutes and state constitutions by state courts.[14]

Gilpin and Walker also argued that the Mississippi decisions had in fact correctly interpreted the language of the state constitution. Gilpin asserted "if . . . the people of Mississippi intended that people might introduce slaves for sale until the 1st of May 1833, but that on that day his right to do so should cease, it seems difficult to imagine how they could have expressed their intention in clearer language. They forbade it. There is nothing in forbidding a thing to be done which requires further action." Similarly, Walker contended that "the clause is not directed to the legislature and is not a mandate in substance or form, but an absolute prohibition, operating proprio vigore." Observing that the state constitution of 1817 had by its terms explicitly armed the state legislature with the power to regulate the slave trade, he contended that "the reason of the change is obvious. The legislature, during the intervening period of fifteen years . . . had never fulfilled the trust confided to them by prohibiting the [interstate slave trade]; and therefore the framers of the new constitution determined to confide this trust no longer to the legislature, but to prohibit this traffic themselves." Gilpin and Walker also noted the contrast between the slave trade provision and other clauses of the 1832 constitution—some involving slavery—that had explicitly been phrased in terms of grants of power to the state legislature.[15]

Turning to the federal constitutional issue, Walker described it as "'a *grave and important question*'; the most so in my judgment which has ever been brought up for the determination." He linked the claims of the original plaintiffs to the abolitionist petitions that had been presented to Congress on the issue. Walker conceded that Congress had thus far dismissed those petitions out of hand. Nonetheless, he declared that "if [the Supreme Court held that] under [the Commerce Clause] congress may forbid or authorize the transportation of slaves from state to state, in defiance of state authority, then, indeed, we shall have reached a crisis in the abolition controversy, most alarming and momentous."[16]

Walker's fears were not entirely unfounded. Sectional conflict over the issue of the interstate slave trade could be avoided only so long as the subject was effectively ignored in Congress. If the issue was openly discussed, many representatives of Northern states would likely have felt political pressure to express their support for federal action that hindered or abolished the interstate trade. In turn, such expressions of support undoubtedly would have provoked cries of outrage from Southern representatives. A decision from the Supreme Court explicitly concluding that Congress had the authority to regulate the interstate slave trade might well have made such an exchange more likely by raising the national profile of the issue, thus making it substantially more difficult for Northerners in Congress to ignore the question. Against this background, Walker asserted that a holding that Congress possessed exclusive authority to regulate the interstate slave trade might lead to "anarchy and civil war," while if the issue were left solely in the hands of the states, "the power of [antislavery] agitators will expire, and [the] decree will be regarded as a re-signing and re-sealing of the constitution."[17]

These considerations no doubt informed the constitutional arguments of both Walker and Gilpin. They noted that states could effectively ban the interstate slave trade by outlawing slavery generally. Given this reality, Walker asserted that to deny similar authority to slave states would undermine the uniformity of the Constitution. He also railed against what he viewed as the unfairness of such a holding to the Southern states, complaining that "the very states which refused within their limits to recognize slaves as property, should claim the power by their votes in congress, to recognize their transportation and sale in other states, is preposterous."[18]

Walker also contended that, given the historical context in which the Constitution was adopted, the framers could not have believed that they were arming Congress with the power to regulate the interstate slave trade. In making this argument, Walker began by recounting the long historical pedigree of state regulation of the slave trade. In addition, noting the intense controversy surrounding the provision dealing with the *international* slave trade, he observed that if the Commerce Clause had been viewed as arming Congress with similar authority one would have expected even more objections from the delegates representing the Deep South. Yet, as he observed, this possibility does not seem to have been considered by the convention, and was rarely mentioned by Southern Antifederalists during the ratification debates.[19]

These historical observations provided the backdrop for a variety of different doctrinal arguments. Walker began by rejecting the analogy to the Slave Trade Clause, arguing that, rather than a limitation on the more general power to regulate foreign commerce, this clause was an affirmative grant of power to Congress to regulate the international slave trade after 1808. He insisted that, for the purposes of both the federal Constitution and Mississippi law, slaves were to be viewed as "persons" rather than "property," and that therefore the prohibition on importation was a regulation of "social relations" rather than "commerce."

Working from this premise, both Walker and Gilpin relied on *Miln* to support their position. Alternatively, they contended that the prohibition on importation should be characterized as the kind of quarantine law to which Chief Justice Marshall had adverted in *Gibbons v. Ogden,* an act of "self-protection" by the state of Mississippi. Gilpin also argued that, even assuming Congress possessed the authority to regulate the slave trade, the states retained concurrent authority in the absence of contrary federal action.[20]

Not surprisingly, the attorneys for the original plaintiffs had a quite different view of the controlling principles in *Groves.* Both Jones and Clay conceded that a series of decisions by the state's highest court on issues of state constitutional interpretation would have bound the Supreme Court, and Webster agreed that such decisions would be entitled to "great attention." However, Jones and Webster characterized the decisions of the Mississippi courts as "contradictory" and argued that the proper interpretation of the constitutional provision "has not been conclusively settled." Similarly, Clay noted that the judges of the states' courts "had not agreed in opinion."[21]

Clay combined this assertion with a nationalistic vision of the relationship between the state and federal courts. Describing the effort to void the promissory notes as an "outrage on justice," he asked rhetorically whether "is this court a Mississippi court, or a court of the twenty-six states?" He then contended that, as "a court of the union," the Supreme Court was "bound to construe the constitution of the state of Mississippi, not by the construction given in times of passion, not on decisions given which may have been biased by the large interests of the state, supposed to be benefitted by the decisions of the state court, but on great principles, and on those of justice and truth."[22]

Clay—whose constituents included a number of traders who had sold slaves in Mississippi—continued his argument with an extraordinary attack on the Mississippi Court of High Errors:

Who are the judges of the courts of Mississippi, and what are the tenure of their offices? They are elected by the people . . . and a court thus constituted are called upon to decide a case affecting a large portion of the citizens of the state, in which strangers to the state, and who have no interest in their appointment, are the claimants! The judges of Mississippi are sitting in their own cause; in the cause of those around them; of those who gave and can take away their offices! The object of the constitution of the United States, in establishing the courts of the United States, and giving to those courts [diversity jurisdiction] was to have such controversies decided impartially, and without the influence of local bias, or that of local courts.[23]

Webster, by contrast, based his argument on an appeal to what he saw as a distinction between statutory interpretation and constitutional interpretation:

A constitution stands on different ground, as to its interpretation, from a statute; a statute is to be construed by the courts, which are intrusted with its execution. A constitution is to stand as it is adopted by the people, from whom it has all its weight and authority. If we have clear evidence to show how the people of Mississippi understood this provision, this should prevail [over contrary state court interpretations].[24]

The plaintiff's attorneys then contended that, until supplemented by enforcing legislation, the state constitutional provision did not in fact bar the importation of slaves into Mississippi for sale. Clay, for example, asserted that "the nature of constitutions is to establish and declare principles; and, except in some particular cases, to leave to the legislature the enactment of laws, to carry out the principles thus declared." Similarly, Jones and Webster emphasized the questions of penalty left open by the constitutional provision.[25]

Clay also focused on what he saw as the unfairness of a decision voiding the promissory notes. He averred that, by imposing a tax on imported slaves, the legislature had "implicitly ratifi[ed]" contracts such as those at issue in *Groves*. Under such circumstances, he argued, to hold that the state constitution invalidated the notes would be an ex post facto law and a "violation of right."[26]

Clay and Webster then turned to the question of whether a state prohibition on the importation of slaves for sale would be constitutional. Their basic argument on this point was straightforward and simple. Both reaffirmed the right of each state to regulate the institution of slavery within its borders, and to outlaw slavery if it wished. At the same time, they contended that, where slavery was recognized by state law, slaves were considered to be property for purposes of federal constitutional law, and that the authority to regulate the interstate trade in such property rested exclusively with Congress.[27]

However, Webster and Clay had strikingly different notions of the scope of congressional power to regulate the slave trade. In 1819, Webster had endorsed the claim that Congress had the plenary authority to regulate or, if it chose, to outlaw the interstate slave trade entirely. His argument in *Slaughter* was entirely consistent with this view. By contrast, in 1839, Clay had expressed the opinion that Congress had the power only to "facilitate and accommodate, but not to obstruct and incommode" the interstate traffic in slaves. Clay's presentation to the Court in *Slaughter* elaborated on this contention. Echoing the debate over slavery in the District of Columbia, he conflated opposition to the interstate slave trade with the movement to outlaw slavery more generally, characterizing his opponents as being on the "abolition side of the question." Moreover, Clay suggested that congressional authority to regulate the interstate slave trade under the commerce power was limited, asserting that "regulation implies continued existence—life, not death; preservation, not annihilation; the unobstructed flow of the stream, not to check or dry up its waters." Thus, in Clay's view, no government had the authority to outlaw or sharply limit the interstate trade in slaves.[28]

The arguments of Robert Walker and Henry Clay highlighted the potential explosiveness of any decision by the Court on the federal constitutional issues implicated by *Groves*. Faced with this reality, a majority of the seven participating justices initially chose to avoid deciding these issues by concluding that the state constitutional provision was not self-enforcing and therefore did not invalidate the promissory notes. Speaking for the Court, Justice Smith Thompson began by rejecting the claim that this conclusion was foreclosed by the decisions of the Mississippi Supreme Court. While apparently conceding that the Court would have been bound to follow a definitive ruling of the Mississippi court on this issue, Thompson focused solely on the decision in *Glidewell v. Hite* and argued that, because Judge James Trotter ultimately concluded that the constitutional provision could not be interposed on collateral attack, Trotter's discussion of the proper interpretation of that provision was dictum.[29]

Thompson then turned to an independent analysis of the state constitutional ban on the importation of slaves. He asserted that the sequence of events between 1833 and 1837 suggested that the provision was "not understood as a prohibition per se, but only directory to the legislature." Echoing Clay's arguments, Thompson also contended that

to declare all contracts made for the purchase of [slaves imported for sale] from the 1st of May, 1833, until the passage of the [1837 statutory prohibition] illegal and void, when there was such an unsettled state of opinion and course of policy pursued by the legislature, would be a severe and rigid construction of the constitution, and one that ought not to be adopted unless called for by the most plain and unequivocal language.

Thus, Thompson concluded that the promissory notes were not void, but rather that they should be enforced.[30]

From a purely legal perspective, Thompson's analysis can be effectively criticized on a variety of different grounds. In particular, his account of the Mississippi cases seems consciously designed to minimize the significance of the pronouncements of the Mississippi judges on the state constitutional issue.

Thompson entirely ignored the *Green II* opinion and the fact that the structure of that opinion strongly suggests that Judge Trotter himself believed that a construction of the constitutional provision was a necessary predicate to an analysis of the collateral attack issue; that Judge William Sharkey—the only other high court judge hearing the case—explicitly noted his agreement with Trotter on the substantive issue; and that, in *Glidewell,* Sharkey had treated the interpretation of the constitutional provision as settled law. In short, the interpretation of the Mississippi constitution by the state courts was far more definitive than the terms of the *Groves* opinion would suggest.

Nonetheless, the approach of the majority had the virtue of resolving the dispute in *Groves* without exacerbating sectional tensions over slavery-related issues. While dissenting, Justices John McKinley and Joseph Story were almost equally circumspect. Although implicitly concluding that the state constitutional prohibition was self-enforcing and within the authority left to the states by the federal constitution, they issued no opinion that would potentially have inflamed the political situation.

Justice John McLean, however, was not moved by such considerations. Despite the fact that he joined in the majority opinion, McLean refused to be deterred from discussing the question of whether state governments could constitutionally prevent the importation of slaves from other states.

McLean began his opinion by rejecting the claim that states possessed concurrent power to regulate interstate commerce, contending that the issue had been resolved by *Gibbons v. Ogden* and asserting that "unless the [commerce] power be not only paramount, but exclusive, the constitution must fail to attain one of the principal objects of its formation." At the same time, McLean strongly defended the constitutionality of the Mississippi prohibition on the importation of slaves, contending that the authority to regulate the interstate slave trade rested solely with the states. On this point, McLean's argument was much like that of Robert Walker. McLean distinguished sharply between the interstate and foreign slave trades, asserted that slaves were persons rather than property for constitutional purposes, and noted the apparent unfairness of denying slave states the right to prohibit the importation of slaves while leaving the nonslave states free to exercise the same power. McLean concluded with a strong reaffirmation of state authority in this regard:

Each state has a right to protect itself against the avarice and intrusion of the slave-dealer; to guard its citizens against the inconveniences and dangers of a slave population. The right to exercise this power, by a state, is higher and deeper than the constitution. The evil involves the prosperity, and may endanger the existence of a state. Its power to guard against, or to remedy the evil, rests upon the law of self-preservation; a law vital to every community, and especially to a sovereign state.[31]

McLean's precise motives for gratuitously discussing the constitutionality of the Mississippi state constitutional provision were not entirely clear. Despite his personal opposition to slavery, the opinion was anything but a ringing endorsement of the most advanced antislavery positions. Instead, it is perhaps better understood as a salvo in the ongoing struggle over the issue of the exclusivity of the federal commerce power.

McLean was a strong advocate for the view that Congress possessed exclusive authority to regulate interstate commerce. At the same time, he recognized that, at least in the abstract, that principle would threaten the ability of the Southern states to make their own independent decisions regarding the desirability of allowing the interstate slave trade to continue—a regime that no Southern justice was likely to countenance. McLean's solution was to argue that issues relating to the authority over the interstate movement of slaves were sui generis in legal terms, thus allowing him to combine an argument for the principle of exclusive federal power to regulate interstate commerce generally with an assurance that the adoption of that principle would not threaten the authority of the Southern states to deal with slavery-related issues within their jurisdictions.

In any event, McLean's opinion brought a sharp retort from Henry Baldwin. Baldwin began by condemning McLean's decision to address the substantive constitutional issue related to the interstate slave trade at all, declaring that such questions "are of the highest importance to the country, and in my opinion ought not to be considered by us unless a case arise in which their decision becomes indispensable."[32] Nonetheless, once McLean had addressed those issues, Baldwin felt compelled to respond.

Baldwin joined McLean in asserting that the Constitution vested Congress with exclusive authority to regulate interstate commerce. However, unlike McLean, he derived the constitutional principles that applied to the regulation of the interstate slave trade from those applicable to regulations of interstate commerce more generally. Beginning with this premise, Baldwin's argument tracked that which had been made by Henry Clay. Contending that slaves should be viewed as property for constitutional purposes, Baldwin analogized the interstate slave trade to the international slave trade and asserted that, by analogy to the Slave Trade Clause, Congress clearly had authority to regulate the interstate trade. He further contended that federal power was exclusive but "conservative in its character, for purposes of protecting the property of the citizens of the United States," and did not include the authority to interdict the trade. At the same time, he argued that any effort to prohibit the interstate slave trade would be a taking of property in violation of the Fifth Amendment. Thus, in essence, Baldwin concluded that the right to engage in the interstate slave trade was protected by the Constitution, and that the effort by the state of Mississippi to interfere with the slave trade ran afoul of the Dormant Commerce Clause.[33]

The other participating justices clearly had no appetite for a potentially in-flammatory debate over the constitutional standards that governed regulations of the interstate slave trade. Like Baldwin, Chief Justice Taney expressed regret that McLean had chosen to state his views on the constitutional issues at length, but he felt compelled to briefly express his own views in response. Taney challenged McLean's assertion that the issue of the exclusivity of the commerce power had been settled by prior case law. However, on the specific issue before the Court, Taney contented himself with a brief assertion that the power to reg-ulate the interstate slave trade rested exclusively with the states. Justices Story, Thompson, Wayne, and McKinley were even less forthcoming, joining in a brief statement that read simply that the Mississippi state constitution did not run afoul of the Commerce Clause.[34]

Taken as whole, *Groves* fits comfortably into the model of a Court whose justices were generally averse to exacerbating the sectional conflict through their decisions. To be sure, in at least one sense, the pattern of opinions was unbal-anced in favor of the Southern perspective. Three of the justices expressed the view that Congress lacked the power to interfere with the interstate slave trade, while none explicitly took the contrary position, leading one Southern news-paper to declare that "one point of the abolition controversy (and that the most important one) is solemnly settled in favor of the South."[35] However, at least four of the seven participating justices (including two of the three participating Southerners) initially went to great lengths to avoid discussing *any* constitu-tional issue on the merits, and a different group of four justices (once again, including two Southerners) contented themselves with upholding the Missis-sippi provision without comment, even after McLean issued his provocative opinion. In short, even when provoked, the justices in *Groves* generally chose to avoid interjecting themselves into a sectional controversy.

In some contexts, however, this option was not available to the justices. When presented with a dispute involving fugitive slaves in 1842, the justices could not avoid deciding a series of constitutional issues that had significant ramifications for sectional relations. Faced with such a problem, justices from both sections crafted a solution that was in part a simple application of dis-tinctively legal principles but was also designed to minimize the tensions be-tween the free and slave states.

CHAPTER 7

The Problem of Fugitive Slaves

Throughout the Jacksonian era, the problem of fugitive slaves was a major source of sectional tension. Escapees from bondage in the slave states often sought refuge in the North, either permanently or en route to Canada. Southerners complained that Northern residents interfered unduly with efforts to apprehend these fugitives, while some Northerners asserted that free blacks were too often kidnapped and sent into slavery under the pretense of being escapees.[1] In constitutional terms the dispute focused on the proper interpretation of Article IV, Section 2, paragraph 3—the Fugitive Slave Clause.

The Fugitive Slave Clause was the most unambiguously proslavery provision to emerge from the Constitutional Convention of 1787. To be sure, many commentators have argued that a number of other sections of the Constitution favored Southern interests. However, the Fugitive Slave Clause was the only provision that explicitly granted slaveowners rights that they had not theretofore possessed. Under the Articles of Confederation, each state could, if it wished, free any putative slave found within its borders. By contrast, the new Constitution both forbade states from declaring escaped slaves free and guaranteed slaveowners the right to recover runaways.

Moreover, the Fugitive Slave Clause limited the potential impact of the 1772 English decision in *Somerset v. Stewart,* the case that would ultimately become the bulwark of antislavery legal theory. In *Somerset,* a slave had been transported from Virginia to England, which had no legislation either establishing or prohibiting slavery. The slave escaped, only to be recaptured by his master, who then attempted to place him on a ship for the purpose of being sent to Jamaica for sale. Lord Mansfield issued a writ of habeas corpus ordering that the slave be released from the custody of the ship's captain, declaring famously that "the state of slavery is of such a nature that it is incapable of being introduced on any reasons, moral or political. . . . It is so odious that nothing can be suffered to support it but positive law."[2]

Although Mansfield himself may have seen the decision in more limited terms, *Somerset* came to stand for the proposition that any slave who was brought into England gained his freedom at the moment that he entered the country, by whatever means and for whatever purpose.[3] By its terms, the Fugitive Slave Clause forbade the full implementation of this principle in the United States.

Nonetheless, at the time that it was adopted, the Clause itself was almost entirely uncontroversial. On August 28, 1787, after the convention had committed itself to a provision requiring states to extradite fugitives from justice, Pierce Butler and Charles Pinckney of South Carolina moved to require "fugitive slaves and servants to be delivered up like criminals." James Wilson of Pennsylvania observed that "this would require the executive of the state to do it, at public expense," and Roger Sherman of Connecticut complained that he "saw no more propriety in the public seizing and surrendering a slave or a servant than a horse." Butler then withdrew his motion "in order that some particular provision might be made, apart from [the Extradition Clause]." On August 29, his motion to insert a separate clause was adopted without objection, and on September 12 the Committee on Style and Arrangement produced language that was essentially identical to that which is currently in the Constitution. After a minor change in wording on September 15, the Fugitive Slave Clause became part of the convention's proposal without apparent dissent.[4]

This new protection for slaveholders played little role in the struggle over ratification. Some Southern Federalists did point to the Clause as a benefit to the South.[5] However, the reaction of Northern Antifederalists stands in marked contrast to their treatment of other provisions of the new Constitution that they viewed as proslavery. While Northern opponents of the Constitution vociferously attacked both the apportionment of the House of Representatives and the Slave Trade Clause, their reaction to the Fugitive Slave Clause was, with few exceptions, a resounding silence.

The basic idea of a Fugitive Slave Clause was by no means a novel concept. As early as 1643, the New England Confederation mandated intercolonial cooperation in the rendition of fugitive slaves. However, by the time the Constitutional Convention met in Philadelphia, the possibility of conflict over the issue had been greatly magnified by the developing sectional divide over the issue of slavery more generally. The drafters of the Constitution faced a situation in which the momentum of the emancipation movement was accelerating in the Northern states while in some areas of the South, particularly in the Deep South, support for the institution of slavery remained strong. Further, by 1787, Massachusetts had already become a refuge for runaways from the South. In the absence of some constitutional provision to the contrary, as slavery was abolished in other states, they too might become such refuges, inevitably creating sectional tensions that could threaten the unity of the nation. The lack of opposition to the Fugitive Slave Clause suggests that unionists of all stripes accepted the need to forestall this danger.

In short, unlike provisions such as the Three Fifths Clause and the Slave

Trade Clause, the Fugitive Slave Clause was not a sectional compromise between the positions of delegates who began with opposing conceptions of the appropriate course of actions. Instead, the Fugitive Slave Clause was an embodiment of a basic premise that underlay the long-term success of any union between the Northern and Southern states. Even by the late eighteenth century, when slavery remained legal in most of the Northern states, it had become clear that the economic and social system in the South was based on principles quite different than those which prevailed in the North. Union between North and South was simply not plausible if the governments of the North were committed to undermining the slavery-based systems of the South. In essence, the Fugitive Slave Clause defined the minimum degree of tolerance for Southern institutions that Southerners required of their Northern brethren.

At the same time, the language chosen for the clause created a variety of interpretational difficulties. Despite the protestations of Roger Sherman, the wording of the Fugitive Slave Clause was clearly patterned on that of the Extradition Clause. Both clauses were premised on the theory that the state from which the alleged fugitive came was the proper venue for determining his ultimate status. Conversely, the function of the government of the state in which he was found was simply to detain the alleged fugitive and deliver him to the appropriate party.

However, the two clauses differed in one critical respect. Fugitives from justice are alleged to have offended against the public order. Thus, the Constitution requires that the request for extradition be made by the "executive authority" of the state from which the fugitive had allegedly fled. One would normally expect that the governor would not make such a request unless a criminal prosecution had been begun in good faith against the fugitive, and that the fugitive would have an opportunity to have the charges against him adjudicated by a criminal court after his extradition.

By its nature, any invocation of the right to recover a fugitive slave implicated a more complex set of interests. In the case of a putative slave, the claimant would not be a government official, but rather a private party who had a pecuniary interest in the assertion of a right to hold that person to service. This incentive created the specter of Southerners possibly invoking the constitutional mandate in support of dubious claims, or even seeking to enlist the aid of Northern state governments in outright kidnapping schemes. Conversely, antislavery Northerners seized on the need to protect free blacks as justification for the passage of state laws that placed obstacles in the path of those seeking the return of blacks who were in fact "fugitives from service." These issues provided the backdrop for congressional action in the early 1790s.

Ironically, the sequence of events that led to the passage of the Fugitive Slave Act of 1793 began with the kidnapping of a free black man, John Davis.[6] Sometime in the 1770s, Davis, who was at that time a slave, had been brought by his master from Maryland to what the master believed to be a part of Virginia. At the time, however, the border between Virginia and Pennsylvania was uncertain, and on August 31, 1779, representatives of the two states determined that the area in which Davis had settled was in fact part of Pennsylvania. Although the agreement was not finally ratified until April 1, 1784, both John Davis and his master thus became subject to the provisions of Pennsylvania's Gradual Emancipation Act of 1780.

Under the terms of that statute, all children born to slaves in Pennsylvania after March 1, 1780 became free after a period of indenture. By contrast, masters were allowed to retain all slaves that they owned in Pennsylvania as of March 1, 1780, provided that the slaves were registered with a court clerk prior to November 1, 1780. All slaves not so registered became immediately free. In 1782, recognizing the uncertainties faced by slaveowners in areas previously claimed by Virginia, the Pennsylvania legislature amended the statute to allow those slaveowners until January 1, 1783 to register their slaves.

John Davis's master did not take advantage of the registration opportunity. Instead, in 1788, he hired John out to a Mr. Miller in Virginia. Some of John's neighbors, purportedly members of the Pennsylvania Abolition Society, soon found John in Virginia and returned with him to Pennsylvania. In turn, Miller hired Francis McGuire, Baldwin Parsons, and Absalom Wells—all Virginians— to bring John back to Virginia. McGuire, Parsons, and Wells succeeded in locating John and forcibly returning him in May 1788. John was then sold to a planter in eastern Virginia.

In November 1788, McGuire, Parsons, and Wells were indicted for kidnapping in Pennsylvania state court. In June 1791, at the request of the Pennsylvania Abolition Society, Pennsylvania Governor Thomas Mifflin sent Virginia Governor Beverly Randolph a copy of the indictment and a request for the extradition of the men who were accused in the indictment. Randolph referred the request to James Innes, the state attorney general, who issued a report concluding that, for a variety of reasons, the Extradition Clause of the federal Constitution did not require Randolph to grant the request. Relying on this report, in July 1791 Randolph sent a formal refusal to Mifflin.

Mifflin then appealed for aid to President George Washington, who referred the matter to Attorney General Edmund Randolph. Attorney General Randolph concluded that the initial request for extradition was technically deficient, but that if these deficiencies were remedied, Governor Randolph should extradite the fugitives. Mifflin sent a new request with the changes that had been suggested by the attorney general. Nonetheless, Governor Randolph continued to refuse to cooperate, in part because state legislators from McGuire's district complained that John Davis was in fact a slave who had been lured from Virginia by members of the Pennsylvania Abolition Society, and that the case involved nothing more than a prosecution for the justifiable recapture of a fugitive slave. Thus, rather than granting the extradition request, Governor Randolph complained to Mifflin that Pennsylvanians were "seducing and harboring the slaves of the Virginians."

The dispute over John Davis provided the background for congressional action on both the extradition of fugitives from justice and the recovery of fugitive slaves. On October 27, 1791, President Washington sent Congress copies of his correspondence with Governor Mifflin and the report that had been prepared by Attorney General Randolph. On October 31, the House of Representatives referred the issue to a committee composed of three members—Reps. Theodore Sedgwick and Sherarjashbub Bourne of Massachusetts and Rep. Alexander White of Virginia. The committee was charged with the task of preparing a bill to provide the means for both the extradition of fugitives from justice and the rendition of fugitive slaves. On November 15, Sedgwick reported a bill that addressed both issues.[7]

Under the procedures established by the bill, one who claimed a putative fugitive slave could present an application to the governor of the state in which the alleged fugitive was found. The application was required to be supported by depositions of two persons who affirmed that the person identified was in fact a fugitive slave. Upon receipt of such an application, the governor was instructed to issue an arrest warrant that would be enforced by the appropriate officials in the latter state, who would then arrest the alleged fugitive and deliver him to the person who had originally applied for the warrant. State officials who refused to enforce the arrest warrants would have been subject to stiff fines in federal court.

The Sedgwick bill was read twice on November 15 and scheduled for a third reading. However, for unknown reasons, the third reading never took place, and the bill died without a vote. The following year, the Senate took the lead.[8] In March 1792, a committee comprised of Sens. George Cabot of Massachusetts, Roger Sherman of Connecticut, and Ralph Izard of South Carolina was appointed to consider the issues of extradition of fugitives from justice and rendition of fugitive slaves. At the beginning of the next session, the Senate appointed a new committee consisting of Cabot and Sens. George Read of Delaware and Samuel Johnston of North Carolina to consider the same subject.

On December 20, the new committee reported a bill that was in some respects more favorable to claimants than the proposal that had died the previous year in the House of Representatives. The Senate bill required state officials to arrest an alleged fugitive slave and turn him over to a claimant on the basis of a single deposition and made law enforcement agents who refused to aid claimants subject to fines. In addition, private citizens who "harboured" or "concealed" fugitive slaves were to be subject to penalties for each day that the citizens aided the fugitives, and claimants also retained the right to sue those who aided fugitives for damages.

After debate, on December 28, the Senate recommitted the bill to a committee that was expanded to include Sherman and Sen. John Taylor of Virginia. On January 3, 1793, the reconfigured committee reported a bill that was radically different from the December 20 proposal. While allowing owners or their agents to seize putative runaways without first obtaining government permission, the new bill required anyone seized as a fugitive slave to be brought before a judge or magistrate before being removed from the state. In most cases, a certificate of removal was to be granted if the claimant provided "proof to the satisfaction" of the presiding officer, either in the form of sworn testimony or an affidavit. However, no such certificate was to be granted if the alleged fugitive had been a resident of the state for a certain number of years. In that case, the putative runaway could be removed only after a trial by jury in the state in which he was found. Like the December 20 bill, the January 3 bill provided for monetary damages against law enforcement officials who failed to cooperate in the rendition process, as well as fines and imprisonment for private citizens who interfered with claimants' efforts to recover fugitives.

Although the precise content of the discussions was not recorded, the January 3 bill was apparently very controversial. Between January 14 and January 16, the Senate reconfigured the bill into a form that was more acceptable to both sides of the debate. In this form, the bill passed the Senate on January 18. The House of Representatives passed the bill in slightly amended form on February 4, and the Senate concurred in the House amendment on the same day.[9] On February 12, 1793, President George Washington signed the bill into law.

According to the Fugitive Slave Act of 1793, a slaveowner or his agent was "empowered to seize or arrest [the] fugitive from labour" and to bring him before a federal judge or "any magistrate of a county, city or town corporate" where the fugitive had been found. Upon "proof to the satisfaction" of the official, which could be provided either by affidavit or oral testimony, the official was required to issue a certificate that allowed the claimant to remove the alleged fugitive from the state where he was found to the state from which he allegedly had escaped. Any person who concealed a runaway or interfered with efforts to recover the fugitive was made subject to a $500 penalty, payable to the slaveowner.

Neither side was entirely satisfied with the regime established by the 1793 statute. Many Southerners believed that the statute provided insufficient protection for the rights of slaveowners. Some Northerners, by contrast, argued that free blacks in the North were left vulnerable to being kidnapped and sent into slavery. Advocates of these positions sought to have their concerns addressed by additional legislation at both the federal and state levels.

One of the Southerners' complaints was that Northern employers were aiding fugitives by providing them with employment. Seeking to address this problem, on December 17, 1801, Rep. Joseph Nicholson of Maryland introduced a bill that would have imposed heavy fines on those who employed an African American unless the employee carried a certificate of freedom that had been authenticated by the local government. The bill would also have required employers to publish a description of the new employee in two newspapers within a month of hiring him. However, Northerners objected to the burden that the requirement would impose on employers, and on January 18, 1802, the bill was defeated on a 46 to 43 vote, with only six Northerners voting in favor of the bill and only two Southerners in opposition.[10]

Beginning in late 1817, Southerners made a concerted effort to obtain more comprehensive protection for the rights of those who sought to recover fugitives from service. On December 17, on the motion of Rep. James Pindall of Virginia, who described the protections embodied in the 1793 statute as "little more than nominal," the House of Representatives appointed a committee to inquire into the issue, and on December 29, the committee reported a bill designed to strengthen the mechanisms available to slaveowners. The Pindall bill would have allowed a slaveowner seeking to recover an alleged fugitive to obtain a certificate from a judicial officer in his home state. Once presented with such a certificate, a federal or state judge in the state in which the alleged fugitive was located was required to issue a warrant for the arrest of the alleged fugitive. If the claimant or his agent identified the seized person as the person named in the original certificate, the alleged fugitive would be delivered to the claimant for transportation to the claimant's home state.[11]

Consideration of the bill produced sharp exchanges in both the Senate and the House of Representatives. Rep. Charles Rich of Vermont unsuccessfully sought to use the bill as a vehicle to eliminate the right of "recaption," that is, the right to seize and remove an alleged fugitive without benefit of formal legal process. Rich proposed an amendment that would have made it unlawful to seize and transport "any negro, mulatto, or person of color" without first obtaining a certificate from a judge or magistrate. More often, opponents of the Pindall bill argued that the bill threatened the rights of free blacks in the North and challenged the constitutionality of its provisions.

Opponents conceded in general terms that Congress had the right to pass legislation implementing the Fugitive Slave Clause. However, Sen. James Burrill Jr. of Rhode Island and Rep. Clifton Claggett of New Hampshire contended that the bill unduly restricted the use of the writ of habeas corpus by denying judges the authority to inquire into the question of whether the alleged fugitive was *in fact* the property of the claimant. In addition, both Claggett and Sen. David Morrill of New Hampshire argued that the bill unconstitutionally delegated federal judicial power to the state officials who were called upon to issue the original certificate in the slaveowner's home state. By contrast, Southerners such as Sen. William Smith of South Carolina argued that the writ of habeas corpus was designed to do nothing more than to ensure that a detained person was held by virtue of the procedures established by law, and Pindall responded to the objection raised by Claggett and Morrill by observing that Congress often relied on the state courts to execute federal laws.[12]

The bill was also supported by some Northerners. For example, Rep. Jonathan Mason of Massachusetts asserted that "the judicial tribunals of the South . . . would decide on the cases as correctly as those of the North, perhaps more so [because] so great a leaning was there against slavery that, the juries of Massachusetts would, in ninety-nine cases out of a hundred, decide in favor of the fugitive," and that "he wished not, by denying just facilities for the recovery of fugitive slaves, to have [Boston], infested, as it would be, without an effectual restraint, with a great portion of the runaways from the South." Similarly, Rep. John Holmes of Massachusetts asserted that the Pindall bill "was necessary to preserve the Constitutional rights of a large portion of the States" and that "he did not think it competent in Massachusetts to try a question between a Southern master and his slave."[13]

Against this background, on January 30, the Pindall bill passed the House by a vote of 84 to 69. On March 12, the Senate passed a slightly amended version of the bill by a vote of 17 to 13, as Sens. Harrison Gray Otis of New York, Nathan Sanford of New York, and William Taylor of Indiana joined a united South to provide the margin of victory.[14] However, the two Houses failed to resolve their differences, and the bill did not become law.

The failure of efforts to strengthen the Fugitive Slave Act did not end the dispute over the shape of federal law. The constitutionality of the 1793 statute itself was questioned in a variety of different fora. The federal courts uniformly upheld the validity of the statute. However, the state courts were divided. While the highest courts of Massachusetts and Pennsylvania rejected the constitutional challenges with little discussion,[15] the arguments received a much fuller airing in New York and New Jersey.

Three different New York state judges addressed the issue in *Jack v. Martin*.[16] *Jack* arose from the case of a Louisiana slave who had escaped and come to live in New York. His master, Mary Martin, came to New York, obtained a certificate by following the procedures outlined in the Fugitive Slave Law, and had Jack seized by the local sheriff. Jack then challenged his seizure in state court, seeking to obtain a writ of *de homine replegiando*—personal replevin—as provided by state law.

In 1834, the case came before Judge Samuel Nelson, who would later serve on the Supreme Court of the United States. Nelson first observed that, if the Fugitive Slave Act was constitutional, the state law could not stand. He contended that the Fugitive Slave Clause "implies a doubt whether [the states] would, in the exercise of unrestrained power, regard the rights of the owner, or properly protect them by local legislation," and that the clause should "receive the construction that will operate most effectually to accomplish the end consistently with the terms of it." Nelson then asserted:

It is very clear that, if [enforcement is] left to [the states] the great purpose of the provision might be defeated. . . . The states might omit any legislation on the subject, and thereby leave the owner without any known means by which to assert his rights; or they might so encumber and embarrass the prosecution of them, as that their legislation on the subject would be tantamount to a denial.

Given this possibility, Nelson concluded:

The idea that the framers of the constitution intended to leave the regulation of this subject to the states, when the provision itself obviously sprung out of their fears of partial and unjust legislation by the states in respect to it, cannot readily be admitted. It would present an inconsistency of action and an unskillfulness in the adoption of means for the end in view, too remarkable to have been overlooked by a much less wise group of men.[17]

Thus, Nelson rejected Jack's petition for a writ of *de homine replegiando*.

The following year, the judges of the New York Court for the Correction of Errors agreed that, on the facts of *Jack* itself, the petition for personal replevin should be denied. However, they differed sharply on the constitutionality of the Fugitive Slave Act more generally. Senator Issac W. Bishop's argument was much like Nelson's.

Difficulties of the most perplexing and harassing character, in reference to fugitive slaves, had occurred previous to the adoption of the constitution; and it is absurd to suppose that the members of the convention representing the interests of [the Southern] states, did not intend carefully to guard against a recurrence of similar evil; and it seems to me to be a fair inference from the proceedings of the convention, that they supposed they had done so effectually by the adoption of the [Fugitive Slave Clause] and that they intended to confer full power upon congress to regulate the whole matter.

By contrast, Chancellor Reubin H. Walworth took a quite different tack. Walworth focused not only on issues of federal-state relations but also on what he saw as the inadequate procedural protections afforded to those who were claimed as fugitives, asserting that

I find it impossible to bring my mind to the conclusion that the framers of the constitution have authorized the congress of the United States to pass a law by which the certificate of a justice of the peace of the state, shall be made conclusive evidence of the right of the claimant, to remove one who may be a free native born citizen of this state, to a distant part of the union as a slave; and thereby to deprive such person of the benefit of the writ of *habeas corpus,* as well as of his common law suit to try his right of citizenship [by jury] in the state where the claim is made.[18]

Noting that the Constitution by its terms did not explicitly vest Congress with the authority to adopt enforcing legislation, Walworth analogized the Fugitive Slave Clause to the Privileges and Immunities Clause of Article IV (the Comity Clause) and asserted that "the object of the framers of the Constitution was not to provide a new mode by which the master might be enabled to recover the services of this fugitive slave, but merely to restrain the exercise of a power, which the state legislatures respectively would otherwise have possessed, to deprive the master of [the] pre-existing right of recaption." Walworth scoffed at the notion that the states were likely to unduly impede the ability to recover fugitives, arguing that "the members of the state legislatures, as well as other state officials, both executive and judicial, being bound by oath to support the constitution, it cannot be legally presumed that they will violate their duty in this respect" and that "the supreme court of the United States . . . is possessed of ample power to correct any erroneous decision which might be made in the state courts against the rights of the master."[19]

The following year, in 1836, Chief Justice Joseph C. Hornblower of New Jersey elaborated on many of the same themes in *State v. Sheriff of Burlington.*[20] *Sheriff of Burlington* was a habeas corpus proceeding seeking the freedom of Alex Helmsly, a black man being held by a local official on the claim that he was a fugitive slave. Helmsly was being held pursuant to the provisions of a

New Jersey statute establishing rendition procedures. Nonetheless, Hornblower began with an assessment of the federal statute, which he asserted "[establishes] a summary and dangerous proceeding, and affords but little protection or security to the free colored man, who may be falsely claimed as a fugitive from labor, or whose identity may be mistaken."

Hornblower carefully parsed the various provisions of Article IV of the Constitution, noting that the convention had explicitly vested Congress with the authority to adopt legislation enforcing the Full Faith and Credit Clause of Section 1 but had not included a similar provision in the Fugitive Slave Clause. He averred "that the constitution has in express terms given the right of legislation to Congress in reference to [the Full Faith and Credit Clause] and remained silent in respect to [the Fugitive Slave Clause] is to my mind a strong argument that no such power was to be given in connection with [the latter]." Like Walworth, Hornblower dismissed the assertion that states would refuse to adopt procedures that would adequately protect the legitimate claims of masters, noting that "such refusal would amount to a violation of the national compact, and is not to be presumed or anticipated."[21]

Hornblower then turned to the adequacy of the procedures established by the New Jersey rendition statute. Although characterizing the provisions of the state law as "more humane and better calculated to prevent frauds and oppression than the federal statute," he nonetheless found that the statute violated the state constitution. Hornblower noted that the alleged fugitive was to be "delivered up" only if service was actually due to the claimant—a question of fact. In Hornblower's view, the putative slave was constitutionally entitled to have that question determined by a jury. Since the New Jersey statute did not provide for a jury trial, Hornblower found the statute to be constitutionally deficient— a conclusion that would clearly have applied equally to the federal Fugitive Slave Act.[22]

In 1842, *Prigg v. Pennsylvania*[23]—the last of the trilogy of important slavery cases of the early 1840s—brought many of the same issues before the Supreme Court. *Prigg* was a challenge to the constitutionality of Pennsylvania's revised antikidnapping statute. The evolution of the state statute mirrored the development of similar statutes in a number of other Northern states.[24] In 1820, with sectional tensions rising over the issue of slavery in Missouri and a number of prominent citizens expressing displeasure with the provision for summary proceedings in the Fugitive Slave Act, the state legislature passed a law that strengthened the protections that had been provided to free blacks by the antikidnapping statute of 1788. The new statute stiffened the penalties for the kidnapping of free African Americans. More importantly, it prohibited local aldermen and justices of the peace from taking jurisdiction of cases involving runaways. Thus, the 1820 statute made it substantially more difficult for claimants to locate an official who could act to enforce their rights under the federal Fugitive Slave Act of 1793.

Officials in the neighboring slave state of Maryland were very disturbed by the 1820 statute. They sent commissioners to the Pennsylvania state legislature, who carried with them proposed revisions that were far more favorable to those seeking to recover alleged fugitives. An intense political struggle ensued, and in 1826 a revised state law dealing with fugitive slaves was adopted by the legislature. The new law was clearly a compromise between the demands of Maryland slaveholders and those of the antislavery forces in Pennsylvania. While abolishing the common law right of recaption in Pennsylvania, the new law also reinstated the jurisdiction of local judicial officials over actions to recover fugitives. At the same time, the procedural requirements for the issuance of a certificate of removal by those state officials were much more stringent than those mandated by the federal law. The alleged runaway could not be detained without an affidavit from the claimant that provided a detailed description of the basis for the claim. Moreover, the oath of the owner or other interested persons would not suffice to support a certificate of removal, and the alleged slave was entitled to introduce evidence to refute the slaveowner's claim.

Although one of the Maryland commissioners described the Pennsylvania law as "eminently useful . . . because it is a pledge that the states will adhere to the original obligations of the confederacy," the representatives of the state of Maryland were far from entirely satisfied with the substance of the new Pennsylvania statute. Thus, it should not be surprising that the issue of fugitive slaves continued to be a source of tension between the two states. The facts of *Prigg* reflected this tension.[25]

Prigg arose from the forcible removal of Martha Morgan from southern Pennsylvania to northern Maryland. Martha had been born late in life to a black man and woman who were enslaved to John Ashmore in Maryland. In 1812, prior to Martha's birth, her parents had been allowed to retire and continue to live on the Ashmore estate. After the parents' retirement, Ashmore purportedly asserted on a number of occasions that he had set Martha's parents free. Moreover, he never attempted to exercise any dominion over Martha herself. Further, when Ashmore died intestate in 1824, the inventory of his estate listed two other slaves, but made no mention of Martha. Nonetheless, because Ashmore never took the formal steps required to emancipate either Martha or her parents, Martha apparently remained a slave under the laws of Maryland, and thus part of the estate that passed to Ashmore's widow, Margaret.[26]

Sometime prior to John Ashmore's death, Martha married Jerry Morgan, a free black man. She bore several children to Morgan in Maryland. In 1832, they moved to York County, Pennsylvania, where she bore several more children. In February 1837, a party of four Marylanders came to Pennsylvania with the intent to return Martha to Maryland. Included in the party were Edward Prigg and Nathaniel E. Bemis, who was Margaret Ashmore's son-in-law. They obtained a warrant from Thomas Henderson, a justice of the peace in Pennsylvania, authorizing William McCreary, a constable in York County, to bring Martha and her children before Henderson. McCreary then brought the entire Morgan family, including Jerry, to Henderson's residence. In turn, Henderson determined that he lacked jurisdiction to adjudicate the matter under the relevant Pennsylvania statute.[27]

Faced with this turn of events, the Marylanders released Jerry Morgan, telling him that if he would return home they would meet him in the morning. However, after Jerry left, Prigg, Bemis, and the remainder of their party brought Martha Morgan and the children into Maryland, where they were sold to a slave trader. Subsequently, in May 1837, Martha sued for her freedom in a Maryland county court. On August 30, a jury concluded that, because John Ashmore had never formally emancipated Martha, both she and her children were indeed slaves owned by Margaret Ashmore. Shortly thereafter, they were sold.[28]

The Morgan affair caused a considerable uproar in Pennsylvania. After receiving complaints from Jerry Morgan and a number of other citizens of the state, Pennsylvania Governor Joseph Ritner demanded that Maryland Governor Thomas W. Veazey deliver the Marylanders to stand trial for violating Pennsylvania's antikidnapping law. Veazey initially refused the demand on the ground that Prigg, Bemis, and their compatriots had not been indicted. Subsequently, an indictment was returned and an order to arrest the members of the party was issued. However, they were "always absent when called for."

In 1838, seeking to resolve the matter and reduce tensions with its neighbor to the north, the Maryland state legislature established a commission to negotiate with the Pennsylvania state government "to make such arrangements as may be necessary to refer the questions involved to the Supreme Court of the United States, without compromising the liberty of the accused" and to secure changes in the Pennsylvania statute. Finally, on May 23, 1839, the Pennsylvania legislature passed a statute that essentially authorized a pro forma trial at which Prigg would be found guilty through a process ensuring that the issues raised by the case could ultimately be resolved by the Supreme Court.[29]

Prigg required the justices to grapple with the complex issues raised by the Fugitive Slave Clause. The competing ideological and jurisprudential impera-

tives were fully discussed in the arguments before the Supreme Court. Prigg
was represented by Jonathan Meredith and John Nelson of Maryland, while
State Attorney General Ovid F. Johnson and Deputy Attorney General Thomas
C. Hambly spoke for the state of Pennsylvania. The attorneys for both sides
emphasized the wide-ranging implications of *Prigg*. For example, Meredith declared that "the case was one of vital interest to the peace and perpetuity of the
Union itself," while Johnson asserted that "in all the solemn constitutional
questions which have been adjudicated before [the Supreme Court] no one has
arisen of more commanding import, of wider scope in its influence, or on
which hung mightier results for good or ill for this nation." On the merits, however, they differed radically on the principles to be applied.[30]

Meredith's strategy was dictated by the context in which *Prigg* came to the
Court. The specific question of whether states might adopt legislation designed
to aid slaveowners in recovering those who escaped from service was not before
the Court. Instead, Meredith's only goal was to overturn Prigg's conviction for
violating the Pennsylvania antikidnapping statute by demonstrating that that
statute was unconstitutional. Early in his presentation, Meredith signaled his
strategy by asserting that "to the interference of state legislation, might justly
be ascribed much of that exasperation of public sentiment, which unhappily
prevailed upon a subject that seemed every day to assume a more malignant
and threatening aspect."[31] Throughout his argument, Meredith strove to demonstrate that state governments had no role to play in regulating the interstate
rendition of fugitive slaves.

In theory, Meredith might have argued that the Pennsylvania statute was unconstitutional because the Fugitive Slave Clause by its terms was intended to exclude *all* statutory regulation of the rendition process. However, such a regime
would not have been satisfactory to Southern slaveowners, who often sought
government aid in recovering escaped slaves. Thus, Meredith dismissed the possibility that the constitutional provision was designed to be totally self-executing.
He noted that the second part of the clause required both a claim and a delivery,
but did not specify the manner in which the claim was to be made or the procedure for delivery. The only plausible implication, Meredith contended, was
that these details were left to be filled in by legislative action. He argued further
that the situation that had given rise to the Fugitive Slave Act itself was "strongly
illustrative of the difficulties and embarrassments which would continually have
arisen, if the [Extradition Clause] had been left to execute itself," and that the
same issues would have arisen under the Fugitive Slave Clause.[32]

Notwithstanding this conclusion, Meredith contended that the Pennsylvania
statute was unconstitutional because the power to adopt implementing legis-

lation rested solely with the federal government. After reviewing the status of slavery at the time that the Constitution was adopted, he asserted that the Fugitive Slave Clause "was manifestly intended to restore to the south the rights which the customary law had formerly extended to them, in common with the other colonies," rights which he claimed had been abrogated in some of the states in which the process of emancipation had been underway. Meredith further contended:

The apprehension must have forced itself upon every southern mind in the convention, that if the provision were left to be carried out by state legislation, it must prove but a precarious and inadequate protection. The provision, it is true, yielded the right of the owner to reclaim the fugitive, in whatever state he might have sought refuge; but if the power to regulate the mode in which this provision was to be carried into practical effect—if the power of enforcing its execution were left to the states, it could not but have been foreseen, that its whole purpose might be defeated. That the states might either legislate or not; in the one case, leaving the owner without legal means to vindicate his rights; in the other, embarrassing the prosecution of them, so as to delay or defeat them.[33]

Having outlined the objections to vesting the enforcement authority solely in the states, Meredith turned to the problem of deriving a congressional enforcement power from the Constitution. He began his analysis by emphasizing that the Fugitive Slave Act had been passed contemporaneously with the adoption of the Constitution itself, and he also referenced the state court cases that had upheld the constitutionality of the statute. He then sought to characterize the passage of the statute as an exercise of the Article III power to establish tribunals inferior to the Supreme Court. Meredith conceded that the Fugitive Slave Act did not prescribe common law judicial proceedings. Nonetheless, he argued that the summary proceedings mandated by the statute were "of a judicial character," and that Congress possessed the power and even the duty to establish the forums in which those proceedings would take place.[34]

At the same time, Meredith contended that if the Court recognized a concurrent state power to regulate the rendition process, "the constitutional guarantee would . . . become a sounding phrase, signifying nothing," because, in his view, "state legislation upon [the subject of rendition] would become the sport of prejudice." Observing that, by its nature, such legislation would establish "different tribunals, forms of proceeding, and modes of proof . . . in the different states," Meredith asserted that "the pursuing owner would find it utterly impracticable, ignorant of the particular state into which the fugitive had escaped, to meet the requirements of local law." Thus, he concluded that "the nature of the power, and the effect of its actual exercise by the states, raise an implication sufficient to render it exclusive." Meredith also argued that, even if state power were concurrent in theory, the passage of the federal Fugitive Slave Law preempted state legislation on the rendition issue.[35]

Not surprisingly, the attorneys for the state of Pennsylvania took a quite different view of the legal principles that governed *Prigg*. Both Hambly and Johnson argued that the Fugitive Slave Act was unconstitutional because Congress lacked the authority to vest state officials with the judicial power of the United States. Noting that all blacks were presumed free in states where slavery had been outlawed, Hambly also argued that if the Fugitive Slave Clause constitutionalized the right of recaption, it would be inconsistent with both the Fourth and Fifth Amendments. Johnson, on the other hand, emphasized the fact that the Pennsylvania statute was the product of negotiations between Maryland and Pennsylvania. However, like Meredith, both Hambly and Johnson devoted most of their arguments to the issues of federalism that were raised by the case.[36]

The essence of their argument was Johnson's assertion that "the constitution does not aim at any abridgment of the state sovereignties on this subject, except in the single point of prohibiting them from setting fugitive slaves free." Johnson insisted that

different rules on this subject would naturally be established in different states. Less strictness of proof of the right of the master would be satisfactory in a slave state, than would be so in a free state. Some respect is due to the common feelings, or even prejudices of a community, in the enforcement of claims deemed odious in principle to any considerable number of the people. If even compatible with justice, they should not be pressed in a manner to outrage . . . the sympathies of those on whom the demand is made.

Hambly focused his attention on the claim that Congress had no authority to establish procedures for rendition, emphasizing the lack of any specific grant of power and observing that, in general, the entire subject of slavery was left to the states by the Constitution. Johnson, by contrast, based his defense of the Pennsylvania statute on a theory of concurrent authority. He observed that "anterior to the adoption of the Constitution, the power of prescribing the mode of surrendering up fugitive slaves, clearly belonged to the states alone," and he contended that this power "is not taken away by [the Constitution]; it is not inconsistent with any of the powers vested in congress or the general government; it is one of the most necessary attributes recognized and sanctioned by every principle of national law. It belongs to them still."[37]

Johnson then turned to the claim that the Pennsylvania statute was preempted by the Fugitive Slave Act. He argued that "the acts of congress and

Pennsylvania form together an harmonious system, neither jarring nor conflicting in any part of its operation. It is careful of the rights of the slave-holder, and is adapted to the feeling, sympathies and sovereign power of the states." He also insisted that "the states . . . had a right to authorize the actions of their officers . . . on such terms as they please, if they did not contradict the act of congress [and] there was no such contradiction or repugnancy in this case."[38]

A majority of the justices rejected these arguments, concluding that the Pennsylvania statute was unconstitutional. Joseph Story delivered the opinion of the Court. The opinion began with an unusual assertion of the limits of the precedential significance of the analysis which was to follow, declaring that "before . . . we proceed to the points more immediately before us, it may be well, in order to clear the case of difficulty, to say, that in the exposition of this part of the constitution, we shall limit ourselves to those considerations which appropriately and exclusively belong to it, without laying down any rules of interpretation of a more general nature."[39]

On one level, this declaration might be viewed as a simple recognition of the fact that each clause of the Constitution was the product of a unique interaction among factions with differing political agendas, and that the Court's approach to constitutional interpretation generally should reflect this reality. Thus, Story also observed that "perhaps, the safest rule of interpretation, after all, will be found to be to look to the nature and objects of the particular powers, duties and rights, with all the lights and aids of contemporary history; and to give to the words of each just such operation and force, consistent with their legitimate meaning, as may fairly secure and attain the ends proposed."[40]

But at the same time, the explicit attempt to limit the precedential impact of the *Prigg* opinion was at the very least unusual. Further, the use of this device allowed Story to confront the politically explosive questions presented by the case without fear that his approach would unduly distort the Court's approach to federalism-related issues more generally. Nonetheless, the form of his argument in *Prigg* clearly reflected the influence of related conventions of legal analysis.

Parts of Story's approach had been foreshadowed in his *Commentaries on the Constitution*, where he had explicitly rejected the claim that purported fugitives were entitled to a jury trial, concluding instead that the Constitution envisioned a regime which allowed their removal based on "summary administrative procedures." Nonetheless, his opinion in *Prigg* began promisingly for the antislavery forces, adopting the position of *Somerset v. Stewart*,[41] the legal mainstay of the antislavery movement, and declaring that "by the general law of nations, no nation is bound to recognize the state of slavery, as to foreign slaves found within its territorial dominions, when it is in opposition to its own policy and institutions, in favor of other nations where slavery is recognized [because] slavery is deemed to be a mere municipal regulation, founded upon and limited to the range of the territorial laws."[42] However, he then proceeded to outline and defend a set of conclusions that were in many cases more favorable to the proslavery position.

Story began by arguing that the Fugitive Slave Clause was central to the creation and maintenance of the Union. Notwithstanding the fact that the provision engendered very little discussion during the Constitutional Convention or the ratification debates, he declared that the Fugitive Slave Clause was "of the last importance to the safety and security of the southern states and could not have been surrendered by them, without endangering their whole property in slaves," that the clause "was so vital to the preservation of [the Southern states'] domestic interests and institutions that it cannot be doubted that it constituted a fundamental article without the adoption of which the Union could not have been formed," and that, in the absence of the Fugitive Slave Clause, the issue of fugitive slaves "would have created the most bitter animosities, and engendered perpetual strife between the different states." He then described the scope of the clause in sweeping terms, asserting that

> any state law or . . . regulation, which interrupts, limits, delays or postpones the right of the owner to the immediate possession of the slave, and the immediate command of his service and labor, operates, *pro tanto,* a discharge of the slave therefrom. . . . The question is not one of quantity or degree, but of withholding or controlling the incidents of a positive and absolute right.[43]

Story's treatment of the right of recaption followed logically from this characterization. He noted that, under the principles of the common law, the right of ownership in property carried with it the right to recover the property by self-help. He further observed that, by its terms, the Fugitive Slave Clause required even nonslave states to recognize the owner's property right in the escaped slave. Thus, Story had "not the slightest hesitation in holding, that . . . the owner of a slave is clothed with entire authority, in every state in the Union, to seize and recapture his slave, whenever he can do it, without any breach of the peace or any illegal violence."[44]

Having embraced the proslavery position on recaption, Story next addressed the respective roles of the state and federal governments in enforcing the Fugitive Slave Clause. Story began this portion of the opinion by observing that government aid would often be necessary for the claimant to recover the fugitive, and that the Clause itself, which provided that the slave "shall be delivered up, on claim of the [putative master]," seems to contemplate government enforcement.[45] Against the background of this premise, he turned to the question of *which* government was charged with the duty of enforcement.

On this point, Story's argument implicitly drew on Chief Justice John Marshall's treatment of the more general concept of implied powers in *McCulloch v. Maryland*. In *McCulloch*, Marshall had emphasized the need to vest Congress with sufficient authority to fully effectuate the powers that had been specifically outlined in the Constitution. Similarly, in *Prigg*, Story relied on the basic principle that "where the end is required, the means are given; and where the duty is enjoined, the ability to perform it is contemplated to exist, on the part of the functionaries to whom it is entrusted." Thus, Story argued that, since the Fugitive Slave Clause was found in the federal Constitution, "the natural inference certainly is, that the national government is clothed with the appropriate authority and functions to enforce it." He scoffed at the argument that the lack of a specific enforcement provision was fatal to this contention, declaring that "if this be the true interpretation of the constitution, it must, in a great measure, fail to attain many of its avowed objects, as a security of rights and recognition of duties" and noting that "[Congress] has, on various occasions, exercised powers which were necessary and proper as means to carry into effect rights expressly given, and duties expressly enjoined thereby." Thus, after reviewing in detail the specific provisions of the Fugitive Slave Act of 1793, he concluded that, with one exception, the act was "clearly constitutional, in all its leading provisions." Story thereby implicitly rejected the claim that a jury trial was required before an alleged fugitive could be seized and delivered to a claimant.[46]

While emphasizing the power of Congress to enforce the Fugitive Slave Clause, Story downplayed the role which state governments were to play in vindicating the claims of putative owners. First, Story argued that the adoption of the federal statute in 1793 implicitly barred states from legislating on rendition of escaped slaves. In reaching this conclusion, he relied on *Houston v. Moore* to establish the proposition that "where congress have exercised a power over a particular subject given them by the constitution, it is not competent for state legislation to add to the provisions of congress upon that subject; for that the will of congress upon the whole subject is as clearly established by what it has not declared, as by what it has expressed."[47]

Moreover, Story concluded that, even if Congress had not acted, state governments would have had no authority to adopt legislation designed to enforce the Fugitive Slave Clause. In contending that the power to enforce the Clause was vested *exclusively* in the federal government, he purported to apply the principles established in *Sturges v. Crowninshield*, concluding that "the nature of the provision and the objects to be attained by it require that it should be controlled by one and the same will and act uniformly by the same system of regulations throughout the Union." Otherwise, he argued, the right established by the Constitution "would never, in a practical sense, be the same in all the States [but] might be enforced in some States, retarded or limited in others and denied as compulsory in many, if not in all." Thus, in Story's view, states could not pass statutes designed to vindicate the claims of owners under any circumstances.[48]

These elements of Story's opinion in *Prigg* rested almost entirely on the doctrine of federal supremacy. He did make two concessions to the principle of state autonomy, however. First, he argued that state officers could not be compelled to enforce the federal statute, although they were free to do so if required by state law. Second, making an argument much like that of Chief Justice Marshall in *Gibbons*, Story distinguished sharply between regulation of the owner's right to retake fugitive slaves and the police power of the state, concluding that under the latter authority states retained "full jurisdiction to arrest and restrain runaway slaves, and remove them from their borders and otherwise secure themselves against their depredations and evil example."[49]

Taken as a whole, the structure of Story's opinion in *Prigg* reflected the confluence of his beliefs about the nature of slavery as an institution with his vision of federalism and his concern for ameliorating friction between the free states and the slave states. However, Story's values and worldview were not universally shared by his colleagues. The diversity in the respective outlooks of the Taney Court justices produced a variety of approaches to the issues presented by the Fugitive Slave Clause. While some agreed entirely with Story, others took a quite different view of the issues presented in *Prigg*.[50]

Only three justices failed to register a dissent from any of the principles announced in Story's opinion. Neither John McKinley nor John Catron wrote separately in *Prigg*. Both Joseph A. Burke and R. Kent Newmyer have suggested that one can infer that McKinley and Catron probably disagreed with at least some portions of Story's analysis. However, as Paul Finkelman has noted, in the absence of some explicit indication to the contrary, the justices are generally presumed to endorse all aspects of the opinion of the Court.[51] Thus, McKinley and Catron should be seen as concurring fully with Story.

McKinley's decision to concur reflects a theory of federalism that he had expressed in *Bank of Augusta v. Earle*.[52] In that case, dealing with the interpretation of the Commerce Clause, he had contended that the powers of the national government should be construed narrowly but also viewed as exclusive on those matters that were properly within the purview of federal authority.

As a justice from a slaveholding state, McKinley was hardly likely to conclude that the federal government lacked the power to enforce the Fugitive Slave Clause. At the same time, the vision of federalism that led McKinley to embrace the concept of federal exclusivity under the Commerce Clause was equally pertinent to the issue of fugitive slaves.

By contrast, it is difficult to characterize Catron's decision to join silently with Story in *Prigg* as a simple reflection of judicial nationalism. Instead, his concurrence more likely reflected a felt desire to craft a compromise to defuse the tensions to which Justice Story adverted in his opinion for the Court. These concerns were even more clearly expressed in the separate opinion of Justice James Moore Wayne.

While explicitly noting his agreement with Story in all respects, Wayne's opinion was devoted entirely to a defense of the view that the power to enforce the guarantees of the Fugitive Slave Clause rested exclusively with the federal government. Wayne deployed a number of different arguments in support of this conclusion. Some of these arguments were purely formal; he contended that "the surrender of a sovereign right carries with it all its incidents," and he further noted that a decision which relied on state law to conclude that a person was not in fact a fugitive could discharge that person from labor in apparent contravention of the language of the Fugitive Slave Clause itself. Wayne also emphasized the importance of slavery to the Southern states, observing that, without the Fugitive Slave Clause, "all of the property of the citizens would have been protected in every state, except that which was the most valuable in a number of them. In such a case, the states would have become members of the Union upon unequal terms." He further observed that, under the guise of providing additional remedies to owners of fugitive slaves, Northern states might in fact hinder the ability of the owners to reclaim their slaves.[53]

However, the major thrust of Wayne's argument was his claim that federal exclusivity was necessary to minimize the sectional friction created by the issue of fugitive slaves. He began by asserting that state governments were not appropriate agencies to determine the scope of the correlative rights and obligations created by the Fugitive Slave Clause, which were by definition federal in nature, and emphasizing the need for uniformity in the procedures for enforcing the right:

The obligation [created by the Fugitive Slave Clause] is common to all [the states] to the same extent. . . . Shall, then, each state be permitted to legislate in its own way, according to its own judgment, and their separate notions, in what manner the obligation shall be discharged to those states to which it is due? To permit some of the states to say to the others, how the property included in the provision was to be secured by legislation, without the assent of the latter, would certainly be, to destroy the equality and force of the guarantee, and the equality of the states by which it was made. . . . Is it not more reasonable to infer that [the states] meant that the right for which some of the states stipulated, and to which all acceded, should, from the peculiar nature of the property in which some of the states were interested, be carried into execution by that department of the general government in which they were all to be represented—the congress of the United States.

Later, he asserted that the doctrine of federal exclusivity "removes those causes which have contributed more than any other to disturb that harmony which is essential to the continuance of the Union." Wayne concluded by observing that

if there are not now agencies enough to make the assertion of the right to fugitives convenient to their owners, congress can multiply them. But if it should not be done, better is it that the inconvenience should be borne than that the states should be brought into collision upon this subject, as they have been.[54]

Wayne's argument captures what was perhaps the most important principle unifying the four justices who joined the Story opinion in *Prigg*. While differing in their views on slavery and to some extent on the appropriate *structure* of the Union, all were deeply committed to the *idea* of the Union. Moreover, whatever their views on the institution of slavery in the abstract, they were undoubtedly keenly aware that the dispute over slavery was the single issue most likely to disrupt the Union and that the ongoing conflict over the proper treatment of alleged fugitive slaves constantly generated tensions over this issue.

While no approach could totally eliminate these tensions, Story's delicately crafted compromise must have seemed well calculated to dampen the friction created by the problem of fugitive slaves. On one hand, the slaveholders gained a reaffirmation of their right to recapture escaped slaves, the promise of continuing federal aid in the process, and a guarantee that free state governments would not interfere. On the other, while residents of the free states were required to endure the spectacle of their African American neighbors being captured and returned to slavery, Northerners were at least assured that neither they nor their representatives would be required to act as slavecatchers, thus removing a major source of Northern irritation. Finally, to the extent that the Southern states had lingering complaints with the treatment of fugitive slaves and their masters, the Story/Wayne analysis channeled those complaints to the federal government, rather than to their sister states, which might well take offense to these complaints.

Viewed from this perspective, it is not surprising that Story's analysis was attractive to a number of the justices on a Court that was dominated by Jacksonians. Nonetheless, five of the justices had at least some misgivings about Story's conclusions. Their approaches showed a variety of different attitudes toward not only the institution of slavery but also more general concepts of federalism, as well as the influence of the formal conventions of legal analysis.

The opinions of both Justice Smith Thompson and Justice Henry Baldwin reflected their respective differences with Story on issues of federalism generally. Thompson's views on some of the issues in *Prigg* had been foreshadowed in 1835 by his opinion in *In re Martin.*[55] There, sitting on circuit in 1835, Thompson had been faced with a direct challenge to the constitutionality of the Fugitive Slave Act of 1793. The challenge was based upon two of the most important themes that would later figure prominently in the arguments in *Prigg*—that the procedure for issuing a certificate violated the Seventh Amendment guarantee of trial by jury, and that, in any event, Congress lacked constitutional authority to enact legislation implementing the Fugitive Slave Clause.

Thompson rejected both of these arguments. He found the Seventh Amendment inapplicable for two reasons. First, he noted that (at least in formal terms) the certificate issued by the magistrate did not finally determine that the person to be seized was a runaway; rather, it was simply an arrest warrant, allowing the putative slave to be seized and returned to the master's home state where, in theory, a full trial could take place. In addition, Thompson contended that the question of whether the alleged fugitive owed service under the laws of the state from which he had fled was a question of law rather than one of fact.[56]

Considered in isolation, these arguments might be viewed as simple exercises in the technical analysis of rules of law. By contrast, Thompson's discussion of federal power revealed his attitude toward the Fugitive Slave Clause more generally:

It cannot be presumed that it was intended to leave [the issue of fugitive slaves] to state legislation. There is no express injunction upon the states to pass any laws on the subject; and unless they choose [sic] to do it, the great benefit intended to be secured to slaveholders would be entirely defeated. We know, historically, that this was a subject that created great difficulty in the formation of the constitution, and that it resulted in a compromise not entirely satisfactory to a portion of the United States. But whatever our private opinions on the subject of slavery may be, we are bound in good faith to carry into execution the constitutional provisions in regard to it; and it would be an extravagant construction of this provision in the constitution to suppose it to be left discretionary in the states to comply with it or not, as they should think proper.[57]

Taken alone, statements such as these strongly suggest that Thompson, like Story, saw enforcement of the Fugitive Slave Clause as critical to the maintenance of sectional harmony. And indeed, Thompson had no difficulty in concurring with most of Story's opinion in *Prigg*. However, Thompson also saw the case as another skirmish with Story in their ongoing battle over the principle of federal exclusivity. As we have seen, after the departure of Chief Justice Marshall, Story became the foremost exponent of the view that, in general, grants of power to Congress divested states of authority to legislate on the same subject. By contrast, with the sole exception of his position on the regulation of Indian tribes, Thompson was equally persistent in arguing that states typically retained concurrent power in the absence of federal statutes.[58] Thus, in *Prigg* itself, Thompson contended that states retained authority to adopt legislation governing rendition, so long as the state legislation was not in conflict with federal statutes. He filed a brief opinion observing that "legislative provision . . . is essential for the purpose of preserving peace and good order in the community [because] in some parts of our country, [fugitive slave cases] are calculated to excite feelings which, if not restrained by law, might lead to riots and breaches of the peace," and conceding that "this legislation . . . belongs more effectively to congress than to the states, for the purpose of having the regulation uniform throughout the country." Nonetheless, observing that, in theory at least, Congress might choose to repeal the 1793 statute, Thompson also contended that "there is nothing in the subject matter that renders state legislation unfit" and concluded that "the constitution protects the master in the right of possession and service of his slave, and makes void all state legislation impairing that right, but does not make void state legislation in affirmance of the right."[59]

In short, Thompson was, like Story, deeply committed to the view that the constitutional issues related to slavery should be resolved by the principles of ordinary legal and constitutional discourse. Moreover, even more than Story, he viewed the case primarily through the lens of federal-state relations. Although his ultimate conclusions were different, much the same can be said of the approach taken by Justice Baldwin in *Prigg*.

Based solely on his opinions in *Groves* and *Johnson v. Tompkins*, one might have expected Baldwin to produce a strongly proslavery opinion in *Prigg*. However, in his treatise on constitutional law, Baldwin had embraced two general principles of federalism that, in the context of the dispute over fugitive slaves, militated Southern interests. Like McKinley, he had argued that federal power in general should be construed narrowly, but that grants of power to Congress should be deemed exclusive.[60]

These principles underlay his approach to *Prigg*. Baldwin produced no opinion at all in the case; instead, he simply issued a statement declaring that he concurred in the judgment but dissented from Story's analysis. James Moore

Wayne's opinion, however, reported that Baldwin was the only justice who believed that Congress lacked authority to add to the protections provided by the Fugitive Slave Clause itself, but that Baldwin also took the view that, if in fact Congress possessed authority to enact implementing legislation, states would thereby be divested of power to enforce the constitutional.[61] Thus, like Thompson, Baldwin did not view the controversy over the Fugitive Slave Clause as an issue to be governed by unique judicial principles. Instead, he simply applied the same legal theories of federalism and interpretation that he had developed for dealing with constitutional problems more generally. By contrast, other justices were more plainly influenced by their views on the issues of slavery specifically.

John McLean's opinion reflected the influence of both his opposition to slavery and his commitment to judicial nationalism. McLean began by conceding that the Constitution established a federal right to reclaim fugitive slaves from free states. Like Story, he viewed the issue of enforcement of this right primarily in terms of the allocation of authority between the federal and state governments, and he found the power to provide a mechanism for enforcement of the slaveowner's right to be exclusively in the federal government. However, McLean differed from Story on other important issues. First, he took a more nationalistic view on the obligation of state governments, concluding that the federal government could constitutionally require state officials to enforce the federal remedy. At the same time, however, he also agreed that the federal government had no power to coerce state compliance with obligations so imposed.[62]

More importantly, McLean took a strong stance in favor of state authority to vindicate one of the major tenets of antislavery constitutionalism—the idea that states could and should prohibit claimants from attempting to recapture alleged fugitives without satisfying specified procedural requirements. Here the language of state autonomy dominated the McLean opinion. Noting the presumption against slavery in the free states, McLean contended that in states with antikidnapping laws, the choice in recaption cases was between "the presumption of right set up by the master, unsustained by any proof, or the presumption which arises from the law and institutions of the State." Recognizing in each state "a power to guard and protect its own jurisdiction, and the peace of its citizens," McLean concluded that in order to protect free men, states could constitutionally require that slaveowners meet the requirements of the federal statute or the state law prior to forcibly reclaiming fugitives.[63] Thus, notwithstanding his strong commitment to judicial nationalism generally, on this issue McLean's opinion was not only antislavery but also clearly more state-centered than Story's analysis.

Although he did not embrace the most advanced elements of antislavery constitutionalism, McLean's approach provides the clearest example of the influence of antislavery thought in *Prigg*. Not surprisingly, proslavery thought also clearly impacted the views of some members of the Court in *Prigg*. This impact is most clearly reflected in the opinions of Justice Peter V. Daniel and Chief Justice Roger Brooke Taney.

In other contexts, Daniel consistently argued against expansive interpretations of federal power. Nonetheless, in *Prigg* he concurred with the view that Congress had the authority to adopt legislation enforcing the Fugitive Slave Clause. At the same time, purporting to rely on the principles established in *Sturges, Houston v. Moore,* and *New York v. Miln,* Daniel joined Smith Thompson in arguing that states also possessed concurrent authority to provide for rendition of escaped slaves.[64] But unlike Thompson, Daniel strongly supported the adoption of state legislation.

Daniel emphasized the practical importance of the support of state officials, observing that "whenever the master, attempting to enforce his right of seizure under the constitution, shall meet with resistance, the inconsiderable number of federal officers in a state, and their frequent remoteness from the theatre of action, must, in numerous instances, at once defeat his right of property, and deprive him also of personal protection and security." In addition, he focused on the symbolic effect of Story's theory of federal exclusivity, arguing that the ban on state laws vindicating the rights of the master might buttress the arguments of those urging interference with legitimate efforts to recover escapees from service.

Suppose that a fugitive from service should have fled to a state where slavery does not exist, and in which the prevalent feeling is hostile to that institution; there might, nevertheless, in such a community, be a disposition to yield something to an acknowledged constitutional right—something, too, in the preservation of that right; but let it once be proclaimed from this tribunal, that any concession by the states toward the maintenance of such a right is a positive offence, the violation of a solemn duty, and I ask what pretext more plausible could be offered by those who are disposed to protect the fugitive, or to defeat the rights of the master? The constitution and the act of congress would thus be converted into instruments for the destruction of that which they were designed especially to protect.

Finally, Daniel rejected the argument that states might, under the guise of legislation purportedly designed to protect the rights of slaveowners, actually impede the recovery of fugitives, observing that analogous arguments might be made against the grant of enforcement power to the federal government, and that "should . . . abuses be attempted, the corrective may be found . . . in the controlling constitutional authority of this court."[65]

Taney's opinion reflected an even stronger commitment to the protection of Southern interests. Taney rejected the argument that the Fugitive Slave Clause was largely concerned with allocating authority between Congress and the state governments, asserting instead that the clause "does not purport to be a distribution of the rights of sovereignty by which certain enumerated powers of government and legislation are exclusively confided in the United States [but] provides merely for the rights of individual citizens and places them under the protection of the general government; in order more effectually to guard them from invasion by the States." Not surprisingly, like Story, he concluded that the Fugitive Slave Clause not only constitutionalized the right to recaption but also vested Congress with the power to pass legislation to vindicate the rights of slaveowners. Unlike Story, however, Taney analogized the Fugitive Slave Clause to the Comity Clause, and he concluded that the states had not only the power but also the duty to supplement federal protection of the slaveholders' rights.[66]

The analyses of McLean, Daniel, and Taney reflected the sectionalist impulses that threatened the stability of the national political process in the 1840s. Conversely, Story's opinion embodied the views of those who sought to dampen sectional tensions through a process of accommodation and compromise. But while Story himself is reported to have characterized his opinion as "a triumph of freedom," modern commentators have often characterized the opinion as leaning heavily toward the South. R. Kent Newmyer, for example, concludes that "*Prigg* went to the South, or at least a plain reading of [Justice Story's] opinion would indicate," while Don E. Fehrenbacher describes Story's opinion as "emphatically proslavery in tone and substance," and Paul Finkelman declares that the decision was "a sweeping victory for slavery."[67]

Such assessments rest in substantial measure on Story's vindication of the right of recaption and correlative invalidation of state personal liberty laws. For example, Finkelman complains that

by striking down Pennsylvania's Personal Liberty Law and by extension the personal liberty laws of other states, Story left the Northern states without the weapons or the legal authority to prevent the kidnaping of blacks. . . . Story further endangered blacks in the North by asserting that the Constitution gave the master a right of self-help "to seize and recapture his slave" anywhere in the nation regardless of state or federal statutory law.

Similarly, Thomas D. Morris asserts that Story "seemed to withdraw from free blacks north of the Mason-Dixon the equal protection of the laws, and to deny them standing to invoke the procedures used to secure personal liberty," and Akhil Reed Amar claims that, under the rules established in *Prigg,* "it was open season on free blacks everywhere in America."[68]

In fact, Story's treatment of these issues did not deprive free blacks of any of the legal protections available to other persons in the Northern states. Typically, people are protected against kidnapping not by procedural devices, such as those contained in the personal liberty laws, but rather by the generally applicable criminal statutes and common law principles that prohibit one person from holding another against his will. Story's opinion does not suggest that the Fugitive Slave Clause somehow abrogated these statutes with respect to free blacks in the North. To the contrary, he analogized the master's right to exercise self-help to recapture an escaped slave to a parent's right to recover a runaway child—a case where the kidnapping statutes clearly retained their significance. An adult found in possession of a child claiming to be restrained against his will could clearly be arrested, and could only escape criminal liability by proving that he was in fact the parent of the child.

Similarly, as Justice James Moore Wayne clearly implied in his concurrence, the vindication of the right of recaption in no way vitiated a slave hunter's liability for kidnapping a *free man.* Of course, if the slaveowner or his agent was arrested on a charge of kidnapping an African American, like the plaintiff in *Johnson v. Tompkins,* he would be free to assert, as an affirmative defense, that the person whom he had seized was in fact an escaped slave and that he had done nothing more than exercise his right to self-help in regaining his property. However, if he failed to prove that the seized person was in fact a fugitive from service, then the slave hunter would be subject to criminal liability for the seizure. To be sure, in practice slave hunters were rarely if ever prosecuted for pretextually seizing free blacks. But the basic point remains; the constitutionalization of the right of recaption in no way deprived free blacks of the protection of generally applicable laws against kidnapping.[69]

Against this background, Story's conclusions on the right of recaption and the constitutionality of the state personal liberty laws were dictated by a distinctively legal analysis of the language of the Fugitive Slave Clause and the background principles of the common law. In forbidding nonslave states from freeing slaves who escaped into their jurisdiction, the Fugitive Slave Clause essentially declared that escapees remained the property of their former masters. Further, the common law provided the owner of property with the right to self-help to recover that property, wherever the property might be found. Thus, the only logical conclusion is that the slaveowner would have a right to recapture a fugitive under the same circumstances that he might be entitled to retake any other type of property, free of the additional hindrances mandated by state personal liberty laws. Story's positions on these issues requires no more.

Story's critics can more plausibly claim that his treatment of the Fugitive Slave Act of 1793 placed free blacks at risk. A slave hunter could have no liability for kidnapping if he had first obtained an order from a responsible government agency giving him the right to seize the putative slave. By its terms, the Fugitive Slave Act of 1793 established a process by which the slave hunter could obtain such an order.

Story's critics have raised two quite different objections to his conclusion that the federal statute was almost entirely constitutional. First, they have assailed Story's claim that the procedures established by the Fugitive Slave Act were sufficient to satisfy constitutional minima, contending that the federal statute denied to putative slaves rights protected by the Due Process Clause of the Fifth Amendment and the guarantee of trial by jury in the Sixth Amendment.[70] However, the language of the Fugitive Slave Clause creates substantial difficulties for the argument. The wording of the clause is quite clearly patterned on that of the Extradition Clause, and the proof required by the statute for the issuance of a certificate of removal is almost precisely analogous to the evidence which is required to support extradition. The reason that the proof is deemed sufficient in an extradition case is that extradition does not purport to be a final determination of guilt. Similarly, even after an alleged fugitive was returned to the home of the slaveowner, he was still able to bring a suit for freedom in the courts of that state—an option that was ultimately pursued (albeit unsuccessfully) in the courts of the state of Maryland by Martha Morgan, the slave whose removal gave rise to the litigation in *Prigg* itself.

More plausibly, some critics of *Prigg* claim that Congress lacked the power to adopt any statute designed to effectuate the Fugitive Slave Clause. They note that the Constitution does not explicitly vest Congress with the authority to adopt such a statute. Thus, for example, Barbara Holden Smith observes that "Article IV is generally not concerned with the powers of the national government," and also asserts that "if the Framers had intended to confer on the national government the power to enact legislation to aid the states in their duty to return fugitive slaves, it is fair to assume they would have explicitly said so in the Fugitive Slave Clause." In addition to relying generally on the doctrine of enumerated powers, some antislavery theorists analogized the Fugitive Slave Clause to the Comity Clause, and observed that no one would argue that Congress had authority to pass a statute protecting the rights guaranteed by that provision.[71]

The problem with the latter argument is that the analogy to the Comity

Clause is inapt. While the first part of the Fugitive Slave Clause established a right similar to those guaranteed by the Comity Clause, the source of authority for the 1793 statute was not that part, but rather the language that requires escapees to be "delivered up on Claim of the [master]." This language is drawn almost verbatim not from the Comity Clause but rather from the Extradition Clause, which requires states to apprehend and deliver those charged with crimes in other states. Indeed, the Fugitive Slave Act itself was included in the same statute that established the procedures to be followed in making a theoretically binding request for the extradition of a person charged with a crime. Thus, a holding that Congress could not pass legislation implementing the Fugitive Slave Clause would imply a similar lack of authority to define the procedural requirements of the Extradition Clause—a conclusion with which even the antislavery forces were uncomfortable.

Still, the conclusion that the federal government had the power to pass enforcement legislation is somewhat problematic in legal terms, and can plausibly be viewed as a concession to the slave states. But at the same time, a majority of the slave state justices were also willing to make important concessions in *Prigg*. Each of the three Southern justices who wrote opinions in *Prigg* clearly realized that, without the aid of state government officials, the recapture of fugitive slaves would be substantially more difficult. Yet a majority of the five slave-state justices—Wayne, McKinley, and Catron—chose to concur fully with Story in concluding that states could not establish their own rendition schemes, and that state officials could refuse to cooperate in implementing the procedures established by the federal Fugitive Slave Act.

As Wayne's opinion indicates, the decision of these justices is best understood as an effort to defuse sectional tensions over the issue. To be sure, distinctively legal principles played some role in the analysis. For example, the conclusion that the passage of the federal Fugitive Slave Act implicitly barred states from adopting supplemental legislation might aptly be characterized as a simple application of the legal rules that had been previously established in *Houston v. Moore*. But Story's main emphasis was on the claim that states could not have adopted such legislation even in the absence of a federal statute. While Story could plausibly rely on *Sturges v. Crowninshield* to support this conclusion, the principles established in *Sturges* cannot be said to have definitively resolved this issue in *Prigg*. Moreover, Story cited *no* legal authority to support the conclusion that state officials could not be required to aid in the enforcement of the federal statute.

In short, both legal and political forces contributed to the decision in *Prigg*. Ultimately, however, Story's opinion is best characterized as a true compromise between the interests of the North and the South on the issue of fugitive slaves. Particularly when considered together with *Groves* and *The Amistad,* the opinion reflects the views of a Court controlled by justices committed to the views of those who sought sectional accommodation in the early 1840s.

CHAPTER 8

Assessment

All of the slavery-related decisions of the early 1840s represented victories for those who favored sectional accommodation. However, each of the decisions reflected a unique decision-making dynamic. These dynamics were byproducts of the specific nature of the issues presented to the Court.

The decision in *The Amistad* is best understood as the product of the influence of distinctively legal principles. Particularly noteworthy were the actions of the Southern justices who unanimously joined Justice Story in voting to free the blacks found on the slave ship. From an ordinary political or cultural perspective, one might have expected some or all of the Southerners on the Court to be sympathetic to the claims of the shipowners. Yet instead, all joined with Story in vindicating the claims of the Africans and their abolitionist allies. A commitment to the ideology of legal reasoning provides the most plausible explanation for this seeming incongruity.

But at the same time, the long-term significance of the resolution of the case by the Supreme Court was by its nature limited. The decision in favor of Cinque and his comrades had no impact on either the balance of sectional political power or the ability of the Southern states to maintain their institutions without interference from the North or the federal government. Under these circumstances, Chief Justice Taney and Justices McKinley, Wayne, and Catron were apparently willing to ignore the political sentiments of slave-state residents in order to vindicate the Southern justices' commitment to the ideology of legal reasoning.

The political context created a quite different decision-making dynamic in *Groves v. Slaughter*. In the early 1840s, the disagreement over the status of the interstate slave trade, which gave rise to *Groves,* played only a minor role in the disputes between the North and South. At the same time, the justices clearly understood that any of their pronouncements on the issue of congressional power to regulate the domestic slave trade had the potential to raise the profile of the issue and thereby exacerbate sectional tensions. Faced with this reality, a bisectional majority of the justices was initially willing to distort the clear import of Mississippi state law in order to avoid confronting the basic federal constitutional issue. Even when John McLean, the justice with the strongest antislavery convictions, felt the need to address the general issue of federal exclusivity, he was careful to link his basic theory of the commerce power with the argument of Mississippi slaveowner Robert Walker in order to assure Southerners that his analysis would not imperil the Southern states' ability to regulate the slave trade. Conversely, although they believed themselves forced to confront the constitutional issues related to the interstate slave trade after McLean announced his opinion, the Southerners on the Court were careful to defend the slave-state position in the blandest, most inoffensive terms available.

By contrast, avoidance of the issues raised by the Fugitive Slave Clause was a much less attractive option for accommodationists in *Prigg*. From the time that the Constitution was drafted, the efforts of slaveowners to recover putative slaves who had allegedly escaped northward created ongoing tensions between the free states and the slave states. Against this background, the diverse approaches of the justices reflected a variety of different influences. Henry Baldwin, for example, viewed the case entirely through the prism of distinctively legal principles, while Roger Brooke Taney and John McLean each sought to use *Prigg* as a vehicle to advance a sectional agenda. Taney argued that the Constitution required state officials to participate in the rendition of fugitive slaves, a regime that was likely to have been unacceptable to many Northerners. Conversely, the framework outlined by McLean would have been offensive to many Southerners. Although McLean agreed that Congress had the power to pass legislation implementing the Fugitive Slave Clause, he would have prohibited Northern states from providing additional remedies to slaveowners while at the same time allowing the same states to interpose procedural obstacles to the exercise of the right of recaption.

But a majority of the justices rejected all of these approaches. In theory, the accommodationist majority might have limited itself to consideration of the constitutional status of the state personal liberty laws and the right of recaption, the only issues raised directly by the case. But a narrow opinion would have left unanswered a variety of important questions related to the fugitive slave controversy, which carried within them the seeds of further conflict. While no pronouncement from the justices could entirely still this conflict, a broad opinion at least had the potential to ameliorate tensions.

Against this background, while Story and his allies were clearly influenced by distinctively legal principles, many of his conclusions are best understood as part of an effort by a bisectional coalition of accommodationist justices to craft a global solution that would be widely accepted in both the free states and the slave states. Story's assertion that state officials could not be required to participate in the enforcement of the federal Fugitive Slave Act is particularly striking in this regard. He might have claimed that the vindication of the constitutionality of the Fugitive Slave Act itself was a necessary predicate to the invalidation of the Pennsylvania Personal Liberty Law under a theory of federal exclusivity. But the refusal of the justice of the peace to issue the certificate of removal was not before the Court; therefore, the discussion of this issue was pure dictum. Story's decision to analyze this issue is thus best understood as a part of a unified strategy to provide a plausible compromise under which Southerners would retain the right of recaption and be allowed to take advantage of the federal statute if they chose, but Northerners would be assured that they could prevent their government officials from being enlisted as slavecatchers.

In purely political terms, Story's framework was apparently attractive to a narrow majority of five justices—Story himself, Smith Thompson of New York, James Moore Wayne of Georgia, John McKinley of Alabama, and John Catron of Tennessee. But, apparently for distinctively legal reasons that transcended the dispute over fugitive slaves itself, Thompson opposed the effort to ensconce the principle of federal exclusivity into constitutional law. Thus, this principle only became the institutional doctrine of the Court because it was also embraced by John McLean, who provided the necessary fifth vote on this point, thus creating majority status for Story's entire opinion.

In short, the decision in *Prigg* was produced by a dynamic much like that of the national political system as a whole in the early 1840s. While the balance of power was held by those who advocated sectional accommodation, accommodationists at times had to rely on sectionalists from the North or South to pass legislation or win elections. However, the commitment of both judges and politicians to sectional accommodation would come under increasing pressure in the decade following *Prigg* as a series of events led to an upward spiral in the tensions between North and South.

Part Three

The Conflict Escalates, 1843–1853

CHAPTER 9

Slavery and Territorial Expansion

For the Whig Party, the election of 1840 brought not only the election of a president but also governing majorities in both houses of Congress. Not surprisingly, most Whigs looked forward confidently to implementing their economic program. Their hopes were dashed when William Henry Harrison became ill and died only one month after his inauguration and John Tyler ascended to the presidency. Despite having been a strong supporter of the candidacy of the nationalist Henry Clay for the Whig nomination in 1840, Tyler was a stalwart of the states' rights wing of the Whig Party. He broke with Henry Clay and most of the party establishment after vetoing bills that would have rechartered the Bank of the United States and postponed the cuts in rates mandated by the Compromise Tariff of 1833. By mid-1843, Tyler had been formally excommunicated from the party.[1] Soon thereafter, an effort to acquire Texas became the centerpiece of his administration.[2]

The sequence of events that led to the dispute over Texas can be traced to the Adams-Onis Treaty of 1819, in which the United States renounced its claims to Texas and, in return, the Spanish government agreed to sell Florida to the United States. Subsequently, efforts were made to purchase Texas by the administrations of both John Quincy Adams and Andrew Jackson. However, the Mexican government rebuffed these overtures. The situation became more complex after Texas declared its independence from Mexico in 1836. The victories of the Texans on the battlefield and the request of their fledgling government for annexation in November 1836 set off a politically charged debate in the United States over the appropriate course of action for the American government.

The debate over Texas took on a strong sectional tone. Many Southerners favored annexation, while Northern opinion was generally hostile. Northern opponents included not only antislavery Whigs but also Van Buren Democrats, who (though often derided by modern scholars for deferring unduly to their Southern counterparts) worried that a serious effort to annex Texas would disrupt the sectional harmony that they strove mightily to preserve. Against this background, a petition circulated widely by the American Anti-Slavery Society complained that "six or eight" slave states might ultimately be carved out of Texas, which the society claimed would leave the South in complete control of the national government. In addition, the governments of eight Northern states formally protested against annexation. Conversely, on January 4, 1838,

Sen. William C. Campbell of South Carolina offered a resolution urging the annexation of Texas whenever it could be done "consistently with the public faith and treaty stipulations of the United States" and without disrupting relations with Mexico. On June 14, seven senators from the slave states joined with their united Northern colleagues to table the resolution by a vote of 24–14.[3] With neither party's leadership having any apparent inclination to press the issue, the prospects for annexation seemed dim.

However, after replacing Harrison, Tyler pursued the annexation of Texas with an enthusiasm that stemmed in part from a sincere commitment to the principle of national expansion and in part from a desire to use the issue to create an independent power base for his administration. His representatives, led by Secretary of State Abel P. Upshur, a Calhounite from Virginia, successfully negotiated a treaty of annexation, which was signed on April 12, 1844.[4] The treaty was submitted to the Senate for ratification on April 22, 1844.

The submission of the treaty set off an intense political struggle. Supporters argued that annexation would provide economic benefits to the nation as a whole and claimed that, if not acquired by the United States, Texas would become part of the British Empire. Opponents, by contrast, contended that the treaty was unconstitutional, that annexation would inevitably bring war with Mexico, and that the debt which the government of Texas had incurred would impose a crushing financial burden on the federal government. In addition, issues of slavery and sectional relations unquestionably played a major role in the dispute.

The importance of the slavery issue was magnified by the famous Packenham Letter, in which John C. Calhoun of South Carolina, who had become secretary of state on April 1, 1844, explicitly defended the treaty on the ground that annexation was necessary to protect the South from the abolitionist designs of the British. Calhoun's motives for making this intemperate assertion have been extensively debated by historians.[5] But whatever its purposes, publication of the letter provided impetus to the claim that annexation was simply a device to enhance the position of the slave power in the federal government.

Against this background, on April 17, 1844, Henry Clay—who by this time had become the presumptive Whig presidential nominee for the upcoming election of 1844—announced his position on the annexation issue. In 1819, Clay had bitterly denounced the provisions of the Adams-Onis Treaty that renounced American claims to Texas. By contrast, noting the sectional animosity that had been aroused by the issue, he opposed the treaty of annexation in 1844. Clay described the treaty as "a measure compromising the national character, involving us certainly in a war with Mexico, dangerous to the integrity of the

Union . . . inexpedient in the present financial condition of the country, and not called for by any general expression of public opinion."[6] On April 27, Martin Van Buren, Calhoun's hated political enemy and the leading candidate for the Democratic presidential nomination, also declared against immediate annexation, discounting the British threat and focusing primarily on the danger of war with Mexico. At the same time, however, Van Buren announced that he would acquiesce in the acquisition of Texas if he became convinced that it had widespread public support.[7]

With the leaders of both major parties having declared their opposition to immediate annexation, the treaty had no chance of obtaining the two-thirds majority necessary for ratification by the Senate. Instead, the treaty was overwhelmingly rejected by a vote of 35–16. Despite the importance of the slavery issue, the pattern of the votes clearly indicates that other considerations were significant as well. With the sole exception of Sen. John Henderson of Mississippi, both Northern and Southern Whigs followed Clay's lead and voted solidly against the treaty. Conversely, all slave state Democrats except Sen. Thomas Hart Benton of Missouri voted for the treaty. Only free state Democrats were split, with five out of twelve voting in favor of ratification.[8]

The defeat of the treaty did not signal the end of the controversy over the annexation of Texas. In substantial measure because of Van Buren's position on the Texas issue, the Democratic Convention passed him over in favor of James K. Polk, a relatively obscure, proannexation former governor of Tennessee, and adopted a platform that strongly favored the acquisition of Texas. As expected, the Whigs nominated Henry Clay to succeed Tyler. The electorate was thus presented with a clear choice on the issue of annexation.

Unfortunately for Clay and the Whigs, James Birney, once again the nominee of the Liberty Party, also based his campaign largely on opposition to the annexation of Texas. Although receiving less than 2 percent of the votes nationwide, Birney may have siphoned off enough votes from Clay in New York to give the victory to Polk, who gained a plurality in the popular vote of less than 40,000 out of more than 2.7 million votes cast and a margin of 170 to 105 in the electoral college. The overall pattern of the voting belies any effort to characterize annexation as a purely sectional issue. To be sure, Polk swept the Deep South, including Georgia, which the Democrats had not carried since 1832. But Clay carried most of the Upper South, and Polk also was successful in Indiana, whose electoral history was similar to that of Georgia, as well as Pennsylvania and Michigan, both of which had been carried by Harrison in 1840. The results thus suggest that attitudes regarding Texas were determined as much by party as by section.[9]

In any event, Polk's election substantially changed the political dynamic of the annexation issue. Annexationists claimed a popular mandate for their position. However, although the strength of the Whigs in the Senate had been substantially reduced by the election, even in the new Congress Democrats would be well short of the two-thirds majority necessary to ratify a treaty. Thus, the only viable option was to proceed by admitting Texas as a state through a joint resolution of Congress—an idea that Tyler had entertained even before the defeat of the treaty.

Issues of constitutionality aside, the use of this device brought the issue of slavery even more clearly to the fore. Although under most proposals the entire area of Texas was initially to be admitted as a single slave state, at the time people generally seem to have believed that the new state would not remain undivided indefinitely. Instead, both supporters and opponents of annexation acted on the assumption that, as its population grew and dispersed more widely, Texas would eventually be divided into a number of smaller states. Fearing that this eventuality would unduly enhance the power of the South in Congress, Northerners pressed for assurances that slavery would be outlawed in at least some of the states that would be created from Texas.

Against this background, Whig Rep. Milton Brown of Tennessee proposed a solution that basically incorporated the principles of the Missouri Compromise, allowing the formation of up to five states from the territory of Texas, but also providing that slavery would be barred from any state formed out of territory that was wholly north of the Missouri Compromise line. Opponents of slavery rejected the Brown proposal as inadequate, noting that the part of Texas north of the line was minuscule at best. This reality led twenty-eight Northern Democrats to vote against the Brown proposal. Moreover, House Whigs generally remained adamant in their opposition to any scheme for annexation, with only seven Southern Whigs supporting Brown. Nonetheless, his proposal gained a 120 to 98 majority.[10]

Supporters of annexation faced a more difficult task in the Senate. There, the Whigs continued to hold a slender majority in the lame duck session. Thus, annexationists could not prevail without some Whig defections. In addition, they would need the support of the seven Van Buren Democrats who had opposed the annexation treaty.

The leader of the Van Burenites was Sen. Thomas Hart Benton of Missouri—the only slave state Democrat who had voted against the treaty. Early in the session, Benton put forth a resolution that would have authorized the president to negotiate with the government of Mexico for the acquisition of Texas, while at the same time providing that, if acquired, Texas would ultimately be divided equally between free states and slave states. Later, under pressure from both the Missouri state legislature and Andrew Jackson, Benton introduced a quite different resolution, authorizing the president to negotiate annexation with the government of Texas.

Southerners remained dissatisfied because the new resolution did not resolve the issue of slavery. They suggested to Benton that he include the territorial provisions of the Brown resolution in his proposal. However, Northern Democrats objected to this suggestion. The impasse was resolved by combining the Benton and Brown resolutions, giving the president the option of either offering annexation to Texas under the terms outlined in the House proposal or reopening negotiations. Believing they had assurances that Polk would pursue the Benton option, the Van Burenites threw their support behind the combined proposal. It was adopted by the Senate by a vote of 27–25, with three Southern Whigs joining the united Democrats to provide the margin of victory, and then passed the House 132–76 on an almost straight party-line vote.[11]

The belief that Polk would renegotiate the conditions of annexation was critical to Democratic unanimity, and thus to the success of the resolution in the Senate. In essence, this belief allowed the Van Buren Democrats to satisfy the demands of loyalty to the party platform without committing themselves to acquiescence in annexation under terms they believed unacceptable. In particular, the Benton alternative left open the option of refighting the battle over the division of Texas into free and slave states when the renegotiated terms were once again presented to Congress. Indeed, it was quite possible that renegotiation would doom the entire project. Calhoun, for example, feared that pursuit of the Benton alternative would ultimately result in the submission of a new treaty, which would likely die in the Senate because of Whig opposition.[12]

However, subsequent events did not follow the course envisioned by Benton and his allies. They were stunned when the lame duck Tyler presented the government of Texas with the terms of the Brown resolution. Polk chose not to disavow Tyler's actions, and Texas accepted Tyler's offer. Thus, Texas was admitted to the Union, with the division between potential free and slave states determined by the pattern of the Missouri Compromise.

The controversy over the acquisition of Texas left a residue of sectional bitterness that was exacerbated by subsequent clashes over the further acquisition of territory. The first of these acquisition-related issues involved the resolution of a dispute with the British over the status of the Oregon Territory, an area that ran from the southern boundary of the modern state of Oregon north to the latitude of 54 degrees, 40 minutes. The British claim was based on its citizens having been the first from any European power to land on the coast of Vancouver Island. Americans, by contrast, had been the first to discover the mouth of the Columbia River and to explore the lower valley of the river. The United States had also acquired Spanish claims to Oregon through the Adams-Onis Treaty, and argued that, prior to 1819, the Spanish in fact had possessed the best claim to the entire coast.[13]

Prior to 1844, the United States and Great Britain had made a number of efforts to resolve the dispute through negotiation. Seeking to gain control of the harbor at Puget Sound, the United States had repeatedly offered to divide the territory at the 49th parallel. The British, by contrast, argued that the boundary should be established by the Columbia River, much of which is below the 47th parallel. In the absence of a permanent settlement, in 1827 the parties had agreed that the entire territory would be open to the citizens of both countries. However, this "joint occupation" agreement was subject to abrogation by either party on a year's notice.

The election of 1844 brought the issue of Oregon to a head. Seeking to counter the argument that Democratic support for the annexation of Texas was a surrender to the slave power, the Democratic platform for the election also called for the United States to demand the entire Oregon territory. While by no means as prominent as the debate over Texas, the issue had some traction in the Northwest. After Polk's victory, on a party line vote, the lame duck session of the House of Representatives passed a measure calling for the abrogation of the joint occupation agreement and the establishment of a territorial government for Oregon.[14] However, this measure was opposed by the outgoing Tyler administration and was not taken up by the Senate.

Whatever the motives for the reference to Oregon in the platform, Polk himself was committed to pressing for a final resolution of the controversy on terms that were favorable to the United States. He rallied Northern Democrats behind the view that "our title to [all of] the country of Oregon is 'clear and unquestionable.'" Polk's Democratic supporters were joined by Rep. Joshua Giddings of Ohio and a small handful of other radical antislavery Whigs, who pressed for the annexation of the entire Oregon territory as a counterweight to the newly admitted Texas. By contrast, concerned about the possibility of a war with England, many Southern Democrats and most Whigs of all stripes pressed for a more conciliatory approach.[15]

A protracted struggle ensued in both the House of Representatives and the Senate. Ultimately, in April 1846, the House of Representatives and the Senate agreed on a resolution that authorized the President to give notice "at his discretion." Against the background of the threat of abrogation and potential war, the British made new concessions, and a treaty resolving the dispute was signed on June 15. Under the terms of the treaty, the 49th parallel was established as the boundary between the United States and Canada, with the exception of the southern tip of Vancouver Island, which did not become part of the United States. Further, the right to free navigation of the Columbia River was limited to the ships of the Hudson Bay Company, which had long maintained a number of fur-trading outposts on the river.

By any objective standard, the treaty was a diplomatic triumph for the United States, which gained almost everything that it had requested in previous negotiations. Indeed, Lord Palmerston, who soon thereafter became Britain's Foreign Secretary, observed that "it would have been strange if the Americans had not been pleased with an arrangement which gives them everything which they ever really wanted." Nonetheless, Northern Democrats rebelled against the treaty. The depth of their anger was revealed when the Senate voted on the treaty on June 17. While only two slave state Democrats voted against the treaty, it was opposed by Northern Democrats by a 12–2 margin. The treaty was ratified only because it was supported unanimously by Senate Whigs.[16]

The bitterness of Northern Democrats was fueled largely by what they saw as the disparate treatment of Texas and Oregon. Northerners pointed out that they had ultimately provided unanimous support for the annexation of Texas (albeit with the understanding that annexation would be under the terms of the Benton proposal), but that many of their Southern colleagues had refused to reciprocate during the Oregon controversy. Thus, Democratic Sen. Edward Hannegan of Indiana complained during the debates that Texas and Oregon "were nursed and cradled in the same cradle—the [Democratic Convention of 1844]. There was not a moment's hesitation, until Texas was admitted; but the moment she was admitted, the peculiar friends of Texas turned, and were doing all they could to strangle Oregon!"[17]

This sense of disparate treatment was magnified by the fact that the Senate was called upon to approve the division of Oregon only after war had been declared upon Mexico. The immediate trigger for the war was a dispute over the boundary between Mexico and Texas. Mexico claimed that the Nueces River formed the southern boundary of Texas, while the United States argued that the border was further south, at the Rio Grande River. War broke out after Polk ordered General Zachary Taylor to march to the Rio Grande, where his army was attacked by Mexican forces. Northern Democrats asked why the administration was willing to divide Oregon in order to avoid war with England, while at the same time refusing to compromise on the Texas boundary in order to avoid war with Mexico.

Nonetheless, dissatisfaction with the settlement of the Oregon boundary dispute did not translate into Democratic opposition to either the Mexican War itself or to Polk's desire to use the war as a device to force Mexico to make territorial concessions to the United States. To the contrary, most of the opposition to the war and the acquisition of additional territory came from the same groups that had been most vociferous in pressing for the Oregon compromise—the united Whigs and a small group of Calhounite loyalists. Conversely, both Northern and Southern Democrats joined in exhortations to extract the maximum territorial gains from the war, in some cases pressing for the annexation of all of Mexico. Much of the territory sought by Polk and his allies was north of the Missouri Compromise line. Nonetheless, Northern Whigs charged that the war was being prosecuted for the purpose of adding slave territory to the United States and thus enhancing the influence of the slave power in the federal government.[18]

It was against this background that Democratic Rep. David Wilmot of Pennsylvania, representing the interests of a small group of Van Burenite Democrats, introduced his famous proviso during the waning days of the first session of the Twenty-ninth Congress on August 12, 1846. The occasion was a bill that would have appropriated $2 million for the purpose of negotiating a treaty to end the Mexican War and acquiring land from Mexico as an incident to the treaty. Wilmot moved an amendment that would have provided "that, as an express and fundamental condition to the acquisition of any territory from the Republic of Mexico . . . neither slavery nor involuntary servitude shall ever exist in any part of said territory, except for crime, whereof the party shall first be duly convicted."[19]

The decision to introduce the Wilmot Proviso was influenced by a number of different factors. In part, it was designed to inoculate Northern supporters of the war against the charge that they were supporting the expansionist aims of the slave power. In large measure, however, the introduction of the Proviso was a response to what many Northern Democrats viewed as unfair treatment by the Polk administration and their Southern colleagues more generally. The grievances of the Northerners were not limited to the denial of the 1844 nomination to Van Buren and the decision to compromise on the Oregon boundary. In addition, Van Burenites generally believed that Polk had unfairly favored their political enemies in the selection of his cabinet. Northeasterners were angered by the failure of the Walker Tariff to incorporate some of their views. Westerners resented Polk's veto of a River and Harbors Bill that would have benefited their constituents. All of these factors helped create the atmosphere that generated the Proviso.[20]

The rules under which the bill was considered allowed almost no debate, but the votes that followed the introduction of Wilmot's amendment provided a clear portent of things to come. In rapid succession, the House rejected an amendment by Democratic Rep. William W. Wick of Indiana that would have applied the Missouri Compromise line to acquired territories, passed the Wilmot amendment, declined to table the bill as amended, and passed the bill. In each case, the House was divided almost strictly on sectional lines. With the session coming to a close, maneuvering by both pro- and anti-Proviso forces led to the bill dying without action by the Senate.[21]

The issue was rejoined when Congress reconvened in December. Polk once again sought an appropriation for a treaty with Mexico (this time for $3 million), and on January 4, 1847, Democratic Rep. Preston King of New York moved to attach the Wilmot Proviso to the so-called $3 Million Bill.[22] The extensive discussions that followed were in many ways reminiscent of the debate over the status of slavery in Missouri and Arkansas during the crisis of 1819–1820. To be sure, in one respect, the opponents of slavery were in a stronger position in 1847. All parties to the earlier dispute had apparently conceded that, in the absence of positive action by Congress, slavery would have been legal in both Missouri and Arkansas. By contrast, slavery was illegal under Mexican law in all of the territory that would have been covered by the Wilmot Proviso. Thus, the supporters of the Proviso could legitimately claim that they were simply preventing the introduction of slavery into areas where it had not previously existed.

Not surprisingly, Southerners vigorously opposed the Proviso. In the Senate, Calhoun introduced a series of resolutions declaring that, because the territories held by the federal government were the "common property" of all the states in the Union, Southerners could not constitutionally be prohibited from bringing their slaves into those territories.[23] These resolutions were never put to a vote. Instead, Southerners typically pressed for an extension of the Missouri Compromise line to the Pacific Ocean.

Whichever alternative Southerners favored, their opposition to the Wilmot Proviso was based as much on symbolism as on substance. Many Southerners doubted that the land which was likely to be acquired from Mexico (particularly that which was south of the Missouri Compromise line) was suitable for cultivation by slave labor. At the same time, they saw the Proviso as denying them equal status in the Union. For example, although Democratic Rep. David S. Kaufman of Texas observed that "I question very much whether slavery, under any circumstances, would ever be transplanted into California. South of 36 degrees, the territory is comparatively barren, not adapted to slave labor," he also asserted that "*principle* is dearer to us than *interest*" and that the Proviso "violates and outrages the principles of the Constitution, and destroys the compromise proposed to the South in 1820." Similarly, Whig Rep. Alexander Stephens of Georgia described the Proviso as "an *insult* to the South," an "expression to the world" that Southerners "deserve public censure and national odium."[24]

Sentiments such as these were exacerbated by the tone of the rhetoric of some of those who supported the Proviso—rhetoric that echoed the acrimonious debate over the admission of Missouri. Thus, for example, Democratic Rep. Bradley R. Wood of New York declared that "this is a national question. . . . It is one in which the North has a deeper and higher stake than the South possibly can have. It is a question whether, in the government of the country, she shall be borne down by your slaveholding, aristocratic institutions, that have not in them the first element of Democracy." Describing Virginia as a "worn-out, decaying state" and comparing it unfavorably to Pennsylvania, Whig Rep. James Dixon of Connecticut declared that "slavery is the incubus which has crushed the energies of Virginia, and marred her beauty in the very morning of her youth, with the wan decrepitude of old age." Similarly, Wilmot himself explicitly compared Michigan to Arkansas, asserting that "within the past twenty years, the former has assumed a high place among the States of this Union. She exhibits at this day all the elements and resources of a great State, cities, flourishing towns and highly cultivated fields, with a population that outnumbers three or four times that of Arkansas. Yet, Arkansas has even a better soil, and superior natural advantages. What is the cause of this disparity? It is slavery . . . and that alone."[25]

Against this background, the Proviso issue came to a vote in the House of Representatives on February 15, 1847. After once again defeating efforts to adopt the Missouri Compromise line, the House adopted the antislavery language on an almost purely sectional vote of 115–106. The amended $3 Million Bill was then passed and sent to the Senate. There, the Proviso was defeated by a vote of 31–21, as six Northern Democrats joined the united South in opposition. When the unamended appropriation bill was returned to the House, the Polk administration exerted enormous political pressure on Northern Democrats. As a result, seven Democrats who had originally supported Wilmot changed their votes, and six more simply absented themselves at the crucial moment. As a result, an effort to reattach the Proviso was defeated by a vote of 102–97. The unamended $3 Million Bill was then passed and sent to the president by a vote of 115–81.[26]

The dispute over the Wilmot Proviso put tremendous stress on the bisectional coalitions that comprised both the Whig and Democratic parties. As the election of 1848 approached, the explosive issue of slavery in the territories dominated the political landscape. Not surprisingly, Calhoun and his allies

sought to exploit the controversy by calling on Southerners of all political per-
suasions to unite around a proslavery candidate who would protect the residents of the slave states from what Calhoun described as Northern aggression.
Ultimately, however, it was the supporters of the Proviso who would unite to
form the purely sectional Free Soil Party to contest the election.[27]

The impetus for the formation of the Free Soil Party was the dissatisfaction
of many Proviso supporters with the presidential nominees of the two national
parties. When the Democrats met in convention in May 1847, the leading contenders for the party's nomination were three Northerners: Sen. Lewis Cass of
Michigan, Sen. James Buchanan of Pennsylvania, and Supreme Court Justice
Levi Woodbury of New Hampshire. However, in 1847, none of the three could
be counted as supporters of the principles of the Proviso. After initially voting
against the extension of slavery, Cass became the leading proponent of popular
sovereignty—the view that the white settlers in each territory should have the
right to decide for themselves whether to countenance slavery. Buchanan, on
the other hand, consistently supported the extension of the Missouri Compromise line to the Pacific Ocean. While Woodbury had not expressed a view on
the Proviso, he had strong connections to the Southern wing of the party.

Ultimately, Cass prevailed, and the party adopted a platform embracing the
principle of popular sovereignty. This result was anathema to many antislavery
Democrats—particularly the Van Burenites, who also blamed Cass for undermining Van Buren's candidacy in 1844. When Cass's nomination was announced,
Van Buren's supporters from New York—known as Barnburners—walked out
of the convention en masse.[28]

The results of the Whig Convention in June were equally disappointing to
the opponents of slavery. Reasoning that Southern interests would be best protected by a native of a slave state, Southern Whigs united around the candidacy
of General Zachary Taylor, a Louisiana plantation owner with no previous political experience who was one of the heroes of the Mexican War. Taylor had
taken no position on the question of whether slavery should be permitted in
the territory acquired from Mexico, and the convention sought to capitalize on
the ambiguity of his position by simply not adopting a platform. Nonetheless,
Northern Whigs who strongly supported the Wilmot Proviso were appalled by
the idea of a Taylor candidacy. When the convention chose Taylor as the party's
standard-bearer, protests immediately erupted in a number of Northern states.
Anti-Taylor sentiment was particularly strong among Whigs in Ohio and
Massachusetts.[29]

Sectional divisions were further exacerbated by a conflict over the organization of a government for the newly acquired territory of Oregon. The House

of Representatives first considered a bill for the creation of such a government in August 1846, shortly before the Wilmot Proviso was first introduced. On August 6, with little discussion, the House adopted a provision outlawing slavery in the new territory over the objections of forty-three Southerners. The amended bill then passed on a voice vote, but it was never acted upon by the Senate.[30]

By the time the territorial government bill was reintroduced in the House of Representatives in January 1847, the Wilmot Proviso had dramatically altered the political dynamic. As reported from committee, the Oregon Bill effectively barred slavery from Oregon by incorporating the provisions of the Northwest Ordinance by reference. On January 14, Democratic Rep. Armstead Burt introduced a proposal to amend the bill to provide that slavery should be barred "inasmuch as the whole of the said territory lies north of 36 degrees, 30 minutes . . . the line of the Missouri Compromise."[31]

Burt's defense of this amendment is notable for its exposition of what was to become the basic Southern position on slavery in the territories—the argument that the Missouri Compromise was unconstitutional, but that the South was nonetheless willing to accept it because it provided a workable basis for sectional coexistence. Northerners, however, refused to accept any implication that slavery should be allowed in territory south of the Missouri Compromise line. On January 15, the Burt amendment was soundly defeated despite unanimous support from slave state representatives. The next day, the unamended bill was passed over the objections of a majority of the Southern representatives.[32] Once again, however, the Senate failed to act, largely because of a dispute over whether noncitizens should be allowed to vote in Oregon.

When Congress returned to the consideration of the Oregon question in 1848, its deliberations were complicated by the signing of the Treaty of Guadalupe Hidalgo, under which Mexico ceded Upper California and New Mexico to the United States. Many senators were less than entirely satisfied with the terms of the treaty. Whigs continued to argue that territorial acquisitions should be limited to northern California, while a bisectional group of Democrats pressed for the annexation of the entire nation of Mexico. Nonetheless, the Senate recommended ratification on March 10, and Polk signed the treaty on March 16, thereby giving more concrete form to the issues that had been raised by the Wilmot Proviso.[33]

Against this background, on June 27, 1848, with the support of President Polk, Democratic Sen. Jesse Bright of Indiana made an effort to use the dispute over slavery in Oregon as a vehicle to extend the Missouri Compromise line to the Pacific Ocean. This proposal drew fire from both sides of the political spectrum. Antislavery Northerners continued to argue that slavery should be banned from all of the territory that had been acquired from Mexico. Conversely, while disclaiming any intention to actually introduce slavery into Oregon, militant Southerners such as Calhoun and Democratic Sen. Jefferson Davis of Mississippi continued to insist that Congress had no constitutional authority to outlaw slavery in any of the territories.[34]

Once again, the two houses of Congress were initially deadlocked, as the House of Representatives insisted on an unadorned prohibition of slavery and the Senate refused to accept such a provision. The ensuing struggle was highlighted by an effort to pave the way for the Supreme Court to resolve all outstanding questions regarding slavery in the territories. On July 18, a Senate committee chaired by Whig John M. Clayton of Delaware reported a bill that would have created an official territorial government for Oregon and would have continued the ban on slavery that had been adopted by the unofficial provisional government of Oregon unless and until a new territorial legislature acted on the subject. At the same time, the Clayton Compromise would also have established territorial governments for California and New Mexico that would have been specifically forbidden from taking action either to establish or to prohibit slavery. Instead, the bill provided that any putative slave could bring an action for freedom in the territorial courts and that the judgment in such an action could be appealed directly to the Supreme Court. Clayton asserted that "in this dark and gloomy hour [resolution by the Supreme Court] was the dial plate which glittered through and which he trusted would guide us to a safe and harmonious result" and that "the people, being law-abiding, would submit to the decision of that court, which held the highest place in their confidence."[35]

The Clayton Compromise passed the Senate on July 27 by a 33–22 vote, but it was tabled the next day without debate in the House of Representatives by a margin of 112–97. The voting patterns in both houses appeared to reflect a fairly widespread belief that judicial resolution would favor the South. Southern Democrats were solidly in favor of the proposal, while Northern Whigs—the most consistently antislavery faction in Congress—were almost equally solidly opposed. Northern Democrats were split, reflecting the division between the doughface contingent and those with stronger antislavery sentiments.[36]

While most Southern Whigs supported the compromise, some were less sanguine about the implications of Clayton's proposal for slavery. For example, Rep. Alexander Stephens of Georgia reasoned that, in the absence of territorial legislation, the Supreme Court would conclude that the Mexican prohibition on slavery remained in effect in California and New Mexico. Against this background, Southern Whigs split in both houses, with Stephens leading a small group of his compatriots whose votes were crucial to the defeat of the compromise in the House of Representatives.[37]

Ultimately, the antislavery forces prevailed in the Oregon controversy. The stalemate was broken when three slave state Senators broke ranks and agreed to accept the House formulation. On August 14, Polk signed the bill, noting that Oregon lay entirely north of the Missouri Compromise line.[38]

On August 9, as the Oregon controversy was raging, antislavery dissidents from both the Democratic and Whig parties joined with veterans of the Liberty Party in Buffalo, New York to create the Free Soil Party. They chose as their presidential candidate Martin Van Buren—ironically, the same man who had been instrumental in creating the Democratic Party in part to prevent sectional tensions from creating an intolerable strain on the Union. Against the background of the bitter struggle over the Wilmot Proviso, the rapid rise of the inherently sectional Free Soilers threatened to permanently destabilize the bisectional alliances. While Van Buren could not hope to win the presidency outright, he and his supporters hoped to win enough electoral votes to throw the election into the House of Representatives, where at the very least they might play a pivotal role in choosing the new president.

However, the national performance of the Free Soil ticket performance in the election fell far short of these hopes. The clear winners were the bisectional parties, with Taylor emerging victorious in both the popular vote and the electoral college. Van Buren received only 10 percent of the total popular vote and only 15 percent of the votes cast in the free states. While the Free Soilers finished ahead of the Democrats in Massachusetts, New York, and Vermont, Van Buren failed to carry a single state. Although Van Buren was able to rally many erstwhile Northern Democrats to the Free Soil cause, outside of Massachusetts and the Midwest even Whigs of pronounced antislavery sentiments proved to be reluctant to vote for their former nemesis. Thus, 80 percent of Van Buren's support came from voters who had previously identified themselves as Democrats.[39]

Although the presidential campaign of 1848 did not immediately result in the reorganization of the political structure along sectional lines, disputes over slavery continued to threaten the stability of the two-party system even after Taylor's election. While politicians sparred over fugitive slaves and the future of slavery in the District of Columbia, the controversy over the future of the territory acquired from Mexico remained the focal point in the sectional conflict. In the North, the election not only brought a number of Free Soilers into Congress but also stiffened the resolve of many Northern Whigs—fearful of being labeled "soft" on slavery—to insist on the adoption of the Wilmot Proviso. Conversely, Calhoun and his allies continued their efforts to unite Democrats and Whigs in a sectional party committed to the position that slavery must be permitted in all of the newly acquired territories. In December 1848, responding to what they characterized as Northern aggression, Calhoun and Democratic Sen. Henry S. Foote of Mississippi called a caucus of Southern senators and representatives. Only a small majority of Southern legislators actually attended the meeting; nonetheless, forty-six Democrats and two Whigs ultimately signed the "Address to the People of the Southern States," which demanded, among other things, that slavery be allowed in the territories.[40]

The impact of the dispute on the two major political parties emerged clearly when the newly elected House of Representatives convened and sought to choose a speaker in December 1849. The Democrats had a small numerical advantage over the Whigs in the House, but Free Soilers held the balance of power. The Whig caucus chose as its candidate Rep. Robert C. Winthrop of Massachusetts, while the Democrats put forward Rep. Howell Cobb of Georgia. Both Winthrop and Cobb were generally viewed as moderates on slavery-related issues. Nonetheless, some Southern Whigs refused to support Winthrop because he had voted for the Wilmot Proviso, and some Northern Democrats opposed Cobb because he was a Southerner. Conversely, a number of Free Soilers saw Winthrop as insufficiently committed to the antislavery cause, and the idea of replacing him as the party standard-bearer with a slave state Whig who might draw some Southern Democratic support was unacceptable to Northern Whigs generally. Ultimately, Cobb prevailed on the sixty-third ballot, but only after the rules were changed to allow the election to be decided on a plurality vote.[41]

The contest for the speakership reflected the fragility of sectional relationships and demonstrated that any effort to directly confront the issue of slavery in the territories would have potentially explosive consequences. But the evolution of the situation in California made it impossible for Congress to simply ignore the problem. The discovery of gold in early 1848 had prompted a massive influx of immigrants from the east, overwhelming the ability of the provisional military government to cope with the situation. All agreed that Congress needed to act quickly to organize a permanent civilian administration to deal with the problem. The difficulty was that any effort to organize such a territorial government would inevitably reignite the conflict over the Wilmot Proviso. The problem became even more complicated when, without authorization from Congress, Californians themselves organized a convention that, with the private support of Zachary Taylor, petitioned for admission to the Union and drafted a constitution that prohibited slavery.[42]

Tensions were further exacerbated by an acrimonious dispute over the boundary that separated Texas from the unorganized territory that had been acquired from Mexico. Fearing that free states would be formed from the unorganized territory, Southerners generally supported the claims of Texas. For similar reasons, Northerners wished to minimize the size of Texas and maximize the size of the unorganized area.

Even before Taylor took office, accommodationists had begun working furiously to craft a solution that would resolve these issues in a manner that would minimize the strains on sectional relations. For example, in December 1848, Democratic Sen. Stephen A. Douglas of Illinois proposed to admit the entire Mexican Cession as a single state, and Whig Rep. William Ballard Preston of Virginia, who would soon enter Taylor's cabinet as secretary of the navy, introduced a similar bill in the House of Representatives in February 1849.[43] Both bills would have allowed the people of California themselves to resolve the issue of slavery, thereby obviating the need for a corrosive congressional debate that inevitably would have focused on Northern demands for the application of the Wilmot Proviso to the newly acquired territory.

These proposals drew fire from Southern Democrats on the one hand and Northern Whigs and Free Soilers on the other. Recognizing that under the Preston plan California would almost certainly come into the Union as a free state, Mississippi Democratic Rep. Albert Gallatin Brown characterized those who had come to California during the gold rush as "mere adventurers" and complained that "the emigrants whose rights are to be affected by this proceeding—the cotton, sugar and tobacco grower—have not yet started on their journey [to California], and yet you are proposing to force this Territory into the Union as a State, settle its institutions, and forever exclude this better class of emigrants." Conversely, Northern opponents of the Douglas-Preston approach would settle for nothing less than an explicit endorsement of the Wilmot Proviso. In the House of Representatives, Northern congressmen succeeded in adding antislavery language to the Preston bill, thereby effectively killing it. In the Senate, the Douglas bill never even reached the floor.[44]

A long and complex struggle followed when Congress reconvened in December 1849.[45] In two messages sent to Congress in January 1850, Zachary Taylor advocated the admission of both California and New Mexico as states without passing through the territorial stage, with the status of slavery in each to be determined under the principles of popular sovereignty. While Taylor's approach would have avoided a reprise of the discussion of the Wilmot Proviso, all parties to the debate understood that this plan would result in the admission of two free states, giving the free states a clear majority in the Senate in addition to the preponderance that they already enjoyed in the House of Representatives.[46]

Subsequently, Henry Clay made a bid to use the disputes over the admission of California and the Texas boundary as an occasion to settle a variety of ongoing conflicts related to slavery. He introduced a single "omnibus" bill that would have linked the admission of California as a free state to the creation of territorial governments in Utah and New Mexico with no mention of slavery, the settlement of the Texas–New Mexico border dispute, the abolition of the slave trade in the District of Columbia, and the adoption of a new, strengthened federal fugitive slave law. Clay hoped that both Northerners and Southerners might be willing to accept provisions of the bill that they found distasteful in return for concessions on other issues. But when Clay's opponents succeeded in dismembering the omnibus, the Union itself seemed to be at risk, as Southerners threatened to secede rather than accept the admission of California as a free state without some compensation.[47]

In August 1850, Douglas once again took charge of efforts to reach a compromise. Douglas had the strong support of Millard Fillmore, a New York Whig who had ascended to the presidency when Taylor died on July 9. Douglas broke the omnibus into separate parts. While Douglas modified some of the terms originally proposed by Clay, the basic structure of the solution to the territorial problem remained intact. California was to be admitted as a free state, and Utah and New Mexico organized as territories without reference to the status of slavery. Douglas succeeded in creating majority coalitions in support of each bill in the Senate. The House of Representatives quickly followed suit, and on September 17, Fillmore signed the last of the bills into law.[48]

The adoption of the compromise measures temporarily muted the controversy over the expansion of slavery. But the compromise package was less successful in dampening the conflict over the issue of fugitive slaves. Instead, this issue came to the forefront in the early 1850s.

CHAPTER 10

The Controversy over Fugitive Slaves, 1843–1853

Despite the efforts of Story and his compatriots to craft a compromise that would be acceptable to both the North and South, *Prigg* did not provide an adequate framework for dampening sectional tensions over the issue of fugitive slaves. The decision brought comments from a variety of different quarters. Initially, some commentators from both sections failed to grasp the significance of the concessions made to the North. Southerners expressed pleasure with the decision, while adverse comment came primarily from antislavery Northerners. For example, the New York *Daily Express* complained that "the conclusion to which the Court have arrived involves consequences which can by no means be satisfactory to this part of the country." Further, the abolitionist Cincinnati *Philanthropist* described the decision as "revolting" and condemned what the newspaper characterized as an assault on state sovereignty. Similarly, in February 1843, a joint committee of the Massachusetts state legislature complained that Story's opinion "assumes as a rule of practical value, that slavery must . . . be sustained even at the cost of all the safeguards of liberty" and that "a decision which arrives at a result so shocking to the feelings and the principles of every citizen in a land of freedom, must be in its principle erroneous." By contrast, without examining Story's opinion, the *Baltimore Sun* declared that *Prigg* was "all that Maryland can desire, and will be particularly agreeable to the slaveholders of the South."[1]

However, Southerners quickly became dissatisfied with the regime established by *Prigg* and the 1793 statute. In large measure, this dissatisfaction was engendered by incidents in a number of Northern states whose actions largely vindicated the concerns expressed by Chief Justice Taney and Justice Daniel in their separate opinions in *Prigg*. Northern interest in the antislavery aspects of *Prigg* was piqued by a well-publicized incident in Boston. On October 4, 1842, George Latimer, a slave owned by James B. Gray, escaped from Norfolk, Virginia, and was followed by his erstwhile master to Boston. On October 14, Gray obtained the aid of local law enforcement officials in detaining Latimer, and the state courts found that efforts to invoke the state's Personal Liberty Law to obtain Latimer's freedom were barred by *Prigg*. However, faced with massive public demonstrations, Gray consented to sell his rights to Latimer rather than risk having the ex-slave taken from him by force.[2]

Many Southerners were enraged by the outcome of the Latimer affair, and they pressed for new federal laws providing stronger protection for their interests. At the same time, the opponents of slavery realized the extent to which those seeking to recover fugitives relied on the aid of state governments, and that Story had explicitly concluded that state officials could not be compelled to participate in the execution of the Fugitive Slave Act. On February 17, 1843, the Massachusetts legislature adopted a statute that barred state officials from participating in the rendition process and also prohibited the use of state jails to detain fugitives. A number of other Northern states soon adopted similar statutes, and by 1848, those seeking to recover fugitive slaves were also unable to call on state officials for aid in Connecticut, Ohio, Pennsylvania, Rhode Island, or Vermont. At times, antislavery Northerners went even further, mobilizing direct resistance to efforts by slaveowners to reclaim fugitives. In one particularly well-publicized occurrence, the so-called McClintock Riot of 1847, James Kennedy, a Maryland slaveowner, was killed when some residents of Carlisle, Pennsylvania tried to prevent him and a companion from returning to Maryland with three fugitives who had escaped to Carlisle.[3]

Southerners viewed such incidents as evidence of Northerners' disdain for the constitutional obligations that were owed to slaveowners. For example, a Virginia state legislative committee characterized the new round of personal liberty laws as a "disgusting and revolting exhibition of faithless and unconstitutional legislation . . . palpable frauds upon the South, calculated to excite at once her indignation and her contempt." Similarly, in 1849, Calhoun complained that "the attempt to recover a slave, in most of the Northern States, cannot now be made without the hazard of insult, heavy pecuniary loss, imprisonment, and even of life itself," and in 1850, an unidentified commentator asserted that "no decision of the Supreme Court has produced more evil consequences than [*Prigg*]. It has embarrassed the owners of slaves in recovering their property in the free states. It has encouraged the abolitionists in their efforts to increase those embarrassments."[4] In isolation, such expressions of dissatisfaction would have been insufficient to induce a Northern-dominated House of Representatives to acquiesce in a strengthened Fugitive Slave Law. However, in 1850, the renewed dispute over the issue of slavery in the territories created a political climate in which the passage of such a statute was possible.

In the aftermath of the passage of the compromise measures, the dispute over fugitive slaves temporarily moved to center stage in the sectional struggle.

The Fugitive Slave Act of 1850 did little to reduce the tensions between North and South over this issue. Indeed, if anything, the passage of the statute exacerbated those tensions. The difference in the perspectives of the two sections was reflected in the evolution of the statute itself.[5]

Efforts to obtain new legislation on fugitive slaves in the Thirty-first Congress began even before Henry Clay had introduced his compromise resolutions. The bill initially drafted by Democratic Sen. James Mason of Virginia and reported by the Senate Judiciary Committee on January 16, 1850, would have greatly expanded the number of federal officials empowered to issue certificates of removal. Whereas the 1793 statute gave this power only to federal judges and state officials, the Mason bill provided that a certificate of removal could also be issued by "any commissioner, or clerk of [the district] courts, or marshal thereof, or any postmaster. . . . or collector of customs." The Mason bill also doubled the fine imposed on those who aided fugitive slaves.[6]

On January 28, Whig Sen. William Seward of New York responded by introducing a bill that would have mandated jury trials for alleged fugitive slaves, required judges to grant writs of habeas corpus for alleged fugitives that were seized, and imposed stiff penalties on those judges who refused to issue such writs. Just as they had prior to 1850, antislavery Northerners argued that the provision of jury trials was nothing more than an application of ordinary principles of fairness. Thus, for example, Free Soil Sen. John P. Hale of New Hampshire asserted that "I would never consent to purchase peace by the surrender of such a valuable right, as that valuable right, 'formidable,' in the words of the Declaration of Independence, 'to tyrants only.'" Sentiments such as these were widespread in the North. Thus, despite his famous declaration that, on the issue of fugitive slaves, "the South is right, and the North is wrong," even Daniel Webster ultimately introduced a bill requiring jury trials.[7]

Not surprisingly, Southerners had a quite different perspective. For example, viewing the Seward bill as a device to prevent slaveowners from exercising their legitimate right to retake fugitives, Democratic Sen. Henry S. Foote of Mississippi bitterly argued that the bill "was designed to cap the climax of southern wrongs, to cause the oppression at once to overflow, and to force us of the South . . . to secede from the Union, or, remaining in it, to submit to a wanton, heartless and insulting deprivation of all our constitutional rights, such as no free people has ever been known patiently to endure."[8] The proposal on fugitive slaves that emerged from the compromise Committee of Thirteen clearly reflected this view as well.

On May 8, when Clay presented the committee proposals to the full Senate, he began his analysis of the fugitive slave issue by embracing the basic Southern position. Clay first analogized the delivery of escaped slaves to the extradition of fugitives from justice, observing that "the procedure uniformly is summary. It has never been thought necessary to apply, in cases of that kind, the forms and ceremony of a final trial." He also dismissed the possibility that jury trials were necessary to ensure that free blacks would not be kidnapped into slavery under the pretense of being fugitives, noting that "if there have been any instances of abuse in the erroneous arrests of fugitives from service or labor, the committee have not obtained knowledge of them," and averring that "[the committee] believe that none such have occurred, and are not likely to occur." Clay further contended that if a jury trial was required in the state where the alleged fugitive was found, "under the name of a popular and cherished institution . . . there would be a complete mockery of justice, so far as the owner of the fugitive is concerned." He asserted that, even if a jury ruled in favor of the claimant, "[the claimant] would have to bear all the burden and expense of the litigation, without indemnity, and would learn by sad experience, that he had by far better abandoned his right in the first instance, than to establish it at such unremunerated cost and heavy sacrifice." Finally, Clay noted that all of the Southern states provided that alleged fugitives would have a forum to pursue a claim for freedom after they had been returned.[9]

Despite his embrace of the basic Southern perspective, Clay offered two amendments to the Mason bill as concessions to Northern opinion. The first would have required the claimant to carry with him "when practicable" a record, obtained in an *ex parte* proceeding before a court of his home state, describing the alleged fugitive himself and the facts surrounding his escape. Second, when the fugitive denied that he was in fact an escaped slave, the claimant would have been required to post a bond in the state where the alleged fugitive was found, pending a full trial before a tribunal in the claimant's state, where the seized African American would be entitled to introduce evidence rebutting the claimant's assertion that he was in fact an escaped slave. By having these amendments adopted, Clay hoped to allay Northern concerns about potential kidnapping of free blacks, while at the same time maintaining Southern control over the rendition process.[10]

Clay's proposals were not acceptable to either side. Democratic Sen. Pierre Soule of Louisiana observed that the proposals did nothing to obviate the cost to slaveowners associated with full jury trials, and also asserted that imposing such a requirement was tantamount to the assertion of federal control over the state institution of slavery. Conversely, arguing for jury trials in the states where the alleged fugitive was found, Whig Sen. William L. Dayton of New Jersey complained that the Clay proposals reduced Northern officials to "the mere executive, the mere ministerial officers of the slave States, for the purpose of carrying their judgments into effect." Against this background, the compromise proposals were rejected without even a recorded vote on August 19.[11]

Mason then brought forward a revised version of the bill that he had introduced earlier in the session. While Northern Whigs continued to press for a requirement of jury trials, their proposals were easily defeated. An amendment by Whig Sen. Thomas Pratt of Maryland, which would have required the United States government to compensate owners for fugitives who were not delivered, met a similar fate on August 22. Pratt was not only opposed unanimously by Northerners, but also by many Southerners, some of whom objected in principle to the extension of any federal authority over slavery and others who suggested that the proposal amounted to a compensated emancipation scheme. On August 23, Mason's bill passed the Senate by a vote of 27–10, with three Northern Democrats joining a united South. On September 12, the House of Representatives followed suit by a vote of 109–76, as Northern Democrats provided the margin of victory for the bill. With the territorial issue having been settled on relatively favorable terms for the North, many Northerners in both houses simply chose to abstain.[12]

The Fugitive Slave Act of 1850 greatly expanded the number of federal officials empowered to act as commissioners for the purpose of issuing certificates of removal and charged these officials with the duty of hearing claims of putative masters "in a summary manner." Upon receiving "satisfactory proof" of the validity of the claimant's assertion of ownership—defined as either a sworn statement taken by the responsible official himself or a document certifying that appropriate testimony had been given before an official in the state from which the alleged escape had occurred—the federal commissioner was to issue a certificate for removal of the alleged fugitive. The testimony of the alleged runaway himself was explicitly deemed nonadmissible. The commissioner was to be paid $10 per case if he found for the claimant, but $5 if he found against the claimant.

Once a certificate of removal was issued, no court was allowed to interfere with the removal of the alleged fugitive. The claimant was entitled to enlist the aid of federal marshals in securing and returning the alleged fugitive to his home state, and the marshals were to be liable for the full value of any fugitive who escaped. Moreover, the commissioners were empowered to summon ordinary citizens to act as a posse comitatus to apprehend the alleged fugitive. Finally, the statute increased the penalties for those who interfered with the apprehension of alleged fugitives.

For many Southerners, enforcement of the statute was the linchpin of the entire compromise package. Thus, for example, while a convention called in the state of Georgia adopted a platform declaring that Georgia "does not wholly approve, [but] will abide by it as a permanent adjustment of this sectional controversy," the same convention also proclaimed that "it is the deliberate opinion of this Convention, that upon the faithful execution of the Fugitive Slave Bill by the proper authorities depends the preservation of our much loved Union." Making the same point more bluntly, a North Carolina newspaper editor warned the free states to "respect and enforce the Fugitive Slave Law as it stands. If not, WE WILL LEAVE YOU."[13]

Northern opinion, on the other hand, was more divided. Some influential Northerners joined with Daniel Webster and his allies in both defending the constitutionality of the statute and urging full compliance with its provisions. Others, including Free Soilers and many Northern Whigs, shared the views expressed in the New York *Tribune,* which asserted that the Fugitive Slave Act was without constitutional and moral force and predicted that Northerners "will burden its execution with all possible legal difficulties, and they will help slaves to escape all the more zealously."[14] Some Northerners did indeed take this path. Moreover, others went further and resorted to extralegal methods to protect escaped slaves who had found their way to the North.

While some escapees were recovered without serious incident, resistance to the execution of the Fugitive Slave Law in the North was sufficiently common to generate ongoing resentment in the South. Conversely, many antislavery Northerners remained unreconciled to what they saw as the unjust provisions of the statute. Thus, the issue of the finality of the Compromise of 1850 played an important role in the campaign for the presidency in 1852.

At the Democratic Convention that assembled in Baltimore on June 1, the delegates were able to manage the issue without difficulty. Despite the fact that most of the Northern Democrats who had defected to the Free Soil Party in 1848 had returned to the fold, a provision endorsing the finality of the Compromise of 1850 generally and the Fugitive Slave Act in particular was included in the platform without incident. All of the major contenders for the Democratic presidential nomination—Lewis Cass of Michigan, Stephen A. Douglas of Illinois, James Buchanan of Pennsylvania, and William Marcy of New York—were from Northern states, although Buchanan was the clear favorite among Southern delegates. After more than forty ballots produced a deadlock among the favorites, the convention turned to ex-Senator Franklin Pierce of New Hampshire, a supporter of the Compromise who had no difficulty in enthusiastically embracing the principle of finality.[15]

The issue created greater problems for the Whigs when they convened in Baltimore two weeks later. Together, the forces of Millard Fillmore and Daniel

Webster, both of whom strongly favored the Compromise of 1850, controlled a majority of the delegates to the convention, and were able to insert a provision in the party platform that endorsed principles similar to those embraced by the Democrats. However, the delegates ultimately chose Gen. Winfield Scott of Virginia as the party nominee, a hero of the Mexican War who was paradoxically the favorite of the Northern antislavery wing of the party. Moreover, in his acceptance letter, Scott pointedly did not endorse the language in the platform that accepted the finality of the Fugitive Slave Act.[16]

The elections that followed were a disaster for the Whigs. Although winning only slightly more than half of the popular vote, Pierce carried every state in the Union except Vermont, Massachusetts, Kentucky, and Tennessee. John P. Hale, the candidate of the Free Soil Party (renamed the Free Democrats), who explicitly called for the repeal of the Fugitive Slave Act, received the support of only slightly more than half the number of voters who had supported Van Buren in the election of 1848.[17]

Whig losses were particularly severe in the Deep South, where party members stayed away from the polls in droves. As a result, in the newly elected House of Representatives, the number of Southern Whigs—often a force for moderation—was reduced to a mere twenty-two members. In the Democratic party, the size of the already-powerful Southern wing was correspondingly increased.[18] Thus, in addition to weakening the Whig Party, the election of 1852 also increased the sectionalization of American politics more generally.

Nonetheless, an observer in early 1853 might well have concluded that the basic architecture of that system could still survive—that the results of the election of 1852 were nothing more than a part of the ordinary cycle of American politics, and that the Whig Party could yet recover its competitive position in both sections of the country. To be sure, the dispute over fugitive slaves remained largely unresolved. But acrimonious as it was, that issue might have conceivably been managed within the bisectional structures that dominated national politics.

In general, the decisions of the Supreme Court in the late 1840s and early 1850s also remained generally consistent with this bisectional model. During this period, the Court continued to grapple with issues that had the potential to exacerbate the North-South conflict. But while the rhetoric of the advocates that came before the Court at times reflected the increasingly acrimonious tone of sectional relations, the decisions of the justices themselves typically followed the pattern that had been set in *Groves* and *Prigg*.

CHAPTER 11

The Supreme Court in 1846

The makeup of the Court changed significantly in the four years following the decision in *Prigg*. Three of the Northern justices who had filed opinions in the case—Joseph Story, Smith Thompson, and Henry Baldwin—were no longer on the Court. They had been replaced by men whose perspective on slavery-related issues was at times somewhat different from those whom they had succeeded.

Samuel Nelson filled the seat that was vacated by the death of Smith Thompson in December 1843.[1] The effort to replace Thompson was initially handicapped by the complex political situation of the early 1840s. At the time of Thompson's death, the presidency was held by John Tyler, who by that time had thoroughly alienated most members of the Whig Party under whose banner he had been elected. The difficulties in filling Thompson's seat reflected the awkwardness of Tyler's political position.

After considering the possibility of nominating Democrat Martin Van Buren to replace Thompson, Tyler initially nominated John C. Spencer, a New York Whig from his own cabinet. Spencer was a man of great intellectual ability, but he had alienated orthodox Whigs by continuing to serve under Tyler after Tyler's break with the party. Opposition from these Whigs doomed the nomination in the Senate. Tyler then selected Reuben H. Walworth, the chancellor of New York. If he had been confirmed, Walworth would probably have added a strong antislavery voice to the Court. Prior to the *Prigg* decision, in *Jack v. Martin*, he had expressed the view that Congress lacked the authority to pass legislation to enforce the Fugitive Slave Clause.

However, the Senate also failed to confirm Tyler's choice, although Walworth's defeat seems not to have been based on slavery-related issues but rather on his personal unpopularity and the fear that he would be replaced in New York by a Democrat. Finally, in February 1845, Tyler—now a lame duck—turned to Democrat Samuel Nelson, the chief justice of the New York Supreme Court. Nelson was quickly confirmed and took his seat on February 13.

Samuel Nelson was born in 1792 in Hebron, New York. Initially planning to become a minister, Nelson attended Middlebury College, graduating in 1813. Turning to law, he studied in the offices of Savage and Woods in Salem, New York, and then with Judge Woods after Woods moved to Madison, New York. Nelson was admitted to the bar in 1817, entered politics, and served as a postmaster for three years before being appointed a judge of the Sixth Circuit in New York in 1823. In 1831, he was elevated to the state supreme court as an associate justice, eventually becoming chief justice of that court in 1837.

On issues of federalism, Nelson's jurisprudence was much like that of the man that he replaced on the Court. Like Thompson, Nelson was a firm believer in the theory that a grant of power to Congress per se did not generally deprive the states of concurrent power to regulate the same subject. However, Nelson appears to have been at least marginally more sympathetic than Thompson to the South on issues directly related to slavery.

Even before he came to the Supreme Court, Nelson had produced at least one notable opinion on the constitutional issues related to slavery. Like Walworth, Nelson had been called upon to interpret the Fugitive Slave Clause in *Jack v. Martin.* However, unlike Walworth, Nelson had adopted the position that ultimately prevailed in *Prigg,* concluding that Congress possessed authority to adopt legislation enforcing the constitutional rights of claimants. Moreover, once on the Court, his circuit opinions were notable for an apparent lack of zeal in enforcing the federal prohibition on the slave trade.

The appointment of Levi Woodbury had a far more significant impact on the ideological balance of the Court.[2] Woodbury was born in Francestown, New Hampshire, on December 22, 1789. He received his formal education at Dartmouth College, and after studying law with Judge Jeremiah Smith, was admitted to the state bar of New Hampshire in 1812. Woodbury soon entered politics and had a long and distinguished career in public service, at times being seriously considered as a possible candidate for president on the Democratic ticket. He served as a justice of the New Hampshire state supreme court from 1816 to 1823, governor of New Hampshire from 1823 to 1824, speaker of the New Hampshire State House of Representatives in 1825, United States senator from New Hampshire from 1825 to 1831 and 1841 to 1845, and secretary of the navy under Andrew Jackson from 1831 to 1834. Woodbury then succeeded Taney as secretary of the treasury, serving in that capacity under both Jackson and Martin Van Buren from 1834 to 1841. Like Taney before him, he became a key ally in Jackson's war against the Bank of the United States. On December 23, 1845, James K. Polk nominated Woodbury to fill the seat vacated by the death of Joseph Story, and the nomination was confirmed without incident by the Senate on January 3, 1846.

As a committed Jacksonian, Woodbury's ideological perspective differed sharply from that of the conservative Whig whom he replaced. Whereas Story was a strong proponent of federal power, Woodbury hewed to the Jacksonian conception of states' rights. Moreover, Woodbury did not share Story's distaste for slavery. Instead, he was known as a Northern man with pronounced Southern sympathies. Indeed, after Woodbury failed in his bid for the Democratic presidential nomination in 1848, William Seward wrote that "I am quite sure that Judge Woodbury has lost the last nomination that was open to a Judge of the Supreme Court who regarded Emancipation as Fanaticism."[3]

The last of the new justices to join the Court was Robert C. Grier, who succeeded Justice Henry Baldwin after Baldwin died in April 1844.[4] Baldwin's seat was filled only after a long and tortuous search for his replacement. John Tyler first offered the position to Democratic Senator James Buchanan of Pennsylvania. However, Buchanan declined to be formally nominated. Tyler then chose Democrat Edward King, a lower court judge from Pennsylvania who was so undistinguished that Story professed not to even know his name. The Senate refused to act on this nomination, and it died with the election of Democrat James K. Polk to the presidency.

Polk's first choice to fill the vacant seat was George Woodward of Pennsylvania. Woodward, however, was handicapped by a history of outspoken nativism and the enmity of Simon Cameron, a powerful Democratic senator from his home state. When six Democrats joined the opposition Whigs to defeat the nomination, Polk next had discussions with Buchanan, who was then serving as secretary of state. After Buchanan ultimately decided to stay in the Cabinet, Polk turned to Grier.

The new appointee was born on March 5, 1794 in Cumberland County, Pennsylvania. The son of a Presbyterian minister and schoolmaster, Grier received a thorough classical education at home before being admitted to Dickinson College in 1811 and graduating the following year. Grier then returned home to Northumberland to assist his father in operating a school there, assuming full responsibility for the school after his father's death in 1815. After studying law in his spare time, Grier was admitted to the local bar in 1817.

Grier soon moved to the Pittsburgh area, where he became active in politics. Initially he espoused the Federalist cause, but after the collapse of that party, Grier converted to the Democrats and actively supported Andrew Jackson in his presidential campaigns. In 1833, Grier became president judge of the District Court of Allegheny County, where he became known for assertive jury charges that at times resembled more the words of an advocate than those of an impartial judge.

Grier's distaste for abolitionists was well known. On one occasion, when a letter announcing an abolitionist meeting was read in the Presbyterian Church in which Grier was an elder, he rose and objected, condemning the abolitionist cause as unconstitutional and seditious, and declaring that it should be rejected by all good Christians and loyal citizens. These views stood Grier in good stead when Polk was considering a replacement for Baldwin. Four congressmen from the adjoining slave state of Maryland urged Polk to select Grier and identified him as one of those who "acknowledges the right of the master to his slave and will enforce it irrespective of the clogs from time to time attempted to be thrown around it by state legislation"—one of the earliest instances where a nominee was supported explicitly because of his views on slavery.[5] Against this background, Polk sent Grier's nomination to the Senate on August 3, 1846, and it was approved with no apparent opposition the next day.

Grier's circuit court decisions did not disappoint his proslavery supporters. When presented with issues related to fugitive slaves, he made no secret of his own sympathies. At the same time, however, Grier also demonstrated his fidelity to the principle of the rule of law.

Both of these characteristics were reflected in Grier's 1850 charge to the jury in *Oliver v. Kaufman*.[6] There the defendants were charged with violating the Fugitive Slave Act of 1793 by aiding in the escape of a number of slaves. Grier's charge emphasized the importance of the Fugitive Slave Clause in the constitutional scheme. He also specifically warned the jury that "no theories or opinion which you or we may entertain with regard to liberty or human rights, or the policy or justice of a system of domestic slavery, can have a place on the bench or in the jury box." In addition, however, he charged the jury that "the odium attached to the name of 'Abolitionist' . . . should not be suffered to supply any want of proof of the guilty participation of the defendants in the offence charged even if the testimony in the case should satisfy you that the defendants entertained the sentiments avowed by the class of people designated by that name."[7]

At the same time, Grier admonished the jury to "beware . . . that the occasional insolence and violent denunciation of the South be not permitted to prejudice your minds against the just rights guaranteed to them by the constitution and laws of the Union" and that "it is your duty to treat with utter disregard ignorant and malicious vituperation of fanatics and demagogues, whether it comes from North or South, and give to the respective parties such protection of their respective rights as the constitution and laws of our country secure to them."[8]

Grier's approach to *United States v. Hanaway*[9] reflected similar values. *Hanaway* was a trial for treason that was conducted in the aftermath of an incident that took place in Christiana, Pennsylvania, on September 11, 1851. On that day, after obtaining the warrants required by the Fugitive Slave Law, Edward Gorsuch, a slaveowner from Baltimore County, Maryland, led a posse seeking to recover escaped slaves from the house of a free African American in Christiana.

The posse included several of Gorsuch's relatives and three deputy federal marshals. While Gorsuch and his allies were in the house, they were surrounded by a group of two dozen armed free blacks who were determined to prevent the capture of the escapees. A shot was fired, and in the ensuing melee Gorsuch was killed and his son severely wounded.[10]

The Christiana incident brought an intense reaction from Southerners and Southern sympathizers. Residents of Baltimore County insisted that "the authors of the outrage [be] brought to a strict accountability" while the Philadelphia *United States Gazette* declared that the violent confrontation was more than a "murderous riot," but was an "act of insurrection . . . almost a servile insurrection, if not, one of treason." Against this background, a number of the free blacks who were involved in the violence were arrested and charged with a variety of offenses under state law, as were Castner Hanaway and Elijah Lewis, two white men who were present at the disturbance and had expressed support for the blacks but had taken no active part in the violence.[11]

Fillmore, however, determined to take even more aggressive action. He ordered a large number of federal marines and marshals to Christiana, and they arrested almost forty persons in connection with the violence. Seeking to make an example of the prisoners, the administration had Hanaway, Lewis, and twenty-five African Americans indicted by a grand jury and tried for treason in the Federal District Court for the Eastern District of Pennsylvania in Philadelphia. Justice Grier and District Judge John P. Kane presided, and because of the nature of the case the state of Maryland participated through counsel in the prosecution.

Grier's charge to the jury once again reflected his strong support for the Southern position on fugitive slaves. Reiterating the standard claim that Northern acceptance of the Fugitive Slave Clause was the price for Southern acquiescence in the Constitution, he asserted that "if individuals or state legislatures in the North can succeed in thwarting and obstructing the execution of this article of our confederation, and the rights guaranteed to the South thereby, they have no right to complain if the people of the South shall treat the constitution as virtually annulled by the consent of the North and seek secession from any alliance with open and avowed covenant breakers."[12] Apparently treating the contrary discussion in Story's *Prigg* opinion as dictum, Grier then declared that "those states in the North whose legislation has made it a penal offence for their judicial and executive officers to lend their assistance in the execution of this clause of the constitution, and compels them to disregard their solemn oath to support it, have proceeded as far, and perhaps farther, in the path of nullification and secession than any Southern state has yet done." Against this background, Grier concluded that "the real objection with these people [who oppose the Fugitive Slave Act of 1850] is to the constitution itself."[13]

The language of the *Hanaway* charge also reflected the depth of Grier's disdain for abolitionists and the higher law philosophy espoused by many of them.

It is not in this hall of independence that meetings of infuriated fanatics and unprincipled demagogues have been held to counsel a bloody resistance to the laws of the land. It is not in this city that conventions are held denouncing the constitution, the laws and the Bible. It is not here that the pulpit has been desecrated by seditious exhortations, teaching that there is meritorious, murder excusable, and treason a virtue. The guilt of this foul murder rests not alone on the deluded individuals who were its immediate perpetrators, but the blood taints with even deeper dye the skirts of those who promulgate doctrines subversive of all morality and all governments. This murderous tragedy is but the necessary development of principles and the natural fruit from seed sown by others, whom the arm of the law cannot reach.[14]

Despite his strong opinions about the Christiana incident and the issue of the Fugitive Slave Clause generally, Grier again proved unwilling to abandon fundamental legal principles in order to appease Southern opinion. Although he stated that "the testimony in this case has clearly established that a most horrible outrage upon the laws of this country has been committed" and "that it is the duty of the state of Pennsylvania, or of the United States, or of both, to bring to condign punishment those who committed this flagrant outrage on the peace and dignity of both cannot be doubted," Grier also strongly intimated that, in his view, the actions of the defendants did not rise to the level of treason, observing that "it would be dangerous precedent . . . to extend the crime of treason by construction in doubtful cases, and [such a] decision would probably operate in the end to defeat the purposes of the law, which the government seeks to enforce." Such statements can only be viewed as reflecting a strong commitment to the rule of law, which overbore Grier's distaste for those who openly opposed the enforcement of the Fugitive Slave Act. His charge led to the acquittal of the defendants in *Hanaway*.[15]

In short, none of those who ascended to the Court in the mid-1840s was likely to generate enthusiasm among antislavery Northerners. But sympathy for the interests of slaveholders was not the only factor that would influence the decisions of these new appointees. Not only did they feel bound by the concept of the rule of law, but as Jacksonians they were committed to the maintenance of sectional harmony. The same values would inform the decisions of the Court as a whole in the late 1840s and early 1850s.

CHAPTER 12

Revisiting the Commerce Power

In the late 1840s, the Court continued to struggle with sectionally charged issues related to the scope of the commerce power. In 1847, in *Rowan v. Runnels*,[1] the justices were asked to revisit the substantive issue that had been raised in *Groves v. Slaughter*. *Rowan* presented the Court with a suit based on another promissory note given in consideration for the sale of slaves imported into Mississippi in 1836. In the interim between *Rowan* and *Groves*, however, the Mississippi Supreme Court had clearly held that the state constitutional prohibition on the interstate slave trade was self-enforcing. The defendants contended that, notwithstanding the decision in *Groves*, the Supreme Court was bound to follow the rulings of the state supreme court on the meaning of its own constitution. The plaintiffs, by contrast, insisted that *Groves* remained the controlling precedent.

The 1842 decision in *Swift v. Tyson*[2] provided the jurisprudential backdrop for the consideration of *Rowan*. *Swift* began as a prosaic diversity action filed in New York federal court. The substantive issue in the case was whether the plaintiff was entitled to recover on a promissory note that had been endorsed to him. Prior to 1842, the Court had uniformly held that the legal issues surrounding such a claim would be determined according to the common law of New York, pursuant to the Judiciary Act of 1789, which provides that "the laws of the several states, except where the constitution, treaties or statutes of the United States shall otherwise require or provide, shall be regarded as rules of decision, in trials at common law, in the courts of the United States, in cases where they apply."

Speaking for the majority in *Swift*, Justice Joseph Story took a different view of the import of the Judiciary Act. He determined that decisions of state courts would not bind the Supreme Court on issues of "general commercial law" that were not governed by state statutes. But at the same time, Story also reaffirmed the view that the Supreme Court was bound to follow state court decisions with respect to "the positive statutes of the state, and the construction thereof adopted by the local tribunals, and to rights and titles to things having a permanent locality."[3]

Rather plainly, the questions presented by *Rowan* fell into the latter category. And indeed, speaking for the Court, Chief Justice Taney conceded that "this court will always feel itself bound to respect the decisions of the State courts, and from the time they are made will regard them as conclusive in all cases upon the construction of their own constitution and laws." Nonetheless, with only Justice Daniel dissenting, the *Rowan* Court concluded that it should continue to follow the principles first laid down in *Groves v. Slaughter* and held that the Mississippi constitutional provision was not self-executing. In defense of this view, Taney asserted that

we ought not to give to [state court decisions] a retroactive effect, and allow them to render invalid contracts entered into with citizens of other States, which in the judgment of this court were lawfully made. For, if such a rule were adopted, and the comity due to State decisions pushed to this extent, it is evident that the provision in the constitution of the United States, which secures to the citizens of another State the right to sue in the courts of the United States, might become utterly useless and nugatory.

In doctrinal terms, the Court's holding was quite extraordinary. *Rowan* was not a case in which the Mississippi Supreme Court had in any way changed its view on the proper characterization of the state constitutional provision that was at issue. Even under the view taken by the *Groves* majority, the most that one could say was that, prior to *Groves*, the state supreme court had yet to definitively establish a position on the question of whether the ban on the importation of slaves for sale was self-enforcing. Moreover, none of the parties in *Rowan* could assert a plausible claim to have relied upon the rule announced in *Groves*. All of the relevant transactions in *Rowan* had been fully consummated before *Groves* was decided. In short, the Court's decision in *Rowan* rested on nothing more than a raw preference for its own position rather than the conclusion reached by the body that had ultimate responsibility for interpreting the Mississippi state constitution, whose decisions the Court itself conceded were binding. From a purely legal perspective, such a conclusion is almost inexplicable.

Rowan is thus best understood as a reflection of the Taney Court's continuing reluctance to exacerbate the sectional conflict unnecessarily. If the Court had felt bound to conclude that the state constitutional provision was self-executing, the justices would have been forced to confront the Dormant Commerce Clause issue that they had striven so mightily to avoid six years earlier in *Groves*, and with it the explosive attendant question of whether the federal government possessed the power to regulate the interstate slave trade. Rather than pursue such a course, they apparently chose to distort the appropriate relationship between state and federal courts on issues of state constitutional law.

But despite these exertions, the Court could not entirely disengage its Commerce Clause jurisprudence from issues related to slavery. The problem reemerged in a different context two years later, as the justices confronted the

Passenger Cases.[4] By their terms, the *Passenger Cases* had no direct connection to the dispute over slavery or the sectional conflict more generally. Instead, they involved the efforts of the states of New York and Massachusetts to deal with the large influx of immigrants that passed through their ports in the mid-nineteenth century. Many of these immigrants immediately moved westward to the less densely inhabited lands of the American frontier. But some also remained in port cities such as New York and Boston, and of this group a significant number became public charges.

The statutes at issue in the *Passenger Cases* were at least in form designed to generate resources to deal with this problem. *Smith v. Turner* was a challenge to a New York statute—purportedly aimed at raising funds for the establishment of a marine hospital—that required the master of each vessel arriving from a foreign port to pay one dollar and fifty cents for each cabin passenger and one dollar for each steerage passenger. In addition, masters of vessels involved in the coastal trade were required to pay twenty-five cents for each passenger. Similarly, in *Norris v. City of Boston,* the Court was called upon to consider a Massachusetts statute that provided for the inspection of incoming ships and forbade the landing of any person determined to be a "lunatic, idiot, maimed or infirm person" unless a bond was posted to ensure that the person did not become a public charge. In addition, prior to landing, all passengers were required to pay a tax of two dollars "to be appropriated as the city or town may direct for the support of foreign paupers."

While the statutes themselves did not differentiate between immigrants on the basis of race, the constitutional challenges also potentially threatened the continued vitality of the Negro Seamen's Acts that were then in force in a number of Southern states. These statutes had been adopted in response to the discovery of a plan by Denmark Vesey, a free black who lived in Charleston, to foment a slave rebellion in 1822. The statutes required that black crewmen of any ship coming into a port where the statute was in force be held in jail until the ship departed, with the cost of incarceration to be paid by the ship's captain.

Almost from their inception, the Negro Seamen's Acts drew protests from the governments of Great Britain and Massachusetts, both of whose ships often employed African Americans as sailors. Representatives of these governments claimed that the statutes were not only unjust but also unconstitutional. In 1823, while sitting on circuit, Justice William Johnson concluded that the South Carolina statute ran afoul of the dormant Commerce Clause, and in 1824 Attorney General William Wirt issued an official opinion to the same effect. However, Johnson's decision was not appealed to the Supreme Court, and in 1831 Attorney General John Berrien reached a contrary conclusion.[5]

In 1843, in response to a memorial from a number of citizens of Boston, a committee of the House of Representatives considered the same issue. While seven of the nine members of the committee concluded that the Negro Seamen's Acts violated the Constitution, two members disputed this contention, arguing the statutes were a legitimate exercise of the states' police powers. Ultimately, the full House of Representatives voted to table the report without debate.[6]

Despairing of the possibility of congressional action, the following year the Massachusetts state legislature dispatched Samuel Hoar to South Carolina and Henry Hubbard to Louisiana with the intention of mounting legal challenges to the Negro Seamen's Acts that would ultimately be resolved by the Supreme Court. Neither Hoar nor Hubbard was able to complete this mission, however. After the South Carolina state legislature condemned Hoar as "the emissary of a foreign government" and declared that the state had the right "to exclude from their territories seditious persons or others . . . dangerous to their peace," Hoar fled the state under threat of mob violence. Hubbard quickly left Louisiana under a similar threat.[7] These events formed the backdrop for the Court's consideration of the *Passenger Cases.*

The New York case was first argued in December 1845. Before the justices ultimately came to a decision, each case was argued three times, culminating in December 1848. These arguments engaged the talents of some of the most prominent advocates of the day. Arrayed against the statutes were Daniel Webster and Rufus Choate of Massachusetts, as well as David B. Ogden and J. Prestcott Hall of New York. They were opposed by John Davis and George Ashmun of Massachusetts, together with Attorney General Willis Hall of New York and John Van Buren, the son of the former president.

Issues related to slavery played an important role in the arguments in both the Massachusetts and New York cases. The parties jousted over the implications of both the Slave Trade Clause and *Groves v. Slaughter* for the constitutional analysis to be applied. The challengers argued that, by its terms, the Slave Trade Clause vested Congress with plenary power to tax incoming immigrants, while those who defended the statutes insisted that the clause was applicable only to the importation of slaves, and in any event did not deprive the states of concurrent power. Conversely, the attorneys for Massachusetts and New York contended that the principles accepted by the majority in *Groves* vindicated the state statutes, while their opponents reminded the Court that the majority opinion in the case had held only that the state constitutional provision was not self-executing.[8]

In addition, all of the parties to the *Passenger Cases* were well aware of the implications of the decisions for the Negro Seamen's Acts. Like those who attacked the Negro Seamen's Acts, the plaintiffs in the *Passenger Cases* contended that the New York and Massachusetts statutes trenched on the exclusive power of Congress over interstate and foreign commerce. Conversely, like the attorneys for the states of New York and Massachusetts, the defenders of the Negro Seamen's Acts contended that the power to regulate commerce did not rest exclusively with the federal government and that the statutes were a legitimate exercise of state police power. Thus, in the course of their arguments, Davis, Hall, and Van Buren reminded the Court that a decision striking down the New York and Massachusetts statutes could threaten the Negro Seamen's Acts as well.[9]

Against this background, the *Passenger Cases* spawned opinions from each of the nine justices, with five justices in each case ultimately concluding that the state law ran afoul of the dormant Commerce Clause. The Court was divided by political ideology rather than by section; the majority included three Southern justices and two Northerners, while the dissenters were split evenly between natives of free states and slave states, respectively. The opinions generally reprised the arguments of the attorneys. Two of the justices specifically addressed the relevance of the decision to the continued vitality of the Negro Seamen's Acts.

Georgian James Moore Wayne, who wrote the opinion of the Court, took pains to reassure Southerners that the Court's decision neither threatened those statutes nor implied that Congress could constitutionally force the Southern states to allow the immigration of free blacks. Like McLean before him in *Groves,* Wayne essentially argued that issues related to slavery were sui generis, to be governed by a unique set of constitutional standards. He asserted that "the fear expressed, that if the States have not the discretion to determine who may come and live in them, the United States may introduce into the Southern States emancipated negroes [*sic*] from the West Indies and elsewhere, has no foundation." Rejecting the view that the judiciary should be governed "by the summary logic of ifs and syllogisms," Wayne contended that, instead, "the Constitution is to be interpreted by what was the condition of the parties to it when it was formed, by their object and purpose in forming it, and by the actual recognition in it of the dissimilar institutions of the States" and that "[it] is a very narrow view of the Constitution which supposes that any political sovereign right given by it can be exercised, or was meant to be used, by the United States in such a way as to dissolve, or even disquiet, the fundamental organization of either of the States. The Constitution is to be interpreted by what was the condition of the parties to it when it was formed, by their object and purpose in forming it, and by the actual recognition in it of the dissimilar institutions of the States." Finally, Wayne contended that it will be found, too, should this matter of introducing free negroes into the Southern States ever become the subject of judicial inquiry, that they have a guard against it in the Constitution, making it altogether unnecessary for them to resort to the casus gentis extraordinarius, the casus extremoe necessitatis of nations, for their protection and preservation. They may rely upon the Constitution, and the correct interpretation of it, without seeking to be relieved from any of their obligations under it, or having recourse to the jus necessitatis for self-preservation.[10]

In short, while generally espousing a strongly nationalistic view of the scope of both the commerce power and the dormant Commerce Clause, Wayne argued that slavery was a special case, whose domestic aspects were left solely in control of the state governments.

By contrast, rejecting the view that slavery-related issues could be governed by a different set of constitutional standards, Levi Woodbury asserted in dissent that "it is a mistaken view to say, that the power of a State to exclude slaves, or free blacks, or convicts, or paupers, or to make pecuniary terms for their admission, may be one not conflicting with commerce, while the same power, if applied to alien passengers coming in vessels, does conflict. Slaves now excepted, though once not entirely, they are all equally and frequently passengers, and all oftener come in by water in the business and channels of ocean commerce than by land." In its analysis of the *Passenger Cases,* the *Charleston Mercury* expressed similar fears, declaring that "if we correctly understand the points decided . . . they sweep away . . . all our laws made to prevent free colored persons—'citizens of Massachusetts,' or whatever abolition region—from entering our ports and cities."[11]

The decision in the *Passenger Cases* ended the Supreme Court's involvement with the Commerce Clause issues that directly impacted the sectional conflict. While the disputes over the interstate slave trade and the Negro Seamen's Acts continued to create tensions between North and South, the Court never definitively resolved the constitutional questions raised by these disputes. By contrast, during this period the Court was once again called upon to elaborate more fully on the constitutional principles arising from the dispute over fugitive slaves.

CHAPTER 13

The Ongoing Struggle
over Fugitive Slaves

In the late 1840s and early 1850s, antislavery Northerners continued to mount constitutional challenges to the statutes that were designed to facilitate the recovery of fugitive slaves. The legal theories on which they relied were developed largely by Salmon P. Chase of Ohio, a Democrat who was one of the most prominent leaders of the radical wing of the antislavery movement. Chase's efforts on behalf of escaped slaves and those who aided them had earned him the nickname "Attorney General of Fugitive Slaves." In 1847, he brought the issue of fugitive slaves back to the Supreme Court in *Jones v. Van Zandt*.[1]

Van Zandt arose from the efforts of nine slaves to escape from service to their master, Kentuckian Wharton Jones. The would-be escapees crossed into Ohio and were picked up outside Cincinnati by John Van Zandt, a farmer who was driving his covered wagon to market. One of the fugitives, Andrew, drove the wagon, while the remaining eight, including one named Letta, rode inside with Van Zandt himself. Approximately fifteen miles later, they were accosted by two men named Heffernan and Hargrave, who recognized the wagon as belonging to Van Zandt and suspected that it was being used to transport fugitive slaves. At Van Zandt's urging, Andrew sought to outrun the pursuers. However, the wagon was overtaken, and all of the escapees except Andrew himself were captured and returned to Kentucky, where Heffernan and Hargrave received a $450 reward from Jones.

Heffernan and Hargrave were indicted for kidnapping in Ohio state court, but their cases never came to trial. A number of those who aided them did face trial, but were ultimately acquitted. Van Zandt, on the other hand, faced civil actions in federal court for allegedly violating the federal Fugitive Slave Act. Sitting on circuit, Justice John McLean found for the plaintiffs, and this decision was appealed to the Supreme Court.[2] There, Van Zandt was represented by both Chase and William H. Seward, the equally prominent antislavery Whig who had served as governor of New York and would later lead the Senate opposition to the passage of the Fugitive Slave Act of 1850.

Chase and Seward filed separate written briefs in *Van Zandt*. Each began with the claim that Van Zandt had not in fact violated the Fugitive Slave Act and also that, in any event, the complaint did not include the allegations that were necessary to find such a violation. This argument was followed by a short section devoted to the claim that, even if otherwise constitutional, the Fugitive Slave Act could not constitutionally be applied in a case involving one who escaped from Kentucky to Ohio. The remainder of the briefs were full-bore assaults on the constitutionality of the Fugitive Slave Act itself.

The arguments in the first part of the briefs were highly technical. Chase, for example, began by contending that the Fugitive Slave Act was a penal statute, and that as such both the statute itself and the allegations made under the statute must be strictly construed. Against this background, he argued that the complaint in the case did not adequately allege that Andrew and Letta were in fact escapees, that Van Zandt did not have the required notice that they were in fact escaped slaves when he aided them, and that he had not "harbored or concealed" them within the meaning of the statute.[3]

Van Zandt's attorneys then turned to the broader issues that were implicit in the case. Both Chase and Seward began with an argument that, depending on one's perspective, might be characterized as either ingenious or implausible. The argument was based on the fact that the state of Ohio had been created from the territory covered by the Northwest Ordinance, and the claim that the Fugitive Slave Act (and, by implication, the Fugitive Slave Clause itself) violated the section of the ordinance which provided that "there should be neither slavery nor involuntary servitude within the territory, otherwise than in the punishment of crimes." Characterizing the ordinance as "a solemn covenant between the original states . . . and the people and the states that were to occupy it," Chase contended that "the constitution of the United States, neither did, nor could, of itself, and without the consent of the people and states of the territory, repeal, impair, abridge or alter the terms of the compact," while Seward asserted that "the Thirteen States who united in forming the Constitution could not change [the Northwest Ordinance] though all agreed." They recognized that the ordinance also contained a Fugitive Slave Clause, which qualified the prohibition on slavery itself. However, they noted that this provision of the ordinance by its terms only applied to those who had escaped from the *original* states, and that Kentucky, the home of Wharton Jones, was not one of those states. Thus, Chase and Seward concluded that the Fugitive Slave Act could not constitutionally be applied under the specific facts in *Van Zandt*.[4]

Chase then turned to the question of the constitutionality of the Fugitive Slave Act more generally. He was, of course, immediately forced to confront the decision in *Prigg*. Noting that *Prigg* was not an action under the Fugitive Slave Act, but rather a challenge to the constitutionality of Pennsylvania's Personal Liberty Law, Chase sought to characterize the discussion of the constitutionality of the Fugitive Slave Act as nonbinding dictum. But he saved his harshest criticism for the holding that the Fugitive Slave Clause constitutionalized the right of recaption, declaring that "the right is placed, by the opinion of the court, upon a ground so repugnant to the feelings of all classes of men in the north and northwest, and so subversive of the sovereignty and independence of the states, that it encounters, at this moment, a degree of jealousy and hostility beyond all former precedent." Chase raised the specter of

the slave hunter, ranging, at will, through the free states, and clothed with a power, above the control of state laws and state constitutions, and state authorities, to seize and drag beyond state limits, without legal process, and without any judicial sanction, state or federal, persons, who, for aught that appears beyond his bare assertion, are as much entitled to the protection of the law as he is himself, is a portentous anomaly, not to be contemplated, without alarm and irritation.[5]

Both Seward and Chase also reprised a number of the legal arguments that had been made by the attorneys for the state of Pennsylvania in *Prigg*. They argued that the Fugitive Slave Act unconstitutionally vested the judicial authority of the United States in state officials, and that Congress lacked power to adopt enforcing legislation. At the same time, they were careful to minimize the potential implications of their argument for the resolution of other constitutional issues—most notably, questions arising under the Extradition Clause.

On their face, the issues raised by the Extradition Clause were closely analogous to those presented by the Fugitive Slave Clause. At the Constitutional Convention, Pierce Butler and Charles Pinckney of South Carolina analogized the rendition of fugitive slaves to the extradition of accused criminals, and the wording of the two clauses is in many respects strikingly similar. Moreover, the Fugitive Slave Act of 1793 was married with the Extradition Act of the same year.

Nonetheless, Seward made a strenuous effort to distinguish the Fugitive Slave Clause from the Extradition Clause. In making this argument, Seward chose to essentially ignore the second part of the former. He contended that, while the Extradition Clause plainly required state action to deliver the fugitive from justice, the Fugitive Slave Clause "is merely negative, imposes no such obligation or duty, and is content with merely denying to the legislative authority of the several States, power to hinder or obstruct citizens of other States in the assertion of lawful claims to labor or service."[6]

Van Zandt's attorneys also reiterated the view that the constitutionalization of the right of recaption violated a number of the provisions of the Bill of Rights. Like Thomas Hambly before them, they invoked the strictures of both the Fourth and Fifth Amendments. In addition, both Seward and Chase asserted that the procedures established by the statute violated the guarantee of a jury trial in the Seventh Amendment. Moreover, Chase made the startling suggestion that the Fugitive Slave Clause "should be construed as providing only for the enforcement of the 'obligations of free persons,' and not for reconsigning men to the 'condition of slaves.'"[7]

All of these legal arguments were presented with eloquence and passion. In addition, in sharp contrast to the appeals for sectional harmony and respect that had marked the arguments on both sides in *Prigg*, the briefs of Seward and Chase in *Van Zandt* featured vigorous attacks on the institution of slavery itself and, by extension, the Southern states in which slavery was a central element of the social and economic system. Seward inveighed against "slavery, with its odious form and revolting features, and its dreadful pretensions for the present and for the future," while Chase described the peculiar institution as "a pernicious parasite . . . which, planted by the side of the constitutional oak, by other hands than those of the Founders of the Republic, and nurtured with malignant care, has twined itself around the venerable tree, and now displays its poisonous fruits and foliage from every branch." Invoking natural law in a manner reminiscent of John Quincy Adams's argument in *The Amistad*, Chase also declared that

no Legislature is omnipotent. No Legislature can make right wrong; or wrong, right. No legislature can make light, darkness, or darkness, light. No Legislature can make men, things; or things, men. Nor is any Legislature at liberty to disregard the fundamental principle of rectitude and justice.

Chase concluded that "I see not how the judicial enforcement of the claim to property in man can be at all reconciled with these principles."[8]

Given the makeup of the Court, even Seward and Chase themselves could hardly have expected that their arguments would carry the day. Indeed, Seward conceded as much, observing that "we dare not hope, we do not expect, that principles which seem to us so reasonable, so just, and so truthful, can all at once gain immediate establishment in this tribunal, against the force of many precedents and the weight of many honored names."[9] Thus it was no surprise when, without even deigning to hear oral arguments, the Court unanimously affirmed the lower court judgment in *Van Zandt*.

Levi Woodbury's opinion for the Court was much more restrained in tone than the antislavery briefs. Most of Woodbury's analysis was devoted to the technical requirements of the Fugitive Slave Act. Nonetheless, he also addressed the claim that the application of the provisions of the act to Van Zandt was forbidden by the Northwest Ordinance, explicitly rejecting the assertion that the ordinance could not have been intended to change the duties that states formed from the Northwest Territory owed to the residents of other states.[10]

In addition, echoing Story and McLean, Woodbury also condemned the view that the Court should exalt natural law arguments over the text of the Constitution. He described the Fugitive Slave Clause as "one of [the Constitution's] sacred compromises, and which we possess no authority as a judicial body to modify or overrule" and asserted that "whatever may be the theoretical opinions of any as to the expediency of some of those compromises, or of the right of property in persons which they recognize, this court has no alternative, while they exist, but to stand by the constitution and laws with fidelity to their duties and their oaths. Their path is a strait [*sic*] and narrow one, to go where that constitution and the laws lead, and not to break both, by travelling [*sic*] without or beyond them."[11]

Although the Supreme Court's decision went against Van Zandt, his fate was not the prime concern of his attorneys. Instead, Seward and Chase viewed the case primarily as a platform from which they might launch rhetorical salvos in the increasingly bitter sectional conflict of the mid-1840s. Thus, even before the Court rendered its decision, Chase had observed that "even though [Van Zandt] be sacrificed, the great cause of humanity will be a gainer by his loss."[12]

Chase and Seward no doubt hoped that the official report of *Van Zandt* would become a vehicle to disseminate their ideas. However, the reporter, Benjamin Howard, refused to include the briefs in the official report. Nonetheless, Chase's brief was published independently and became well known as a classic exposition of both the radical antislavery position on the Fugitive Slave Clause and the reason that many antislavery Northerners found Story's analysis in *Prigg* unacceptable.

Five years later, Chase sought to turn *Prigg* to his advantage in *Moore v. Illinois*.[13] The sequence of events that eventually brought *Moore* to the Supreme Court began in 1843, when Richard Eells was convicted and fined $400 for violating an Illinois statute that forbade state residents to "harbor or secrete" a person legally held to service in either Illinois or some other state or to "in any wise hinder or prevent the lawful owner or owners of such slaves or servants from retaking them." The jury found that Eells was in fact guilty of "harboring and secreting" an unnamed slave from Missouri who had fled from the service of one Chauncy Durkee. Representing Eells in his appeal to the Illinois Supreme Court, attorney George Dixon first interposed technical challenges to the sufficiency of the indictment, contending that the indictment was defective both because it failed to name the slave whom Eells had harbored and to allege that Eells knew that the person was a slave. Dixon then raised a number of constitutional objections. First, citing *Prigg,* he noted that Congress had exclusive power to enforce the Fugitive Slave Clause, and contended that, insofar as the Illinois statue punished those who secreted slaves from outside the state, the statute trenched on this federal power. Dixon argued that, in that context, the statute was not a simple exercise of the police power because it was not aimed at protecting the property of Illinois residents, but rather "affects other states, its subject matter is connected with other states; it is a regulation to benefit other states [and] to protect that which is property there, but not here."[14]

Dixon also asserted that the Illinois statute was in conflict with the federal Fugitive Slave Law because it dealt with the same subject as the federal statute, imposed different penalties, and did not require proof of knowledge and willfulness. In addition, he claimed that the state statute subjected Eells to double jeopardy because it subjected him to punishment under both the state and federal statutes for the same offense. Finally, Dixon appealed to the same ideal of sectional harmony that had figured so prominently in the opinions in *Prigg* itself, asserting that

the idea of crimination [*sic*] and recrimination, of retaliation, conflagration, and unlawful depredation will only inflame passion, exasperate prejudice, and lead to border war and bloodshed, and result in shaking the security and consequently depreciating the value of slave property. The power of congress is ample for every beneficial purpose, and we ought to rely upon its wisdom and patriotism with the most explicit confidence.[15]

The Illinois Supreme Court's decision in *Eells* reflected the fault lines along which Northern society generally was divided. By a 4–3 vote, the Court upheld the judgment of the trial court. Speaking for the accommodationist four-justice majority was the newly appointed Justice James Shields, a Democrat who had only the year before challenged Abraham Lincoln to a duel over an unflattering newspaper article. Shields first brushed aside the objection to the form of the indictment. He noted that the description of the alleged fugitive slave would have been deemed sufficient in an indictment for larceny, and contended that the requirement of scienter was implicit in the language of the statute and would have been understood by the jury. Shields also gave short shrift to the double jeopardy argument, observing that the violations of the federal and state laws "are separate and distinct; [they are] violations of distinct and different laws, and the punishment inflicted by different sovereignties."[16]

Shields conceded that the objection based on federal exclusivity was "of a more serious nature." Nonetheless, he had a twofold response to Dixon's argument on this point. First, characterizing Story's discussion of this point as nonbinding dictum, Shields contended that Taney had the better of the argument on this issue, asserting that the enforcement of the Fugitive Slave Clause "was a matter of strict moral, political and international obligation, which rested upon each state." In addition, noting that Story himself had conceded that states retained the power to protect themselves from the "depredation and evil example" of fugitive slaves, Shields characterized the Illinois statute as an exercise of the police power that had been validated in *Miln*.[17]

Whig Justice Samuel D. Lockwood spoke for the three dissenters. Appointed to the court in 1828, by 1843, Lockwood had apparently moved to a strong antislavery position. The same year, dissenting in *Willard v. The People,* he had rejected the right of slave transit, concluding instead that erstwhile slaves became free the moment that they were voluntarily brought into the state of Illinois.[18] His opinion in *Eells* was also suffused with antislavery sentiment.

Lockwood began his opinion by noting that all persons were presumed free in the state of Illinois, and observing that, in *Prigg,* Story himself had emphasized the limited scope of laws recognizing slavery. Against this background, Lockwood concluded that the indictment was fatally defective both because it failed to explicitly charge that Eells had acted with knowledge that the person that he was harboring was a slave and because the indictment had not named that person. He also argued that the statute should not be construed to punish offenses covered by the federal Fugitive Slave Law, declaring that "to punish criminally for the same offense more than once is a violation of a great fundamental principle." Finally, taking the view that a criminal statute could not be considered a "mere police regulation," Lockwood argued that the Illinois statute was unconstitutional because it sought to regulate a matter that was within the exclusive authority of Congress. He asserted that, in *Prigg,* six justices had agreed that "the power to legislate on the subject of fugitive slaves was vested exclusively in congress."[19]

Eells quickly petitioned the Supreme Court for a writ of error, but for unknown reasons the Court proved to be in no hurry to resolve the appeal. The record and a written argument on Eells's behalf were filed by George Dixon in September 1845, and an argument for the state of Illinois by Attorney General James A. McDougall was submitted in February 1846. Nonetheless, the case was continued for a number of terms, until George Dixon was replaced as counsel for the defendant by Chase, who had since entered the Senate as a representative of Ohio. Opposing Chase during the oral argument was James Shields, who had left the Illinois Supreme Court and was a member of the Senate from Illinois. By the time that the case was finally argued in December 1851, Eells had died. In his place stood Thomas Moore, the executor of his estate.[20]

The arguments for Moore tracked the dissent in the Illinois Supreme Court, with Chase emphasizing in particular the contention that the Illinois statute was void under the principle of federal exclusivity established in *Prigg.* McDougall and Shields, on the other hand, premised their argument largely on *Miln.* The written brief analogized free blacks to paupers and convicts, observing that "negroes [*sic*] have been and continue to be regarded as constituting a vagabond population; and to prevent their influx into the State, restrictive laws have been from time to time passed."[21]

Moore attracted considerable attention from the antislavery forces. Asserting that "no one can fail to see the important political bearing that this case must have," the *New York Times* predicted that, unless the Court overruled *Prigg,* "one of two things must result—either all State enactments on the subject must fade from the statute books and [Eells] be relieved from his sentence, or the very Fugitive Slave act of Congress, which so recently convulsed the country, must be declared invalid."[22] The Supreme Court itself, however, took a different view, affirming Eells's conviction on an 8–1 vote.

The Court unanimously rejected the claim that the Illinois statute should be struck down on the authority of *Prigg v. Pennsylvania,* although John McLean dissented only on the double jeopardy issue, reaffirming a position that he had taken in 1847 in a case that was unrelated to slavery. Robert Grier spoke for the Court. In addition to rejecting the double jeopardy claim, Grier argued that the Illinois statute was an exercise of the police power and thus expressly permitted by the language of Story's opinion in *Prigg.* Grier also noted that the Illinois statute neither interfered with the federal enforcement scheme nor directly aided the claimant in the recovery of the fugitive. In addition, he took the opportunity to emphasize the importance of the statute not only to the domestic tranquility of the state of Illinois itself, but also to the maintenance of amicable North-South relations:

Experience has shown . . . that the results of such conduct as that prohibited by the statute in question are not only to demoralize [the] citizens who live in daily and open disregard of the duties imposed upon them by the Constitution and laws, but to destroy the harmony and kind feeling which should exist between citizens of this Union, to create border feuds and bitter animosities, and to cause breaches of the peace, violent assaults and murder. No one can deny or doubt the right of a State to defend itself against evils of such magnitude, and punish those who perversely persist in conduct which promotes them.[23]

From this perspective, the theme of the majority opinion in *Moore* was much like that of the opinions of both Story and Wayne in *Prigg.*

Nonetheless, the *National Era* complained bitterly of what it described as the inconsistency between *Moore* and *Prigg,* asserting that the former provided new evidence that the Supreme Court was "one of the bulwarks of slavery." Similarly, Carl B. Swisher contends that *Moore* "devitalized" the doctrine of federal exclusivity advanced by the *Prigg* majority. Such assertions misconceive the import of Story's opinion on this point.

The statute considered by the *Moore* Court did not raise any of the issues that the Court had addressed in *Prigg.* *Prigg* limited the power of state governments in two ways. First, Story concluded that state governments could not interfere with the exercise of the private right of recaption. Second, emphasizing the need for uniformity in rendition procedures, he determined that only the federal government could establish the procedures to be followed by slaveowners in order to invoke the power of government officials in the rendition process:

If . . . the states have a right, in the absence of legislation by Congress, to act upon the subject, each state is at liberty to prescribe just such regulations as suit its own policy, local convenience, and local feelings. The legislation of one state may not only be different from, but utterly repugnant to and incompatible with that of another. The time, and mode, and limitation of the remedy; the proofs of the title, and all other incidents applicable thereto, may be prescribed in one state, which are rejected or disclaimed in another. One state may require the owner to sue in one mode, another in a different mode. One state may make a statute of limitations as to the remedy, in its own tribunals, short and summary; another may prolong the period, and yet restrict the proofs: nay, some states may utterly refuse to act upon the subject at all; and others may refuse to open its Courts to any remedies in rem, because they would interfere with their own domestic policy, institutions, or habits. The right, therefore, would never, in a practical sense be the same in all the states. It would have no unity of purpose, or uniformity of operation.[24]

While Grier suggested that the Court might be willing to reconsider the general principle of federal exclusivity in a later case, the Illinois statute that was challenged in *Moore* had no impact on these issues. The state enactment did not purport to regulate rendition procedures, or indeed any aspect of the rendition process. Nor was the statute inconsistent with any of the policies embodied in the Fugitive Slave Act. Instead, the Illinois law simply criminalized the act of hiding fugitive slaves—no more and no less. As such, the statute fell precisely within the category of state enactments that Story himself had clearly indicated were constitutional despite the presence of the Fugitive Slave Clause, observing in *Prigg* that

we entertain no doubt whatsoever, that the states, in virtue of their general police power, possess full jurisdiction to arrest and restrain runaway slaves, and remove them from their borders, and otherwise to secure themselves against their depredations and evil example, as they certainly may do in cases of idlers, vagabonds, and paupers. The rights of the owners of fugitive slaves are in no just sense interfered with, or regulated by such a course; and in many cases, the operations of this police power, although designed essentially for other purposes, for the protection, safety, and peace of the state, may essentially promote and aid the interests of the owners.[25]

Thus, far from being a retreat from *Prigg, Moore* was in fact a relatively straightforward application of the principles established by Story's 1842 opinion.

Still, the tenor of many of the arguments in both *Van Zandt* and *Moore* reflected the ever-increasing sectional tensions of the late 1840s and early 1850s. The impact of these tensions had been even more apparent the year before the decision in *Moore,* when the Supreme Court focused on a different slavery-related issue in *Strader v. Graham.*[26]

CHAPTER 14

Prelude to *Dred Scott*

Strader v. Graham and the Doctrine of Reattachment

In 1851, the Supreme Court for the first time encountered another irritant in the sectional conflict—the question of the status of putative slaves who had been brought voluntarily by their masters into states in which slavery was prohibited. All agreed that the erstwhile slaves became permanently free in that situation if the master established permanent residence in the free state—in legal terms, when the master became a domiciliary of that state. The problems arose when the slaveowner was what was often described as a "mere sojourner," that is, one who was simply passing through a free state in transit or whose residence in that state was only temporary.

The issues presented by these cases were in some ways analogous to those raised by the disputes over fugitive slaves. Some Northerners objected to any regime that would allow Southerners to project the institution of slavery into the free states, even temporarily and at the margins. Slaveholders, on the other hand, saw the need to travel northward with their slaves for some purposes as essential to their status as full partners in the Union.[1]

During the process of drafting the Constitution, Charles C. Pinckney of South Carolina had urged the convention to include explicit protection for the interests of slaveowners on this issue in the Comity Clause. However, the delegates from the other states showed no interest in Pinckney's proposal, and the language that was ultimately adopted made no mention of the issue. By contrast, British common law precedent was at least arguably relevant. In the 1772 decision in *Somerset v. Stewart*, a slave had been transported from Virginia to England, which had no legislation either establishing or prohibiting slavery. The slave escaped, only to be recaptured by his master, who then attempted to place him on a ship for the purpose of being sent to Jamaica for sale. Lord Mansfield issued a writ of habeas corpus ordering that the slave be released from the custody of the ship's captain, declaring famously that "the state of slavery is of such a nature that it is incapable of being introduced on any reasons, moral or political. . . . It is so odious that nothing can be suffered to support it but positive law."[2]

Although Mansfield himself may have seen the decision in more limited terms, *Somerset* came to stand for the proposition that any slave who was brought into England gained his freedom at the moment that he entered the country, by whatever means and for whatever purpose. By its terms, the Fugitive Slave Clause forbade the full implementation of this principle in the United States. Moreover, for much of the early part of the nineteenth century, the governments of the Northern states generally refused to fully embrace *Somerset* even when slaves were brought voluntarily into their jurisdiction.

To be sure, even during this period, the attitudes of the Northern states with respect to this issue were far from uniform. Prior to 1841, a New York statute provided that slaveholders could bring their bondsmen into the state for up to nine months without fear of having the slaves emancipated, and until 1847, Pennsylvania granted slaveholders a six-month grace period. By contrast, in the 1836 decision in *Commonwealth v. Aves,* the Massachusetts Supreme Court concluded that erstwhile slaves brought into the state for even a short period became free by operation of law. However, even the *Aves* court was careful to note that it was not dealing with the situation in which slaves were brought through Massachusetts in transit between the state of domicile and some other destination, and in 1843 the Illinois Supreme Court concluded in *Willard v. The People* that the right to slave transit was guaranteed by the Constitution.[3]

As sectional tensions mounted, the Northern states became less hospitable to Southerners who brought their slaves voluntarily into free territory. The case of Jonathan Lemmon created a particularly intense controversy. In 1852, Lemmon, his wife, and their eight slaves embarked on a voyage by steamboat from Virginia to New Orleans, from whence they intended to travel to Texas. No steamships ran directly from Virginia to New Orleans; thus, the Lemmons and their party were forced to voyage first to New York City, where, after a three-day layover, they intended to board another vessel for the trip to their final destination. After arriving in New York on Saturday, November 6, the Lemmons lodged their party in a hotel in the city to await the arrival of the New Orleans–bound vessel.[4]

Upon learning of the arrival of the Lemmons, Louis Napoleon, a free black New Yorker seeking to free the Lemmon slaves, petitioned Judge Elijah Paine of the New York Superior Court for a writ of habeas corpus. The parties were brought before Judge Paine, and arguments were heard in the case on November 6 and once again on November 8. On November 13, in *Lemmon v. The People,* Paine freed the erstwhile slaves, contending that a statute passed in 1841 freed all slaves within the state's territorial limits except fugitives.[5]

The reactions to Judge Paine's ruling divided along predictable lines. Describing the decision as "one of marked importance," the *New York Times* also contended that "no man who has ever examined the law under which it was to be given, and whose regard for law was greater than his hatred of negro freedom, had the slightest doubt as to what it would be." The abolitionist New York *Evangelist* was even more ebullient, characterizing the decision as "nobly vindicating the law and policy of New York as a free state, and as settling another legal principle in favor of liberty."[6]

Not surprisingly, Southerners and their supporters had a different perspective. Thus, for example, the *Washington Union* described the decision as "a most grievous injury and flagrant outrage upon the South and the bond of the Union," while the *Richmond Daily Dispatch* asserted that if the ruling was upheld on appeal "we should conclude that the States were no longer bound by the Federal compact . . . we should, therefore, recommend reprisals upon any and all property belonging to New York." Similarly, Virginia Governor Joseph Johnson declared in a message to the state legislature that the decision was "contrary to the spirit of all law [and] at war with the relations that should subsist between the sister States of the Union." Howell Cobb, the governor of Georgia, expressed similar sentiments, averring that "[such] a denial of . . . comity is unheard of among civilized nations, and if deliberately and wantonly persisted in, would be just cause for war."[7]

The trial court's decision did not end the controversy. For the next eight years, *Lemmon* wended its way slowly through the New York judicial system and was ultimately affirmed by two higher state courts. However, the Civil War intervened before the case reached the United States Supreme Court, and the Court never passed directly on the constitutionality of the denial of the right to slave transit.[8] *Strader,* however, arose from the application of a closely related legal concept—the doctrine of reattachment.

Reattachment cases involved the status of ex-slaves who had become free by operation of law due to their presence in free states but had later returned voluntarily to states in which slavery was legal. These cases did not implicate the sectional struggle as directly as those involving the status of those who were enslaved in Southern states but were currently present in free states. By their nature, reattachment cases did not involve the projection of slavery into Northern states, even in a limited sense. Instead, these cases simply focused on the status of African Americans while they were present in states which permitted slavery. Such issues were generally of only marginal interest to mainstream Northern politicians—even those who opposed slavery in the abstract.

Moreover, the idea that each state generally has the authority to define the status of its own residents was deeply engrained in the common law. Further, prior to the Civil War, the Constitution did not place general limits on this authority. Since the Due Process Clause of the Fifth Amendment did not apply to the states,[9] the federal Constitution typically did not even prevent states from reducing free citizens to the status of slaves. In some reattachment cases, however, antislavery theorists at times argued that the courts of a slave state were constitutionally required to defer to the law of a free state that granted freedom to an erstwhile slave.

Against this background, the evolution of the Southern approach to reattachment closely paralleled that of the Northern approach to comity. The leading English precedent was *The Slave, Grace,* an 1827 decision for the High Court of Admiralty. There a slave accompanied her mistress to England, but after a one-year visit returned voluntarily to Antigua. In rejecting the claim that the slave's sojourn in England prevented her reenslavement, Lord Sowell conceded that Grace had a right to freedom while in England. Nonetheless, he concluded that this right "totally expired when that residence ceased and she was imported into Antigua" and that her "temporary freedom" was "superseded upon the return of the slave [to a jurisdiction where slavery was legal]."[10] Put another way, the status of slavery was said to have "reattached" to Grace when she returned to Antigua.

Just as the Northern states did not fully embrace *Somerset* in the early nineteenth century, *The Slave, Grace* was at first of only limited significance in Southern jurisprudence. Prior to the 1840s, Southern courts often rejected the application of the doctrine of reattachment, holding instead that an ex-slave who became free under the law of a Northern state which he had visited with the permission of his master retained that freedom even after returning to the slave's Southern domicile.[11] But just as the Northern states moved closer to the principle of *Somerset* in the 1840s and 1850s, *The Slave, Grace* and the doctrine of reattachment generally became more prominent in Southern jurisprudence during the same period. The decision of the lower court in *Strader* provides one of the most significant examples of this trend.[12]

Strader began as an action for damages under a Kentucky statute that made owners of boats liable for taking any slave out of the state without the permission of his master. The African Americans in question, Henry, Reuben, and George, had been enslaved to Kentuckian James Graham. When Henry and Reuben were in their late teens, Graham had sent them to Louisville, Kentucky, to live with a free black man named Williams and be trained as musicians. Graham gave written permission for Williams to bring Henry and Reuben to Cincinnati, Ohio, and New Albany, Indiana, in order to play with Williams. Under this arrangement, Henry and Reuben performed as musicians once in Cincinnati, two or three times in New Albany, and twice in Madison, Indiana. After each of these performances, they returned voluntarily to Kentucky and to the custody of Graham. However, in January 1841, they joined George on a steamboat from Louisville to Cincinnati, from whence the three African Americans escaped to Canada. Graham brought the action for damages against the owner of the steamboat. The owner of the steamboat defended on the ground that the escapees had in fact no longer been slaves because they had become free by the laws of Indiana and Ohio during their sojourns in those states and had remained free when they returned to Kentucky.

On October 14, 1844, reversing a judgment in favor of the defendant with respect to Henry and Reuben, the Kentucky Court of Appeals rejected this defense. Speaking for the court, Judge Thomas A. Marshall first questioned whether the defendants in *Strader* had standing to interpose a claim for freedom on behalf of Henry and Reuben when the erstwhile slaves had not themselves ever asserted such a claim in a judicial proceeding. Marshall also questioned whether the laws of Indiana and Ohio dissolved the master/slave relationship under *Strader*-like circumstances, as opposed to simply denying the master the aid of state authorities in imposing his dominion over the slaves. But in any event, citing *The Slave, Grace* and *Aves,* Marshall concluded that Kentucky should apply the doctrine of reattachment even if Henry and Reuben would have been deemed free under the laws of Indiana and Ohio, declaring that "if our law on the subject might meet so little respect in a foreign State, surely it would be carrying the principle of comity to a most unwarrantable length, to deprive [a slaveholder] of his property here, when he has brought it back without any appeal having been made to the foreign law while the subject was within its territorial jurisdiction."[13]

The case was remanded to the trial court, and after a judgment for the plaintiff, came before the Kentucky Court of Appeals once again in 1847. Just as in 1844, Thomas Marshall (who had since ascended to the chief justiceship of the state supreme court) spoke for the court, this time affirming the judgment of the lower court. Marshall emphasized that his earlier opinion had not conceded that Henry and Reuben had become free under the laws of Ohio and Indiana, but had simply concluded that the two escapees would have remained slaves under the law of Kentucky in any event.[14] The second judgment of the Court of Appeals came before the United States Supreme Court on a writ of error.

Representing Strader and the other defendants before the Court, Walter Jones at times focused on the specific facts of the case. He asserted that "if a master voluntarily hire his slave to a citizen of a non-slaveholding state, to perform service and labor in such non-slaveholding state, and if he in fact send the slave there for that purpose, the slave becomes free." Jones observed that "if the citizens of non-slaveholding states could . . . introduce slaves under contracts of hire, they would violate the settled policy of their state by bringing slave labor in competition with the poor." He also cited a variety of cases in which the courts of slave states had concluded that persons in the position of Henry and Reuben remained free by virtue of state law even after returning voluntarily to their homes in those states.[15]

Other parts of Jones's argument, however, made clear that he was advocating a much broader principle. He contended that "by force of the [Northwest] Ordinance, and of the Constitution . . . and the acts of Congress for the admission of Ohio and Indiana," "as soon as Reuben, Henry and George touched the soil of Indiana or Ohio, with the consent of their master, the quality of freedom attached to their persons, and could never be afterwards dissociated from them," no matter what the character of their presence in the nonslaveholding state. Jones later averred that "it is a monstrosity in morals and in law, that a man who has been made free by the operation of law can make himself a slave [simply by voluntarily returning to a slave state]. On the coming of the slave into the free state, by the mere force of the prohibition [on slavery] his shackles fall from him. . . . If he be free in Ohio and Indiana, how shall he be a slave elsewhere?"[16]

The implications of Jones's argument were startling. Essentially, he was contending that, under the guise of establishing a framework for the administration of the Northwest Territory in 1787, the Continental Congress had vested the federal government with a power that was possessed by no state government—the authority to permanently change the status of the domiciliaries of other states, and to force the domicile state to acquiesce in that change. Further, he was suggesting that this regime had been established at a time when the overwhelming majority of the states recognized slavery.

Moreover, Jones explicitly rejected the position that the character or duration of a putative slave's presence in a state north of the Ohio River was relevant to the analysis, asserting that "there [is] no distinction . . . to be drawn from the mere duration of commorancy, if the removal to a free state was voluntary on the part of the slave and with the permission of the master" and that "the instant . . . the slave came within the boundaries of such states, the laws of those states took effect upon his condition, and *eo instanti* he became clothed with every attribute of freedom."[17] Thus, in Jones's view, a slave state would be required to recognize the freedom of a slave even if the master and slave had only passed through Ohio in transit between two slave states. Moreover, under Jones's theory, the states of the Old Northwest would have been *required* to deny the right of slave transit. If the Northwest Ordinance and the statutes admitting Ohio and Indiana forced Kentucky to recognize the freedom of putative slaves that had been present in the two free states, surely it had the same import for the states at which the two statutes were explicitly directed.

Speaking in opposition to Jones, John J. Crittenden of Kentucky, the attorney general in the Fillmore administration, denied that the Northwest Ordinance had any relevance to the case. Instead, Crittenden insisted that the case was governed solely by the laws of Kentucky. He highlighted the fact that the defense was based solely on the view that the three putative slaves had gained their freedom by virtue of temporary stays in Indiana and Ohio. Crittenden also emphasized the potentially divisive impact of a reversal of the Kentucky court's decision, contending that such a reversal "would give to [the Northwest Ordinance] the effect of creating a border warfare" and would "destroy that amenity of intercourse, that interchange of social courtesies, which now exist, and which do so much to preserve those kindly and fraternal feelings upon which the success of our institutions so much depends."[18]

The Supreme Court unanimously concluded that the appeal should be dismissed for want of jurisdiction. Chief Justice Taney's opinion noted that the Court lacked authority to revise or overturn the holding of the Kentucky Supreme Court on issues of state law, and emphasized that states retained broad authority to apply the doctrine of reattachment. He asserted that "it was exclusively in the power of Kentucky to determine for itself whether [the] employment [of slaves] in another state should make them free on their return" and that "there is nothing in the Constitution of the United States that can in any degree control the law of Kentucky upon this subject."[19]

Taney then turned to a discussion of the impact of the Northwest Ordinance. He first observed that "the Ordinance . . . if still in force could have no more operation than the laws of Ohio in the state of Kentucky, and could not influence the decision upon the rights of the master or the slaves in that state, nor give this court jurisdiction over the subject." But he also concluded that, in any event, the Northwest Ordinance had ceased to have any legally binding effect when Ohio was admitted as a state. Indeed, Taney argued that some provisions of the ordinance had been invalidated by the subsequent adoption of the Constitution itself. Echoing the position taken by some slave state representatives during the debates over the admission of Missouri, he suggested that the perpetual prohibition on slavery was unconstitutional because it would have "place[d] [the states of the Old Northwest] in an inferior condition as compared with the other states, and subject[ed] their domestic institutions and municipal regulations to the constant supervision of this court."[20]

The implication that the antislavery provisions of the Northwest Ordinance were in part unconstitutional was understandably anathema to an antislavery

Westerner such as John McLean. McLean agreed that those provisions had been superseded by the state constitution when Ohio was admitted to the Union, and that the Court lacked jurisdiction over *Strader* for that reason. However, he also asserted that "anything that is said in [Taney's] opinion beyond this . . . is . . . extra-judicial."[21]

The public reactions to *Strader* divided along predictable lines. The *National Era* saw the decision as an example of "the vigilance with which [the Supreme Court] guards the interest of Slavery." By contrast, the *Washington Union* happily declared that *Strader* "settles the law on two very important questions, and *maugre* the grumbling of the abolitionists, will meet the general approbation of the country."[22] But in any event, *Strader* was only a minor skirmish in the conflict over slavery. Six years later, a state court's application of the doctrine of reattachment would lead to a far more portentous decision in *Dred Scott v. Sandford.*

CHAPTER 15

Assessment

In general, proslavery Southerners had good reason to be pleased with the positions take by the Supreme Court from 1845 through 1853. Their positions were adopted without reservation by the unanimous or near-unanimous decisions in *Van Zandt*, *Moore*, and *Strader*. To be sure, some Southerners were uneasy about the broad vision of the federal commerce power enunciated by James Moore Wayne in *The Passenger Cases*. But even in that case, Moore was careful to explain that his approach would not in any way jeopardize the ability of Southern state government to exercise exclusive control over the ingress of slaves and free blacks.

At the same time, the import of the Southern victories during this period should not be overstated. *Van Zandt* and *Moore* were simply straightforward applications of the principles that had been established in *Prigg*, and the holding in *Strader* did nothing more than ratify the basic principle that each state government in general retained exclusive authority to define the status of its domiciliaries who were also within the state's territorial boundaries. The most potentially controversial aspect of *Strader*—Taney's assertion that the antislavery provisions of the Northwest Ordinance had been superseded by the Constitution—does not seem to have attracted significant comment at the time, perhaps because this assertion was of no practical import, and arose only indirectly in the context of a decision dealing with the power of a slave state over its own citizens.

Indeed, the most significant aspect of these cases may not have been the actual holdings of the Court, but rather the aggressively sectionalist tenor of some of the arguments made by antislavery attorneys—most notably, the brief of Salmon P. Chase and William Seward in *Van Zandt*. Particularly when taken together with Taney's unnecessary attack on the Northwest Ordinance in *Strader*, the *Van Zandt* brief served as a pointed reminder that the sectional truce that was still nominally in place in 1853 was extremely fragile, and that both Northern and Southern sectionalists stood ready to take any opportunity to attack that truce. Indeed, the truce would not survive the dramatic events of 1854.

Part Four

The Sectionalization of
American Politics, 1853–1859

The Kansas-Nebraska Act, the Anthony Burns Affair, and the Demise of the Second-Party System

Although Stephen Douglas and his allies hoped that the bills passed in 1850 would provide a final solution to the issue of slavery in the territories, in fact the adoption of the compromise measures provided only a temporary respite. In part, this reality derived from the fact that even those who supported the territorial provisions of the Compromise of 1850 differed on the import of congressional silence regarding the issue of slavery. Northern members of Congress believed that the Utah and New Mexico statutes embodied the principle of popular sovereignty, leaving territorial legislatures the option of banning slavery if they so chose. Thus, Douglas announced to his constituents in Chicago that the settlement recognized the "right" of territorial residents to regulate "their own internal concerns and domestic institutions in their own way." By contrast, Southerners such as Whig Sen. Robert Toombs of Georgia took the view that nonintervention implicitly authorized slaveholders to bring their slaves into the territories, declaring that the Utah and New Mexico bills "contained all [the South] did demand."[1] Ultimately, however, it was a quite different issue that would unravel the short-lived peace achieved through the Compromise of 1850. The issue was the future of the Missouri Compromise.

During the early 1850s, Southerners and their allies would sometimes claim that the Compromise of 1850 had implicitly repealed the Missouri Compromise.[2] From a purely formal perspective, such claims were insupportable. To be sure, Southerners persistently advocated the extension of the Missouri Compromise line to the Pacific Ocean, and that proposal was rejected in 1850. But the repeal of the Missouri Compromise itself was simply not an issue in the struggle over the admission of California and the organization of the Utah and New Mexico territories.

All of the relevant statutes were by their terms territorially limited. The Missouri Compromise dealt only with the land acquired through the Louisiana Purchase. By contrast, each of the other bills that were adopted focused specifically on parts of the territory subsequently acquired through the Treaty of Guadalupe Hidalgo that ended the Mexican War. Moreover, even a suggestion that any of the latter bills would alter the disposition of the lands of the Louisiana Purchase would have led to the bills' demise. Indeed, the issue was not even discussed. Thus, subsequent claims that the Compromise of 1850 formally repealed the Missouri Compromise are simply not consistent with either the facts or the historical context in which the former was adopted.

On another level, however, the Compromise of 1850 had a profound impact on the continuing effectiveness of the arrangements that had been agreed upon in 1820. The Missouri Compromise did not establish territorial governments in any part of the area north of 36 degrees, 30 minutes. Instead, the creation of each territorial government required separate legislation that could, in theory at least, modify or abrogate the terms of the Missouri legislation. At least in the Senate, Southern cooperation was needed to adopt the necessary legislation without such modifications. Prior to 1850, such cooperation was provided without incident.

The events of 1850 and the immediately preceding years dramatically changed the political dynamic. In the long struggle over the organization of Oregon and the Mexican Cession, Southern efforts to extend the Missouri Compromise line to the Pacific Ocean had been conclusively rejected. In essence, Northerners had refused to adhere to the general principle of territorial division underlying both the Northwest Ordinance and the Missouri Compromise itself. Moreover, continuing to acquiesce in the organization of free states from the area of the Louisiana Purchase would have virtually guaranteed that Southerners would soon find themselves at the mercy of the representatives of the free states. Further, the events in the years that culminated in the adoption of the Compromise of 1850 hardly augured well for the consideration of Southern interests under those conditions. Against this background, many Southerners believed themselves absolved from any duty to cooperate in the organization of new territories from which slavery was excluded.

Initially, Southern reluctance to cooperate was expressed through a refusal to agree to the organization of the Nebraska Territory, all of which was located north of the Missouri Compromise line. In the House of Representatives, proponents of a territorial government were able to overwhelm Southern opposition in early 1853 and approve the Nebraska Bill on a vote of 98 to 43. However, when Stephen Douglas introduced a similar bill in the Senate, it was tabled by a vote of 23 to 17 in March 1853, with Southern senators voting against Douglas by a margin of 19 to 2.[3] Douglas nonetheless remained determined to organize the territory in order to secure a central route for the transcontinental railroad. Thus, he determined to reintroduce the Nebraska Bill in the Thirty-Third Congress, thereby setting in motion the series of events that would ultimately destroy any hope of sectional harmony.

As the price for their support, Southerners insisted that the Nebraska Bill explicitly provide for the repeal of the Missouri Compromise. Douglas himself apparently would have preferred that slaves not come into the territories and believed that natural conditions would prevent slavery from taking hold west of the Mississippi. However, he was sincerely committed to the principle of popular sovereignty and more concerned with obtaining the support necessary for the establishment of the territorial government. When he introduced the bill on January 4, it did not specifically address the question of slavery, but simply provided for admission of states carved from the territory "with or without slavery, as their constitution shall prescribe at the time of their admission."[4]

Representatives of the slave states found this formulation unacceptable because it would have created a situation in which slaveowners could vote for a proslavery constitution, but would have been barred from bringing slaves into the territory prior to the admission of the newly created states. Douglas next proposed to add a clause which stated that "all questions pertaining to slavery in the Territories . . . are to be left to the people residing therein, through their appropriate representatives."[5] Southerners remained unmollified, because the prohibition of 1820 would have remained in effect until superseded by the actions of a territorial legislature that would presumably be elected without the influence of slaveowners, who would be unlikely to emigrate to the territory unless the ban on slavery was removed.

Against this background, on January 16, Kentucky Whig Archibald Dixon announced that he would offer an amendment that not only would have repealed the prohibition on slavery in the Missouri Compromise but also would have explicitly allowed slaveholders "to take and hold their slaves within any of the Territories of the United States." After consultations with both Dixon and Southern Democrats, Douglas responded by altering his bill so that, when finally reported to the Senate floor on January 23, 1854, it explicitly declared that the Missouri Compromise had been repealed by the Compromise of 1850 and was therefore "inoperative and void." The revised bill also split the newly organized territory into Kansas in the south and Nebraska in the north—a decision that was widely perceived as setting the stage for the ultimate admission of one slave state and one free state.[6]

Not surprisingly, a fierce debate ensued.[7] The supporters of the bill fell into two camps. Southerners railed against what they saw as the unjustness of the Missouri Compromise line. For example, Dixon asserted that the restriction that had been imposed in 1820 "tramples the great doctrine of equality of States underfoot, and tears asunder the chart upon which the liberty of the people is written." Others saw the principle of popular sovereignty not only as right in itself but also as providing the best possibility for removing the question of slavery from national politics. Thus, Democratic Rep. Moses McDonald of Maine asserted that under a regime of popular sovereignty, "the question [of slavery] becomes local. No longer will there be any inducements, and most certainly no propriety, in discussing the question at the North, or in non-slaveholding communities."[8]

The opponents of the bill were no less vehement. Whig Rep. Aaron Harlan of Ohio complained that "the barricades and bars heretofore erected to obstruct the progress of slavery are to be broken down, and a great highway is to be opened up to facilitate its progress by the passage of [the] bill." In the Appeal of the Independent Democrats, a group of radical antislavery congressmen and senators described the Kansas-Nebraska Bill as "a gross violation of a sacred pledge . . . a criminal betrayal of precious rights . . . part and parcel of an atrocious plot" to turn the territory into a "dreary region of despotism, inhabited by masters and slaves."[9]

Despite protests such as these, Douglas and his allies were ultimately successful in driving the Kansas-Nebraska Bill through Congress. In the Senate, the bill carried by a vote of 37 to 14, as fourteen Northern Democrats joined a near-unanimous South in defeating a polyglot alliance of seven Northern Whigs, four Northern Democrats, one Free Soiler, and two maverick Southerners. Resistance in the House of Representatives was much stiffer. For a time it seemed possible that Southern Whigs in the House would unite in voting against the bill. However, as Michael F. Holt has observed, the wide circulation of the Appeal of the Independent Democrats had raised the political cost of this course of action by associating opposition with the most radical antislavery elements in Northern politics. Thus, with the support of Democratic President Franklin Pierce, the Douglas proposal prevailed by a vote of 113 to 100. Sixty-nine of seventy-eight slave state representatives voted for the bill, including seven of the nineteen Southern Whigs who voted. Half of the Northern Democrats in the House supported the bill as well. By contrast, Northern Whigs were unanimously opposed.[10]

Prior to the Missouri Compromise, the idea of popular sovereignty had implicitly governed the entire Louisiana Purchase without creating great consternation in any of the territories. However, against the background of the disputes of the 1840s and 1850s, the reinvigoration of the same formula proved to be a recipe for disaster. Representatives of both free states and slave states recruited settlers for Kansas, with each group hoping to secure the territory for its camp. Violence between the two groups became commonplace, and in the first election for a territorial legislature Missourians crossed the border in droves to fraudulently cast votes for proslavery candidates. In short, rather than dampening sectional tensions, as its partisans hoped, the move to popular sovereignty exacerbated the conflict between North and South.[11]

The bitter conflict over the Kansas-Nebraska Act also had a spillover effect on the dispute over fugitive slaves. Some Northerners who had hitherto supported the Fugitive Slave Act of 1850 felt betrayed and considered themselves absolved from the obligation of aiding slaveowners who sought to recover escapees. Thus, for example, Amos Lawrence, a conservative Whig from Massachusetts, warned that the passage of the Kansas-Nebraska Act would render the Fugitive Slave Act a dead letter in the North.[12]

The widely discussed case of Anthony Burns further roiled sectional relations.[13] In March 1854, Burns, who was enslaved to Charles F. Suttle of Alexandria, Virginia, stowed away on a ship in Richmond and found his way to Boston. After learning of Burns's whereabouts, Suttle and William Brent arranged for the city police force to arrest Burns on a charge of robbing a jewelry store. The arrest took place on Wednesday, May 24, and Burns was delivered into the custody of United States Marshal Watson Freeman at the courthouse. The next day, Burns was brought before United States Commissioner Edward G. Loring for a hearing, but the hearing was postponed until May 27 at the request of Burns's attorneys Richard H. Dana Jr. and Charles Mayo Ellis.

The antislavery forces called a public meeting to mobilize support for Burns. The meeting was held in Faneuil Hall on the evening of Friday, May 26. A group of abolitionists led by Thomas Higginson and Martin Stowell determined to use the meeting as a springboard to launch a rescue of Burns. Those who attended first listened to inflammatory speeches from Samuel G. Howe, Wendell Phillips, Frances W. Bird, John L. Swift, and Theodore Parker, and were informed that an effort was being made to free Burns. Many then rushed to the courthouse. Higginson led a small group who broke down the door but were repulsed by defenders, one of whom was killed in the struggle.

Order was restored after the mayor called in local military units. Marshal Freeman then brought in federal forces to protect the courthouse. After being informed of the situation, President Fillmore also ordered Secretary of War Jefferson Davis to send in marines, cavalry, and artillery to Boston. In addition, Fillmore directed a federal revenue cutter to stand by in Boston Harbor to transport Burns back to Virginia in the event that Suttle was issued a certificate of removal.

When the hearing was resumed on May 27, a large crowd had gathered in the Court Square. After three more days of hearings, on Friday, June 2—three days after the Kansas-Nebraska Act was signed into law—Loring concluded that Suttle was entitled to take possession of Burns and return with him to Norfolk. Burns was then taken under military guard to the revenue cutter as a crowd of an estimated 50,000 hostile Bostonians looked on. Burns was returned to Norfolk, where he was bought by a North Carolina speculator. Ultimately, the free black community in Boston purchased Burns's freedom in 1855.

The combination of the passage of the Kansas-Nebraska Act and the Anthony Burns affair had a profound impact on the structure of national politics. Already riven by sectional dissension over the passage of the Compromise of 1850 and shaken by a massive influx of immigrants who overwhelmingly supported the Democratic Party, the Whig Party disintegrated as a national organization after the events of 1854. Many Northern Democrats who had opposed the repeal of the Missouri Compromise also sought a new political identity.

In the wake of these developments, a number of different political organizations competed for the allegiance of the erstwhile Whigs and antislavery Democrats. One group sought to create a bisectional American or "Know-Nothing" party organized around nativist principles. Southern Democrats sought to lure formerly proslavery Whigs into their party. In the North, antislavery leaders worked to unite their previously disparate forces under the banner of what would become known as the Republican Party.

The Republican Party was entirely sectional. While some Republicans supported racial equality more generally, the party as a whole emphasized the immorality of slavery specifically and the need to protect the interests of white Northerners. Indeed, some Republicans argued that, because most blacks in the United States were slaves, preventing the spread of slavery was the best way to preserve the character of the country as a white nation. Thus, for example, one Republican newspaper declared that "the Republicans mean to preserve all of this country that they can from the *pestilent presence of the black man.*"[14]

In narrow programmatic terms, the party vigorously supported the principles of the Wilmot Proviso and the approach to the issue of fugitive slaves that had been outlined by Chase in *Jones v. Van Zandt*. Republicans denied any suggestion that they were abolitionists; instead, they explicitly recognized that the Constitution prohibited the federal government from taking direct action against slavery in the Southern states. Instead, the immediate objective of the party was to reduce or eliminate the influence of the slave power on the federal government itself. But Republicans also openly advocated using all constitutional means to undermine the institution of slavery in the South and encourage the reorganization of Southern society in a manner consistent with the free labor principles of the North.[15] The Republicans' rise to prominence in the North would have a profound impact on the Court as it continued to grapple with slavery-related issues in the late 1850s.

CHAPTER 17

The Supreme Court in the Mid-1850s

As sectional relations continued to deteriorate, the dynamic of the Supreme Court changed as well. This change was in part a byproduct of a turnover in personnel. In addition, however, the increasing tension between North and South triggered a change in the attitudes of a number of the justices who had served on the Court since the early 1840s.

The early 1850s brought two new, powerful legal minds to the Court. The first to arrive was Benjamin Robbins Curtis, who came to the Court in late 1851. Curtis was born on November 4, 1809 in Watertown, Massachusetts.[1] He was educated at Harvard University and Harvard Law School, where he studied under Joseph Story. After briefly practicing in Northfield, Massachusetts, where he was admitted to the bar in September 1834, Curtis associated himself with Charles Pelham Curtis, a distant relative who had an established practice in Boston. Except for his interlude on the Supreme Court, Curtis remained in private practice in Boston until his death.

Like orthodox Massachusetts Whigs generally, Curtis believed that slavery was wrong. However, for Curtis, opposition to slavery was always subordinate to his concern for the maintenance of an appropriate relationship between the states of the Union. Curtis's private correspondence reflects his understanding that disputes over slavery represented a clear threat to this relationship. His awareness of this threat is also reflected in his advocacy of a set of closely related legal and political doctrines designed to ease tensions between free states and slave states. In the legal context, Curtis argued that issues of slavery should not be treated differently than other questions of status. Like his political mentor, Webster, who had turned toward accommodationism in the struggle over the Compromise of 1850, Curtis contended that the Northern states should recognize the importance of slavery to the interests of the South and give those interests substantial consideration in slavery-related policy decisions.

As early as 1836, Curtis showed a willingness to defend what he saw as the legitimate interests of slaveowners, arguing unsuccessfully in *Commonwealth v. Aves* that, under state law, a Louisiana slaveowner should retain dominion over a slave voluntarily brought into Massachusetts on a temporary sojourn.[2] However, prior to his appointment to the Court, Curtis's most important public pronouncement on slavery came in a November 1850 speech counseling obedience to the newly strengthened Fugitive Slave Act. The speech argued that the state of Massachusetts and its citizens were bound to respect the act by virtue of the state's decision to accept the constitutional compact, which included the Fugitive Slave Clause. In addition, Curtis made two points that, taken together, summarized his position on the issue of fugitive slaves generally. First, he contended that Massachusetts owed no obligation to escaped slaves:

With the rights of [fugitive slaves] I firmly believe Massachusetts has nothing to do. It is enough for us that they have no right to be *here.* Our peace and safety they have no right to invade; whether they come as fugitives, and being here, act as rebels against our law, or whether they come as armed invaders. Whatever natural rights they have, and I admit those natural rights to their fullest extent, *this* is not the *soil* on which to vindicate them.

In addition, Curtis emphasized the need to seek accommodation with the slave states—a need which he viewed as deriving as much from geography as from the existence of the Union:

Without an obligation to restore fugitives from service, Constitution or no Constitution, we could not expect to live in peace with the slave-holding states. . . . You may break up the Constitution and the Union to-morrow . . . you may do it in any conceivable or inconceivable way; you may draw the geographical line between slave-holding and non-slave-holding *anywhere;* but when we have settled down, they will have their institutions and we shall have ours. One is as much a fact as the other. One engages the interests and feelings and passions of men as much as the other. And how long can we live in peace, side by side, without some provision by compact, to meet this case? Not one year.

This speech clearly reflected that the importance of living in harmony with the slave states was a dominant theme in Curtis's thinking. Not surprisingly, when the local federal marshals sought a formal legal opinion vindicating the constitutionality of the Fugitive Slave Act, Curtis was the man that they asked to produce the opinion.[3]

His rejection of radical antislavery doctrine served Curtis well when Levi Woodbury died on March 4, 1851, creating a vacancy on the Supreme Court. By custom, Woodbury was to be replaced by a New Englander. President Millard Fillmore sought a person who would "combine a vigorous constitution with high moral and intellectual qualifications, a good judicial mind, and such age as gives a prospect of long service."[4] Moreover, as a strong supporter of the Compromise of 1850, Fillmore was unlikely to choose a nominee from the radical antislavery wing of his party. The forty-two-year-old Curtis thus became a logical choice. With the strong endorsement of Daniel Webster, Curtis was given a recess appointment on September 22, 1851, and he was subsequently confirmed by the Senate over the objections of the radical antislavery forces.

Almost immediately after his appointment, Curtis once again found himself embroiled in the controversy over fugitive slaves. In May and June 1851, sitting in his capacity as circuit justice, Curtis joined District Judge Peleg Sprague in presiding over the trial of Robert H. Morris. Morris was a Boston lawyer who was charged with aiding in the escape of Shadrack Minkins, a fugitive slave who was forcibly removed from the custody of federal marshals in February of the same year. At the Morris trial, Free Soil Sen. John P. Hale of New Hampshire, representing Morris, sought to invoke the concept of jury nullification—the idea that, as representatives of the community, jurors could refuse to convict defendants under laws that the jurors believed were unjust. Hale argued to the jurors that, if they believed that the Fugitive Slave Act was unconstitutional, they should vote to acquit.

Curtis firmly rejected this contention, determining that the statute was constitutional and charging the jury that "the jury were to take the law as stated by the court and apply it to the facts which they find." Nonetheless, Richard Henry Dana, who was co-counsel with Hale, later recalled that, despite Curtis's pro-Compromise views, "there was, on [Curtis's] part, an affirmative determination that the trial be conducted with absolute fairness," and that at one point during the trial Curtis made a crucial comment on the weight of the evidence that favored the plaintiff.[5]

Curtis's charge to the jury clearly reflected his concern with the integrity of the process. He admonished the jury that "Morris, as counsel, had the same rights and privileges as other counsel, and his conduct must be presumed right until proven wrong." Noting that the prosecution had emphasized "the greatness of the crime and its consequences," Curtis further warned that "[while] it was true that a great crime had been committed in the very place where justice is administered, which, if repeated may lead to violence and bloodshed; but, though thus serious, they were not to convict an innocent man, but to consider the evidence with vigilance and fairness. The importance of the consequences to the prisoner should on the other hand guard them against light suspicions; they should act only on proper proof." Based on this charge, Morris was acquitted.[6]

In 1854, Curtis faced similar issues in connection with the Anthony Burns affair. The Pierce administration brought federal criminal charges against a number of the more prominent would-be rescuers, contending that they had either interfered with the service of federal process or had intentionally incited others to interfere. Curtis once more joined Peleg Sprague in presiding over the proceedings. In his charge to the grand jury on June 7, Curtis averred that "it is not my province to comment on events which have recently happened." At the same time, the language of the charge made his views crystal clear. Noting the difference of opinion between the North and South on the issue of fugitive slaves, he continued:

Who can fail to see that the government would cease to be a government, if it were to yield obedience to those local opinions? While it stands, all its laws must be faithfully executed, or it becomes the mere tool of the strongest faction of the place and the hour. If forcible resistance to one law be permitted practically to repeal it, the power of the mob would inevitably become one of the constituted authorities of the State, to be used against any law or any man obnoxious to the interests and passions of the worst or most excited part of the community; and the peaceful and the weak would be at the mercy of the violent.[7]

Based on this charge, the grand jury returned an indictment against the Burns protesters. Nonetheless, despite his antipathy toward the protesters and their tactics, on April 12, 1855, Curtis ordered the indictment to be quashed because it was technically deficient.[8]

The antislavery forces of all stripes were understandably pleased with this result. The *New York Times* cheered the end of what it described as "a grand legal farce, which has been admirably played for all purposes of agitation and excitement, but which in itself has been simply ridiculous from beginning to end." The abolitionists who had led the effort to free Burns were more exultant. Celebrating this "victory over Judge Curtis," Higginson insisted that Curtis had yielded to "all the influence of personal presence and all the weight of public opinion in the state" and had been loath to face Theodore Parker in the courtroom on a daily basis. Parker himself made similar allegations, excoriating Curtis in the strongest possible terms.[9]

More likely, Curtis was guided by the same scrupulous regard for legal formalities that had marked his treatment of the *Morris* case in 1851. Indeed, the attempt to rescue Burns was in principle no different than the more successful effort to prevent the rendition of Shadrach Minkins. In both cases, Curtis demonstrated that his commitment to distinctively legal analysis was more important in his hierarchy of values than his views on the merits of questions related to slavery. Put another way, by 1856 Curtis was probably the justice who was most likely to provide a dispassionate analysis of the legal issues related to the sectional conflict.

In 1853, the Southern contingent on the Supreme Court was strengthened by the arrival of John Archibald Campbell of Alabama, the first Southern justice to be appointed since the decision in *Prigg*.[10] Campbell was born on June 24, 1811, the first child of a prominent family that owned a plantation in Wilkes County, Georgia. At an early age it became clear that Campbell was intellectually gifted. Thus, after only one year at the local school, at the age of eleven he was sent to Athens, Georgia, to study. There he attended a grammar school for one year before entering Franklin College in 1823, graduating in June 1825 with the first honors in his class.

After financial difficulties forced him to abandon his dream of a military career, Campbell decided to become a lawyer. In January 1829, he moved to St. Andrews, Florida, to read law with his uncle, John Clark. Campbell rapidly completed his studies and returned to Georgia, gaining admittance to the bar at the age of eighteen. Seeking better career opportunities, Campbell relocated to Montgomery, Alabama, in March 1830, where he soon established a reputation as one of the ablest lawyers in the state. In both 1836 and 1852, he was offered positions on the Alabama Supreme Court. In each case, he declined.

When John McKinley died on July 19, 1852, the slavery issue played a significant role in determining his successor. President Millard Fillmore first nominated Edward A. Bradford of Louisiana, but the Senate adjourned without considering the nomination. Amidst a widespread belief that Bradford could not be confirmed, Fillmore then turned to Sen. George E. Badger of North Carolina. This nomination was defeated in part because Badger had supported the Wilmot Proviso. In the final days of his presidency, Fillmore next chose William C. Micou of Louisiana, but the Senate—dominated by Democrats—was in no mood to confirm the nominee of a lame duck Whig. After Democrat Franklin Pierce assumed office in March 1853, he nominated Campbell to succeed McKinley on the joint recommendation of Democratic Justice John Catron of Tennessee and Whig Justice Benjamin Robbins Curtis of Massachusetts.[11]

The recommendation of the two sitting justices reflected the uniformly held opinion of Campbell's legal talents. One newspaper compared him favorably with Joseph Story, and even a publication that strongly disagreed with Campbell's political views conceded that "he is chock full of talent, genius, industry and energy. . . . For the last ten years, he has been deservedly at the head of the Alabama Bar . . . exceedingly popular, and as a jurist and a man commands the respect and confidence of everyone."[12] Nonetheless, the issue of slavery created some controversy. Unlike the Badger nomination, however, the concerns about Campbell were raised by Northern antislavery Whigs.

The source of these concerns was the ideological and legal positions that Campbell had expressed both publicly and privately in the years immediately preceding his nomination to the Court. Although his background and temperament differed significantly from Peter Daniel, Campbell was no less committed to the protection of Southern interests. Indeed, unlike Daniel and Taney, who were conventional Jacksonian Democrats at the time that they were nominated to serve on the Court, Campbell was a self-identified "Southern man," whose loyalty to sectional interests dominated his political worldview.

Campbell feared that many northern Democratic politicians would seek to capitalize on rising antislavery sentiment to advance their personal careers. Thus, in the run-up to the elections of 1848, Campbell professed "indifference to the election of any Democrat [from] north of the Potomac" and believed (incorrectly, as proven by subsequent events) that Zachary Taylor—a Whig— was the best available presidential candidate because, as a Southern slaveholder, Taylor would presumably be more sympathetic to Southern interests.[13]

In addition, Campbell was alarmed by the possible implications of the Mexican War. He opposed territorial acquisitions from Mexico, because in his view the land was unsuitable for exploitation through slave labor. Thus he believed that such acquisitions would inevitably destabilize the balance of power in favor of the North. Recognizing that territorial expansion was probably inevitable, as a second choice Campbell believed that either the treaty of cession or congressional action should guarantee slaveowners the right to bring their slaves into any newly acquired territory. Thus, in a letter to Calhoun, he opined that "Slavery is the central point about which Southern Society is formed. It was so understood at the formation of the Constitution. It has been dealt with by the country since in the same spirit. This territory is the fruit of common expenditure and toil. We *must* insist that for the future the same spirit shall be maintained. We *must* have an organization of the territory that admits us as equals."

At the same time, however, in 1848 Campbell also privately expressed the view that Congress was not required by the Constitution to allow slavery in the territories. Instead, he simply contended that slavery should be allowed as a matter of policy.[14]

However, Campbell's legal thought appears to have been radicalized by the crisis of 1850. As a delegate to the Nashville Convention of 1850, he drafted the resolutions which embraced the common property doctrine and declared that

every act of the federal government which places any portion of the property lawfully held in the States of the Union out of the protection of the federal government, or which discriminates in the nature and extent of the protection to be given to different species of property, or which impairs the title of the citizen in any of the territories of the Union, without affording just compensation, is a plain and palpable violation of the obligations of the government, and is contrary to the spirit and meaning of the constitution of the United States.

Even at this stage, however, Campbell was apparently not entirely inflexible on this issue. Despite their insistence on the unconstitutionality of restrictions on slavery in the territories, the resolutions also expressed a willingness to accept the extension of the Missouri Compromise line in order to preserve sectional harmony.[15]

"The Rights of the Slave States," published in 1851, provides a more complete exposition of Campbell's views on the sectional conflict. There Campbell argued that the most important danger to the South lay in what he viewed as the rising tide of abolition in the North, contending that "the abolition of the slave trade and slavery in the District of Columbia, the Missouri and Oregon restrictions, and the dishonest settlement of the questions in regard to the Mexican conquests, are of themselves nothing, compared with the engrossing and pervading evil of anti-slavery agitation." Nonetheless, while observing that he would have "greatly preferred another field for the contest," he also asserted that the struggle over slavery in the territories acquired in the Mexican War "necessarily involved the fate of our institutions." Campbell decried the refusal of the North to recognize the principle that "slavery, as an institution of property, in the States, [is] entitled to the same rank, privilege and protection as every other institution of property" and declared that "the experiment of the fugitive evinces that [Northerners] cannot fulfill their duties under the Constitution." Finally, in addition to calling for Southern unity, Campbell also strongly defended the right to secession, asserting that "the union of twenty willing States, and eleven reluctant or subjugated ones, would be such a commentary upon our principles of self-government, that [not even committed Whigs] could endure the hideous record."[16]

Antislavery politicians were understandably chagrined by the expression of sentiments such as these from a nominee to the Supreme Court. However, even if they had been determined to oppose a nominee with such sterling credentials, they lacked the political power to block Campbell's confirmation by the Senate. Thus, the opponents of slavery could only cling to the hope expressed by the *New York Times*:

Past experience has shown that, once placed [on the Supreme Court] for life, the professions of the partisan soon give place to the convictions and sense of high responsibilities of the jurist. . . . [Wayne and McLean], the highest-toned Federalists on the Bench have been taken from the Democratic ranks, and it will be strange if the views of a gentleman of first-rate legal talent, like Mr. Campbell should prove less conservative.[17]

Even in 1853, with respect to slavery-related issues this prediction rested more on hope than on logic. Campbell was indeed deeply committed to the conventions of legal analysis. At the same time, however, he was equally committed to a constitutional theory that protected the rights of the Southern states in general and slaveowners in particular. Further, he believed that this constitutional theory was entirely consistent with basic principles of legal analysis. Moreover, by 1856, Campbell's attachment to these views can only have been strengthened by the bitter dispute over the Kansas-Nebraska Act and the meteoric rise of the Republican Party.

To be sure, as a judge, Campbell did not uniformly support the more radical elements of the proslavery movement. For example, sitting on circuit in New Orleans in 1854, he vigorously attacked "filibustering" expeditions designed in part to add slaveholding territories such as Cuba to the United States. In his jury charge, Campbell harshly criticized these expeditions as violative of the neutrality laws, and reminded Southerners that Northerners could only be expected to fulfill their obligations under the Fugitive Slave Laws if the Southerners in turn lived up to their obligations under federal law.[18] However, on the core issue of slavery in the territories, a committed Southern sectionalist such as Campbell was inevitably drawn to the position that the Constitution protected Southern rights.

Changes in personnel were not the only factors that created a shift in the Court's attitude. The same political forces that increased the sectionalization of American politics in the late 1840s and 1850s also had an impact on the views of the justices who were holdovers from the Court that had decided *Prigg.* The transformation of Peter V. Daniel provides the most dramatic example of this impact.

Although he was always a strong defender of slavery and Southern interests, prior to 1845 Daniel's sectionalist impulses were tempered by his allegiance to the national Democratic Party. Daniel's political alliance with Martin Van Buren was a model of bisectional cooperation, and his opinion in *Prigg,* while undoubtedly pro-Southern, was relatively moderate in tone. Moreover, Daniel was one of the few Southern Democrats who opposed the movement for the annexation of Texas, viewing it as a Calhounite conspiracy.

At the same time, however, Daniel took offense to Northerners who opposed annexation on the grounds that the addition of Texas would benefit the slave states. In 1844, he expressed his outrage to Van Buren in the strongest terms:

Can anything be more galling to the spirit of honorable men than to be told that it is enough to justify the condemnation of any measure, that its effect may be the promotion of their peculiar interests and welfare: that it may prove advantageous to the holders of slave property? Are we to be placed under the permanent and unrelenting ban of the Federal Government? To be held as less than the *equals* of our miscalled *fellow citizens?* To be regarded as the plague-spot upon our nation, and then required by our oppressors and revilers to shout for our *blessed Union?* A blessed Union indeed it would be upon such terms. No—No—The most temperate among us, would not hesitate to decide, if things have come or are to come to this complexion, to go with our imputed blemishes, our crimes and defilements, apart to ourselves; and leave these exclusively beautiful and moral and clean and immaculate, to their own purity.[19]

The dispute over the Wilmot Proviso crystallized Daniel's outrage. As early as 1845, Daniel privately expressed the view that federal legislation explicitly limiting the right of slaveowners to bring slaves into the territories would be grounds for secession. Nonetheless, similar to many like-minded Southerners, he also affirmed his willingness to accept the general idea of geographical division as a workable compromise. This position changed two years later, after the New York State Democratic Convention adopted a resolution supporting the position that slavery should be outlawed in all of the territory that had been obtained from Mexico. Daniel then wrote to Van Buren seeking clarification of the former president's position on this issue. When Van Buren replied evasively, Daniel (whose wife had recently died from a stroke) responded that, if Van Buren in fact supported the Wilmot Proviso,

I shall have lived to witness a development that even the great and overwhelming and stunning calamity that has come upon me cannot prevent me from contemplating with deep sorrow and alarm. I shall have been constrained to perceive on the part of those, on whom of all the public men in this nation I imposed the greatest trust, what my deliberate convictions compel me to view as the overthrow of the great national compact; as the extreme of injury and oppression in its most galling form, because it declares to me that I am not regarded as an equal.[20]

Daniel's mortification can only have been magnified in 1848, when Van Buren became the presidential candidate of the Free Soil Party.

The impact of Daniel's sense of personal betrayal on the subsequent evolution of his political thought cannot be reliably assessed. What is clear is that, beginning in the late 1840s, Daniel associated all things Northern with the antislavery movement, and hated the North with an obsessive fury that he had hitherto reserved for his Whig political enemies. He refused even to venture north of the Delaware River and became indifferent to the preservation of the Union itself. Thus, when in his presence a great-nephew made a favorable comment regarding those who took antislavery positions, Daniel replied simply, "I fear those people are very wicked." In short, even before the political cataclysm engendered by the dispute over the Kansas-Nebraska Act, Daniel had become, in the words of Don E. Fehrenbacher, "a brooding, proslavery fanatic."[21]

Daniel was not the only Southern holdover who had become increasingly agitated by the dispute over the Wilmot Proviso and the Kansas-Nebraska Act. Privately, Taney complained bitterly about "Northern insult and Northern aggression."[22] While making no such explicit declaration, the normally moderate Wayne and Catron were also no doubt disturbed by the increasing Northern hostility toward the South and the rise of the Republican Party.

Analogous forces had a quite different impact on the approach of John McLean. As the election of 1856 approached, McLean would be influenced not only by his jurisprudential philosophy and lifelong opposition to slavery but also by the exigencies of his ongoing pursuit of the presidency. As early as 1832, McLean had flirted with the idea of running as the candidate of the Anti-Masonic Party. However, prior to the political realignment of the early 1850s, he became closely associated with the Whigs, and was a major factor in the early maneuvering for the Whig nomination for the election of 1848.[23]

During that campaign, McLean began with strong support among Northern Whigs. Thus, one of his primary goals was to draw Southern party members to his banner. In making his case for the nomination, McLean presented himself as a nonideological reform candidate, juxtaposing his candidacy with that of professional politicians such as Clay and Webster. The emergence of the Wilmot Proviso as a major national issue played a significant role in undermining this strategy. Once the question of slavery in the territories assumed such prominence, Southern Whigs were unlikely to support a person such as McLean, whose antislavery credentials were already well established.

After it became clear that he would not become the Whig candidate, many prominent adherents to the Free Soil movement sought to enlist McLean as the candidate of their party. With the Wilmot Proviso being the primary focus of the dispute over slavery in the late 1840s, even radical Free Soilers saw McLean's views as basically consistent with Free Soil doctrine. While his theoretical framework differed from that of most party members, McLean agreed that slavery could not consitutionally be introduced into territories prior to the adoption of a state constitution drafted at the time of admission to the Union.[24] However, understanding that the Free Soil candidate had no real chance to win the election in 1848, McLean himself demurred. He hoped to make another strong run for the Whig nomination in 1852, and believed that running on the Free Soil ticket in 1848 would undermine such a campaign.

Despite his ambitions, McLean never emerged as a serious contender for the nomination in 1852. By 1856, the American political landscape had changed dramatically. The Whig Party had disintegrated, and both the nativist Know-Nothings and antislavery Republicans were seeking to fill the resulting vacuum and emerge as the primary opposition to the Democrats. McLean first courted the Know-Nothings, characterizing nativism as a much-needed reform movement. When Millard Fillmore was nominated as the Know-Nothing candidate in February 1856, McLean and his supporters turned to the Republican Party as the vehicle to advance his presidential ambitions. He and John Fremont soon emerged as the primary contenders for the 1856 Republican nomination.[25]

The tactical problem that confronted McLean and his supporters in 1856 was quite different from that which they had faced in his pursuit of the Whig nomination in 1848. Rather than appealing to Southerners, McLean's task in 1856 was to convince some elements of the Republican Party that his antislavery views were sufficiently radical to merit their support. A number of McLean's opponents asserted (with some justification) that his embrace of Republicanism was as much a matter of convenience as conviction. For example, Republican Sen. Benjamin F. Wade privately complained that "if he is with us at all it is but timidly and feebly." Radicals—whose distaste for the Fugitive Slave Laws of 1793 and 1850 was often as intense as their opposition to the expansion of slavery into the territories—were particularly disturbed by McLean's conclusion that Congress did in fact have authority to adopt legislation enforcing the Fugitive Slave Clause. Thus, McLean's consistent willingness to enforce the provisions of the federal statutes led one Ohio Republican to assert that McLean "has *no sentiment* or *sympathy* with the *principle of universal Liberty.*"[26]

Prior to 1856, some Republicans were also dissatisfied with McLean's position on the Kansas-Nebraska Act and its aftermath. In 1847, he had propounded a view that in essence turned the Southern theory of nonintervention on its head. His argument began with the basic premise of *Somerset,* which held that legally, slavery could not exist in the absence of positive law recognizing the relationship. McLean then contended that Congress lacked the constitutional power to establish slavery in the territories held by the federal government. Therefore, under this theory, slaves could not be held in those territories prior to statehood.[27]

Some Republicans objected that this theory did not establish the power of Congress to pass legislation affirmatively prohibiting slavery in the territories.[28] Indeed, the argument might be taken to imply that Congress lacked such authority, thereby undercutting the contention that Southerners had broken a solemn pledge when they engineered the repeal of the Missouri Compromise. McLean's Republican critics also faulted him for his failure to condemn the tactics employed by the proslavery forces in Kansas. Seeking to blunt these objections, his supporters urged McLean to denounce the repeal of the Missouri Compromise in the strongest terms.

Dred Scott v. Sandford would provide McLean with a very public forum to deliver just such a denunciation. However, for a time it seemed that he might first be required to confront the issue of fugitive slaves once again, as the case of Sherman Booth worked its way to the Supreme Court.

CHAPTER 18

Ableman v. Booth, Part 1
Northern Nullification

For understandable reasons, studies of the Supreme Court's role in the sectional crisis of the mid-1850s generally focus most of their attention on the Court's treatment of the territorial and citizenship issues in *Dred Scott v. Sandford.* However, prior to 1856, the dispute that gave rise to *Dred Scott* had received almost no national attention. By contrast, the conflict that eventually led to the decision in *Ableman v. Booth* had a much higher national profile.

The evolution of this conflict reflected the radicalization of Northern public opinion on the fugitive slave issue in the 1850s. The prelude to the consideration of *Ableman* began prosaically when a slave, Joshua Glover, escaped from Benoni S. Garland, his master in Missouri. Glover then came to live and work in Racine, Wisconsin, in 1852.[1] After receiving the requisite authorization from United States District Judge Andrew G. Miller, on Friday, March 10, 1854—less than a week after the Senate passed the Kansas-Nebraska Act—Garland came to Glover's home in Racine and, with the aid of two deputy United States marshals and four assistants, captured Glover after a struggle and brought him to the county jail in Milwaukee. Glover was held in the jail pursuant to a Wisconsin statute that required county jails to provide facilities to detain persons held under federal law.

On March 11, a large group of residents gathered in Racine to protest Glover's capture. A committee was chosen to draft resolutions. Among other things, these resolutions condemned the "kidnapping" of Glover, demanded that he receive a trial by jury, and, asserting that the Kansas-Nebraska Act had repealed "all compromises heretofore adopted by the Congress of the United States," characterized the "Slavecatching law of 1850" as "disgraceful and *also repealed.*" Copies of the resolutions were sent by telegraph to Sherman M. Booth, an abolitionist newspaper editor in Milwaukee. After first printing a run of inflammatory handbills, Booth rode through the streets of Milwaukee shouting "a man's liberty is at stake!" and also reportedly exhorting "freemen to the rescue!"[2]

By 2:30 P.M., a crowd of several thousand people had gathered outside the jail where Glover was being detained. The crowd passed resolutions which, among other things, demanded that Glover receive a trial by jury. In addition, a vigilance committee was appointed. In the interim, attorneys who had been contacted by Booth persuaded a local circuit judge to issue a writ of habeas corpus, demanding that those who held Glover in custody bring him before the judge and justify the decision to hold Glover. The writ initially was served on Sheriff Herman Page, the county official who had charge of the jail. Page, however, responded that, while Glover was in the county jail, he was not in Page's custody.

The attorneys then returned to the circuit judge and persuaded him to issue a second writ of habeas corpus, this time directed at Deputy Federal Marshal Charles Cotton, who had charge of Glover. On instructions from Judge Miller, Cotton ignored the writ. Miller also informed the representatives of the protesters that a hearing on Glover's status would be held on Monday morning at ten o'clock, and that "no power on earth could take Glover from his jurisdiction."[3] Soon thereafter, one hundred men arrived on a steamboat from Racine and joined the crowd at the jail, which was addressed by Booth and other speakers, all of whom stressed the necessity of opposing the enforcement of the Fugitive Slave Law, but also counseled the crowd against breaking the law.

Booth and the remainder of the vigilance committee then left to take tea. In their absence, the crowd demanded that the jailer surrender the keys to the jail. When the jailer refused, the crowd broke down the door with pickaxes and an improvised battering ram. They led Glover from the courthouse and, with Booth at his side, Glover was taken in a buggy to the underground railway station in Waukesha, from whence he escaped to Canada.

Soon after Glover escaped, Garland and the officials who had originally participated in the capture of Joshua Glover were charged by the sheriff of Racine county with assault and battery, and Garland was jailed. Judge Miller ordered Garland freed on a writ of habeas corpus, concluding that Garland "was aiding the marshal in the service of a warrant, at the marshal's request." Miller's anger at the entire sequence of events was apparent from the language of his opinion, in which he declared that "I view this [arrest] warrant . . . to have been obtained by an officious intermeddler, for the same purpose as the habeas corpus, to effect the rescue of the fugitive Glover" and "I cannot but consider the imprisonment of [Garland], or of the marshal [who was also named in the warrant] a greater outrage than the rescue."[4]

United States District Attorney John R. Sharpstein then lodged criminal complaints against Booth and nine other leaders of the Glover rescue, alleging that they had violated the Fugitive Slave Act by aiding Glover in his escape from custody. When Booth was brought for arraignment before Winfred Smith, a commissioner for the federal district court, bail was set at two thousand dollars. Booth initially posted bail through a surety; however, on May 26, at Booth's own request, the surety delivered him to the federal authorities, and Booth was remanded to the county jail in Milwaukee.

By returning to the custody of the commissioner, Booth placed himself in a position to challenge the constitutionality of the Fugitive Slave Act of 1850 in state court. On May 27, he successfully petitioned Justice Abram D. Smith of the Wisconsin Supreme Court for a writ of habeas corpus. Fearing that ignoring the writ might provoke another confrontation with the citizenry of Milwaukee, Sharpstein chose instead to appear before Justice Smith and mount a defense at a hearing on May 29.

At the hearing, Booth was represented by Byron Paine, an abolitionist attorney. Paine's argument first addressed and rejected the claim that the state courts should not under any circumstances intervene to free a person who was in federal custody. In making this argument, Paine relied heavily on the justification for nullification initially articulated in the 1790s by Thomas Jefferson in the Virginia and Kentucky Resolutions. Paine declared that "when the evil spirits of usurpation and oppression enter into and possess the Federal Power, the States may interpose with such powers as they have to arrest the progress of the evil." Apparently seeking to distance himself from the position taken by South Carolina during the nullification crisis of the early 1830s, Paine also contended that "whatever objections might be urged against the actual exercise of the right of resistance by the legislative and executive departments of the State, cannot be urged with equal force against the actions of its Judiciary." He concluded by asserting that "even if we have no judicial precedents in favor of the right of the States to protect their people against tyranny and usurpation, it is time such a precedent should be made."[5]

Turning to the merits, Paine relied on the standard antislavery critiques of the Fugitive Slave Act. He argued that Congress lacked constitutional authority to pass enforcement legislation, that the statute unconstitutionally delegated judicial authority to commissioners, and that the procedures mandated by the statute violated the Bill of Rights. Paine also excoriated the *Prigg* Court, condemning what he described as "the violence they . . . perpetrate[d] on the established rules of construction" and contending that Story "labor[ed] to arrive at the construction as shall best suit the convenience and accomplish the purpose of the slave-owners."[6]

Paine could not have found a more sympathetic ear for his arguments. On June 7, Justice Smith issued a lengthy opinion which concluded that Booth should be released from federal custody. Smith began his opinion by confronting the assertion that state courts lacked the authority to intervene in favor of a person who was in federal custody. His response to this argument was twofold. First, he contended that "every citizen has a right to call upon the state authorities for protection" and that "it is the duty of the judicial officer, when applied to, to see that no citizen is imprisoned within the limits of the state . . . except by proper legal and constitutional authority." In addition, Smith noted that, while he might have been reluctant to order the release of a prisoner from the custody of a federal judge, he had no such hesitation about asserting his authority over federal commissioners, whom Smith characterized as "subordinate and irresponsible functionaries, holding their office at the will of the federal courts."[7]

Turning to the merits of the habeas petition, Smith initially argued that the arrest warrant under which Booth was being held was fatally defective because it failed to allege that Garland had claimed Glover, and that Booth was entitled to be released for that reason alone. In addition, describing the state courts as "sentinel[s] to guard the outposts as well as . . . citadel[s] of the great principles which [the Constitution] was intended to declare, secure and perpetuate" and proclaiming a duty "to interpose a resistance . . . to every assumption of power on the part of the general government, which is not expressly granted or necessarily implied in the federal constitution,"[8] Smith also mounted a detailed assault on the constitutionality of the Fugitive Slave Act.

The bulk of the opinion focused on the contention that Congress lacked authority to provide a mechanism for the enforcement of the Fugitive Slave Clause. Smith began by decrying increases in federal power generally, declaring that "the last hope of free representative and federative government rests with the states. Increase of influence and patronage on the part of the federal government naturally leads to consolidation, consolidation to despotism and ultimate anarchy, dissolution and all its attendant evils." After reviewing the sparse discussions of the fugitive slave issue during the drafting and ratification process, he juxtaposed the Fugitive Slave Clause with the Full Faith and Credit Clause, with its explicit grant of power to Congress, concluding that there was not "one word of grant, or one word from which a grant [of power to legislate with respect to fugitive slaves] may be inferred or implied" and also that "from the known temper and scruples of the national convention, we may safely affirm, that had it been asked it would not have been granted, and had it been granted, no union could have been formed upon such a basis."[9]

Smith also concluded that the Fugitive Slave Act ran afoul of the procedural requirements outlined in the Bill of Rights. He distinguished sharply between proceedings to extradite fugitives from justice and efforts to recover fugitive slaves, asserting that in the former, "judicial proceedings have already been commenced, and [extradition] is but a species of process to bring the defendant into court," while the Fugitive Slave Clause "contemplates a judicial determination of the lawfulness of the *claim* which may be made."[10] The latter, he insisted, required the full panoply of protections normally associated with due process of law, including a trial by jury.

Smith conceded that his conclusions were inconsistent with the views expressed by the Supreme Court in *Prigg* and its progeny. At this stage, however, he was not defying the Court's authority. Instead, Smith simply urged the Court to revisit its holding in *Prigg* in view of the antipathy toward the Fugitive Slave Act in the North and what Smith saw as the deficiencies in the reasoning of Justice Story's opinion in *Prigg* itself.[11]

Justice Smith's decision was noted widely, and, not surprisingly, hailed as a great victory by abolitionists and radical elements of the more mainstream antislavery movement. The *National Era,* for example, expressed the hope that "this example of judicial independence and integrity [will be] followed in all the State Courts."[12] However, the legal battle in Wisconsin was still in its early stages. Sharpstein, acting on Ableman's behalf, quickly petitioned the full Wisconsin Supreme Court for a writ of certiorari to review the order to release Booth. When the court agreed to hear the case, Sharpstein enlisted the services of Edward G. Ryan, a distinguished Wisconsin attorney, to represent the federal government.

Ryan mounted a far more sophisticated defense of the federal government's position than Sharpstein had originally presented before Justice Smith. Nonetheless, on July 19, in *In re Sherman M. Booth* (*Booth I*), the full court affirmed the order mandating Booth's release. Justice Smith delivered a long opinion reaffirming the views that he had expressed on June 7 in even more emphatic terms. Chief Justice Edward V. Whiton and Justice Samuel Crawford joined Smith in concluding that being held under the authority of a commissioner was not equivalent to being under the jurisdiction of a federal court, and that therefore the state courts could appropriately issue a writ of habeas corpus in Booth's case. They also agreed that the warrant under which Booth was held was fatally defective.[13] By contrast, the court was deeply divided on the question of the constitutionality of the Fugitive Slave Act.

While agreeing with Smith that the statute was unconstitutional, Chief Justice Whiton emphasized different considerations. Unlike Smith, who focused primarily on the argument that Congress lacked authority to pass *any* enforcement legislation, Whiton relied entirely on two other contentions: that the statute unconstitutionally delegated federal judicial power to commissioners, and that it denied alleged fugitives what Whiton characterized as their constitutionally protected right to a trial by jury.

Whiton asserted that, since the Fugitive Slave Act of 1793 had not provided for the appointment of federal commissioners, the *Prigg* majority had not explicitly passed on the first point. By contrast, Whiton conceded that the jury trial argument had been implicitly rejected when the Court upheld the constitutionality of the 1793 statute in *Prigg* and *Van Zandt*. At the same time, he observed that the specific issue before the Court in *Prigg* was the constitutionality of Pennsylvania's Personal Liberty Law and declared that "it would be most unjust to [the Supreme] court to hold that it has decided questions which its judges have not even discussed, and which have not even been before it for adjudication."[14]

Crawford, on the other hand, was unpersuaded by the arguments against the constitutionality of the Fugitive Slave Act. For constitutional purposes, he saw the reliance on commissioners in the 1850 statute as indistinguishable from the use of state officials that the Supreme Court had addressed in *Prigg*. While observing that as an original matter he would have held that the states and the federal government possessed concurrent authority to enforce the Fugitive Slave Clause, he contended that the constitutional issues surrounding the Fugitive Slave Act of 1850 had been "definitively settled" by *Prigg* and its progeny.[15]

Despite Crawford's dissent, the order freeing Booth from the custody of the commissioner was affirmed. Not surprisingly, abolitionists were jubilant about the decision. Predicting that the case would ultimately find its way to the United States Supreme Court, the New York *Evangelist* optimistically speculated that "we have good reasons for expecting that if the decision of the Supreme Court can be procured, it will make a decided rent in this oppressive and cruel, if not wholly unconstitutional law." The Boston *Commonwealth* was more cautious, but nonetheless upbeat. On the one hand, the *Commonwealth* described the Supreme Court as "the agent of the slaveholding power, [which] must be expected to conform in its decisions to the will of that power." But the same newspaper hailed *Booth I* as the "decision of a highly respectable state court . . . evidence of a tendency towards a healthy state on this subject" and predicted that "before long the Northern courts generally will come to the same conclusion; and then, in the face of the mass of judicial opinion in the largest section of the country, the [fugitive slave law] cannot stand, but must be materially modified or repealed."[16]

It soon became clear, however, that the state court's decision in *Booth I* would be only an early skirmish in the legal conflict set in motion by the escape of Joshua Glover. On September 11, noting that similar clashes between state and federal authorities had occurred in other states, United States Attorney General Caleb Cushing of Massachusetts wrote that he had decided that the decision should be appealed to the Supreme Court. After the papers were filed, Chief Justice Roger Brooke Taney issued a writ of error to the Wisconsin Supreme Court, and the state court complied with the demands of the writ, providing a copy of the record to the Court.[17]

In the interim, it had also become clear that, despite its doctrinal and symbolic importance, the decision in *Booth I* had not materially changed the legal situation faced by Booth. On Saturday, July 8, even before the Wisconsin Supreme Court had rendered its decision, a federal grand jury returned an indictment against Booth for aiding and abetting the escape of Joshua Glover. The grand jury also indicted John Ryecraft and John Messenger for their roles in the affair. On July 10, Judge Miller himself issued arrest warrants based on the indictments. Booth was promptly rearrested on the basis of these warrants.

Now represented by James H. Paine, the father of Byron Paine, Booth once again petitioned the Wisconsin Supreme Court for a writ of habeas corpus. However, in *Ex Parte Sherman M. Booth* (*Booth II*), the state supreme court unanimously declined to issue the writ. In his concurring opinion, Justice Abram Smith explained the difference between the two cases, observing that "in [*Booth I,* Booth] was held under the process of an officer who had no power to hear and determine upon the validity of the law, or the allegations of the defendant against its validity. But now he is held under process of . . . a judicial tribunal, having full power and authority to decide upon all the questions and allegations presented in his behalf."[18] Under those circumstances, the court reasoned, considerations of comity required that the action in the federal court be allowed to proceed to its conclusion without interference from a state court.

Southerners and their allies were greatly relieved by the decision in *Booth II.* A correspondent of the *Washington Union,* the official organ of the administration of President Franklin Pierce, praised the Wisconsin Supreme Court for recognizing the exclusive jurisdiction of the federal courts to deal with cases arising under the Fugitive Slave Law. Not surprisingly, those who had supported the decision in *Booth I* took a quite different view. On July 15, the *Milwaukee News* complained that "it was easy to sit on the bench and solemnly decide the [Fugitive Slave Act was] unconstitutional and void. . . . But, when . . . Booth applies for the practical fruits of this solemn adjudication in his favor, the two judges are seized with a spasm of 'comity.' Although the law is wholly void, they can't venture to grant a *writ of habeas corpus!* The unhappy victim must lie in prison as an act of courtesy."[19]

Because Booth was ill, Ryecraft was tried alone in November 1854. Edward Ryan once again represented the federal government. Defending Ryecraft, attorneys George Lakin and Michael Steever appealed to the higher law doctrine and also insisted that the burden was on the prosecution to plead and prove that Glover had in fact been a slave. In addition, like the defense in the *Morris* case in 1851, Lakin and Steever contended that the jury had the right to determine the law as well as the facts.[20]

Judge Miller's charge to the jury on November 18 rejected these contentions and also left no doubt regarding his views about both Ryecraft's guilt and the actions of those who had broken into the jail and freed Glover more generally. Miller began by defending not only the constitutionality of the Fugitive Slave Act of 1850 but also the policy underlying the law, asserting that it was "effective in carrying out the provisions of the constitution [and] is equally so in protecting free colored persons from secret or criminal deportation." He evinced nothing but disdain for the appeal to the higher law doctrine, declaring "if a man willfully violates the laws of his country by the commission of an offense against those laws, he comes with a poor grace before a jury of honest men, sworn to render a true verdict according to evidence, with a plea of 'higher law' or 'rights of conscience.'" Miller also brushed aside the assertion that the members of the jury could act on their own independent interpretation of the law, stating simply that "under the judicial system of the United States, [the members of the jury] take the law from the court in all cases both civil and criminal whether it comports with their individual opinions or not."[21]

Turning to the facts of the case, Miller stated flatly that the testimony demonstrated that Ryecraft had been a member of the vigilance committee and that he was "at the jail, working and assisting to break the door of the jail-yard and the door of the jail."[22] Miller also decried the actions of the members of the committee in inciting the crowd by describing Garland and the deputy marshals as "kidnappers":

If I had ordered the marshal to bring up Glover for hearing, at that time, it certainly could not have been done. Under the cry of kidnapper the rescue would have been effected by the excited crowd, and the personal safety of the officer imperiled. An offer to the judge of protection would be of little avail, after a mob was got up by the cry of rescue, and inflamed by that of kidnapper. . . . The committee was probably the primary cause of that outrage and, if so, each member of it is responsible for the escape.[23]

Against the background of this charge, the jury convicted Ryecraft on November 19.

Despite Ryecraft's conviction, the assertion that the prosecution was required to plead and prove the fact that Glover was a slave in an action under the Fugitive Slave Act created some uneasiness among the representatives of the federal government. Accordingly, in December, prior to bringing Booth to

trial, prosecutors voluntarily dismissed the indictment against Booth and rein-
dicted him, this time adding a count charging him with obstructing, resisting,
and opposing the execution of federal process more generally. Booth struck
back by filing complaints for false imprisonment in state court against both
Miller and Sharpstein, forcing them to post bail in order to avoid being taken
into custody.[24]

The trial of Booth himself took place in a crowded Milwaukee courtroom
from January 10 through January 13, 1855. Despite Miller's earlier ruling that issues of law were matters for the judge rather than the jury, Paine's summation
appealed openly to the concept of jury nullification—the idea that, if necessary
to reach a just result, jurors were free to ignore the strictures of positive law and
vote their consciences. Analogizing the Glover escape to the rescue of Peter
from Herod's prison by an angel, Paine identified the slave power as Herod and
asserted that "men are now indicted for imitating Angels of God" and also proclaimed that "I charge upon this prosecution that they have come into court
before you and confessed that they are engaged in the execution of an infamous
law."[25]

Miller, however, was having none of it. Echoing Justice Curtis's rejection of
jury nullification in the *Morris* case, Miller sternly warned the jurors that they
would be committing "moral perjury" if they disregarded his instructions on
the law, and also reiterated his view that the government was not required to
prove that Glover had in fact been a slave. In addition, Miller commented that
the testimony of the witnesses established a clear case of resistance and opposition to process.[26] Based on this charge, the jury convicted Booth after only
eight hours of deliberations. Booth was not, however, found guilty on all counts
of the indictment; instead, the jury concluded only that he was guilty of aiding
and abetting the escape of Joshua Glover from the custody of the deputy marshals. Moreover, the jurors also appended a statement declaring their solidarity
with Booth:

Resolved, that while we feel ourselves bound by a solemn oath to perform a most painful
duty, in declaring the defendant guilty of the above charge and thus making him liable
to the penalties of a most cruel and odious law, yet at the same time, in so doing we declare that he performed a *most noble, benevolent and humane act* and we thus record
our condemnation of the Fugitive Slave law, and earnestly commend him to the
clemency of the court.[27]

Based on the verdict, after denying defense motions for a new trial, on January
23 Miller sentenced Booth to thirty days imprisonment in the county jail and
a fine of $1,000, and Ryecraft to a term of ten days in jail and a fine of $200.

Assessments of the verdict against Booth and Ryecraft differed widely. Some saw the decision as a victory for the principle of the rule of law. For example, the *Milwaukee News* declared that

we rejoice at this verdict, not because this defendant is made to suffer, but because it is calculated to teach men a fact which they have been too prone to forget, that we live under a government of law, that our institutions of freedom rest upon the observance of law, that the rampant spirit of mob law shall not be tolerated with impunity in the free State of Wisconsin, that the doctrine of a higher law to justify the disregard of the allegiance which each citizen owes to his country is a false doctrine, and he who attempts to put it into operation is taking a straight road and a short one to the penitentiary.[28]

Not surprisingly, antislavery activists had a quite different view, characterizing Booth in particular as a martyr to the cause who was being punished unjustly. On February 1, the New York *Independent* proposed that its readers each contribute one dollar to a fund that would pay Booth's fine. Contributors to the fund included a number of prominent antislavery members of Congress.[29]

Subsequent events soon raised the profile of the case still further. Seeking to have their clients freed from custody, on January 26 the attorneys for Booth and Ryecraft once again petitioned the Wisconsin Supreme Court for writs of habeas corpus. The following day, the court granted the petition, and the writs were served on both Ableman and Samuel Conover, the sheriff of the county jail where the two convicted activists were being held. While specifically declining to acknowledge the jurisdiction of the court, Ableman replied that he could not produce Booth and Ryecraft because they were now in the custody of the county sheriff. Conover, on the other hand, agreed to bring the prisoners to appear before the court in Madison, Wisconsin. On January 30, a crowd of 2,000 supporters marched with Booth and Ryecraft as they were being taken to the Milwaukee train station for their trip to Madison.[30]

The hearing on the petition to free the prisoners was set for February 2. Sharpstein was notified, but did not appear, apparently unwilling to recognize the authority of the Wisconsin court to issue the writ.[31] After hearing arguments from the attorneys for the prisoners, in *In Re Booth and Rycraft* [sic] (*Booth III*),[32] the three justices of the state supreme court concluded unanimously that both prisoners should be freed.

The opinions of Chief Justice Whiton and Justice Smith were largely devoted to defenses of the general proposition that the state courts possessed the power to interpose their authority to free prisoners held in federal custody. Whiton proclaimed that "without this power, the state would be stripped of one of the most essential attributes of sovereignty, and would present the spectacle of a state proclaiming the allegiance of its citizens, without the power to protect them in the enjoyment of liberty upon its own soil." Similarly, Smith declared that "the power to guard and protect the liberty of the individual citizen is inherent in every government; one which it cannot relinquish, which was reserved to the states [and] without which they could not exist, because it is obvious that they could claim no allegiance or support from their citizens whom they had not the power to protect."[33]

It fell to Justice Crawford to provide the justification for the decision freeing Booth and Ryecraft under the specific circumstances of *Booth III*. Crawford, who had voted to sustain the constitutionality of the Fugitive Slave Act in *Booth I*, was careful to limit the scope of his analysis in *Booth III*. He first emphasized that the state court could intervene only in a case in which the federal court lacked jurisdiction, noting that "if it had such jurisdiction, it matters not how illegal, unjust or arbitrary the proceedings in that court may have been, nor how many errors may have been committed upon the trial; if the court had jurisdiction . . . it is by no means my duty as a judicial officer of this state to revise the decision or correct the errors." Second, he focused on the fact that, rather than being common law courts of general jurisdiction, the federal courts had only the "special and limited" jurisdiction established by statute, and thus that "the facts necessary to give them jurisdiction must appear affirmatively on the face of their proceedings, and cannot be presumed."[34]

Crawford conceded that some of the counts of the indictments had alleged facts sufficient to provide the court with jurisdiction to determine if Booth and Ryecraft had violated the Fugitive Slave Act of 1850. However, the two antislavery activists had not been convicted under those counts. Instead, their confinement rested solely on the counts of the indictments that charged that they had assisted Joshua Glover in escaping from federal custody, but did not allege that Glover had owed service and labor to Garland. Crawford contended that the statute required such allegations and that the relevant portions of the indictment had therefore not charged the two defendants with a federal crime. Analogizing *Booth III* to a case in which the federal court had lacked personal jurisdiction over the defendant, Crawford reasoned that only such a charge could vest the federal courts with jurisdiction to try the cases, and that therefore the Wisconsin Supreme Court could free Booth and Ryecraft in a habeas corpus proceeding.[35]

Crawford was able to characterize his opinion as limited in scope only by conflating the jurisdictional inquiry with an examination of the merits. The gravamen of a jurisdictional objection is the claim that the court lacks power to adjudicate the legal issues that have been brought before it. Yet Crawford did not assert that the federal district court had no authority to determine whether the indictment sufficiently alleged a violation of the Fugitive Slave Law. Instead, he simply concluded that the district court had interpreted the statute incorrectly by not requiring that Glover's status be pleaded and proven—a quintessential decision on the merits.

Moreover, Crawford's approach was flatly inconsistent with the Supreme Court's decision in *Ex Parte Watkins*.[36] In *Watkins,* after being convicted of a crime in a federal court in the District of Columbia, the petitioner sought a writ of habeas corpus from the Supreme Court, alleging that "the indictments under which he was convicted and sentenced to imprisonment charged no offense for which the prisoner was punishable in the lower court or of which that court could take cognizance"—essentially the same claim that was being made by Booth with respect to his conviction. In holding that the Court would not entertain the petition, Chief Justice John Marshall had asserted that "it is universally understood that the judgments of the courts of the United States, although their judgment be not shown in the pleadings, are yet binding on all the world. . . . The judgment of [a federal] court, in a criminal case, is, of itself, evidence of its own legality and requires for its support, no inspection of the indictment on which it is founded."[37] Similarly, the judgment against *Booth* was "evidence of its own legality" and was not subject to review in state court through the issuance of a writ of habeas corpus.

Not surprisingly, analysis of these legal niceties found little place in the commentary that followed *Booth III.* The New York *Journal of Commerce,* closely allied with the Democratic Party, described the decision as an "utter subversion of the powers of the Federal Judiciary," and Judge Miller himself warned that "some state or county judge or state court commissioner may follow this precedent, and upon some vague notion of the unconstitutionality of acts of Congress, or of error in the proceedings of this court . . . discharge all the United States convicts and prisoners from the prisons and jails of this state." By contrast, the staunchly antislavery New York *Tribune* declared that "the Judges of [Wisconsin] have won a lasting title to regard and admiration by their late decision in [*Booth III*]. . . . The example which Wisconsin has set will be as rapidly followed as circumstances admit . . . we anticipate a race among the other Free States in the same direction, till all have reached the goal of State independence."[38]

Against this background, federal government officials considered their options. Since Ryecraft had already been confined in the county jail for ten days, *Booth III* had no practical impact on his situation. By contrast, Booth had not yet served the full thirty-day sentence that had been imposed by Judge Miller.

In theory, the federal marshals could have made an effort to rearrest Booth immediately. But this course of action would quite likely have engendered violent resistance, and in any event the federal authorities would have had to find some alternative venue in which to incarcerate him. Thus, the Pierce administration chose instead to appeal *Booth III* to the United States Supreme Court.[39]

The effort to prosecute the appeal met resistance from the Wisconsin Supreme Court, whose attitude had hardened considerably since the appeal of *Booth I* the year before. When the Supreme Court sent its writ of error to the Wisconsin Supreme Court, the state court judges instructed their clerk to ignore the writ and not to record it in the official records of the court. This action was far more extreme than the actual decision in *Booth III* itself. By refusing to honor the writ of error, the Wisconsin court essentially asserted the authority to nullify section 25 of the Judiciary Act of 1793, which provided for appeals by writ of error. The refusal also implicitly challenged the premises of the Supreme Court's 1816 decision in *Martin v. Hunter's Lessee*,[40] which had established the Court's authority to hear and definitively resolve appeals from state courts. Nonetheless, the Wisconsin courts continued to receive support and encouragement from at least some elements of the national antislavery movement. For example, the *Chicago Tribune* declared that "we owe to the Supreme court of Wisconsin the respect and reverence due to a judicial tribunal which has had the courage to avow, and will have the virtue to maintain, the fundamental principles of State Rights and Personal Liberty."[41]

The Wisconsin Supreme Court's maneuver ultimately failed in its intended effect only because the Pierce administration had anticipated the ploy and acted in advance to counteract it. Prior to the issuance of the writ of error, Sharpstein, following instructions from Washington, had approached the clerk of the Wisconsin Supreme Court and requested an authenticated copy of the record in *Booth III*. Sharpstein did not disclose the motivation for his request, and the clerk complied.[42] After the state court refused to honor the mandate of the writ of error, Attorney General Cushing petitioned the Court to act on the copy of the record that Sharpstein had obtained.

Instead, the justices proceeded more cautiously. Speaking for a unanimous Court on May 12, 1856, Taney did note that the refusal of the clerk to comply with the writ of error could not prevent the exercise of the Court's appellate jurisdiction. However, he also concluded that "in a matter of so much gravity and importance," the Court should not proceed to the merits without first giving the clerk another opportunity to provide an official copy of the record of the lower court proceedings.[43] Accordingly, the Court issued an order directly to the clerk of the Wisconsin Supreme Court, mandating that he provide a copy of the state court record. In a companion opinion, the Court also postponed consideration of the appeal in *Booth I* so that the two cases could be considered together.

However else one might characterize this ruling, one point should be clear: The decision was anything but that of a Court that was anxious to intervene decisively in the sectional conflict in early 1856. This point emerges particularly clearly when *Ableman* is considered together with the Court's initial approach to *Dred Scott v. Sandford.*

CHAPTER 19

Dred Scott, Part 1

The Road to the Supreme Court

Sometime in the late eighteenth or early nineteenth century, Dred Scott was born enslaved to Peter Blow, the owner of an 860-acre farm in Virginia.[1] Scott was a dark-skinned man who reportedly grew to slightly over five feet tall. In 1818, he moved with the Blow family to Alabama, where the Blows raised cotton, and in 1830 relocated with the family to St. Louis, Missouri, where Peter Blow opened a boarding house. There, Scott was sold to Dr. John Emerson. The circumstances of the sale are not entirely clear; while some of the evidence indicates that the transaction was consummated by Peter Blow himself, other sources suggest that Scott was sold by Blow's daughter, Elizabeth, shortly after Blow died following a brief illness on June 23, 1832. But in any event, the sale clearly took place sometime before the end of 1833.

Scott's new master was a physician who was born in Pennsylvania in 1802 or 1803 and received his medical degree from the University of Pennsylvania in 1824. Emerson apparently lived for a time in the South before settling in St. Louis sometime prior to August 1831. While in St. Louis, he sought an appointment as a medical officer in the army. After serving in the military on a temporary basis from September 28, 1832 through June 5, 1833, Emerson was appointed assistant surgeon of the army on October 25, 1833. Accompanied by Dred Scott, on December 1, 1833, Emerson reported for duty at Fort Armstrong, which was located on Rock Island in the middle of the Mississippi River within the territorial boundaries of the state of Illinois. When Fort Armstrong was vacated by the army in 1836, Emerson was transferred to Fort Snelling, located in what was then the Wisconsin Territory on the west bank of the Upper Mississippi, near the subsequent location of St. Paul, Minnesota. The fort was located in the territory acquired from France via the Louisiana Purchase. Thus, slavery was prohibited there by the terms of the Missouri Compromise.

Accompanied by Dred Scott, Emerson arrived at Fort Snelling on May 8, 1836. While at Fort Snelling, Scott met Harriet Robinson, a much younger African American woman who was a slave to Major Lawrence Taliaferro, the local Indian agent. Dred and Harriet determined to marry and, unlike many other slaves who formed permanent relationships, solemnized their union in a formal civil ceremony sometime prior to September 14, 1837. Taliaferro, who was also a justice of the peace, presided over the ceremony. Taliaferro then either gave or sold Harriet to Emerson.[2]

On October 20, 1837, Emerson was transferred to Jefferson Barracks in St. Louis. However, because of the difficulty of travel conditions, both Dred and Harriet Scott were left behind, with Emerson planning to send for them later. During this stage of Emerson's travels, Dred and Harriet were hired out to other people at Fort Snelling.

Emerson was posted to St. Louis for only a very short time. On November 22, he reported to his new assignment at Fort Jesup, Louisiana. There he met Eliza Irene Sanford, a St. Louis woman who was visiting her sister, the wife of another officer who was stationed at the fort. After a very short courtship, John and Irene were married in Natchitoches, Louisiana on February 6, 1838. Emerson also sent for Dred and Harriet Scott, and they joined him and his new wife at Fort Jesup in April 1838.

Despite his marriage, almost from the moment that he arrived in Louisiana, Emerson bombarded the surgeon general with requests for reassignment. Eventually, Emerson persuaded the authorities to send him back to Fort Snelling, and John, Eliza, Dred, and Harriet departed Fort Jesup in September 1838. The party landed in St. Louis on September 21, and then left St. Louis on the steamer *Gipsey* on September 26, arriving at Fort Snelling on October 21. While the party was en route on the *Gipsey*, a child, Eliza, was born to the Scotts. While historians have differed on the precise location of Eliza's birth, the weight of the evidence strongly suggests that Harriet gave birth when the steamer was north of the northern boundary of Missouri—once again, in territory from which slavery was forbidden by the Missouri Compromise.

The Emersons and Scotts remained together at Fort Snelling for more than a year and a half, when Dr. Emerson was ordered to Florida, where the Seminole War was being fought. They left Fort Snelling together on May 29, 1840, but Irene Emerson did not accompany her husband to Florida. Instead, together with the Scotts, she remained in St. Louis, living with her father, Alexander Sanborn. John Emerson remained in Florida until he was honorably discharged from the army in the fall of 1842 and spent the rest of his life as a civilian. He returned briefly to St. Louis and eventually moved with his wife to Davenport, Iowa, where he died on December 29, 1843.

The Scotts did not accompany the Emersons to Iowa. Instead, they were apparently loaned or hired out to Captain Henry Bainbridge, the brother-in-law of Irene Emerson, who was stationed at Jefferson Barracks in 1842. Dred Scott may very well have accompanied Bainbridge when he was transferred first to Florida in 1843 and then to Fort Jesup in 1844 and to an unspecified location in

Texas in 1845. In any event, all members of the Scott family were clearly in St. Louis in March 1846, when Irene Emerson hired them out to Samuel Russell.

On April 6, 1846, Dred and Harriet Scott initiated legal actions to establish their freedom in the Missouri state circuit court in St. Louis.[3] Following the standard model, the complaints were in form actions in trespass for assault and false imprisonment. For example, Dred Scott's complaint alleged that he was a free person held in slavery by Mrs. Emerson, and that he was entitled to $10 in damages because she had "beat, bruised and ill-treated" him and had falsely imprisoned him for twelve hours. The papers were initially filed on behalf of the Scotts by Francis B. Murdoch. However, as the state court action progressed, the Scotts were represented by a number of different attorneys. After Murdoch emigrated to California in 1847, he was replaced by Charles Daniel Drake. When Drake in turn moved to Cincinnati in June of that year, Samuel Mansfield Bay, formerly attorney general of Missouri, took on the suit. In July 1847, Alexander P. Field and David N. Hall entered the case, and by March 1848 they had become the Scotts' sole legal representatives.

Irene Emerson's legal affairs were generally handled by Benoni S. Garland, the Sanborn family attorney, who was also, ironically, the erstwhile master of Joshua Glover, whose escape had ultimately given rise to *Ableman v. Booth*. To defend against the Scotts' suit for freedom, Garland retained George W. Goode, a native Virginian who was prominent in proslavery political circles. Goode handled the defense until 1849. He was then replaced by Hugh A. Garland (no relation to Benoni) and Garland's law partner, Lyman D. Norris. Garland and Norris were responsible for carrying the state court action to its conclusion.

Based on existing Missouri law, the attorneys who represented Irene Emerson must have believed that they faced an uphill struggle. In order to be successful in his suit for freedom, Scott had to prevail on two related but analytically distinct issues. Scott first had to demonstrate that during the course of his service in Illinois and the Wisconsin Territory he had in fact become free under the law in force in either or both of those jurisdictions. He also had to show that he remained free after his return to Missouri. On both of these issues, the law seemed to favor Scott at the time that he instituted his suit in state court.

Although the Missouri courts had maintained that a master had a constitutional right to pass through free territories without losing dominion over his slave, they had also consistently held that residence in a free state for even a short period of time could effectively prevent the reattachment of the status of slavery when the former slave returned to Missouri. Moreover, in its 1836 decision in *Rachel v. Walker*, the court had held that Missouri would recognize the freedom of an African American under almost precisely the circumstances that gave rise to *Emerson* itself. In *Rachel,* the court had concluded that the plaintiff had become free by virtue of the Northwest Ordinance and the Missouri Compromise when, in the course of the performance of his duties, an army officer had brought her to Fort Snelling, Minnesota and Prairie du Chien, Michigan to be his servant, and that the doctrine of reattachment did not apply after the servant returned voluntarily with her master to Missouri.[4]

Nonetheless, on November 19, 1846, Mrs. Emerson pleaded not guilty to the complaint. Almost from its inception, the Scotts' suit was beset by procedural complications. In order to prevail under Missouri law, a plaintiff in a suit for freedom was required to prove that he was held or claimed as a slave by the defendant—in this case, Mrs. Emerson. However, Samuel Russell—the witness on whose testimony the Scotts had hoped to rely to prove this point—ultimately admitted that he had no personal knowledge of any facts that would create an inference that would support such a conclusion. Faced with this lack of evidence, the jury returned a verdict for the defendant.

On July 1, 1847, Samuel Mansfield Bay, who had recently replaced Charles Drake as the attorney for the Scotts after Drake relocated to Cincinnati, moved for a new trial on the ground that the testimony of the witness had been a surprise and that Mrs. Emerson's claim of ownership could easily be proven. On the same date, Scott's attorney also filed a new suit naming both Russell and Alexander Sanford as defendants in addition to Emerson, reasoning that Scott could prevail if any one of the three could be shown to have asserted a claim to him. On July 31, the presiding judge ordered Scott's attorney to choose between the duplicate lawsuits, and the attorney chose to pursue the initial motion for a retrial. This motion was granted on December 2. Mrs. Emerson's attorney promptly appealed this decision to the Missouri Supreme Court, but in June 1848, that court dismissed the appeal, holding that the grant of a new trial was not appealable because it was not a final judgment and clearing the way for a retrial of Scott's suit for freedom.

For reasons that have never been fully explained, the new trial was twice postponed and did not resume until January 12, 1850. At the second trial, Scott's counsel produced a new witness who testified that Mrs. Emerson had exercised dominion over Scott by hiring him out to Samuel Russell. Against this background, the jury concluded that Scott should be declared a free man. Mrs. Emerson's attorney promptly appealed the judgment to the Missouri Supreme Court.

The appeal came to the court in the midst of the political upheaval that ultimately led to the adoption of the Compromise of 1850. In Missouri, the dispute had exacerbated a split in the Democratic Party between the supporters and opponents of Democratic Senator Thomas Hart Benton, the Van Burenite who had opposed the annexation of Texas and who alone among slave-state senators had consistently supported the principle of popular sovereignty during the long struggle over the fate of the Mexican Cession. Two of the three members of the court in 1850—William B. Napton and James H. Birch—were strong supporters of the proslavery, anti-Benton faction of the party, and they may have seen in *Scott v. Emerson* an opportunity to strike a political blow at their adversaries.[5]

Birch at first favored an opinion that would have declared the restrictions on slavery in the Missouri Compromise unconstitutional. Napton, however, convinced him that the better course was simply to overturn the Missouri precedents rejecting the doctrine of reattachment and to hold in favor of Mrs. Emerson on that more limited ground. Initially, John F. Ryland, the third member of the court, intended to dissent. Nonetheless, he ultimately agreed to concur in the conclusion that, notwithstanding their travels, both Dred and Harriet remained slaves under Missouri law.[6]

Despite all of this maneuvering, none of the three judges who initially heard *Scott v. Emerson* ever filed an opinion in the case. Although briefs were filed in March, the court deferred consideration of the appeal until its October term. The opinion was then assigned to Judge Napton, but he was unable to produce an opinion prior to the election of September 1851, in which new judges were elected to replace both him and Judge Birch. Thus, the case had to be reargued, and it was not until March 22, 1852, that the state supreme court finally handed down its ruling.[7]

Judge Harry Gamble (who, ironically, had represented the army officer in *Rachel v. Walker*) concluded that the decision of the lower court should be affirmed. In Gamble's view, the case was governed by a straightforward application of the doctrine of *stare decisis.* Relying on *Rachel,* he declared that "I regard the question [presented in *Scott v. Emerson*] as settled by repeated adjudications of this court." Moreover, he observed that *Rachel* and similar cases had been decided "when the public mind was tranquil," and he argued that the principles which those cases espoused had not been in any way discredited by subsequent events.[8]

Judge Ryland joined the newly elected Judge William Scott in reaching a contrary conclusion. Speaking for the majority, Scott began by conceding that a variety of Missouri decisions had previously enforced the rules of nonslave states by recognizing the freedom of African Americans in positions similar to that of the Scotts. However, Judge Scott also observed that, however widespread the practice, the decision of one state to respect the internal laws of another state was entirely voluntary. He then complained that it is a humiliating spectacle, to see the courts of this State confiscating the property of her own citizen by the command of a foreign law. If Scott is freed, by what means will it be effected, but by the constitution of Illinois, or the territorial laws of the United States? Now, what principle requires the interference of this court? Are not those governments capable of enforcing their own laws; and if they are not, are we concerned that such laws should be enforced, and that, too, at the cost of our own citizens?

Later, he adverted to the increasing political tensions between North and South:

Times are not as they were when [decisions such as *Rachel v. Walker*] were made. Since then not only individuals but States have been possessed with a dark and fell spirit with respect to slavery, whose gratification is sought in the pursuit of measures, whose inevitable consequence must be the destruction and overthrow of our government. Under such circumstances, it does not behoove the State of Missouri to show the least countenance to any measure which might gratify this spirit.[9]

This inflammatory rhetoric provided the context for two more standard legal arguments. First, Judge Scott argued that the relevant portions of the Illinois constitution and the Missouri Compromise were penal laws, and noted that penal laws were generally enforced only within the territorial limits of the jurisdictions in which they had been adopted. In addition, citing *The Slave, Grace,* and the state court decision in *Strader v. Graham,* he contended that the doctrine of reattachment applied in any event. Thus, Judge Scott concluded that Dred Scott and his family were not entitled to their freedom under Missouri law.

At this point, one might have thought that the logical next step for Dred Scott and his lawyers would have been to appeal to the Supreme Court of the United States. Such an appeal was never taken. Instead, *Scott v. Emerson* was remanded to the lower court for a new trial, to be governed by the principles established by the state supreme court. However, the new trial was never held. Rather, almost two years later, an entry in the circuit court record for January 25, 1854 reported that the *Scott v. Emerson* case was "continued by consent, awaiting decision of Supreme Court of the United States."[10] The decision to which the entry referred was an expected appeal from *Dred Scott v. Sandford,* a separate action for freedom filed on November 2, 1853, in the United States Circuit Court for the state of Missouri.

The choice to file the new action rather than appeal from the decision of the Missouri Supreme Court was made by Roswell M. Field, who had succeeded Alexander F. Field and David N. Hall as Scott's attorney. Field wrote privately that the reason that he pursued this strategy was to circumvent what he saw as the implications of the Supreme Court's treatment of *Strader,* where the Court had cited jurisdictional considerations in dismissing the Kentucky state court's decision to invoke the doctrine of reattachment. Field feared that the Court would take a similar view of an appeal from the decision of the Missouri Supreme Court in *Scott v. Emerson* and dismiss the appeal for want of jurisdiction. Field wrote that he instituted the suit in federal court in the hope of eventually forcing the Court to a decision on the merits on the question of whether long-term residence in a free state or a territory in which slavery was prohibited by the Missouri Compromise established a claim to freedom that all states were required to honor.[11]

To appreciate the rationale underlying this strategy, one must first understand the precise nature of the legal argument that Field and the other attorneys for the Scotts were making on behalf of their clients. None of the Scotts' lawyers ever contended in court that a federal statute or the Constitution required the state of Missouri to recognize the freedom of slaves who resided in either a state where slavery was prohibited by state law or in a federal territory where slavery was prohibited by the Missouri Compromise. Instead, the contention was that, as a matter of *common law,* the Scotts were entitled to their freedom under the circumstances of the case. As the Supreme Court had held in *Strader v. Graham,* the Court lacked authority to reverse a judgment on appeal from a state supreme court on these grounds. In such an appeal, the Court could only correct errors in federal law.

The posture of a case initiated in a federal trial court was quite different. Under the Supreme Court's 1842 decision in *Swift v. Tyson,* in many common law cases the federal courts were not required to apply the law of the state in which they were located. Instead, federal judges were to use their own best judgment in ascertaining the appropriate rule to be applied.[12] Field hoped that the Supreme Court would ultimately reach a conclusion different from that of the Missouri Supreme Court on the question of whether African Americans in the position of the Scotts could retain their freedom after returning to a slave state.

In pursuing his strategy, Field was immediately confronted with a problem. The Constitution and the applicable statutes limit the types of cases that may be heard by the lower federal courts. The only conceivable basis for jurisdiction in the new federal case envisioned by Field would be diversity of citizenship— a claim that the plaintiff and the defendant were citizens of different states. Since both Dred Scott and Irene Emerson were residents of Missouri, a suit for freedom in federal court would have been dismissed immediately for want of jurisdiction. However, the complaint filed by Field in the federal court in St. Louis alleged that title to Scott had been conveyed to John F. A. Sanford, the brother of Mrs. Emerson and the executor of Dr. Emerson's will. Sanford had recently moved to New York City and was therefore the resident of a different state than Dred Scott. The fortuity of this coincidence, together with the lack of a paper trail documenting the conveyance, has led some historians to conclude that the sale to Sanford in fact never took place and that he somehow colluded with Field to create the appearance of diversity of citizenship.[13] But whatever the reality of the situation, Sanford admitted being the owner of Dred Scott, and this issue never became a subject of controversy in federal court.

By contrast, another aspect of the jurisdictional issue eventually took on central importance in the resolution of *Dred Scott*. Speaking for Sanford, on April 3, 1854, attorney Hugh Garland filed a plea in abatement, asserting that the court lacked jurisdiction because Scott was not a citizen.[14] By its terms, this plea raised the question of whether even free African Americans could be citizens who were entitled to invoke diversity jurisdiction in order to gain access to the federal courts under Article III of the Constitution and the existing jurisdictional statutes.

Prior to *Dred Scott*, this question had rarely if ever been raised in diversity actions initiated by free blacks. Instead, the dispute over the constitutionality of the Negro Seamen's Act had provided the backdrop for much of the debate about the citizenship of African Americans. In addition to arguing that these statutes were inconsistent with the Commerce Clause, the government of Massachusetts in particular complained that the African American crew members from that state were citizens of Massachusetts, and thus that applying the Negro Seamen's Acts to them denied them the rights guaranteed by the Comity Clause.[15]

The basic Southern response to this line of attack rested on the contention that free blacks were not citizens under the Constitution, and thus were not entitled to the protections of the Comity Clause. On this point Southern theorists relied on two analytically distinct arguments. Some used a state-centered theory of citizenship, contending that national citizenship was derivative of state citizenship and that free blacks generally lacked the rights normally associated with citizenship in their home states and thus would not be considered citizens in those states. Other Southern theorists took a different view, asserting that citizenship for Comity Clause purposes was defined by national standards that excluded African Americans.[16]

Neither approach was free from difficulty. First, any rights-focused definition of citizenship required the definition of a core set of rights that constituted the sine qua non of citizenship. Admittedly, many Northern states denied a wide variety of rights to their free black inhabitants, particularly political rights. However, those same rights were also generally denied to women and children, whom all conceded had the status of citizens under the Constitution. Conversely, some states allowed noncitizens to vote if they met certain other qualifications. Indeed, in the antebellum era, the most widely held view was that all free inhabitants who owed allegiance to a particular sovereign were citizens of that sovereignty. Under this definition, free blacks clearly qualified as citizens—a point recognized even by some slave-state courts in the early nineteenth century.[17]

Further, even if one could specify a set of rights that were indispensable to citizenship, defining citizenship by reference to these rights would not have completely solved the Southern problem. The nature of the rights enjoyed by free blacks varied greatly even among the nonslave states. Although the legal regime of states such as Indiana was almost as hostile to free blacks as that of the Southern states themselves, a number of nonslave states allowed African Americans to vote even prior to the Civil War. Massachusetts also allowed free blacks to serve on juries. Thus, if the status of United States citizenship was derived from the possession of state-created rights, Southern theorists would have had to concede that at least *some* free blacks could claim the protection of the Comity Clause.

Finally, any state-centered approach to federal citizenship had to contend with troubling structural anomalies. By its nature, the constitutional definition of citizenship had only limited significance under the antebellum regime. It had no impact on purely domestic issues—most notably, the relationship between a state and its own citizens. Therefore, no definition of federal citizenship could threaten core principles of state autonomy. Instead, what was at stake was the enjoyment of some of the specific rights entrusted to the federal government by the Constitution. To have state governments control access to these rights necessarily created some tension with the basic idea that the federal government was supreme within the sphere of influence allocated to it by the Constitution.

There were different problems posed by the argument that federal citizenship might be defined independently from state citizenship. On their faces, the wording of both the Comity Clause and the Diversity of Citizenship Clause appear to be inconsistent with the notion that a person who is recognized as a citizen by his home state might not be considered a citizen for constitutional purposes. Neither clause refers to citizens of the United States per se. Instead, the Comity Clause provides that "the Citizens of *each State* shall be entitled to all Privileges and Immunities of Citizens in the several States," while the Diversity of Citizenship Clause vests the federal courts with jurisdiction to hear cases "between Citizens *of different States*." These complex theoretical problems provided the background for the consideration of Garland's plea in abatement.[18]

The plea was not skillfully drafted. It did not allege that Scott had remained a slave or had been born a slave. Nor did Garland specify the state in which Scott had been born. Instead, the plea asserted only that, because Scott was a descendant of African American slaves, he could not be considered a citizen of the state of Missouri for purposes of diversity jurisdiction. These omissions helped shape the arguments on citizenship in both the Circuit Court and subsequent proceedings in the Supreme Court.

On April 14, Field demurred to the plea, effectively contending that the complaint in the case alleged facts sufficient to support the exercise of jurisdiction. When the issue was argued on April 24, Garland cited a number of cases which had held that free African Americans were not citizens for purposes of the Comity Clause. He contended that the principles animating these decisions applied equally to the Article III, Section 2 concept of diversity of citizenship for jurisdictional purposes. Field, by contrast, observed that African Americans had all the rights of citizens in *some* states, and that, in any event, citizenship for Article III purposes required no more than simple residence.[19]

The following day, presiding Judge Robert W. Wells, a slaveholder who at one point had been the attorney general of the state of Missouri, sustained the demurrer, finding the plea in abatement presented insufficient grounds for dismissing the complaint. Wells argued that one need not be a citizen for the purposes of Article IV in order to qualify for diversity jurisdiction under Article III. In Wells's view, for purposes of the latter provision, one need be no more than a resident with the capacity to own property. Otherwise, he observed, a free African American would not only be unable to avail himself of diversity jurisdiction as a *plaintiff*, but would also be immune from the exercise of such jurisdiction over him as a *defendant*. Unwilling to countenance this conclusion, Judge Wells found that the court had jurisdiction over the claims of Dred Scott and his family.[20]

Having lost on the jurisdictional issue, Sanford's attorney defended the case on the merits. Field and Garland agreed on a statement of facts which, while not entirely accurate, conveyed the sense of the travels of Dred Scott and his family with Dr. Emerson and described the later conveyance of Scott to John Sanford. No additional witnesses or evidence were introduced at the brief jury trial that was held on May 15. At that trial, Field argued that Scott was free by virtue of the operation of the Northwest Ordinance, the constitution of Illinois, and the Missouri Compromise. Conversely, Garland's argument tracked the reasoning of the Missouri Supreme Court in *Scott v. Emerson*. Believing himself bound by that case and the Supreme Court's decision in *Strader v. Graham*,

Judge Wells charged the jury that the law was with Sanford, and the jury quickly returned a verdict in Sanford's favor.[21]

This decision was in a very real sense only preliminary. From the moment that the case was filed in the Circuit Court, it was no doubt clear to all of the parties that *Dred Scott* would find its way to the Supreme Court. After his motion for a new trial was denied, Field filed an appeal with the Court on December 30, 1854. Although a crowded docket delayed consideration of the case for more than a year, the fate of Dred Scott and his family would ultimately be decided by the nine justices in Washington, D.C.

By the time that the *Dred Scott* case was argued before the Supreme Court, both sides had obtained volunteer assistance from attorneys with prominent national reputations. On October 14, 1854, Hugh Garland died. He was replaced as counsel for Sanford by Reverdy Johnson of Maryland and Henry S. Geyer of Missouri. Johnson, a former United States senator who had served as attorney general under Zachary Taylor, was generally recognized as one of the leading constitutional lawyers in the country. Geyer had served as a senator from Missouri and was regarded as perhaps the greatest lawyer in the state.

Geyer and Johnson were opposed by Montgomery Blair of Maryland. Blair was an apt choice to represent the Scotts in the Supreme Court. Born in Kentucky in 1813, Blair was a former slaveowner whose personal odyssey epitomized the impact of disputes over slavery on the structure of American politics more generally. His father, Frances Preston Blair, was a member of Andrew Jackson's "kitchen cabinet." After moving to St. Louis in 1836, Montgomery became a protege of Thomas Hart Benton. In the wake of the bitter dispute over the Wilmot Proviso, Blair temporarily abandoned the Democratic Party in 1848, supporting Free Soil candidate Martin Van Buren in preference to Lewis Cass, the Democratic nominee. Soon thereafter, Blair returned to the Democratic fold and campaigned enthusiastically in support of Franklin Pierce for president in 1852. Blair moved to Washington, D.C., in 1853, and in early 1855, Pierce selected him to be the solicitor for the newly created Court of Claims. Nonetheless, by 1856 the escalating conflict in Kansas had once again alienated Blair from the dominant faction in the Democratic Party and led him to join the newly formed Republican Party. He would later serve as postmaster general under Abraham Lincoln.[22]

Field had written to Blair requesting his aid as early as May 24, 1854. After Field repeated his request on December 24, emphasizing the importance of the principles involved in the case, Blair agreed to represent Dred Scott without payment on December 30—the same day that Field filed his appeal with the Supreme Court. Blair in turn persuaded Gamaliel Bailey, the editor of the abolitionist *National Era,* to raise the funds necessary to cover court costs and incidental expenses.

The Court itself did not finally reach the *Dred Scott* case until February 1856. On February 7, Montgomery Blair filed the only written brief of which there is any surviving record. In his attack on the lower court decision, Blair did not advert directly to *Strader v. Graham.* Nor did the brief make any mention of the time that Scott had spent at Fort Snelling. Instead, Blair focused solely on Scott's residence in Illinois as the basis for the claim that Scott should be declared a free man. Blair rejected the assertion that the Illinois prohibition on slavery should be viewed as a penal law, and also the view that Scott's status as a slave had simply been suspended while he lived in Illinois. Rather, Blair argued that, by choosing to bring Scott to live for an extended period in Illinois with the knowledge that slavery was forbidden there, Emerson had in effect voluntarily emancipated Scott, and that, prior to the decision in *Scott v. Emerson,* the Missouri courts had consistently recognized such emancipations as final. Scott, Blair argued, was entitled to the benefit of these pre-*Emerson* rules, which, he noted, were consistent with the principles that had been adopted by a variety of other slave states.[23]

From the perspective of some modern commentators, Blair's decision to rely solely on Dred Scott's time in Illinois seems almost inexplicable. Paul Finkelman, for example, argues that Blair could have relied on Scott's journey to Fort Snelling to distinguish *Strader.* The Court in *Strader* had held only that Kentucky was not bound to respect the freedom of erstwhile slaves that had been granted by the law of another state (Ohio). By contrast, during his time at Fort Snelling, Scott became free by virtue of a *federal* statute—the Missouri Compromise. Finkelman asserts that, in this context, Blair should have argued that Missouri was bound by the Supremacy Clause to vindicate Scott's freedom upon his return to that state.[24]

However, to Blair, the idea that the Missouri Compromise would have a more expansive extraterritorial effect than the law of Illinois seems to have been inconceivable. Indeed, although a similar argument had been made in *Strader,* no one appears to have made such a claim at any stage in *Dred Scott.* Against this background, if the status of only Dred Scott himself had been at issue, the tactical decision to ignore the time spent at Fort Snelling would have been entirely plausible. Given the makeup of the Court and its recent decision in *Strader,* Blair faced an uphill struggle in any event, particularly with respect to the Southern members of the Court. Adverting to the politically explosive issue of the status of the Missouri Compromise would have created the danger of alienating these justices.

Moreover, from this perspective, invocation of Dred Scott's residence at Fort Snelling would have added nothing to the strength of his case. If the courts of Missouri were entitled to disregard the Illinois prohibition on slavery, in Blair's view they had no greater obligation to recognize Scott's freedom based on his residence in the Wisconsin Territory. Indeed, as Field observed in a letter to Blair, the argument based on Scott's time in Illinois was actually stronger than that founded on his time in the Wisconsin Territory. While the Missouri Compromise simply provided that slavery "shall be and is . . . forever prohibited" north of 36 degrees, 30 minutes, the Illinois state constitution explicitly stated that the introduction of slavery into the state would result in the emancipation of the slave. In short, the discussion of the Missouri Compromise may well have appeared to carry substantial risks with little hope of a corresponding reward.[25]

However, when Harriet and Eliza are considered in the equation, the glaring flaw in Blair's strategy emerges clearly. Neither had ever lived in the state of Illinois. The antislavery provisions of the Missouri Compromise provided the *only* basis on which they could claim their freedom. It seems highly unlikely that Blair made a conscious decision to sacrifice Dred Scott's wife and daughter for a tactical advantage; the most plausible explanation for his strategy is that he simply did not focus on the difference between the relative legal positions of Dred Scott himself and that of his family.

In any event, the majority of the brief was not devoted to the issue of Scott's freedom at all, but instead focused on a defense of the lower court's conclusion that he could be considered a citizen of Missouri for the purpose of diversity jurisdiction.[26] One conceivable explanation for this rather curious strategy is that Blair might have been seeking to preempt an anticipated attack on the lower court ruling by Sanford's attorneys. But if this was Blair's motivation, his execution was singularly inept. His argument dealt only with the *substance* of the claim that the lower court had jurisdiction over the case as an initial matter, tracking the argument of Judge Wells and citing a number of lower court decisions that had allowed free African Americans to participate in diversity actions both as plaintiffs and defendants. Blair failed to even mention the possibility that the jurisdiction issue was not properly before the Supreme Court at all—an argument which, as we will see, had considerable force and even turned out to be persuasive to a number of the justices.

Alternatively, Blair may have been influenced by a letter from Roswell Field that suggested that a favorable ruling by the Supreme Court on the substance of the jurisdiction question could have important collateral benefits. Field believed that, if free African Americans were deemed to be citizens for purposes of diversity jurisdiction, a putative slave seized and held under the provisions of the Fugitive Slave Act of 1850 could obtain a jury trial in the state where he was captured by the simple expedient of instituting a suit in federal court for freedom against the person who claimed him. Jurisdiction for such a lawsuit would be based on the theory that the African American who had been seized was a citizen of the state where he had been found.[27]

If vindicating this position was in fact Blair's motivation for failing to advert to the procedural bar to consideration of the jurisdiction issue, then he was guilty of sacrificing the interests of his client in order to make a speculative attempt to advance the goals of the broader antislavery movement. Moreover, while some modern commentators have accepted Field's argument at face value,[28] the success of this strategy would have been far from certain, even if free African Americans had been held to be citizens for purposes of diversity jurisdiction.

Field appears to have mistakenly believed that the federal courts were required by the Constitution to take jurisdiction over all cases based upon diversity of citizenship. In fact, in order to bring an action in federal court, one must satisfy not only the relevant constitutional minima but also the statutory requirements imposed by Congress. Courts would have probably held that the general diversity jurisdiction established by statute could not be used to circumvent the more specific provisions of the subsequently adopted Fugitive Slave Act of 1850. Under this view, an alleged escapee might have been able to prosecute his suit for freedom in federal court but only in the state where his master resided, *after* the putative escapee had been returned to that state. Nonetheless, Field clearly believed that a favorable ruling on the merits of the citizenship issue would benefit fugitive slaves, and a similar belief may have informed Blair's tactics as well.

In any event, in seeking to vindicate the lower court's ruling on African American citizenship, Blair observed that, in many cases prior to *Dred Scott,* federal courts had recognized free African Americans for purposes of diversity jurisdiction without even discussing the issue. He conceded that "there is a recognised social distinction which excludes [African Americans] from association with whites on equal terms in all the States," and that in many states free blacks were denied political rights. Blair contended, however, that citizenship was not premised on the possession of these rights, but that any person who was "a freeman . . . not a foreigner, not a slave" should be considered a citizen for constitutional purposes. He also observed that, while Congress had generally limited naturalization to free whites, specific treaties had granted American citizenship to members of a number of Indian tribes and to the inhabitants of Louisiana and California without regard to race.[29]

Against the background of these written arguments, *Dred Scott* was first argued before the Supreme Court on February 11, 12, 13, and 14. While normally each attorney was allowed two hours to make his argument, on the motion of Reverdy Johnson, the Court extended the allotted time to three hours. Although the newspaper reports of the arguments were very brief, one point emerges clearly. Whether gratuitously or because of the situation of Harriet and Eliza, Johnson and Geyer contended that Congress lacked the authority to prohibit slavery in the territories acquired from France through the Louisiana Purchase.[30] This marked the first time that such an argument was made during the litigation over the status of Dred Scott and his family.

The introduction of this argument fundamentally changed the nature of the *Dred Scott* litigation. By challenging the constitutionality of the Missouri Compromise, Johnson and Geyer were doing nothing less than inviting the Court to involve itself directly in the political crisis that was deeply dividing the country. Not surprisingly, for the first time, the popular press began to take notice of the case. Thus, for example, on February 15, Horace Greeley reported in the New York *Tribune* that the Supreme Court would soon decide "a most important case, involving the validity (in its day) of the Missouri restriction." Nonetheless, public discussions of *Dred Scott* at this point were far less numerous and prominent than newspaper accounts of other aspects of the sectional conflict, including cases such as *Lemmon v. The People* from New York and the *Booth* cases from Wisconsin.

In hindsight, the relative lack of attention paid to *Dred Scott* in early 1856 seems almost perverse. Yet viewed from the perspective of most observers at that time, one can easily see how the *Booth* and *Lemmon* cases might have seemed to be of greater significance. *Booth* arose from the efforts of the state of Wisconsin to nullify the Fugitive Slave Act of 1850, while in *Lemmon* a New York court had freed the slaves of a Virginia resident who was doing nothing more than passing through New York while in transit to Texas. In each case, the relationship between the fact situation and the sectional conflict was direct and apparent. By contrast, on its face, *Dred Scott* involved nothing more than the efforts of a Missouri court to determine the status of an African American who was in Missouri and was a resident of that state. The sectional implications of the case emerged only indirectly and required more explanation.

Moreover, prior to arguments of February 1856, none of the courts that had dealt with the case had focused on the constitutionality of the Missouri Compromise. Further, even after the issue had been raised in the arguments of Geyer and Johnson, it was far from clear that the Supreme Court would reach that question. Indeed, the decision to discuss the Missouri Compromise came only after a complex series of deliberations that reflected the interaction of nine justices with widely differing views on both the morality of slavery generally and the relationship of slavery to the sectional conflict more specifically.

The Court discussed *Dred Scott* in conference a number of times between the completion of the oral arguments and May 12. For John McLean, the case presented a golden opportunity to advance his presidential campaign by making a strong statement in favor of the constitutionality of the Missouri Compromise and allay the concerns of those Republicans who doubted the depth of his commitment to antislavery principles. From the beginning, he appears to have been prepared to issue just such an opinion. By contrast, other justices were less anxious to enter the political fray on this issue.

In an account that seems to be confirmed by the private correspondence, James Harvey, a confidant of Justice John McLean, reported in the New York *Tribune* that the Southern justices planned to decide the case on narrow grounds, avoiding a discussion of the Missouri Compromise altogether, but that McLean and perhaps other Northern justices would vindicate the constitutionality of the Compromise in dissent. Similarly, in a letter to George Ticknor on April 8, Justice Benjamin Robbins Curtis wrote that "the court will not decide the question of the Missouri Compromise line—a majority of the judges being of opinion that it is not necessary to do so."[31] Thus, once again, at this stage, most of the justices apparently had no inclination to take an assertive role in the sectional conflict.

Ironically, however, a dispute over the proper application of distinctively legal principles would set in motion a chain of events that would ultimately lead to an overtly political decision in *Dred Scott*. After the initial argument, the justices were deeply divided over a technical issue—the question of whether the issue of Dred Scott's citizenship was properly before the Court. In 1856, state courts generally would have held that the defendant clearly waived all objections to jurisdiction by defending on the merits. However, some of the justices believed that, because the subject matter jurisdiction of the federal courts was limited by the terms of the Constitution itself, a different rule should apply in cases in which a challenge to diversity of citizenship was raised.

The justices were evenly divided on this question, with one of their number—Northern Democrat Samuel Nelson—uncertain. Purportedly in order to allow Nelson to resolve his uncertainty, the justices agreed unanimously to have the case reargued, and on May 12—almost simultaneously with the decision to postpone consideration of *Ableman*—the Court issued the requisite order. The attorneys were directed to give special attention to the questions of whether the plea in abatement was properly before the Court, and, if the decision on jurisdiction was reviewable, whether Dred Scott could be considered a citizen for purposes of diversity jurisdiction.[32] Thus, a final decision in the case would be rendered against the background of a dramatically changed political environment.

CHAPTER 20

The Court on the Brink

In May 1856, the Southern justices and their allies had an extraordinary opportunity to intervene actively in the dispute over slavery. For the only time in the antebellum era, both of the major irritants in the sectional conflict were directly implicated by cases under consideration by the Court. *Ableman v. Booth* arose from the most extreme form of Northern resistance to the recapture of fugitive slaves, while the arguments in *Dred Scott* invited the Court to address the explosive issue of slavery in the territories. On both issues, the sympathies of a majority of the justices were unquestionably with the South.

Against this background, the near-simultaneous postponements of *Ableman* and *Dred Scott* can only be seen as the actions of a Court that was dominated by justices who were not anxious to intervene in the increasingly acrimonious sectional conflict. Some have suggested that the Court's relative passivity was itself at times designed to serve the interests of the opponents of the nascent Republican party. Thus, in one of the few public comments on the order for reargument in *Dred Scott*, a disappointed McLean supporter complained bitterly that "the black gowns have come to be artful dodgers. The minority were prepared to meet the issue [of slavery in the territories] broadly and distinctly; but the controlling members were not quite ready ... to open the opportunity for a demolition of the fraudulent pretenses that have been set up in Congress on this question." Prominent Republicans would later repeat this charge in a number of different contexts.[1] However, the evidence belies any such interpretation of the Court's decision.

First, in May 1856, while a decision on the merits of *Dred Scott* might have advanced McLean's personal ambitions, such a decision would not have measurably advanced the cause of Republicans generally and might well have worked to the detriment of the party. The majority had decided not to discuss the territorial issue, and there was no reason to believe that an opinion by McLean on the issue would have been of any great benefit to the Republican cause. By contrast, consideration of the merits of the citizenship issue in *Dred Scott* would have presented Southerners and Northern Democrats with an opportunity to strike a political blow at the Republicans in the North. A high-profile decision by the Supreme Court concluding that free blacks could not be citizens of the United States might well have had great symbolic importance, highlighting the difference on this issue between Democrats and Republicans and giving force to the argument that the political struggle was not simply about slavery (which most Northerners opposed) but also about the status of African Americans more generally (whom most white Northerners were not inclined to accept as equals).

Against this background, the divisions over the relevant procedural issues strongly suggest that ordinary political considerations were not the dominant factor in the justices' deliberations. In considering the question of whether the citizenship issue was properly before the Court, the justices were not split along predictable sectional or political lines. On one hand, a group of four justices, including the two most committed Southern sectionalists on the Court (Taney and Daniel), an accommodationist Southerner (Wayne), and an accommodationist Northern Whig (Curtis), concluded that the merits of the citizenship issue should be considered. On the other, the contrary position was taken by an even more diverse group that included both sectionalist and accommodationist Southerners (Campbell and Catron, respectively), a Northern Democrat (Grier), and the strongest antislavery voice on the Court (McLean). Moreover, the vote to order reargument was unanimous. This pattern can only be seen as a reflection of the dominance of distinctively legal considerations in the consideration of these points.

At the same time, the justices must have been aware that any discussion of the merits of *Dred Scott* in mid-1856 ran the risk of further exacerbating sectional tensions. The desire to avoid unduly roiling the political process may also have influenced the Court's decision not to immediately consider the appeal in *Ableman v. Booth*. The Southern justices in particular must have found the events that gave rise to *Ableman* to have been extraordinarily provocative. Not only had the antislavery forces forcibly prevented a slaveowner from recovering a fugitive from service, but the state courts had in effect countenanced the unlawful behavior of the rescuers, denied the authority of the federal government to aid in the return of fugitive slaves, and defied the Supreme Court itself. One can hardly imagine a more blatant repudiation of what Southerners viewed as the constitutional obligations of the Northern states toward slaveowners and the Southern states more generally.

Moreover, Cushing's motion to act on the copy of the record that he had obtained provided the Southern justices and their allies with a clear opportunity to strike a rhetorical blow at those who opposed the enforcement of the Fugitive Slave Law. The Southerners and Northern Democrats could have proceeded based on the copy of the record that had been obtained by John R. Sharpstein, the district attorney, and justified their action with an opinion that branded Booth and the members of the Wisconsin Supreme Court as lawless nullifiers who were prepared to defy even the Supreme Court of the United States. But the Court declined the invitation, choosing instead to request that the Wisconsin Supreme Court reconsider its decision to ignore the writ of error. Thus, once again, as in *Dred Scott*, the Court showed a reluctance to rush to a decision that might further strain relations between North and South.

Taken together, the treatment of *Dred Scott* and *Ableman* demonstrates that in May 1856, the justices were generally reluctant to inject themselves too deeply into the sectional conflict. To be sure, John McLean would have been prepared to deliver a provocative antislavery opinion in *Dred Scott*, and it would not have been surprising if Peter Daniel had produced an at least equally strident proslavery opinion. But the Court's decision-making process was clearly dominated by those who advocated a far more cautious posture, most likely fearing that any precipitous action would only exacerbate the increasingly bitter sectional divide.

The Court did not revisit *Ableman* until 1859. By contrast, *Dred Scott* was reargued in 1856. But even by that time, extrajudicial events had radically changed the political dynamic, and with it, the attitude of the Southern justices in particular toward a more aggressive judicial posture.

CHAPTER 21

Sectionalism on the March

In the interim between the issuance of the order for reargument in *Dred Scott* and the reargument itself in December 1856, a number of factors intervened to substantially change the dynamic that would determine the Court's resolution of the case. The first significant development was jurisprudential. Only two days after the order for reargument, the Court handed down its decision in *Pease v. Peck*. On its face, *Pease* was entirely unrelated to the dispute over slavery in the territories. Instead, the case (which had begun as a diversity action) revolved around a highly technical issue of Michigan statutory law. All members of the Court conceded that, even under the regime of *Swift v. Tyson*, the case should be governed by Michigan law. The problem was that the most recent interpretation of Michigan law by the state supreme court was apparently inconsistent with prior decisions from the same court. Over the dissents of Justices Campbell and Daniel, Justice Grier concluded for the Court that, under those circumstances, the Supreme Court was not bound to follow the most recent rule laid down by the state supreme court but was instead free to make an independent judgment on the proper rule to be applied.[1]

George Ticknor Curtis would later claim that Justice Grier contemporaneously informed a confidant that *Pease* had been decided specifically to release the justices in *Dred Scott* from the obligation to follow the principles laid down by the Missouri Supreme Court in *Scott v. Emerson*.[2] It is difficult to discern the tactical advantage that Grier and the other justices who would later form the *Dred Scott* majority hoped to gain by undermining the authority of the Missouri decision. But whatever motives actually underlay the *Pease* decision, its doctrinal significance was unmistakable. Even if a justice concluded that the nonconstitutional issues in *Dred Scott* should be governed by state law, he could still cite *Pease* and argue that the Scotts should be deemed free under Missouri law.

The political developments between May and December had an even greater impact on the judicial dynamic. At the time that the Court postponed *Ableman* and ordered reargument in *Dred Scott*, the emergence of the Republican Party as the primary opposition party in the North was far from certain. The performance of self-identified Republicans in the state and local elections of 1855 had been uneven at best, and the future of the party seemed heavily dependent on the course of events in Kansas. To be sure, Republicans had gained a signal victory in engineering the election of Rep. Nathaniel Banks of Massachusetts to the post of Speaker of the House when the 36th Congress was organized in early 1856. But while Congress continued to wrangle over the future of Kansas, the winter of 1855–1856 failed to produce the kind of dramatic events that would further galvanize the antislavery faithful and convince wavering Northerners to put aside their previous political differences and join together in a crusade against the influence of the slave power. If antislavery sentiment could be subsumed in some reconstitution of Whiggery or a Northern party devoted to nativism, temperance, or some other political issue, the possibility of a renewed accommodation between the sections no doubt seemed very real to some contemporary observers—perhaps including some of the justices themselves.[3]

However, the level of sectional tension increased greatly between May and December of 1856. On May 19 and 20, Sen. Charles Sumner of Massachusetts delivered an intemperate speech in the Senate condemning what he described as "the crime against Kansas" and launching vicious personal attacks against a number of important Democrats, including Senator Andrew P. Butler of South Carolina. Two days later, Sumner was caned on the Senate floor by Rep. Preston Brooks of South Carolina, a distant relative of Butler's, provoking a furious response from antislavery Northerners. Almost simultaneously, proslavery forces attacked the antislavery bastion of Lawrence, Kansas, creating an incident that the Republican press seized upon to dramatize what they described as the aggressive nature of the slave power.[4]

These events paved the way for the collapse of the Northern wing of the American party the following month. Sectional tensions within the party had come to the fore as early as June 1855, when Southern representatives at a meeting of the National Council in Philadelphia had pushed through what became known as the "Twelfth Section," which indirectly approved both the Fugitive Slave Act of 1850 and the Kansas-Nebraska Act by endorsing existing laws as the final solution of the slavery question. This decision provoked a walkout by the majority of Northern delegates, who renewed the struggle over the Twelfth Section when the national party reconvened in Philadelphia in February 1856. After failing to persuade the convention to adopt a proposal condemning the Kansas-Nebraska Act, antislavery Know-Nothings once again revolted, leaving the conclave and vowing to oppose Millard Fillmore, the convention's candidate for president, and to assemble once again in June to select their own candidate.[5]

The Know-Nothing movement thus became irrevocably divided between North Americans and South Americans. Nonetheless, until the events of May 1856, it still seemed possible for the North Americans to emerge as the dominant opposition party in the free states, or at the very least to remain an important

independent force in Northern politics. But the reaction to the sacking of
Lawrence and the caning of Sumner virtually guaranteed that the dispute over
nativism would be subordinated to the clash over slavery in shaping Northern
politics, essentially dooming the Know-Nothings to marginal status.

Still, the timing of the North American convention—two weeks before the
Republican convention—posed a delicate tactical problem for Republican
strategists. If Republicans chose a different candidate from the North Americans, the two would split the antislavery vote in the North, virtually assuring
victory for the Democrats. If, on the other hand, Republicans selected a standard bearer after the same person was nominated by the North Americans, the
candidate would inevitably be associated with Know-Nothing ideology and
would thereby lose many antislavery Catholic and immigrant votes. Republican
operatives devised an ingenious solution to this problem. They maneuvered to
have the Northern American convention select Nathaniel Banks as the Know-
Nothing party's candidate, with the private understanding that Banks would
withdraw from the race after the Republican Convention and throw his support
to the Republican nominee.[6]

After the North Americans selected Banks, the Republicans turned to the
business of choosing their own nominee. McLean remained a strong contender
for the nomination. With *Dred Scott* no longer available as a vehicle for courting
support among Republicans, McLean sought to establish his antislavery bona
fides through other means. Shortly after the Court ordered that *Dred Scott* be
reargued, the *National Intelligencer* published an exchange between McLean
and Lewis Cass in which McLean defended the authority of Congress to ban
slavery from the territories. At the urging of his supporters, McLean followed
up with another letter, which was published on June 14—only three days before
the opening of the convention itself. While this second letter neither opposed
the admission of new slave states nor explicitly urged that Congress ban slavery
from the territories, it described the conflict in Kansas as "the fruits of the ill-
advised and mischievous measure—the repeal of the Missouri Compromise"
and called for the immediate admission of Kansas under a constitution that
prohibited slavery.[7]

Ultimately, however, McLean's efforts proved unavailing. The convention
turned to John Fremont, a former Democrat who was politically inexperienced
but had gained widespread fame as an explorer and supporter of California's
revolt against Mexican rule. The platform that the convention adopted was un-
compromisingly sectional, condemning "those twin relics of barbarism—
Polygamy, and Slavery," denying "the authority of Congress, of a Territorial
Legislature, of any individual, or association of individuals, to give legal exis-

tence to Slavery in any Territory of the United States," and declaring that any effort by Congress to countenance slavery in the territories would violate the Due Process Clause of the Fifth Amendment.

Meeting in Cincinnati, the Democrats had selected their nominee earlier in June. Pierce and Douglas were both serious contenders, but both were closely associated with the Kansas-Nebraska Act, and many delegates feared that this association would be a political liability in the Northern states in the general election. Instead, the convention turned to James Buchanan, who had a long, distinguished record of public service and had been American minister to Great Britain during the struggle over Kansas-Nebraska and thus had not been directly involved in the passage of the statute.

As a former senator from Pennsylvania, Buchanan was well positioned to carry that crucial state. At the same time, Buchanan was eminently acceptable to the South. He had been an advocate of the extension of the Missouri Compromise line to the Pacific Ocean in the 1840s, but now he supported a party platform that embraced the concept of popular sovereignty, declaring that the principles of the Kansas-Nebraska Act embodied "the only sound and safe solution of the slavery question" and advocating "the uniform application of the Democratic principle to the organization of territories and the admission of new states, with or without domestic slavery, as they may elect." The platform also endorsed the Fugitive Slave Act of 1850, asserting that "being designed to carry out an express provision of the constitution," the Act "can not, with fidelity thereto, be repealed, or so changed as to destroy or impair its efficiency."[8]

On one critical point, the language of the platform on the territorial issue was deliberately ambiguous. Southern Democrats typically argued that the issue of slavery could only be definitively resolved at the point at which the people of a territory petitioned for admission as a state and adopted a state constitution, and that until that point slavery must be permitted in the territory. Northern Democrats, by contrast, took the view that a popularly elected territorial legislature could bar slavery at any point in the process. By not explicitly choosing between these positions, the convention created a platform that could be supported by both wings of the party—the accommodationist Northerners and the sectionalist Southerners.

This coalition carried the Democrats to a narrow victory in the 1856 presidential election. Sectionalists were clearly dominant in the lower South, where Buchanan won a series of overwhelming victories over Millard Fillmore, the accommodationist Know-Nothing candidate who sought to focus the country's attention on nativism rather than the sectionally divisive conflict over slavery. Similarly, the sectionalist Republican John Fremont swept the states of New

England and the upper Midwest, where Fillmore was not a major factor and Fremont easily bested Buchanan.[9]

The key battleground states were in the upper South and the lower North. Although Fillmore was competitive throughout the upper South, he carried only Maryland, leaving Buchanan with the vast majority of electoral votes from that region. The dynamic of the election in the lower North was more complicated. Buchanan and Fremont were clearly the main contenders, but although Fillmore did not come close to winning any of the free states, he retained considerable support, receiving more than 20 percent of the popular votes in New York, New Jersey, and California and more than 15 percent of the vote in Pennsylvania. Ultimately, Buchanan emerged victorious in all of the lower Northern states except Iowa, New York, and Ohio and defeated Fremont by a vote of 174–114 in the electoral college.[10]

Although Buchanan's election was a victory for the bisectional Democratic party, the results of the election could not have been particularly comforting for either Southerners or accommodationists generally. The clear loser was the Know-Nothing Party—the one organization that sought to downplay the dispute over slavery and instead focus the debate on issues that cut across sectional lines. At the same time, the purely sectional, anti-Southern Republican Party viewed the election as a "victorious defeat." The party had gained a clear majority in the North, and it looked forward to the possibility of defeating the Democrats in 1860 by taking Pennsylvania and either Indiana or Illinois.[11] Conversely, the Democratic Party itself was increasingly dominated by Southerners who were committed to the proslavery agenda.

In December, outgoing President Franklin Pierce added fuel to the fire in his last annual message to Congress. Pierce devoted much of the message to a vitriolic attack on the Republican Party, describing the Missouri Compromise as "a mere nullity. . . . a monument of error. . . . a dead letter in law," and including remarks that suggested to some that Fillmore believed that existing Supreme Court precedent vindicated the Southern position on the constitutional issues raised by *Dred Scott.* Pierce's message provoked a sharp exchange in Congress over these constitutional issues.[12] These events formed the backdrop for the Court's reconsideration of *Dred Scott* itself.

CHAPTER 22

Dred Scott, Part 2

Reargument and Reconsideration

With sectional tensions thus exacerbated, the attorneys made their new presentations to the Court in *Dred Scott* in December 1856. Geyer filed a written brief on December 2, and Blair followed suit on December 15. While still not widely discussed in newspapers, the significance of the case had become clear to political insiders. Thus, when Blair opened oral arguments on December 15, he spoke for three hours before a packed courtroom. The next two days were occupied with arguments by Geyer and Johnson. On December 18, the time was divided between Blair and George Ticknor Curtis, a prominent Massachusetts attorney who was the brother of Justice Benjamin Robbins Curtis. The new addition to Scott's legal team was hardly an antislavery zealot. Instead, he was a conservative Whig who had supported the Compromise of 1850. Nonetheless, at the last moment he agreed to join Blair in the defense of the constitutionality of the restriction on slavery in the Missouri Compromise.[1]

Curtis openly proclaimed his moderate position and took pains to limit his presentation to distinctively legal issues. Given the geographical and political makeup of the Court, Blair would no doubt have been well served by taking a similar approach. However, his presentation is striking for its characterization of *Dred Scott* as a part of the ongoing struggle between the slave power and the defenders of freedom. Blair asserted that

the natural division among men wherever born is into those who sympathise with power and dread the people, on one side, and those who dread tyranny and fear the people less, on the other. The power party naturally associates itself with property interests, and institutions which create political privileges. The other naturally allies itself with the advocates of personal rights, and opposes privileges. The contest going on under the issue here presented is but one phase of this ever-continued and ever-varying strife.

Slavery is an institution which vests political power in the few, by the monopoly of the soil, wealth, and knowledge which it creates. This is the most obvious effect on the society or States where it exists, and an obvious consequence is the concentration of power in the hands of those to whom the authority of such societies or States is entrusted in the confederacy of which they form part.

And it is the sense of inequality and privilege which it creates which lies at the bottom of the contest now going on to decide whether new communities of this character shall be created on the unoccupied lands of the confederacy.[2]

Full transcripts of the arguments of Sanford's attorneys were never published. However, reports of the arguments clearly indicate that Geyer and Johnson also took quite different tacks. Geyer emphasized the doctrine of popular
sovereignty, connecting it to the values underlying the Revolution. By contrast,
Johnson's presentation bristled with Southern indignation against what slaveholders saw as demeaning restrictions on slavery in the territories, condemning
"unequal, disparaging and insulting legislation," characterizing the Missouri
Compromise as the "law of the stronger attempted in the exercise of the con-
queror's right," and declaring that "the people of the South do not stand in the
relation of servant to the North."[3]

Despite the tenor of these arguments, in theory at least, *Dred Scott* was to
be decided on the basis of distinctively legal doctrine rather than political considerations. In making their arguments, the attorneys were required to address
five separate issues.

1. Was the Issue of Dred Scott's Citizenship Properly
before the Court?

Blair argued that Sanford had waived his right to appeal the jurisdictional issue
by pleading to the merits. Geyer and Johnson contended that the defendant did
not have the authority to in effect vest the court with jurisdiction by addressing
the merits, and that the Court therefore was required to dismiss the case if the
pleadings on their face did not state facts sufficient to support jurisdiction based
on diversity of citizenship.[4]

2. Assuming That the Court Should Address the Question,
Were the Scotts Citizens for Purposes of the Jurisdictional
Requirements of Article III?

Attorneys for both sides could cite a variety of authorities to support their respective positions. Expanding on the arguments that he had made in 1855, Blair
argued, first, that the term "citizen" generally meant nothing more than "free
inhabitant" for federal constitutional purposes; second, that the essence of citizenship was not the possession of political rights but rather "the right of protection of life and liberty, to acquire and possess property, and equal taxation";
and finally, that even if free blacks were not citizens for purposes of the Comity
Clause, they nonetheless should be considered citizens for purposes of diversity

jurisdiction. By contrast, Geyer and Johnson argued that free blacks generally were not citizens, and that, in any event, Dred Scott and his family *specifically* were not citizens because (a) as slaves, they were not citizens at birth and (b) even assuming they were emancipated by Emerson, Emerson had no authority to confer upon them the political status of citizenship.[5]

3. Assuming That the Court Had Jurisdiction over the Case, Was the Court Bound to Follow the Decision of the Missouri Supreme Court in Scott v. Emerson?

Geyer and Johnson argued that this issue was governed by the principles enunciated in *Strader v. Graham* and that the Court was bound to follow *Scott v. Emerson*. Blair, by contrast, observed that the *Strader* Court had decided only that the *Strader* case presented no federal question, and reiterated his position that, under the rule of *Swift v. Tyson,* the Court should apply the general federal common law in *Dred Scott,* particularly in view of the fact that the decision in *Scott v. Emerson* was inconsistent with prior Missouri case law.[6]

4. Assuming That the Court Was Not Bound by the Decision in Scott v. Emerson, *Had the Scotts Established Their Right to Freedom?*

On this point, Blair delivered a much more sophisticated argument than he had when the case was first presented to the Court. First, in sharp contrast to his initial brief, Blair carefully distinguished the situation of Dred from those of Harriet and Eliza. Blair continued to rely primarily on Dred's residence in Illinois as the basis for his claim to freedom. At the same time, the argument acknowledged that Harriet's and Eliza's claims could only rest on the antislavery provisions of the Missouri Compromise. Blair also argued that, unlike Dred and Harriet, Eliza had *never* been a slave, because she was born in a jurisdiction where slavery was prohibited by law.[7]

Moreover, for the first time, Blair sought to exploit a crucial omission from the agreed statement of facts. Even Geyer and Johnson conceded that, if Emerson had in fact been domiciled in free territory with the Scotts, then the erstwhile slaves were entitled to their freedom. Blair pointed out that the statement of facts nowhere explicitly stated that Emerson had been domiciled in Missouri at the time that he had entered military service. Under those circumstances, Blair argued, the Scotts were entitled to rely on the common-law presumption that a person was domiciled in the jurisdiction in which he lived—in this case, at different times, the state of Illinois and the Wisconsin Territory—and the Scotts were entitled to their freedom for that reason.[8]

Blair also returned to an argument that he had made when the case was first considered. He contended that, by voluntarily bringing the Scotts into jurisdictions in which slavery was prohibited by law, Emerson had in effect emancipated the Scotts. Thus, Blair reasoned, the Scotts could not legally have been reenslaved upon their return with Emerson to Missouri. He sought to distinguish *The Slave, Grace* on the ground that, unlike England, slavery was prohibited by statute in both the state of Illinois and the Wisconsin Territory.[9]

Geyer and Johnson took issue with virtually all of Blair's conclusions. While conceding that Dred Scott at least might have been entitled to his freedom if Emerson had in fact been domiciled in Illinois, Sanford's representatives focused on the general principle that a person who came to a jurisdiction solely because of a military assignment did not become domiciled there. They also denied that the Scotts were voluntarily emancipated by being brought to reside in free territory, citing a number of authorities for the proposition that Emerson's right to coerce the Scotts had simply been suspended during their common tenure in free territory. Relying heavily on *The Slave, Grace,* Geyer and Johnson concluded that, even leaving constitutional considerations aside, the Scotts were not entitled to their freedom.[10]

5. Was the Restriction on Slavery in the Missouri Compromise Constitutional?

In defending the constitutionality of the Missouri Compromise, Blair and Curtis both focused on Article IV, Section 3, paragraph 2 of the Constitution, which states that "Congress shall have power to dispose of and make all needful Rules and Regulations respecting the Territory or other Property belonging to the United States." They argued that this provision armed Congress with plenary authority to govern the territories, including the authority to ban slavery. Curtis provided a detailed account of the evolution of this clause at the Constitutional Convention. Blair, on the other hand, emphasized the long history of Southern acquiescence in such measures, and contended that Southerners could not first accept the Missouri Compromise as the price for the admission of Missouri as a slave state and then, thirty years after Missouri had been admitted, repudiate the terms of the bargain by arguing that the restriction on slavery was unconstitutional.[11]

Geyer and Johnson responded by arguing that the power granted by Article IV, Section 3, paragraph 2 extended only to the acquisition and disposition of land itself, rather than regulations of the people living on the territory owned by the United States. They conceded that, as an incident to its power to admit new states under Article IV, Section 3, paragraph 1, Congress could institute a temporary government to administer the territories until they had met the prerequisites for statehood. However, Geyer and Johnson contended that, as an implied power, this authority should be interpreted narrowly and did not encompass the prohibition of slavery, which was in no sense necessary for the maintenance of order within the territories. They also relied on the common property doctrine, characterizing Southern acquiescence in previous limitations as expedient compromises in which Southerners had shown a willingness to forgo the enforcement of their rights in the interest of preserving the Union and maintaining sectional harmony.[12]

Unlike the proceedings of the previous February, the December arguments in *Dred Scott* were noted widely in the national press. The quality of Curtis's presentation was almost universally praised, while the efforts of the other attorneys received mixed reviews. Most commentators expected the Court to rule against Dred Scott and his family. Predictably, the reaction to the potential of such a decision split generally along partisan lines. Democratic newspapers typically looked forward hopefully to a final settlement of the dispute over slavery in the territories. By contrast, Republicans such as Horace Greeley complained that a Court with a majority of Southern justices was hardly in a position to issue an impartial decision on the issue of slavery in the territories.[13]

The tenor of these observations reflected the intensification of the sectional struggle that had marked the latter half of 1856. But despite the worsening of sectional relations, an outside observer might well have concluded that accommodationists retained the upper hand on the Court itself. Northern Democrats such as Justices Samuel Nelson and Robert Grier no doubt wished that the issue of slavery in the territories would simply disappear from the national political consciousness, and Benjamin Robbins Curtis of Massachusetts, who had been left without a party when the Whigs disintegrated, had consistently advocated a conciliatory policy toward the South. Conversely, while both James Moore Wayne and John Catron were undoubtedly proslavery, they were also prototypical Southern moderates who in *Prigg* had shown a willingness to cooperate with their Northern brethren in an effort to reach a workable compromise on the issue of fugitive slaves.

The difficulty was that the dispute over slavery in the territories did not readily lend itself to the kind of compromise that Justice Story attempted to craft in *Prigg*. Moreover, any effort by the Court to interpose itself into the dispute risked creating a backlash among those who might be dissatisfied with the Court's position, thereby exacerbating sectional tensions. The only certain method of avoiding this danger was for the *Dred Scott* Court to find an approach analogous to that taken by Justice Thompson in *Groves* and avoid discussion of the constitutionality of the Missouri Compromise altogether.

Theoretically, those justices who wished to avoid confronting the issue of slavery in the territories in *Dred Scott* had two doctrinal paths available to them. First, they might have avoided the merits of the case altogether by concluding that the Scotts were not citizens within the meaning of the Diversity Clause and dismissing the case for want of subject matter jurisdiction. Alternatively, an accommodationist justice could determine that the Court was bound to follow the Missouri decision in *Scott v. Emerson* and conclude that, even if they had been free under the laws of Illinois and the Wisconsin Territory, the status of slavery reattached to Dred Scott and his family when they returned voluntarily to Missouri. Under this view of the case, no discussion of the constitutional issues would be necessary.

Initially, a majority of the justices appeared ready to adopt the latter approach. The deliberations of the Court were delayed after the wife of Justice Daniel was burned to death in a horrible accident on January 3, 1857. Daniel, who himself suffered minor burns in the incident, was understandably griefstricken and did not attend another session of Court until the middle of February. Accordingly, *Dred Scott* was not considered by the full Court in conference until February 14. Before the first conference, the Court seemed poised to issue a narrow decision. On February 3, President-elect James Buchanan had written to his friend, Justice John Catron, asking if the Court would hand down a decision in *Dred Scott* to which Buchanan should refer in his upcoming inaugural address. After first telling Buchanan that the Court had not yet reached a decision, on February 10 Catron wrote the president-elect that the Court would probably decide the case at the February 14 conference, and that the Court would probably not reach the issue of the constitutionality of prohibiting slavery in the territories.[14]

This judgment was initially vindicated at the February 14 conference. First, Samuel Nelson, who earlier had been inclined to the view that the issue of Scott's citizenship was properly before the Court, changed his mind and joined Catron, John McLean, Robert Grier, and John Campbell to create a majority supporting the view that the objection to jurisdiction had been waived. Second, although some of the Southern justices may have preferred a broad opinion even at this stage, the majority of the Court concluded that the case should be decided against the Scott family on grounds that did not require discussion of the constitutionality of the Missouri Compromise. Instead, Nelson was assigned the task of writing an opinion that concluded that under *Strader v. Graham,* the status of the Scotts was determined by Missouri state law, and that the Court was bound to follow the ruling in *Scott v. Emerson.*[15]

Even if Nelson's approach had ultimately been accepted by a majority of the justices, some discussion of the more explosive issues presented by *Dred Scott* would likely have ensued. As early as February 6, Justice Catron predicted in a letter to President Buchanan that Justice Daniel intended to deliver a long opinion in the case.[16] Moreover, the most obvious course of argument for any justice who was inclined to hold in favor of the Scotts required a discussion of the Missouri Compromise. While a judgment against the Scotts could have been based simply on a decision to defer to the Missouri Supreme Court on the issue of Missouri law, a decision in favor of Harriet required a finding that she had become free during her time at Fort Snelling. In the absence of some legal sleight-of-hand, this conclusion could only be reached if slavery was in fact illegal in the Wisconsin Territory, which in turn was most plausibly based on the view that Congress had the authority to adopt the Missouri Compromise. While Curtis might have been politically and temperamentally inclined to craft a solution that would have avoided this eventuality, McLean was less likely to feel similarly constrained. But at the very least, antislavery Northerners would have been spared the indignity of having the Court as an *institution* enlisted against their cause.

In any event, sometime prior to February 19, while Nelson was writing his opinion, the deliberations took a sharply different turn. On the motion of Justice James Moore Wayne, the Southern justices united around the view that Chief Justice Taney should write a majority opinion that addressed the constitutional issues raised by restrictions on slavery in the land acquired in the Louisiana Purchase.

Historians have speculated widely about the forces that shaped Wayne's decision to press for a broad opinion in *Dred Scott.* Commentators have at times theorized that the blandishments of other Southern political figures played a major role in the decision. Some have suggested that Rep. Alexander H. Stephens, an erstwhile Whig from Wayne's home state of Georgia, might have been particularly influential. In prior years, Stephens had steadfastly maintained that legislation was necessary to legalize slavery in the territories. Moreover, in 1847, fearing the outcome of a lawsuit dealing with the issue, he had been instrumental in killing the Clayton Compromise. But the events of the 1850s had clearly altered Stephens's views. In December 1856, Stephens wrote privately that he was "urging all influences [he] could bring to bear on the Supreme Court" to reach the issue of the constitutionality of the Missouri Compromise, and he was confident that, if the issue was considered, the Court would strike down the congressional restriction on slavery.[17]

Still, Wayne was in many respects an unlikely candidate to press for a broad, confrontational opinion. Based on Wayne's record, one would have thought that he was the least likely of all of the Southern justices to wish to provoke a confrontation with the North by explicitly addressing the issue of the constitutionality of the Missouri Compromise. Although he clearly opposed any effort to limit the power of the Southern states over slavery within their own borders, Wayne also argued that the slave states should make concessions in order to preserve sectional harmony. Wayne's willingness to accommodate Northern concerns had emerged clearly in *Prigg,* when he endorsed the anti-slavery aspects of Story's opinion as necessary to prevent friction between North and South.

In the abstract, one possibility might have been that the disputes of the 1840s and 1850s had radicalized Wayne, much as they had turned Daniel against the North. However, Wayne's actions during the subsequent secession crisis and the Civil War belie this interpretation of events. Unlike John Campbell, who resigned from his position on the Court after his home state left the Union, Wayne remained on the Court even after Georgia formally seceded. Moreover, Wayne subsequently provided the crucial fifth vote to uphold Lincoln's power to blockade the South in *The Prize Cases,*[18] and in *Ex Parte Milligan* later joined an opinion that would have vindicated the wartime decision to suspend the writ of *habeas corpus* in Indiana.[19] These votes are impossible to square with the vision of Wayne as a sectionalist zealot.

A more plausible explanation is that Wayne viewed a broad opinion in *Dred Scott* as a step toward *restoring* sectional harmony. The results of the election of 1856 clearly indicated that the issue of slavery in the territories had the potential to drive a permanent wedge between the free states and the slave states and increase the danger of secession. Moreover, with the Republican party emerging as a dominant force in the North and sectionalist Democrats increasingly in control of Southern politics, the political process seemed unlikely to yield a settlement that would be acceptable to both sides. Wayne may have viewed *Dred Scott* as an opportunity to break the deadlock.[20]

In addition, the deliberations of the Court itself could easily have increased Wayne's unease. While most of the justices who were inclined to rule against the Scotts were initially reluctant to discuss the territorial question, Peter Daniel was prepared to issue an inflammatory opinion supporting the Southern position on this issue. At the same time, the claims of Harriet Scott and the children could only be vindicated if the Missouri Compromise was constitutional. Therefore, in conference, Justices Curtis and McLean had apparently indicated their determination to address the constitutional question in their opinions. Moreover, Wayne must have known that McLean in particular was likely to be unsparing in his criticism of the Southern position on the Missouri Compromise. With the issuance of politically charged opinions inevitable, Wayne may well have concluded that a solution imposed by the Court as an institution (albeit one with a clear Southern bias) provided the best hope of finally resolving the issue, undermining the arguments of secessionists in the South, and paving the way for sectional reconciliation.

This explanation is supported by several different accounts of Wayne's motivation. In separate, private letters to Buchanan in February 1857, both John Catron and Robert Grier reported that Wayne felt that he had been "forced up" to a discussion of the territorial issue by the decisions of Curtis and McLean to address the Missouri Compromise. Conversely, while Curtis strongly opposed Wayne's motion and argued in conference that a judicial decision dealing with the issue of slavery in the territories would only exacerbate sectional tensions, he is reported to have later characterized Wayne's motion as an error in judgment rather than an attempt to strike a blow at the North, asserting that Wayne had emphasized "how very important it was to get rid of the question of slavery in the territories, by a decision of the Supreme court, and that this was a good opportunity to do so." Similarly, in 1870, John Campbell stated that Wayne had reached his decision independently in the belief that the final resolution of the dispute over slavery in the territories was necessary for the good of the country, and that a broad decision by the Court was the only way that such a resolution could be achieved. Moreover, Wayne himself is reputed to have expressed the view that "if the Supreme Court could be brought to make a unanimous decision in the Dred Scott case . . . it would settle the question for all time to come."[21]

Of course, while John Catron may well have shared Wayne's sentiments, the motives of at least some of the other Southern justices were no doubt less benign. Peter Daniel clearly wished to strike a blow against the North, and the sectionalism of both Campbell and Roger Brooke Taney had no doubt only been hardened by the events of 1856. Nonetheless, the unanimous support of the slave state justices for Wayne's motion cannot be viewed as a simple expression of radical Southern sectionalism. Rather, it was the product of a coalition between the most militant sectionalists and those who were making a misguided effort to resolve the dispute over slavery in the territories and restore amicable relations between North and South.

When confronted with Wayne's motion, the two Northern Democrats—Samuel Nelson and Robert Grier—faced a complex political problem. Clearly, a permanent resolution of the territorial dispute would sap the lifeblood of the Republican Party, creating an opportunity for large Democratic gains in the free states. But at the same time, rather than defusing sectional tensions, a decision to join an opinion on a Southern-dominated Court that embraced the Southern position might provide Republicans with additional ammunition for the charge that Northern Democrats were nothing more than tools of the slave power. Nelson was plainly concerned about the latter problem. In conference, he joined with Curtis in urging that Wayne's motion not be adopted because the open embrace of the Southern position on slavery in the territories would inflame public opinion in the North.[22]

Ultimately, Grier took a different view, but only under political pressure. On February 19, Catron once again wrote to Buchanan, informing him that a broad decision was forthcoming and asking him to urge Grier to join the majority on this point. Buchanan wrote to Grier with such a request and, after consulting with Taney and Wayne, Grier agreed, declaring in a February 23 letter to Buchanan that "I am anxious that it should not appear that the line of latitude should mark the line of division in the court."[23] Grier's willingness to cooperate with the Southern justices apparently extended not only to the territorial issue but also to a willingness to abandon his previously expressed opposition to the consideration of the merits of the citizenship issue. Against this background, in Buchanan's inaugural address on March 4, the newly elected president was able to state with perfect equanimity that

a difference of opinion has arisen in regard to the point of time when the people of a Territory shall decide [whether to allow slavery] for themselves.

This is, happily, a matter of little practical importance. Besides, it is a judicial question, which legitimately belongs to the Supreme Court of the United States, before whom it is now pending and will, it is understood, be speedily and finally settled. To their decision, in common with all good citizens I shall cheerfully submit, whatever this may be.[24]

Neither Buchanan nor the country at large would have to wait long for the decision to which he referred. Moreover, the decision did indeed prove to be one to which Buchanan and his allies could "cheerfully submit." It would be nothing less than a full-bore assault on the fundamental political creed of Buchanan's political adversaries.

CHAPTER 23

Dred Scott, Part 3

The Opinions of the Justices

Once the decision had been made to address the broader issues presented by *Dred Scott,* Chief Justice Taney assigned to himself the task of writing an opinion for the Court. The case also generated a veritable blizzard of concurrences and dissents. While Justice Grier contented himself with a brief statement noting his concurrence in the conclusions of the majority, all of the other justices took the opportunity to express separate opinions on at least some of the issues presented by the case. Ultimately, seven justices concluded that the Scotts remained slaves, while two believed that Dred Scott and the other members of his family were legally entitled to their freedom.

On March 6, 1857, Taney delivered the opinion of the Court. He first dealt with the issues raised by Scott's assertion that the federal courts had jurisdiction based on diversity of citizenship. Taney began this part of his opinion by discussing the procedural posture of the claim that the case should be dismissed for want of diversity of citizenship. He conceded that, in an ordinary common law court, a decision to defend on the merits would have effectively waived all jurisdictional objections. However, he argued that the rule should be different in federal court.

Taney observed that jurisdiction is ordinarily presumed to lie in common law courts. By contrast, he noted, plaintiffs in federal courts were required to affirmatively plead the facts which brought a diversity case within the limits of subject matter jurisdiction of the federal courts established by Article III of the Constitution, and that this requirement could not be waived by the opposing party. Thus, Taney concluded, once the existence of jurisdictional facts had been put in issue in the trial court, a decision to defend on the merits did not bar an appellate court from reconsideration of the jurisdictional question.[1]

On the merits of the citizenship question, Taney's argument paralleled the unpublished 1832 opinion that he had prepared as attorney general. He began his discussion of the issue by defining the scope of the inquiry in the most sweeping terms. Declining to consider the possibility that the definition of Article III citizenship might be broader than that of federal citizenship for other purposes under the Constitution, he stated that "the question is . . . Can a negro, whose ancestors were imported into this country and sold as slaves, become a member of the political community formed and brought into existence by the Constitution of the United States and as such become entitled to all the rights, and privileges, and immunities, guaranteed by that instrument to the citizen [including] the privilege of suing in a court of the United States."[2]

Taney then differentiated sharply between state citizenship and federal citizenship. He contended that, while a state could declare anyone to be a citizen for its own purposes, the states lacked authority to "introduce a new member into the political community created by the Constitution of the United States." That status, according to Taney, was to be determined by a federal standard and limited to members of two groups: (1) "every person, every class and description of persons, who were at the time of the adoption of the Constitution recognised as citizens in the several States"; and (2) those foreigners whom Congress might choose to naturalize under the authority granted to it by the Constitution.[3]

Taney next turned to an extended historical discussion of the status of free blacks in the late eighteenth century, beginning with his oft-quoted (and misquoted) observation that "they had no rights which the white man was bound to respect."[4] He insisted that free blacks lacked fundamental rights at the time the Constitution was adopted and therefore could not have been viewed as citizens at that time.

In reaching this conclusion, Taney drew on a number of different sources. First, he argued that the laws of the various states limiting the rights of blacks during the founding period were inconsistent with the status of citizenship. Second, he claimed that the Fugitive Slave Clause and the clause limiting the power of Congress over the slave trade "point directly and specifically to the negro race as a separate class of persons . . . not regarded as a portion of the . . . citizens of the Government [formed by the Constitution]." Third, he contended that early actions of the federal government seemed to reflect the view that free blacks were not citizens. Finally, he argued that, during the founding period, many states would have been unwilling to allow transient black inhabitants from other states the privileges and immunities guaranteed to citizens by the Comity Clause.[5]

Taney bolstered his argument by emphasizing what he viewed as the undesirable practical consequences of establishing a regime in which free blacks were considered citizens. He contended that if states were required to recognize sojourning blacks as citizens, the states in particular would be forced to abandon restrictions on free blacks that the Southern states in particular viewed as essential to the preservation of slaveholding society:

[The Comity Clause] would exempt them from the operation of the special laws [and give them the right] . . . to go where they pleased at every hour of the day or night without molestation, unless they committed some violation of law for which a white man would be punished and . . . the full liberty of speech in public and in private upon all subjects upon which [the state's] own citizens might speak; to hold public meetings upon political affairs, and to keep and carry arms wherever they went. And all of this would be done in the face of the subject race of the same color, both free and slaves, and inevitably producing discontent and insubordination among them, and endangering the peace and safety of the State.[6]

Similarly, he later asserted that

if [a person] ranks as a citizen of the State to which he belongs, within the meaning of the Constitution of the United States, then, whenever he goes into another State, the Constitution clothes him, as to the rights of person, with all privileges and immunities which belong to citizens of the State. And if persons of the African race are citizens of a State, and of the United States, they would be entitled to all of these privileges and immunities in every State, and the State could not restrict them; for they would hold these privileges and immunities under the paramount authority of the Federal Government, and its courts would be bound to maintain and enforce them, the Constitution and laws of the State to the contrary notwithstanding.[7]

Based on these historical and practical considerations, Taney concluded that the descendants of slaves could not become citizens of the United States, and that the lower court had erred in declining to dismiss the case for want of jurisdiction.

From a purely legal perspective, the opinion clearly could have stopped at this point, sending the case back to the trial court to be dismissed on jurisdictional grounds. But since he was determined to reach the question of whether or not the Scotts were slaves, Taney faced another procedural problem. Since he had decided that the federal courts lacked jurisdiction over the lawsuit, it was at least arguably inappropriate for him to discuss the merits of the case. Taney dealt with this problem by recasting the issue of the status of the Scotts in jurisdictional terms.

He noted that, if the undisputed facts established that the Scotts were slaves, they could not be citizens, and the federal courts would lack jurisdiction on that ground as well. While the plea in abatement had not asserted that the Scotts were slaves, Taney contended that the Supreme Court could nonetheless legitimately consider this issue. Distinguishing *Dred Scott* from appeals of state court judgments, Taney asserted that "it is the daily practice of this court, and of all appellate courts where they reverse the judgment of an inferior court for error, to correct by its opinions whatever errors may appear on the record material to the case; and they have always held it to be their duty to do so where the silence of the court might lead to misconstruction or further controversy, and the point has been relied on by either side, and argued before the court."[8]

Not surprisingly, most of Taney's discussion of the Scotts' status focused on the constitutional challenge to the Missouri Compromise. He began this part of the opinion with a long discussion of the scope of congressional power under Article IV, Section 3, which vests Congress with the power to "make all needful Rules and Regulations respecting the Territory or other Property belonging to the United States." Taney contended that the Territories Clause applied only to territory already claimed by the United States at the time the Constitution was ratified and was thus inapplicable to the land acquired through the Louisiana Purchase. Therefore, in Taney's view, the Territories Clause granted Congress no power to adopt the limitation on slavery in the Missouri Compromise.[9]

In making this argument, Taney was forced to confront the seemingly contrary authority of *American Ocean Insurance Co. v. Canter,* in which Chief Justice Marshall had declared that while Florida remained a territory, it was "governed by that clause of the Constitution which empowers Congress to make all needful rules and regulations respecting the territory or other property of the United States"—that is, the Territories Clause.[10] Since Florida had also been acquired after the ratification of the Constitution, Taney was faced with the problem of explaining why the same principle should not apply to the Louisiana Purchase. He attempted to resolve this difficulty by claiming that this passage had to be read in the context of the entire *Canter* opinion, and that other language in the opinion suggested that the scope of the Territories Clause remained an open question.[11]

Disposing of the textual provision that seemingly granted Congress plenary power over the territories was an important step in Taney's argument. It did not, however, conclusively establish the constitutional case against the Missouri Compromise. Taney himself observed that Congress had authority "to organize society [in the territories], and to protect the inhabitants in their persons and property"—a power that he viewed as implicit in the Article IV, Section 3, clause 1 power to admit new states. Moreover, he conceded that Congress had great discretion in determining the proper form of government for each territory. In the absence of some contrary constitutional provision, this implied power should have been sufficient to justify a prohibition on slavery.[12]

Taney's solution to this problem was twofold. First, he made his well-known appeal to the doctrine of substantive due process. Noting that the Fifth Amendment provided that "no person shall . . . be deprived of life, liberty, or property, without due process of law," he argued that "an act of Congress which deprives a citizen of the United States of [his] property, merely because he came himself or brought his property into a particular Territory of the United States, could hardly be dignified with the name of due process of law."[13]

Standing alone, this argument is quite weak. Even under Taney's conception of the power of Congress over the territories, the federal government must have had authority to forbid ownership of some types of property whose possession would be legal in some states. Therefore, the protections of the Due Process Clause could be implicated only if slavery had some special constitutional status.

Taney found evidence of this status in the Fugitive Slave Clause and the guarantee of the right of importation of slaves until 1808. In his view, these constitutional provisions demonstrated that "the right of property in a slave is distinctly and expressly affirmed in the Constitution." Moreover, he asserted that "no word can be found in the Constitution which gives Congress a greater power over slave property, or which entitles property of that kind to less protection than property of any other description. The only power conferred is the power coupled with the duty of guarding and protecting the owner in his rights." The special constitutional status of slavery was the linchpin of both Taney's argument and the Southern position on slavery in the territories generally. Taney also invoked the common property doctrine, declaring that the Louisiana Purchase "was acquired by the General Government, as the representative and trustee of the people of the United States, and it must therefore be held in that character for their common and equal benefit . . . until it shall be associated with the other States as a member of the Union."[14]

Having disposed of the issue of the constitutionality of the Missouri Compromise, Taney then turned to the claim that Dred Scott was free because of his residence in Illinois. Taney left the detailed analysis of this issue to the concurring opinion of Justice Samuel Nelson. Taney's own discussion of this point was so brief as to be almost perfunctory. He simply relied on *Strader v. Graham* and asserted that the Court was bound by the Missouri Supreme Court's decision in *Scott v. Emerson*. Against this background, Taney concluded that Dred Scott and his family remained slaves and therefore could not be citizens entitled to invoke the diversity jurisdiction of the federal courts. Taney thus determined that the complaint should have been dismissed on jurisdictional grounds.[15]

Unlike Taney, Nelson chose not to discuss the issue of the constitutionality of the Missouri Compromise. Instead, Nelson remained committed to the narrow opinion that he had prepared before his colleagues made the decision to address the broader constitutional issues potentially implicated by *Dred Scott.*

He declined to discuss the question of whether the descendants of slaves could become citizens of the United States, arguing that the validity of the original plea in abatement was not properly before the Court. Further, while observing that "many of the most eminent statesmen and jurists of the country" had questioned the constitutionality of the Missouri Compromise, in *Dred Scott* he proceeded on the assumption that Congress possessed authority to ban slavery from the territories. Finally, Nelson concluded that the facts demonstrated that Dr. Emerson had not established a domicile in any state or territory in which slavery was outlawed by either state or federal law.[16]

Proceeding from these assumptions, the analysis in Nelson's opinion closely tracked the argument that Taney had made in *Strader*. Nelson began with the commonplace observations that, in general, "every State or nation possesses an exclusive sovereignty and jurisdiction within her territory; and her laws affect and bind all property and persons residing within it" and that "no State . . . can enact laws to operate beyond its own dominions, and, if it attempts to do so, it may be lawfully refused obedience." Thus, in the absence of constitutional limitation, he noted that "it belongs to the sovereign State of Missouri to determine by her laws the question of slavery within her jurisdiction, subject only to such limitations as may be found in the Federal Constitution." Relying directly on *Strader*, Nelson then concluded that the power of Congress over slavery in the territories had no constitutionally binding extraterritorial effect, noting that "Congress has no power whatever over the subject of slavery within [a] state" and arguing that to hold otherwise would be "subversive of the established doctrine of international jurisprudence . . . that the laws of one Government have no force within the limits of another."[17]

Nelson next turned to an examination of the law of the state of Missouri itself. He characterized the decision in *Scott v. Emerson* as generally consistent with the overall pattern of state law, contending that, in general, the Missouri cases that had denied operation of the doctrine of reattachment had involved situations in which the master had established a domicile in a free state. The one exception was *Rachel v. Walker*, where he conceded that the Missouri courts had held that a slave had gained permanent freedom in a factual situation strikingly similar to *Dred Scott* itself. However, Nelson argued that the state court was free to reexamine the *Rachel* doctrine and that, in any event, *Rachel* itself was contrary to the decisions of other courts that had considered the issue. Thus, Nelson concluded that Scott and his family remained slaves.[18]

Both Grier and Wayne delivered short opinions noting their complete agreement with the conclusions reached by Taney and Nelson. Neither opinion added materially to the analysis of the substantive issues raised by the case.

Wayne did, however, launch a spirited defense of the appropriateness of discussing the question of the constitutionality of the Missouri Compromise. Distinguishing sharply between appeals from state courts and those from lower federal courts, Wayne argued that, once the issue of the jurisdiction of the lower federal court was properly placed before the Supreme Court, the Court was empowered to consider the entire record in determining whether the lower court had in fact been authorized to take jurisdiction by the Constitution and the relevant federal statutes.[19]

In contrast to Nelson, Grier, and Wayne, Justices Daniel, Campbell, and Catron each filed detailed opinions addressing both the question of the constitutionality of the Missouri Compromise and the larger question of the power of Congress to prohibit slavery in the territories. Each of the three justices joined Taney in concluding that the Missouri Compromise was unconstitutional. However, the arguments that they deployed differed significantly from those on which the chief justice relied.

The intensity of Daniel's emotional commitment to Southern institutions and interests was clearly reflected in his concurrence.[20] From a purely substantive perspective, Daniel's ultimate conclusions were no different from those of Chief Justice Taney. The tone of the concurrence, however, was much more extreme than that of the majority opinion.

Daniel began with a disparaging characterization of African Americans, which he saw as based upon "truths which a knowledge of the history of the world, and particularly of that of our own country compels us to know," asserting that

the African negro race never have been acknowledged as belonging to the family of nations; that as amongst them never has been known or recognized by the inhabitants of other countries anything partaking of the character of nationality, or civil or political polity; that this race has been by all the nations of Europe regarded as subjects of capture or purchase; as subjects of commerce; and that the introduction of that race into every section of this country was not as members of civil or political society, but as slaves, as *property* in the strictest sense of the word.[21]

Daniel then argued that neither emancipation per se nor the actions of state governments could transmute slaves into citizens of the United States. He noted that emancipation was simply an act of an individual—the owner of a slave—and that private parties lacked authority to confer the status of citizenship. This conclusion by its terms was not particularly noteworthy. Nonetheless, given Daniel's strong commitment to states' rights generally, his analysis of the relationship between state and federal citizenship was particularly striking. He contended that national citizenship was not derived from state citizenship but was instead an independent status whose parameters were defined by national standards, asserting that

> the States, in the exercise of their political power, might, with reference to their peculiar Government and jurisdiction, guaranty the rights of person and property, and the enjoyment of civil and political privileges, to those whom they should be disposed to make the subjects of their bounty, but they could not reclaim or exert the powers which they had vested exclusively in the United States. They could not add to or change in any respect the class of person to whom alone the character of citizen of the United States appertained at the time of the adoption of the Federal Constitution. They could not create citizens of the United States by any direct or indirect proceeding.[22]

The language of Daniel's opinion became more intemperate as he turned to the question of whether Dred Scott remained a slave. He derided the "vaunted" *Somerset* decision, sarcastically commenting that it was often cited as "the proud evidence of devotion to freedom under a Government which has done as much perhaps to extend the reign of slavery as all the world besides."[23] Turning more specifically to the question of the power of Congress to outlaw slavery in the territories, he relied primarily on the common property doctrine:

> Nothing can be more conclusive to show the equality of [the right to settle in the territories] with every other right in all the citizens of the United States, and the iniquity and absurdity of the pretension to exclude or disfranchise a portion of them because they are the owners of slaves, than the fact that the [Constitution], which imparts to Congress its very existence and every function, guaranties to the slaveholder the right to his property, and gives him the right of reclamation throughout the entire extent of the nation; and farther, that the only private property which the Constitution has *specifically recognized,* and has imposed it as a direct obligation on the States and the Federal Government to protect and *enforce,* is the property of the master in his slave; no other property is placed by the Constitution on the same high ground, nor shielded by a similar guaranty.
>
> Can there be imputed to the sages and patriots by whom the Constitution was framed, or can there be detected in the text of the Constitution, or in any rational construction or implication deducible therefrom, a contradiction so palpable as would exist between a pledge to the slaveholder of an equality with his fellow-citizens, and a warrant given . . . to another, to rob him of that property, or to subject him to proscription or disfranchisement for possessing or for endeavoring to retain it? The injustice and extravagance necessarily implied in a supposition like this, cannot be rationally imputed to the patriotic or honest, or to those who were merely sane.[24]

In sharp contrast to the tone of Daniel's concurrence, Campbell's opinion was a measured defense of the states' rights arm of proslavery constitutionalism distilled to a precise, lawyerly argument.[25] Campbell eschewed any discussion of the issue of the citizenship of free blacks, beginning instead with an analysis of the status of Dred Scott under state law. Campbell appeared to concede that, if Scott's master had in fact become a domiciliary of a free state, Scott could have been permanently emancipated through the operation of that state's law. However, Campbell argued that, in *Dred Scott* itself, there was no evidence that the master had in fact established a domicile in either Illinois or Minnesota. From this perspective, although taking the opportunity to extensively criticize *Somerset*, Campbell ultimately characterized this aspect of the decision in *Scott v. Emerson* as a perfectly orthodox application of the doctrine of reattachment recognized in *The Slave, Grace.*[26]

Turning to the issue of the constitutionality of the Missouri Compromise, Campbell, like Taney, began by arguing that the Territories Clause granted Congress only limited authority—in Campbell's words, the power to take "such administrative and conservatory acts as are necessary for the preservation of the public domain, and its preparation for sale or disposition." In particular, he argued:

Whatever [the states'] Constitution and laws validly determine to be property, it is the duty of the Federal Government, through the domain of jurisdiction merely Federal, to recognise to be property. . . . This principle follows from the structure of the respective governments, State and Federal, and their reciprocal relations. They are different agents and trustees of the people of the several States, appointed with different powers and distinct purposes, but whose acts, within the scope of their respective jurisdictions, are mutually obligatory. They are respectively the depositories of such powers of legislation as the people were willing to surrender, and their duty is to co-operate within their several jurisdictions to maintain the rights of the same citizens under both Governments unimpaired. A proscription, therefore, of the Constitution and laws of one or more States, determining property, on the part of the Federal Government, by which the stability of its social system may be endangered, is plainly repugnant to the conditions on which the Federal Constitution was adopted, or on which that Government was designed to accomplish.[27]

Since in his view the Missouri Compromise was unconstitutional, Campbell concluded that Scott remained a slave, and as such was not entitled to maintain a suit in federal court pursuant to diversity of citizenship.

Interestingly, however, Campbell specifically limited his discussion to the constitutionality of congressional enactments. He explicitly refused to comment on the powers of territorial legislatures, suggesting that the judiciary lacked the competence to determine the limits of their power. Thus, although Campbell had nothing but contempt for the doctrine of popular sovereignty in political terms, unlike Taney, he implied that the people of the territories themselves possessed the authority to ban slavery.[28]

John Catron's opinion clearly reflected the impact of the developments of the 1850s on the structure of American politics in general and Southern attitudes in particular. In 1848, Catron had privately advocated the extension of the Missouri Compromise line to the Pacific Ocean and declared that if he were a member of Congress he would have voted to exclude slavery from Oregon. Catron no doubt viewed this approach as a means to permanently resolve the territorial issue on a relatively amicable basis, much as the supporters of the Missouri Compromise had believed that they had found a means to remove the irritant of the territorial issue from national politics.[29] However, like Wayne, Catron apparently concluded that, in the wake of the passage of the Kansas-Nebraska Act and the rise of the Republican Party, only the constitutionalization of the Southern position could still the ongoing disruptions in American politics generated by the territorial question.

Despite this conclusion, Catron's opinion took a quite different tack than those of his Southern brethren. At the outset of the opinion, Catron flatly refused to entertain the question of Scott's citizenship, concluding that any objection to the jurisdiction of the Court had been waived by the choice to actively defend on the merits. In addition, he rejected Taney's claim that the Territories Clause was not by its terms broad enough to empower Congress to outlaw slavery in the territories under its control.[30] Nonetheless, Catron ultimately concluded that the Missouri Compromise violated the rights of slaveowners who wished to bring their property into the Northern portion of the Louisiana Purchase.

Catron based this conclusion on two separate arguments. First, he cited a provision of the treaty of cession itself, which provided that, until "incorporated into the Union," "the inhabitants of the [Louisiana] territory . . . shall be maintained and protected in the free enjoyment of their liberty, property, and the religion which they possess." Noting that slavery was well established in the Louisiana territory at the time of the cession, Catron argued that this provision protected the right to hold slaves not only of those resident in the territory in 1803 but also of those who moved into the territory subsequent to its purchase by the United States.[31]

Taken alone, this argument would have left the issue of slavery in the Mexican cession untouched. However, Catron also vigorously defended the common property doctrine, contending that it was embodied in the Comity Clause. Rejecting the almost universally accepted view that the clause simply guaranteed that citizens in state A who found themselves in state B would have the same fundamental rights as citizens in state B, Catron instead contended that

the [meaning of] the cited clause is not that citizens of the United States shall have equal privileges in the Territories, but the citizen of each State shall come there in right of his State, and enjoy the common property. He secures his equality through the equality of his State, by virtue of that great fundamental condition of the Union—the equality of the States.[32]

Thus, while not agreeing with the reasoning in the Taney, Campbell, and Daniel opinions, Catron ultimately reached the same conclusion on the issue of the power of Congress to ban slavery from the territories.

Justices John McLean and Benjamin Robbins Curtis both disagreed sharply with Taney and the other Southerners on virtually every issue presented in *Dred Scott*. However, their opinions were as different in tone as those of Daniel and Campbell. When he believed that the *Dred Scott* decision would be handed down before the Republican Convention in June 1856, McLean had informed his supporters that he had prepared an opinion that would allay fears about his commitment to the antislavery cause and improve his standing among more radical elements of the party.[33] Although the decision in the case was postponed until 1857, well after Fremont had gained the Republican nomination and Buchanan had won the general election, McLean apparently did not alter the wording of his dissent (perhaps looking to another potential run at the Republican nomination in 1860). Thus, despite the fact that McLean's basic outlook was that of a conservative Republican, the opinion combined orthodox legal analysis with political rhetoric well calculated to convince Radical Republicans that McLean was an acceptable standard-bearer for the party.[34]

McLean began by making short work of the jurisdictional argument. He first expressed the view that the question of Scott's citizenship was not properly before the Court. However, assuming for the purpose of argument that the issue should be addressed on the merits, McLean adopted the most advanced Republican position on this point, declaring that "the most general and appropriate definition of the term citizen is 'a freeman.' Being a freeman, and having his domicil in a state different from that of the defendant, [Scott] is a citizen . . . and the courts of the Union are open to him."[35]

Not surprisingly, the bulk of McLean's opinion was devoted to the issue of slavery in the territories. He premised his argument on the basic tenets of antislavery constitutionalism, asserting that "all slavery has its origins in power, and is against right" and relying on *Somerset* for the proposition that slavery was a local institution that could only exist where established by positive law. He then contended that, at the time the Constitution was drafted, "it is a well-known fact that a belief was cherished by the leading men, South as well as North, that the institution of slavery would gradually decline, until it would become extinct." Against this background, McLean reiterated the argument that he initially had made in 1847, declaring that "there is no power in the Constitution by which Congress can make either white men or black men slaves."[36]

Of course, in *Dred Scott* itself, the only issue was whether Congress could constitutionally *bar* slavery from the territories. Thus, McLean was able to take a position which, while in some tension with the views he had expressed in 1847, was nonetheless more consistent with his basic nationalist perspective. Characterizing the Court's opinion in *Canter* as dispositive, he emphatically rejected Taney's contention that Chief Justice Marshall's sweeping vindication of congressional power to govern the territories in that case was dictum. Instead, analogizing *Dred Scott* to *Canter*, McLean concluded that "if Congress may establish a Territorial Government in the exercise of its discretion, it is a clear principle that a court cannot control that discretion. This being the case, I do not see on what ground the act is held to be void. It did not purport to forfeit property, or take it for public purposes. It only prohibited slavery; in doing which, it followed the ordinance of 1787."[37]

Having disposed of the claim that the Missouri Compromise was unconstitutional, McLean then sought to refute the contention that the Court was bound to respect the Missouri court's conclusion that Scott was a slave under Missouri law. In substantial measure, McLean's disagreement with Nelson was based upon a different characterization of Emerson's status in Illinois. While Nelson viewed Emerson as little more than a mere sojourner in Illinois, McLean contended that Emerson had acquired a domicile in that state.[38] Proceeding from this premise, McLean concluded that the Missouri decision was inconsistent with both common law and constitutional principles.

On the common law issue, McLean argued that the state court decision was inconsistent not only with international law and the decided cases from other jurisdictions but also with the prior decisions of the Missouri Supreme Court itself. McLean appeared to concede that, absent constitutional considerations, the United States Supreme Court would have been required to acquiesce in the enforcement of a state statute that abrogated the common law on this point. However, he noted that in *Pease v. Peck*, Justice Grier had spoken for the Court in establishing the principle that "when the decisions of the State court are not consistent, we do not feel bound to follow the last, if it is contrary to our own convictions; and much more is the case where, after a long course of consistent decisions, some new light suddenly springs up, or an excited public opinion has elicited new doctrines subversive of former safe precedent." Given his anti-slavery sentiments, McLean had no trouble in concluding that this precedent justified reversal of the decision of the Missouri court.[39]

This argument alone would have provided a sufficient basis for holding that Dred Scott should be released from bondage. Nonetheless, McLean also went further, contending that Scott could not constitutionally be returned to slavery in Missouri. McLean founded this conclusion on considerations of horizontal federalism. He argued that the Missouri courts were constitutionally bound to respect the change in status worked by the constitution of Illinois, declaring that

the States of Missouri and Illinois are bounded by a common line. The one prohibits slavery, the other admits it. This has been done by the exercise of that sovereign power that appertains to each. We are bound to respect the institutions of each, as emanating from the voluntary action of the people. . . . Having the same rights of sovereignty as the State of Missouri in adopting a Constitution, I can perceive no reason why the institutions of Illinois should not receive the same consideration as those of Missouri.

He concluded that "I am unable to reconcile [the result in *Scott v. Emerson*] with the respect due to the state of Illinois."[40]

Throughout the opinion, the legal analysis was interspersed with seemingly gratuitous assaults on the institution of slavery itself. For example, McLean asserted that "we need not refer to the mercenary spirit in slaves, to show the degradation of Negro slavery in our country," and that "a slave is not a mere chattel. He bears the impress of his Maker, and is amenable to the laws of God and man." Similarly, in responding to the Southern claim that slavery must be allowed in the territories because the territories were the "common property" of the states, McLean turned the argument on its head, declaring that "the repugnance to slavery would probably prevent fifty or a hundred freemen from settling in a slave territory, where one slaveholder would be prevented from settling in a free Territory."[41] In short, taken as a whole, McLean's opinion, like those some of the Southern justices, was couched in the language of a committed sectionalist, rather than a dispassionate jurist.

Curtis's dissent was in general far more moderate in tone, reflecting his basic ideology, which was both more accommodationist and less nationalist than that of many erstwhile Northern Whigs. After first arguing that the citizenship question was properly before the Court, Curtis steered a middle course in his analysis of the substance of the question. He began by taking issue with Taney's reading of the historical record, contending that at least five states granted free blacks citizenship at the time the Constitution was drafted. Under the Articles of Confederation, these blacks would have been entitled to the privileges and immunities of national citizenship. Thus, for Curtis, the question was whether the Constitution had deprived free blacks of their right to citizenship. After first noting that the Constitution by its terms did not define national citizenship, he expressly considered three other possibilities: that Congress possessed the authority to define citizenship, that all free persons born within the United States were to be considered citizens of the United States, and that each State was to be free to determine "what free persons, born within its limits, shall be citizens of such State, and *thereby* citizens of the United States."[42]

Curtis rejected the first possibility on both practical and doctrinal grounds. He initially observed that, if Congress possessed such a power, it could unduly circumscribe the class of persons eligible to be president, vice president, or members of Congress simply by narrowly defining the term "citizen of the United States." In addition, he noted that the Constitution does not specifically grant Congress general authority to define citizenship. Instead, the only directly relevant provision provides that Congress shall have power "to establish a uniform rule of *naturalization*"—a term that, in Curtis's view, was limited to the removal of the disabilities of alienage from those of foreign birth. Therefore, the doctrine of enumerated powers also mitigated against the theory that Congress had unfettered authority to grant or withhold national citizenship.[43]

Curtis was thus left with a choice between McLean's position—that all native-born free persons were citizens—and the conclusion that each state had the authority to decide (at least as an initial matter) which of its native-born residents should be considered citizens of the United States. In defending the latter theory, Curtis relied in part on a textual argument, observing that, when the Constitution discussed citizenship, it normally referred to state citizenship. Thus, for example, he observed that the Comity Clause provides that "citizens of each *State* shall be entitled to all the privileges and immunities of citizens of the several States"—in effect, choosing state citizenship as the benchmark for the determination that a person was entitled to national protection for the rights appurtenant to that status.[44]

Primarily, however, Curtis grounded his conclusion in fundamental principles of constitutional interpretation. He noted that prior to the adoption of the Constitution, each state possessed the authority to define citizenship as an inherent aspect of its sovereign authority. Further, the states retained all aspects of sovereign authority not granted to the federal government by the Constitution. Since only the power of naturalization was granted to Congress, in Curtis's view the states retained authority to determine the status of native-born residents.

While rejecting Taney's extreme proslavery approach, Curtis's analysis of the citizenship question fell far short of advanced antislavery positions. First, under his theory, if a black person was born in a state that did not consider him a citizen, he could *never* obtain that status, since states would not possess the power to confer national citizenship on persons born outside their borders. Moreover, Curtis repeatedly emphasized that federal power over naturalization extended only to aliens—those born outside the boundaries of the United States. Thus, while in theory Congress could have granted American citizenship to a native African who emigrated to the United States, the federal government was powerless to take similar action with respect to a person who was born a slave in South Carolina and was later emancipated in Massachusetts.

Further, under Curtis's analysis, the Constitution guaranteed only limited rights to those free blacks who were in fact citizens of the United States. Clearly, as citizens they would be entitled to invoke the jurisdiction of the federal courts on the ground of diversity of citizenship, and they could also become candidates for president, vice president, and Congress. The Comity Clause also guaranteed citizens of the United States the right to free ingress and egress to and from all states in the Union—a right that was denied to free blacks by the Negro Seamen's Acts. The question of what other rights free black citizens would enjoy, however, was to be in considerable measure a function of state law.

Curtis embraced the dominant view of the Comity Clause, which both limited the scope of the interests that were protected by that provision and, in many cases, defined the rights of sojourners by reference to those granted by the state to its own citizens. Under this view, if a state imposed some racial restriction on its own black citizens, it could impose a similar restriction on blacks from other states. Thus, responding to the argument that, under his approach, states such as South Carolina would be required to allow free blacks from (for example) Massachusetts to vote and hold office, Curtis first contended that these rights were not protected by the Comity Clause. He then continued:

Privileges and immunities which belong to certain citizens of a State, by reason of the operation of causes other than mere citizenship, are not conferred. . . . It rests with the States themselves so to frame their Constitutions and laws as not to attach a particular privilege or immunity to mere naked citizenship. If one of the States will not deny to any of its citizens a particular privilege or immunity, if it confer it on all of them by reason of mere naked citizenship, then it may be claimed by every citizen of each State by force of the Constitution.[45]

This analysis clearly indicates that states which granted free blacks citizenship could nonetheless place race-based restrictions on the rights of all blacks—

whether domiciliaries or sojourners. Suppose, however, that a state restricted citizenship to white domiciliaries. Could it then deny to black citizens from other states a fundamental right that it granted to all white, native-born citizens—for example, the right to buy real property? Although the language of his opinion suggests that no such discrimination would be constitutional under the Comity Clause, Curtis did not give a definitive answer to this question.

This conclusion, however, was not a reflection of any particular solicitude for the rights of free blacks per se. Instead, it was simply a logical corollary to the same vision of federalism that underlay his approach to the issue of fugitive slaves. From Curtis's perspective, in both cases the Constitution assigned to a single state the authority to make an initial determination regarding status. In the case of national citizenship, that state was the individual's place of birth, and in the case of the master/slave relationship, the relevant state was that of the owner's domicile. From the perspective of other states, the Constitution also assigned a relatively limited significance to that initial determination. Under the Comity Clause, states were required only to provide citizens from other states with the rights common to all state citizens, and under the Fugitive Slave Clause, the state was required to recognize only the owner's claims to recovery of fugitives, as opposed to slaves brought voluntarily into the state. Within the limited scope of the constitutional protection, however, states were not allowed to interfere, whether through the Negro Seamen's Acts or Personal Liberty Laws. The same symmetry of argument would mark Curtis's treatment of the subconstitutional issues of comity implicated by the ultimate determination of the status of Dred Scott.

In analyzing the question of whether Dred Scott and his family were entitled to their freedom, Curtis first criticized the majority's decision to reach the merits at all. Observing that the plea in abatement had not challenged Dred Scott's citizenship on the ground that he was a slave, Curtis argued that this omission left the Supreme Court without the power to reach the issue once it had found that the Court lacked jurisdiction for other reasons. Curtis asserted that "a great question of constitutional law, deeply affecting the peace and welfare of the country, is not . . . a fit subject to be thus reached" and also declared that "I do not hold any opinion of this court . . . binding, when expressed on a question [such as this] not legitimately before it." At the same time, Curtis argued that, because he believed that the Court *did* have jurisdiction, he was compelled to discuss the merits of the case.[46]

On the substantive question, he took issue with virtually all of the arguments of the majority. Curtis described the Territories Clause as "a power to pass all needful laws respecting [the territories]" and declared that "whatever Congress deems needful is so, under the grant of power."[47] At the same time, however, he recognized that the scope of the Territories Clause was not in fact the central issue in the case. As already noted, unless limited by some extrinsic constitutional provision, Congress would have had authority to prohibit slavery in the territories even under Taney's limited view of congressional power. Thus, Curtis dealt extensively with Taney's due process argument.[48]

On this point, Curtis, like McLean, began with the basic antislavery view of the institution of slavery, echoing the language of Justice Joseph Story in *Prigg:* "Slavery, being contrary only to natural right, is created only by municipal law." Further, Curtis noted that, since slavery defined a status, the precise powers, duties, and obligations which grow out of that status must also be defined by municipal law. Thus, in Curtis's view, Taney's argument implied that the Constitution created an anomaly, protecting the institution of slavery in the abstract but not defining the incidents of the status that are an integral part of the institution.[49]

Curtis also contended that the common property doctrine created an even more troubling anomaly, allowing the rights of citizens of slave states in the territories to be judged by one set of municipal regulations, and the rights of citizens from free states to be governed by another. While agreeing that the territories were acquired for the common benefit of all the people of the United States, Curtis argued that the common benefit was to be defined collectively, rather than individually, and that Congress had the authority to determine how best to administer the territories. He concluded his critique of the common property doctrine by declaring that

whatever individual claims may be found on local circumstances, or sectional differences of condition, cannot, in my opinion, be recognised [*sic*] in this court, without arrogating to the judicial branch of the Government powers not committed to it; and which . . . I do not think it fitted to wield.[50]

Curtis thus clearly rejected the proslavery arguments advanced by Taney and the other members of the *Dred Scott* majority. The opinion did not, however, embrace the position espoused by the Republican platform—that the Due Process Clause *prohibited* Congress from granting legal protection to slavery in the territories. While it was unnecessary for Curtis to directly address the Republican position in *Dred Scott,* his argument against the common property doctrine plainly implied that Curtis would have rejected the antislavery analysis as well. In essence, Curtis's position was that the Constitution did not adopt sectional views on the issue of slavery in the territories. Instead, it was left to the "best judgment and discretion of the Congress" to choose from among competing perspectives.[51]

This analysis was no more consistent with the Republican position than with the common property doctrine. Moreover, Curtis did not express a position on the status of slavery in the territories in the absence of congressional action. In short, given the political context, Curtis's opinion could appropriately be described as neither antislavery nor proslavery.

Having vindicated the idea that the Missouri Compromise passed constitutional muster, Curtis turned to an examination of the Scotts' status after they returned to Missouri. Curtis began this part of his opinion with an assessment of the impact of the laws of the Wisconsin Territory on the status of the Scotts. He concluded that those laws did not simply deny recognition to slavery, but instead that they absolutely prohibited the existence of the institution within the Territory. Thus, he reasoned that, under Wisconsin territorial law, Scott's status was that of a free man. The central question was whether Missouri would recognize that change in status.

At one point, Curtis argued that Missouri was constitutionally required to view Scott as a free man. Focusing specifically on Scott's marriage to Harriet, Curtis contended that this marriage was valid under the laws of the Wisconsin Territory and that, in any event, Emerson's consent validated the marriage and effectively emancipated Scott. Curtis noted further that the validity of a marriage is governed by the law of the place at which it was contracted, and that the claim that Scott became a slave once again upon his return to Missouri was inconsistent with the continued validity of the contract of marriage. Thus Curtis concluded that for Missouri to consider Scott a slave not only would be "inconsistent with good faith and sound reason, as well as with the rules of international law" but also would violate the prohibition against impairing the obligation of contract contained in Article I, Section 10, clause 1 of the Constitution.[52]

Most of this portion of the Curtis opinion, however, was devoted to establishing the proposition that Scott's travels had rendered him a free man under the common law. At one point, Curtis seemed to suggest that, under the principles established in *Swift v. Tyson*, the question was to be decided under federal common law. However, like McLean, his primary argument was that the Scotts should have been declared free *under the law of Missouri*. Curtis asserted that, because *Scott v. Emerson* was inconsistent with earlier Missouri Supreme Court decisions, he was not required to treat *Emerson* as an authoritative exposition of Missouri law. Instead, he analyzed the relevant state law issues as if the Missouri courts had never addressed them.[53]

Curtis began with the proposition that, in general, only the domicile of a person has the authority to determine his status and to have that determination recognized by other jurisdictions. He argued that, given the procedural posture in which *Dred Scott* was litigated, Emerson (and thus Scott) should have been deemed to be domiciled in Wisconsin during Emerson's military service there. Moreover, Curtis also argued that in this case, technical domicile was not necessary, because Emerson was a citizen of the United States, residing in a territory of the United States for an indefinite period of time while conducting the business of the United States.[54] Under these circumstances, Curtis concluded, under generally accepted principles of international law, Missouri should have recognized the change in status generated by Wisconsin law.

He conceded that the state of Missouri could have affirmatively chosen to depart from that principle if it chose to do so. He distinguished sharply, however, between the authority of the state itself and that of the state *courts*, arguing that "the judges have nothing to do with the motive of the State. Their duty is simply to ascertain and give effect to its will." While a state court could depart from international law if required to do so by either statute or "customary" law, it could not adopt a new rule because of "any political considerations, or any view it may take of the exterior political relations between the State and one or more foreign States, or any impressions it may have that a change of foreign opinion and action [has occurred] on the subject of slavery." Since Missouri had adopted the common law (and with it, international law) by statute, in Curtis's view *Emerson* was simply wrongly decided.[55]

Modern commentators have generally lavished great praise on Curtis's opinion. Fairman, for example, characterizes the opinion as "written out of the warp and woof of the law" and describes Curtis's performance as "outstanding." Similarly, Fehrenbacher judges the dissent to be "very impressive" and declares that Taney was "badly beaten" by Curtis. On the two largest substantive issues presented by *Dred Scott*—the questions of whether free blacks could be citizens of the United States and whether Congress had authority to prohibit slavery in the territories—Curtis did indeed clearly have the better of the argument. His discussion of these points is beautifully crafted, and his doctrinal and historical critique of Taney's opinion in both areas is unanswerable. On other issues, however, Curtis's analysis is far more problematic.[56]

Curtis's refusal to give controlling effect to *Scott v. Emerson* was dubious at best.[57] In essence, as Taney noted in the majority opinion, the view taken by the dissenters gave plaintiffs an unfair advantage in suits for freedoms where diversity jurisdiction was available. A plaintiff could begin in state court and have his judgment if the state court ruled in his favor. If, on the other hand, the plaintiff proceeded on the state court and was on the verge of losing, he could avoid the strictures of *Strader v. Graham* through the simple expedient of dismissing a state court action prior to judgment and beginning anew in federal court. As *Dred Scott* itself demonstrated, this danger was anything but hypothetical.

Curtis's reaction to Taney's decision to discuss the constitutionality of the Missouri Compromise was in some respects even more problematic. Since it bore on the citizenship question, the discussion of this issue was not technically dictum but rather an alternative ground for decision. Still, some (although not all) of the relevant precedents admittedly suggested that, from a purely legal perspective, Taney erred in choosing to discuss the territorial issue.

The difficulty with the dissent lay not in its conclusion, but rather in the extraordinarily intemperate language that Curtis deployed in his criticism of Taney. Curtis averred that "I do not consider it to be within the scope of the judicial power of the majority of the court to pass upon any question respecting the plaintiff's citizenship in Missouri, save that raised by the plea to the jurisdiction; and *I do not hold any opinion of this court, or any court, binding, when expressed on a question not legitimately before it.*" He also stated that "a great question of constitutional law, deeply affecting the peace and welfare of the country, is not, in my opinion, a fit subject to be . . . reached [given the procedural posture of this case]."[58]

In purely legal terms, Curtis's characterization of the status of the discussion of the Missouri Compromise was simply wrong. The legal effect of this discussion depended on the structure of Taney's opinion, rather than on the soundness of the analysis in the opinion. To illustrate this point, one need look no further than the more general jurisdictional discussion in *Dred Scott* itself. As already noted, although both Taney and Curtis concluded that the issue was properly before the Court, the question of whether the jurisdictional issue should even be considered was a matter of some dispute among the justices. Indeed, although they differed on the merits, both Justices John Catron and John McLean explicitly concluded that the justices could not properly consider the question of jurisdiction pursuant to the writ of error that brought the case before the Court. Yet neither Catron nor McLean even suggested that the jurisdictional analysis of Taney and Curtis was in any sense dictum for this reason. Instead, all of the justices understood that, because Taney and Curtis had concluded that the Court had authority to resolve the jurisdictional issue, their legal analysis of that issue was entitled to full precedential value.

The posture of Taney's treatment of the status of Dred Scott is precisely analogous. Taney may have been wrong in concluding that, as a matter of procedural doctrine, the Court could legitimately consider the issue. But, against the background of that conclusion, his substantive analysis of the question was entitled to its full legal effect. The decision to deliver a pronouncement on the constitutionality of the Missouri Compromise might appropriately be characterized as rash or even intemperate. Nonetheless, even if one considers only Taney's opinion, the pronouncement was most assuredly not extrajudicial in the sense charged by Curtis.

This point emerges even more clearly when Taney's opinion is considered in the context of the other opinions in the case. Of the seven justices in the majority, only four justices were willing to explicitly take the view that free blacks could not be citizens of the United States. Neither Samuel Nelson nor John Catron were willing to discuss the jurisdictional issue at all; John Campbell rested his jurisdictional analysis solely on his conclusion that Dred Scott and his family remained slaves because the Missouri Compromise was unconstitutional; and both McLean and Curtis concluded that Dred Scott should in fact be considered a citizen for purposes of the litigation. Thus, the latter argument was the *only* jurisdictional rationale that commanded the support of a majority of the justices. Given that Taney purported to be speaking for the Court, discussion of this issue could not be considered extrajudicial in any sense.

Normally, one would have expected an attorney who was as technically proficient as Curtis to have appreciated these points. However, he was clearly intent on striking back at Taney and the other Southern justices for reaching the issue of slavery in the territories in *Dred Scott*. As a result, whether knowingly or because his judgment was distorted by the heat of the controversy, Curtis reached for an untenable argument in his effort to discredit Taney.

Moreover, on this point, the dissenting opinion was not simply part of an ordinary skirmish over legal principles. The language chosen by Curtis was nothing more or less than an open invitation for those who disagreed with *Dred Scott* to defy the authority of the Court itself. The fact that such a call issued from the pen of a man such as Benjamin Robbins Curtis speaks volumes about the deterioration of sectional relations in the 1850s and the impact that that deterioration had on the functioning of all national institutions, including the Court. In early 1857, it would have been difficult to find a person who was more committed to either the ideology of legal reasoning or the search for a workable accommodation between North and South. Yet in response to what he perceived as unwarranted aggression from the Southern justices, Curtis was willing to both distort legal doctrine and undermine respect for the Court as an institution.

Of course, Curtis's reaction must be viewed against the background of Taney's initial decision to address the constitutionality of the Missouri Compromise—a decision that was by no means inevitable and that was itself driven by purely political considerations. The point is that, with the possible exception of Nelson's narrow concurrence, the analysis of this issue by *all* of the justices— both proslavery and antislavery—was strongly influenced by political concerns as well as distinctively legal arguments.

Distinctively legal arguments played a more prominent role in the ultimate resolution of the citizenship issue. To be sure, purely political considerations were also a major factor in the Court's treatment of this issue. The opinions of Taney and Daniel can hardly be explained in any other terms, and Grier, who changed positions in early 1857, presumably believed that to express anything less than full concurrence with Taney's opinion would undermine the appearance of bisectionalism that motivated his decision to concur generally. Conversely, McLean's decision to address the substance of the citizenship question after concluding that it was not properly before the Court is best understood as a part of his continuing effort to woo more Radical Republicans. However, given the potential political resonance of the issue, the continued refusal of Catron, Campbell, and Nelson to discuss the status of free blacks must be understood as a product of their doctrinal concerns. Catron expressly argued that the citizenship issue was not properly before the Court, while both Campbell and Nelson pointedly announced that they would not discuss the question.

Although Taney's opinion is typically described as the opinion of the Court on all issues, the open refusal of Campbell and Nelson to discuss the citizenship issue also called into question the legal significance of Taney's conclusion that the descendants of slaves could not be citizens of the United States. This conclusion could qualify as binding precedent only if Taney could legitimately claim to have the support of five justices. Both Wayne and Grier joined Taney's opinion without reservation, while Daniel also expressly asserted that free blacks could not be citizens of the United States. On the other hand, McLean and Curtis disagreed with Taney on the merits, and Catron concluded that the Court lacked jurisdiction to even consider the citizenship question. Thus, on the citizenship issue, Taney could only be said to have been speaking for the Court as an institution if either Campbell or Nelson could be counted as among his supporters.

If, like Catron and McKinley in *Prigg,* Campbell and Nelson had simply been silent, then they would have appropriately been viewed as approving Taney's analysis, notwithstanding the fact that extrajudicial accounts of their views are to the contrary. But the fact that each wrote separately materially changes the equation. Campbell began his opinion by stating he joined the *judgment* rather than the *opinion* of the Court—a phraseology that conventionally signals that he did not agree with some or all of Taney's analysis. Given that Campbell then stated that "my opinion in this case is not affected by the plea to the jurisdiction, and I shall not discuss the questions it suggests," he cannot be seen as supporting Taney on this issue. Nelson also pointedly refused to declare his adherence to Taney's opinion, noting only that he would "state the grounds upon which I have arrived at the conclusion, that the judgment of the court below should be affirmed," and that "it will not be necessary to pass upon [the jurisdictional] question." Therefore, to view Nelson as a member of a majority on the citizenship issue would also be questionable at best.[59]

In any event, technical arguments about precedent had little to do with the political impact of the discussion of citizenship in *Dred Scott*. The simple fact that the issue was featured so prominently in the main opinion in a widely discussed case inevitably raised the profile of the citizenship question in subsequent debates over the proper treatment of free blacks in American society. Nonetheless, not surprisingly, it was the Court's treatment of the question of slavery in the territories that drew the lion's share of the commentary in the immediate aftermath of the *Dred Scott* decision.

CHAPTER 24

Dred Scott, Part 4
The Reaction to the Court's Decision

James Moore Wayne had hoped that a broad opinion in *Dred Scott* would help to ease sectional tensions. In fact, the decision had quite the opposite effect. Rather than definitively resolving the dispute over slavery in the territories, *Dred Scott* itself became another bone of contention in the North-South conflict.[1]

The development of a personal rift between Justice Curtis and Chief Justice Taney prefigured the more general reaction to the decision.[2] The chain of events leading to the rift began with the decision by Justice Curtis to immediately release a copy of his dissenting opinion to the representative of a Boston newspaper who had requested the opinion. In acceding to the request, Curtis later claimed to have been acting on the belief that Taney, like Curtis himself, had already filed a copy of his opinion with the clerk of the court and that this opinion was also available for public distribution. Taney, however, had not yet filed his opinion, and the dissemination of the principal dissent thus provided the opponents of the *Dred Scott* decision with an enormous advantage in the propaganda battle that erupted immediately after the case was decided.

The reason that Taney did not file his opinion immediately is that, contrary to the established practice of the Court, he was busily revising the opinion to bolster his argument against some of the criticisms that Curtis had levied in the dissent that Curtis had delivered from the bench. While denying that he had altered his original opinion to include "any one [new] historical fact, principle, or point of law," Taney subsequently admitted to Curtis that the revised majority opinion included "[additional] proofs and authorities to maintain the truth of the historical facts and principles asserted by the court in the [majority] opinion delivered from the bench, but which were denied in the dissenting opinions." Curtis himself later estimated that the revised opinion contained more than eighteen pages of material that had not been in the majority opinion that Taney had delivered in Court on March 6. By the end of March, rumors that Taney was revising his opinion had reached Curtis.[3]

On April 2, worried that his dissent might need to be changed in order to respond to the revisions in the majority opinion, Curtis wrote to William T. Carroll, the Clerk of the Supreme Court, asking to be provided with a copy of

Taney's opinion as soon as it was printed. On April 6, Carroll responded that he had been instructed by Taney not to provide anyone with a copy of the Chief Justice's opinion before it appeared in the official reports. On April 9, Curtis wrote again, suggesting that the order could not possibly have been intended to apply to him. On April 14, Carroll responded that Taney himself had confirmed that no copy of the opinion should be provided to Curtis.[4]

Between April 28 and June 20, Curtis and Taney exchanged an increasingly frosty set of letters on the subject of the clerk's refusal to provide Curtis with a copy of Taney's opinion. During this exchange, Taney's language was particularly intemperate. Taney contended that Curtis should have obtained the permission of the other justices before releasing his dissent to the press, complaining bitterly that "no one could fail to see that [the release of Curtis's opinion alone] would encourage attacks upon the court and the [other] judges who gave [different opinions] by political partisans whose prejudices and passions were already enlisted against the constitutional principles affirmed by the court." In addition, obviously stung by Curtis's assertion that Taney's discussion of the constitutionality of the Missouri Compromise was not binding, Taney first suggested that Curtis did not actually wish to see the opinion for any reason related to his official duties, but rather "for some other unexplained purpose," which Taney implied was to convey the opinion to Curtis's brother-in-law, Charles C. P. Curtis, a newspaperman whose initial request for a copy of the opinion of the Court had occasioned Taney's directive that it not be released until published in the official reports.[5] By June 20, it was clear that the rift between the two justices was irreparable. Although financial concerns also played a role, the unpleasant exchange with Taney no doubt influenced Curtis's decision to resign from the Court on September 1. Curtis was quickly replaced by Nathan Clifford of Maine, a Buchanan confidant whose sympathy for the South was well known.

The impact of *Dred Scott* on the relationship between Curtis and Taney is an apt metaphor for the effect of the dispute over slavery on sectional harmony more generally. Despite the differences in their respective backgrounds and political orientations, the two justices apparently worked together with no apparent friction prior to 1857, and at times were able to reach workable compromises on important issues that came before the Court. But the issue of slavery in the territories proved impossible to manage without rancor, leading to a permanent breach that undoubtedly left both parties feeling aggrieved.

In the country at large, initial responses to *Dred Scott* broke down along predictable partisan lines.[6] Republicans excoriated the majority. The New York *Tribune* condemned the decision as "wicked" and "abominable," denouncing the "cunning chief" whose "collation of statements and shallow sophistries" showed a "detestable hypocrisy" and a "mean and skulking cowardice." The *Independent* was equally unsparing in its criticism of *Dred Scott,* describing the decision as "a deliberate, willful perversion, for a particular purpose" and "a vain attempt to change the law by the power of Judges who have achieved only their own infamy," and declaring that "if the people obey this decision, they disobey God." Similarly, the *Ohio State Journal* characterized the Court's conclusions as "palpable perversions of the views of the Fathers of the Republic"; the Chicago *Democratic-Press* evinced "a feeling of shame and loathing" for "this once illustrious tribunal, toiling meekly and patiently through this dirty job"; and the Chicago *Tribune* asserted that "we scarcely know how to express our detestation of [*Dred Scott*'s] inhuman dicta, or to fathom the wicked consequences which may flow from it." Sen. William Pitt Fessenden of Maine thus summarized the views of Republicans generally when he proclaimed that "[the] opinion [of the Court], if carried into practice, undermines the institutions of the country."[7]

Conversely, Democrats of all stripes at first hailed the decision as a decisive repudiation of the political creed of the rival Republicans. Northern Democrats greeted the decision with enthusiasm. For example, the *Illinois State Register* declared that "the people who revere the Constitution and the laws ... will hail the decision with satisfaction." Sounding a similar note, the New York *Journal of Commerce* asserted that the decision was "almost the greatest political boon that has been vouched to us since the foundation of the Republic."[8]

Not surprisingly, Southerners were even more ebullient. Thus, the *Richmond Daily Enquirer* cheered that "*sectionalism* has been rebuked, and abolitionism has been staggered and stunned," while the *Nashville Union and American* asserted that *Dred Scott* "fully and completely vindicates and sustains the Democratic party in the patriotism and wisdom of its course throughout the entire history of slavery agitation," and that "now every Department of the Government has sanctioned our views, and the principles of the Kansas Nebraska Act has [*sic*] been sanctioned by a majority of Congress, a Northern President and Northern Judges of the Supreme Court." Similarly, the *New Orleans Picayune* claimed with satisfaction that *Dred Scott* "puts the whole basis of the Black Republican organization under the ban of law, stamps its designs as hostile to the Constitution, and forms the basis upon which all conservative men of the Union can unite for the maintenance of the Constitution as it is and the Union as it is."[9]

At the same time, a number of Southern commentators warned against overestimating the significance of their triumph in the Supreme Court. For example, noting continuing Republican defiance, the *Charleston Mercury* admonished Southerners not to "cherish the delusion that [their] cause is triumphant and [their] rights secure," warning that "the Abolitionists are not at all abashed or dismayed; on the contrary, they accept this repulse as another blow in the work of imparting compactness and strength to their organization, and from the fire that consumes *Dred Scott,* they appear to anticipate a conflagration that will again set the popular sentiment of the North in a blaze of indignation." The *Mercury* also accurately predicted that "the Black Republican party will go into the [presidential election] of 1860, strengthened rather than discredited and weakened by the adverse judgment of the Supreme Court."[10]

What the *Mercury* did not predict was that *Dred Scott* would ultimately have a divisive impact on the Democratic Party itself. The source of the problem lay in the underlying difference of opinion between Northern and Southern Democrats on the issue of slavery in the territories. While Northern Democrats generally hewed to the concept of popular sovereignty, Southerners more often adopted the version of the "nonintervention" theory that would have effectively allowed slavery in all of the territories. Prior to the decision in *Dred Scott,* the two wings of the party had agreed to disagree on the issue of the constitutionality of prohibitions on slavery by territorial legislatures.

The specific issue that divided Democrats had not been raised by the facts of *Dred Scott.* Nonetheless, while Campbell had explicitly concluded that the courts should not overturn territorial legislative actions, Taney had stated that such legislation was unconstitutional, and the logic of the arguments of Daniel and Catron seemed to lead to the same conclusion. While Taney's discussion of the issue was clearly dictum, Southerners took the view that *Dred Scott* had vindicated their position. This conclusion was anathema to many Northern Democrats, who remained firmly committed to the doctrine of popular sovereignty.[11] The sectional divide within the party would assume greater importance as the debate over *Dred Scott* became subsumed in a renewed struggle over the fate of Kansas.[12]

In February 1857—one month before Buchanan took office and the Supreme Court decided *Dred Scott*——the Kansas territorial legislature, still dominated by proslavery politicians, passed legislation designed to pave the way for the admission of Kansas to the Union. The legislation called for a census to be held in March, an election of delegates to a constitutional convention to be held in June, and a convention to be held in September. By this time, antislavery forces were clearly in the majority in Kansas. Nonetheless, fearing that the process would be conducted unfairly to their detriment, free staters decided to boycott the election.

To deal with this explosive situation, Buchanan appointed Robert J. Walker of Pennsylvania to be the territorial governor of Kansas. Based on his background, one might have thought that the new governor would be sympathetic to Southern interests. Walker was a former Mississippi slaveowner who had served as a senator from that state from 1835 to 1845 and as secretary of the treasury in the Polk administration from 1845 to 1849. Moreover, he had written one of the most influential tracts advocating the annexation of Texas in 1844.

However, soon after assuming the governorship of Kansas, Walker publicly took positions that infuriated the political leadership of the slave states. He asserted that, for geographical reasons, Kansas was destined to be a free state, and that Congress would under no circumstances admit Kansas as a slave state or a free state unless "a majority of the people of Kansas shall have fairly and freely decided [the question of slavery] by a direct vote on the adoption of the Constitution, excluding fraud and violence."[13] Despite these comments, antislavery residents of Kansas remained determined to boycott the June elections for delegates to the constitutional convention. As a result, the convention was dominated by supporters of slavery.

Instead of taking the conventional route of adopting a single constitution and submitting it to a referendum for approval or rejection, the convention, which met in the town of Lecompton, produced two documents and asked the voters of the territory to choose between a constitution "with slavery" and a constitution "without slavery." The difficulty was that, although the "without slavery" version prohibited the further importation of slaves into Kansas, it also provided that the two hundred slaves already in the state would remain enslaved, as would their descendants. In addition, both versions of the constitution prohibited amendments to the slavery-related provisions for a period of seven years.

For obvious reasons, these provisions were unacceptable to the antislavery forces in Kansas. They boycotted the December 21 referendum, and the more extreme, "with slavery" version of the constitution was approved by an overwhelming majority of those voting and sent to Congress for approval. Buchanan then threw his support behind the Lecompton constitution. On February 2, 1858, he submitted the document to both houses of Congress, together with a message urging the admission of Kansas under its provisions.

Predictably, Southern Democrats vigorously supported Buchanan. They argued that the logic of the doctrine of popular sovereignty required the admission of Kansas. Brushing aside the clear evidence that a majority of Kansans in fact opposed slavery, Southerners emphasized the formal legality of the process by which the constitution had been adopted. They were supported by some

Northern Democrats, who also emphasized the regularity of the process and took the view that the admission of Kansas was the best hope for reducing sectional tensions.

Other free-state Democrats, led by Stephen A. Douglas, took a different view. Douglas described the process by which the Lecompton constitution was adopted as "a system of trickery and jugglery, designed to defeat the fair expression of the will of the people." Arguing that the principle of popular sovereignty required that the voters have an opportunity to consider all of the provisions of a proposed state constitution, rather than simply those relating to slavery, Douglas asserted that to support the admission of Kansas would require him "to forfeit my faith and my honor in order to enable a small minority of the people of Kansas to defraud a majority of that people out of their elective franchise."[14]

Republicans, on the other hand, were completely united. To them, Buchanan's initiative was anathema. They denounced the effort to admit Kansas under the Lecompton constitution as further evidence of the influence of the slave power in American politics in general and the Democratic Party in particular.

Not surprisingly, references to *Dred Scott* played an important role in this characterization. Thus, for example, Sen. John P. Hale of New Hampshire accused the supporters of the Lecompton constitution of "proposing to carry out this Dred Scott decision by forcing upon the people of Kansas a constitution against which they have remonstrated, and to which, there can be no shadow of doubt, a very large portion of them are opposed." Similarly, Sen. William H. Seward of New York characterized the decision as an example of "judicial usurpation [that] is more odious and intolerable than any other among the manifold practices of tyranny."[15]

Seward also focused on two of the major themes in the more general Republican assault on *Dred Scott*. First, he contended that, because the Court had first concluded that it lacked jurisdiction because free blacks were not citizens, the discussion of the constitutionality of the Missouri Compromise was dictum. Second, he characterized the decision as part of a larger slave-power conspiracy to defend slavery and the interests of the slave states, darkly adverting to "whisperings" between Chief Justice Taney and President Buchanan at Buchanan's inauguration, and noting that the next day (the day before the decision in *Dred Scott* was announced), "without even exchanging their silken robes for courtiers' gowns," the justices visited Buchanan at the White House. Not surprisingly, such attacks engendered equally vigorous defenses of the merits of the *Dred Scott* decision by Southern Democrats, at times accompanied by vigorous denunciations of what Sen. Judah Benjamin of Louisiana described as the "violence [and] recklessness" of some of the charges levied against Taney and his compatriots by some Republicans.[16]

Despite such exchanges, *Dred Scott* does not seem to have played a central role in the dispute over the admission of Kansas. Notwithstanding the strenuous efforts of the Buchanan administration, Congress refused to approve the Lecompton constitution. While the Senate voted 33–25 to admit Kansas under the disputed constitution, the House of Representatives adopted a measure that would have submitted the proposed state constitution to an up or down vote by the people of Kansas. The Senate refused to concur, and a conference committee was formed. On March 23, the committee reported a bill attributed to anti-Lecompton Democrat William H. English of Indiana that would have provided for the admission of Kansas as a state, provided that voters in the territory agreed to a reduction in the federal land grant that had been requested by the Lecompton convention. If the voters rejected the reduction, then Kansas would not become a state until its population was equal to that normally required for one representative in the House.[17]

All parties to the controversy understood that antislavery voters in Kansas would seize on the referendum as an opportunity to prevent admission of Kansas as a slave state. Nonetheless, Southerners realized that the English proposal provided them with a chance to gain at least a symbolic recognition of the legitimacy of the Lecompton constitution—the most that they could possibly achieve under the circumstances. Thus, the English bill passed both houses of Congress, and the subsequent rejection of statehood in the August 2 referendum effectively removed the issue of Kansas as a sectional irritant.[18]

Northern Democrats paid a heavy political price for the effort to vindicate the Lecompton constitution. Whereas fifty-three free state Democrats were elected to the House of Representatives in 1856, only thirty-two survived the election of 1858.[19] The same election saw the contest for a Senate seat from Illinois between Stephen Douglas, who had joined Republicans in opposing the English bill, and Abraham Lincoln, the Republican candidate. *Dred Scott* played an important role in the series of memorable debates between the two candidates that marked that contest.

Well before the debates began, Douglas had made his views on *Dred Scott* crystal clear. He outlined those views at length on June 12, 1857 in a major speech in Springfield, Illinois. In that speech, he enunciated what Fehrenbacher has described as the doctrine of "residual popular sovereignty." While conceding that *Dred Scott* established the right of Southerners to bring slaves into the federal territories without congressional interference, Douglas also declared that it necessarily remains a barren and a worthless right, unless sustained, protected and enforced by appropriate police regulations and local legislation, prescribing adequate remedies for its violation. These regulations and remedies must necessarily depend entirely upon the will and wishes of the people of the Territory, as they can only be prescribed by the local Legislatures. Hence, the great principle of popular sovereignty and self-government is sustained and firmly established by the authority of [*Dred Scott*].

In addition, Douglas lavishly praised the assertion that free blacks could not be citizens of the United States, asserting that the framers of the Constitution had understood the Declaration of Independence as applying only to whites and echoing Taney's assertion that, in the late eighteenth century, black people had universally been regarded as inferior beings.[20]

The latter view formed the basis for Douglas's attacks on Lincoln's reaction to *Dred Scott*. Noting that Lincoln had challenged Taney's conclusion that the descendants of slaves could not be citizens of the United States, Douglas declared that "I do not believe that the almighty ever intended the negro to be the equal of the white man" and "I am opposed to negro citizenship in any and every form." Conversely, he advised that, "if you desire negro citizenship, if you desire to allow them to come into the State and settle with the white man, if you desire them to vote on an equality with yourselves, and to make them eligible to office, to serve on juries, and to adjudge your rights, then support Mr. Lincoln and the Black Republican party."[21]

This assault created something of a dilemma for Lincoln. On one hand, to be viewed as being in favor of "negro equality" was a substantial political liability in the racist American society of the antebellum era—particularly in a state such as Illinois, which had gone so far as to outlaw the immigration of free blacks. On the other, accepting Taney's analysis of the citizenship issue might soften the force of Lincoln's critique of *Dred Scott* as a whole. Faced with this problem, Lincoln temporized. While declaring himself personally opposed to granting citizenship to free blacks, Lincoln argued that Taney had taken the wrong approach to the citizenship issue because the chief justice had applied a national standard on the citizenship issue, rather than allowing each state to decide for itself whether resident free blacks could be considered citizens. Thus, in the fourth debate in Charleston, Illinois, on September 18, 1858, Lincoln asserted that "my opinion is that the different States have the power to make a negro a citizen under the Constitution of the United States if they choose. The Dred Scott decision decides that they have not that power. If the State of Illinois had that power I should be opposed to the exercise of it."[22]

Lincoln made a quite different use of *Dred Scott* in his attack on Douglas.

The core of this attack was a claim that Lincoln had made in his famous House Divided speech, where he had asserted that "the introduction of the Nebraska bill into Congress [by Douglas] was [part of] a conspiracy to make slavery perpetual and national," and that

we see a lot of framed timbers, different portions of which we know have been gotten out by different workmen—Stephen [Douglas], Franklin [Pierce], Roger [Brooke Taney] and James [Buchanan] . . . and when we see they exactly make the frame of a house or a mill, all the tenons and mortices exactly fitting . . . we feel it impossible not to believe that Stephen and Franklin, and Roger and James, all understood one another from the beginning, and all worked upon a common plan or draft drawn before the first blow was struck.

While conceding that Douglas may not have specifically discussed *Dred Scott* with either Buchanan or Taney, Lincoln suggested that Douglas "had as perfect an understanding [of the conspiracy] without talking as with it."[23]

Throughout the debates, Lincoln also asserted that the Supreme Court had not completed its role in the slave power conspiracy with the decision in *Dred Scott* itself. He predicted darkly that, having proclaimed in *Dred Scott* that slavery was a constitutionally protected species of property, the Court would next hold it unconstitutional for any *state* to outlaw slavery within its borders. This indeed had been the view of *Dred Scott* taken in an article published on November 17, 1857 in the *Washington Union*—the official organ of the Buchanan administration. Although far more extreme than the views expressed by most supporters of *Dred Scott* and explicitly repudiated by Douglas, the publication of this assertion in such a prominent Democratic newspaper gave some credence to Lincoln's claim that Taney's opinion was merely an intermediate step toward the full nationalization of slavery.[24]

The specter of a vast, slave power conspiracy provided the backdrop for the famous exchange between Lincoln and Douglas during the debate at Freeport, Illinois, on August 27, 1858. Lincoln posed four specific questions to Douglas during that debate, two of which related directly to the implications of *Dred Scott*. In question two, Lincoln asked, "Can the people of a United States Territory, in any lawful way, against the wish of any citizen of the United States, exclude slavery from its limits prior to the formation of a State Constitution?" Drawing upon the slave power conspiracy theory, in question three he asked Douglas, "If the Supreme Court of the United States shall decide that States cannot exclude slavery from their limits, are you in favor of acquiescing in, adopting and following such decision as a rule of political action?" In answering question two, Douglas reiterated the position that he had taken in Springfield in May 1857. By contrast, he refused to answer question three directly. Noting that even Southerners had condemned the *Washington Union* article, Douglas declared that "there never was but one man in America, claiming any degree of intelligence or decency, who ever for a moment pretended such a thing," and that "[Lincoln] casts an imputation upon the Supreme Court, by supposing that they would violate the Constitution of the United States. . . . It would be an act of treason that no man on the bench could ever descend to."[25] These answers helped preserve Douglas's seat in the Senate. Although Republicans actually received a majority of the votes cast in the elections for the state legislature, Democrats won control of a majority of the seats in both houses of the legislature, and were thus able to reelect their chosen candidate for the Senate seat.

Lincoln and Douglas would have a rematch in 1860—this time, in a contest for the presidency. In the interim, the Supreme Court would finally come to grips with the merits in *Ableman v. Booth*.

CHAPTER 25

Ableman v. Booth, Part 2
The Court Decides

Predictably, the Wisconsin Supreme Court did not accept the invitation to co-operate in the *Ableman* appeal that the Court offered in May 1856. Instead, the state court continued to ignore the writ of error, and on March 6, 1857—the same day that *Dred Scott* was decided—the Supreme Court agreed to proceed on the basis of the record filed by the attorney general. By the time that *Ableman v. Booth*[1] was argued before the Court on January 19, 1859, relations between North and South had been strained almost to the breaking point by the *Dred Scott* decision and the conflict over the Lecompton constitution. Against this background, the United States was represented by Jeremiah S. Black, the attorney general in the Buchanan administration. By contrast, no counsel appeared on behalf of either Booth or the state of Wisconsin.

Black was a particularly apt choice to make the case against the intervention of the Wisconsin Supreme Court. Four years earlier, while serving on the Pennsylvania Supreme Court, he had delivered a strongly worded opinion refusing to issue a writ of habeas corpus on the petition of Passmore Williamson, who had been imprisoned by a federal court after having been alleged to have unlawfully aided in the escape of a slave. Although the full text of his argument in *Ableman* was never published, Black was reported to have denounced the actions of the Wisconsin Supreme Court in the strongest terms, darkly suggesting that the state judges could be cited for contempt but "magnanimously" indicating that the government would not pursue such a course.[2]

Even if sectional considerations had not been implicated, the actions of the Wisconsin court would almost certainly have been condemned by the Supreme Court. Despite their disagreements on the nature of American federalism, no justice had ever espoused the extreme vision of state autonomy that animated the state court decisions in the Booth cases. When the distaste of the majority of the justices for antislavery activity was factored into the equation, the outcome of the case was never really in doubt.

In the abstract, Justice Peter Daniel might have found the Wisconsin Supreme Court's perspective on federalism somewhat attractive. However, given his views on slavery and the sectional conflict, Daniel was hardly likely to countenance state interference in a prosecution under the Fugitive Slave Act.

Conversely, despite John McLean's opposition to slavery, he had consistently resisted efforts to undermine the enforcement of the Fugitive Slave Act. Indeed, as late as 1855, in *Ex Parte Robinson*,[3] McLean had incurred the wrath of more radical elements of the antislavery movement by ordering the release of a federal marshal who had been jailed by Ohio officials for rearresting a fugitive slave whom the state courts had ordered released on a writ of habeas corpus. Thus, in marked contrast to *Dred Scott*, Taney was able to rally a unanimous Court behind an opinion reversing the judgments of the Wisconsin court.

Taney began by assailing the basic premises underlying the disposition of both *Booth* cases by the Wisconsin court. Observing that "the paramount power of the State court lies at the foundation of [both] decisions," he emphasized that the federal government could not function effectively if state interference were permitted, contending that the regime envisioned by the Wisconsin Supreme Court would destroy the Union itself.

It would seem to be hardly necessary to do more than state the result to which these decisions of the State courts must inevitably lead. It is, of itself, a sufficient and conclusive answer, for no one will suppose that a Government which has now lasted nearly seventy years, enforcing its laws by its own tribunals and preserving the union of the States, could have lasted a single year, or fulfilled the high trusts committed to it, if offences against its laws could not have been punished without the consent of the State in which the culprit was found.[4]

Taney then turned specifically to the claim that the Wisconsin court possessed the authority to free Booth from federal custody, strongly assailing the position taken by the state supreme court. Taney argued that because the United States was an entirely separate sovereign entity from the state governments, the state courts had no power to interfere with the sovereign activities of the federal government.

The powers of the General Government, and of the State, although both exist and are exercised within the same territorial limits, are yet separate and distinct sovereignties, acting separately and independently of each other within their respective spheres. And the sphere of action appropriated to the United States is as far beyond the reach of the judicial process issued by a State judge or a State court, as if the line of division was traced by landmarks and monuments visible to the eye. And the State of Wisconsin had no more power to authorize these proceedings of its judges and courts than it would have had if the prisoner had been confined in Michigan, or in any other State of the Union, for an offence against the laws of the State in which he was imprisoned.[5]

Taney conceded that the state courts had authority to issue writs of habeas corpus in order to inquire into the reasons that a person was being held in custody and that the responsible federal officials should provide an explanation in writing. But Taney also asserted that "after the return is made and the State judge or court judicially apprized [*sic*] that the party is in custody under the authority of the United States, they can proceed no further. They then know that the prisoner is within the dominion and jurisdiction of another Government, and that neither the writ of habeas corpus nor any other process issued under State authority can pass over the line of division between the two sovereignties." Any errors in the federal proceeding—including jurisdictional errors—could be corrected only on appeal. Moreover, Taney declared that it was the duty of federal officials to resist, by force if necessary, any effort to remove a prisoner from their custody to bring the prisoner before a state court in a habeas proceeding.[6]

Taney's critique of the state court's decision to free Booth from custody did not rest on a theory of federal supremacy. Instead, it was based on what might be described as a theory of concurrent sovereignty—the view that the state and federal governments should be seen as coequal sovereigns, and that, under principles of comity, each should respect the judicial proceedings of the other. The same theory would suggest that the federal courts should also generally refrain from interfering with ongoing state criminal proceedings, even in the face of allegations that the proceedings somehow implicated federal rights.

By contrast, Taney's response to the Wisconsin Supreme Court's failure to comply with the writ of error emphasized the place of the United States Supreme Court in the judicial hierarchy. On this point, his argument mirrored Story's analysis in *Martin v. Hunter's Lessee*. After noting that the Constitution's grant of appellate jurisdiction by its terms applied to cases from *all* courts—not simply federal courts—Taney contended that

it is manifest that [the establishment of] ultimate appellate power in a tribunal created by the Constitution itself was deemed essential to secure the independence and supremacy of the General Government in the sphere of action assigned to it, to make the Constitution and laws of the United States uniform, and the same in every State, and to guard against evils which would inevitably arise from conflicting opinions between the courts of a State and of the United States, if there was no common arbiter authorized to decide between them.

Taney also contended that, when the Constitution was drafted in 1787, "it was manifest that serious controversies would arise between the authorities of the United States and of the States, which must be settled by force of arms unless some tribunal was created to decide between them finally and without appeal." Finally, after stating flatly that the Fugitive Slave Act was constitutional and that the actions of the commissioner in taking Booth into custody were entirely lawful, Taney averred that "if any argument was needed to show the wisdom and necessity of this appellate power, the cases before us sufficiently prove it, and at the same time emphatically call for its exercise."[7]

Taney also denied that recognizing the ultimate authority of the Supreme Court in any way denigrated the sovereignty of the states. He first observed that "neither this Government nor the powers of which we are speaking were forced upon the States. The Constitution of the United States, with all the powers conferred by it on the General Government and surrendered by the States, was the voluntary act of the people of the several States, deliberately done for their own protection and safety against injustice from one another." He then argued that "the highest honor of sovereignty is untarnished faith. And certainly no faith could be more deliberately and solemnly pledged than that which every State has plighted to the other States to support the Constitution as it is, in all its provisions, until they shall be altered in the manner which the Constitution itself prescribes" and that "no power is more clearly conferred by the Constitution and laws of the United States than the power of this court to decide, ultimately and finally, all cases arising under such Constitution and laws, and for that purpose to bring here for revision, by writ of error, the judgment of a State court, where such questions have arisen, and the right claimed under them denied by the highest judicial tribunal in the State."[8]

Despite its powerful reassertion of the Supreme Court's authority over state courts, *Ableman* should not be read as an endorsement of a strong vision of federal power more generally. Indeed, observing that the Court also had the power to invalidate federal statutes, Taney explicitly noted that "th[e] judicial power was justly regarded as indispensable not merely to maintain the supremacy of the laws of the United States, but also to guard the States from any encroachment upon their reserved rights by the General Government."[9] Thus, although the Supreme Court is clearly a department of the federal government that derives its power solely from the federal Constitution, Taney conceptualized the Court as a neutral arbiter that was well positioned to mediate conflicts between the state governments and the other branches of the federal government. It was this function that he viewed as having been compromised by the actions of the Wisconsin Supreme Court in the *Booth* cases.

In any event, Taney's opinion, with its strongly worded rejection of the actions of the Wisconsin Supreme Court and vindication of the Fugitive Slave Act of 1850, was certainly everything that the proslavery forces could desire. But in the main, the rebuke to the state court was by no means simply an embodiment of sectionalist proslavery legal doctrine. Indeed, a contrary decision could only have been reached by rejecting bedrock principles underlying the Court's own jurisprudence and accepting the extreme state-centered vision of federalism that had been embraced not only by the most radical elements of the antislavery cause but also by Calhoun and his allies during the nullification crisis of the early 1830s.

From this perspective, the decision of John McLean to concur silently with Taney was one of the most telling features of the *Ableman* decision. In 1859, McLean may have harbored the hope that he could obtain the Republican nomination for President in 1860. A strong dissent in *Ableman* might well have enhanced his standing with the radical wing of the party. But to voice such an opinion would have resulted in abandonment of the principles that McLean had repeatedly espoused in the fugitive slave cases that had come before him throughout his judicial career. Despite his lifelong ambition to attain the presidency, McLean was unwilling to take such a hypocritical stance. Instead, he implicitly reverted to the more moderate antislavery stance that had characterized most of his tenure on the Court.

Against the background of judicial unanimity, modern legal scholars have typically viewed the *Ableman* opinion as a classic exposition of mainstream constitutional doctrine. They have generally heaped lavish praise on Taney's performance. For example, Charles Warren characterizes *Ableman* as "the most powerful of all [of Taney's] notable opinions," while Carl B. Swisher asserts that the opinion "marked the Chief Justice at his best [and] was thoughtful, measured and disciplined to the last degree."[10]

Still, the opinion also contained evidence of the continued willingness of the chief justice and his allies to engage in the escalating sectional conflict—most notably, in his decision to speak out on the constitutionality of the Fugitive Slave Act of 1850. As Taney himself noted, the Court need not have discussed this question in order to resolve the controversy that was before the justices in *Ableman*. Despite this concession, Taney declared that "it is proper to say that, in the judgment of this court, the act of Congress commonly called the fugitive slave law is, in all of its provisions, fully authorized by the Constitution of the United States, that the commissioner had lawful authority to issue the warrant and commit the party, and that his proceedings were regular and conformable to law."[11] Of course, unlike the aggressive doctrinal innovations that marked Taney's opinion in *Dred Scott*, this conclusion could aptly be viewed as implicit in the holdings of *Prigg* and its progeny. Nonetheless, the fact that the justices addressed the constitutionality of the Fugitive Slave Act in a case where the issue could have been avoided or ignored reflects the attitude of a Court that now showed no hesitance to take sides in the escalating conflict.

Not surprisingly, against this background, reactions to *Ableman* broke down largely along political lines. Southerners and Northern Democrats unanimously supported Taney. Describing the actions of the government of Wisconsin as "totally illegal and virtually revolutionary," the *Cleveland National Democrat* stated that "we trust that [*Ableman*] will be read with careful, and in the case of men willing to violate the law prayerful attention, for the sound law and truthful doctrines it preaches." Sounding the same note, *The States* of Washington, D.C., declared that, while Taney had "lived long and done much for honor and fame," *Ableman* was "the summit. He will never surpass the wisdom and value of [that] opinion." Similarly, Democratic Sen. Robert Toombs of Georgia praised the Supreme Court's decision, while at the same time condemning the Wisconsin courts for "leap[ing] over all established principles, all securities that men have set up to defend order, liberty, or right."[12]

Republicans, on the other hand, were split. While the *Philadelphia North American* averred that "the conduct of the Wisconsin Court was such as to preclude any other decree," the New York *Evening Post* complained that "nothing more fatal to the reserved rights of the States, nothing more dangerous to the securities, can well be conceived, than the authority claimed for the [federal courts] in the recent decision of Judge Taney." Predictably, some of the strongest reaction came from the state of Wisconsin itself. On March 19, the state legislature adopted a resolution characterizing the decision in *Ableman* as "an act of undelegated power, and therefore without authority and therefore void and without force" and declaring that the states "being sovereign and independent have the unquestionable right to judge of [the Constitution's] infraction; and that a positive defiance of those sovereignties, of all unauthorized acts done or attempted to be done under color of that instrument, is the rightful remedy."[13]

When the issue was raised in Congress, Republican Sen. James Doolittle of Wisconsin was equally emphatic. Doolittle came to the defense of the actions of the Wisconsin Supreme Court after a blistering attack on the actions of the Wisconsin court by Sen. Robert Toombs of Georgia. Implicitly linking *Ableman* to *Dred Scott*, Doolittle rejected the view that the Supreme Court possessed "the absolute power of construing the Constitution of the United States not only for itself, but for all other departments of the [federal] Government, and for all the courts of the several States." Instead, seeking to wrap himself in the mantle of Thomas Jefferson and Andrew Jackson, Doolittle argued that "it is the right and sworn duty of every court and every tribunal to construe the Constitution . . . as they understand it, and not as it is understood by others."[14]

Not surprisingly, attempts to enforce the Court's judgment met with much the same defiant attitude. The first step in the process was to file the mandate

of the *Ableman* Court with the Wisconsin Supreme Court. Jeremiah Black's efforts to obtain a copy of the opinion and mandates from the Court provoked
a mini-controversy that was in some ways reminiscent of the altercation that
had taken place between Taney and Curtis in the wake of *Dred Scott*. When
Black requested such a copy from the clerk's office on April 26, he was at first
informed that Taney had directed that no copies be given out until the opinion
was officially published. Black responded by sending a written protest to the
clerk demanding the document "in the name and by the direction of the President and for the public use in a matter of great and pressing importance" and
declaring that "regarding this as a public record I respectfully suggest that I
have a legal right to have it for the purpose referred to."[15] The matter was referred to Taney, who authorized the release of the opinion to Black on condition
that it be used for official purposes only.

Black then sent a copy of the mandates to Don A. J. Upham, who had succeeded John R. Sharpstein as district attorney in Wisconsin. On September 22,
Upham moved to have the state supreme court file the mandates. The makeup
of the Wisconsin court was entirely different from that which had decided the
original *Booth* cases. In the election of 1855, Orestes Cole had unseated Samuel
Crawford, the lone dissenter in *Booth I* who had written the majority opinion
in *Booth III*. In the spring of 1859, Chief Justice Edward Whiton died, and Republican Governor Alexander Randall chose Luther S. Dixon to replace him.
Finally, in the elections of 1859, the voters chose Byron Paine, who had represented Booth, to replace Abram Smith, who had declined to seek reelection.
Thus constituted, an equally divided court declined to grant Upham's motion.
Only Dixon voted to file the mandate, defending his position in a long opinion.
Cole voted not to file the mandate, while Paine recused himself.[16]

The significance of this action was largely symbolic. In practical terms, the
critical issue was whether Booth would be rearrested and forced to serve the
remainder of the sentence that had been imposed on him by the federal court.
Upham balked at seizing Booth, fearing renewed unrest and leery of the possibility of a new confrontation with the Wisconsin Supreme Court. Thus, it was
not until March 1, 1860 that Booth was rearrested on Judge Miller's orders and
confined in the federal customs house in Milwaukee. Now represented by Carl
Schurz, Booth once again petitioned the Wisconsin Supreme Court for a writ
of habeas corpus, raising the specter of another potential clash between state
and federal authorities.

Ironically, such a crisis was averted in part because Byron Paine had been
elected to the state court. With Paine forced to disqualify himself because of
his prior involvement with the case, the Wisconsin court once again split evenly,

with Cole supporting Booth and Dixon voting to deny the petition. As a result, the court took no action on Booth's behalf.[17]

By March 23, Booth had served the full term of imprisonment to which he had been sentenced. Nonetheless, he remained confined in the customs house because he adamantly refused to either pay the fine which had been imposed or to allow his supporters to pay the fine for him. Seeking to use his imprisonment as a focal point for continued agitation against the Fugitive Slave Act, Booth penned a series of widely published letters that bitterly protested both the fact of his imprisonment and the conditions under which he was being held. Adding to the outcry, the *Wisconsin Free Democrat* complained that "[Booth] is kept in prison now solely because the State has failed to vindicate its authority and honor, and redeem the pledges it has made to protect his liberty" and that "every hour he remains in prison, while no steps are taken for his release, is a reproach to the Republican party of Wisconsin."[18]

Spurred on by such appeals, a group of armed men forcibly removed Booth from federal custody on August 1. Booth did not go into hiding; instead, he continued to address antislavery gatherings, at times brandishing a pistol that he referred to as his "little *habeas corpus*." After a number of efforts by federal officials to recapture Booth were thwarted by crowds of armed men, he was finally taken back into custody on October 8. Booth remained confined in the customs house until, over the bitter objections of Jeremiah Black, he was granted a pardon by President Buchanan on the day before the inauguration of Abraham Lincoln.[19]

Although the Supreme Court was ultimately successful in vindicating the power of the federal government to punish Booth for his defiance of federal authority, its decision holding that the Fugitive Slave Act was constitutional had little practical effect on the course of the sectional struggle. The people and government of Wisconsin were not alone in resisting the enforcement of the statute; thus, efforts to recover escaped slaves became increasingly problematic. In early 1859, the *New York Times* asserted that "right or wrong, the North will not suffer its operation within its borders. No amount of legal or constitutional lore seems likely to shake its determination on this score." The *Times* further observed that "it has come to be understood that the expense, trouble, odium and risk of such endeavors far outweigh the pecuniary value of the property.... Southern slave-owners have made up their minds, deliberately and finally, so far as we can judge from appearances, that they will make no effort to enforce the Fugitive Slave Law of 1850, in the Northern states."[20]

Moreover, the *Ableman* saga reflected the degree to which even the Supreme Court was dependent on other branches of government. The Southern-dominated *Ableman* Court was ultimately successful in resisting the challenge to its authority only because it had the firm support of the executive branch. The election of 1860 would both complete the sectionalization of American politics and effectively sever relations between the Court and the executive branch on slavery-related issues.

Part Five

The Isolated Court

CHAPTER 26

The Election of 1860

The election of 1860 was marked by the triumph of sectionalists in both the North and the South. The dispute over the Freeport Doctrine and the candidacy of Stephen A. Douglas led to the disruption of the Democratic Party when party representatives met to choose a presidential candidate at the national convention that opened in Charleston, South Carolina, on April 23, 1860.[1] Southern delegates, who controlled the platform committee, inserted a provision condemning Northern efforts to obstruct enforcement of the Fugitive Slave Law and also pressed for a plank that would have declared that "it is the duty of the Federal Government . . . to protect, when necessary, the rights of persons and property in the territories"—a thinly veiled call for the adoption of a slave code by Congress. The Douglas forces, who had a bare majority of the delegates to the convention as a whole, accepted the language on fugitive slaves. However, they succeeded in replacing the provision on slavery in the territories with a formulation recognizing the difference of opinion among Democrats on the issue of the power of the territorial legislatures to ban slavery and declaring that "the Democratic party will abide by the decision of the Supreme Court of the United States upon these questions of Constitutional Law." Rather than accept this plank, all of the delegates from the lower South formally withdrew from the convention.

Because of the two-thirds rule, Douglas was still unable to muster the number of votes necessary to claim the nomination. On May 3, the delegates voted to adjourn and resume their deliberations in Baltimore on June 18. In Baltimore, a majority voted to seat pro-Douglas delegations from a number of the states that had bolted from the Charleston convention, and these delegations provided the necessary votes to nominate Douglas. The Southern dissidents responded by nominating Sen. John Breckenridge of Kentucky, who ran on the proslavery platform that had been rejected in Charleston.

Two other candidates entered the contest in May. The Republicans chose Abraham Lincoln as their standard-bearer and adopted a platform that, like its counterpart in 1856, made no mention of fugitive slaves, focusing instead on events in Kansas and the need to bar slavery from the territories. The newly formed Constitutional Union Party, on the other hand, nominated John Bell of Tennessee, with a platform that stated simply that the party embraced "no political principle other than THE CONSTITUTION OF THE COUNTRY, THE UNION OF THE STATES, AND THE ENFORCEMENT OF THE LAWS."

Although both Douglas and Bell purported to run national campaigns, the election soon devolved in effect into two separate races. In the North, the sectionalist Lincoln confronted the accommodationist Douglas, with Bell a significant factor only in Massachusetts. In the South, Breckenridge represented the forces of sectionalism, while Bell carried the banner of accommodationism. Although Douglas had appreciable support in some slave states, he was truly competitive only in Missouri.[2]

Dred Scott played a significant role in the contest between Lincoln and Douglas. In addition to alienating Southern Democrats, the equivocation of the Douglas platform on slavery in the territories left him vulnerable to attacks from Republicans. From the beginning of the campaign, with no hope of competing in the South in any event, the strategy of the Republicans was to paint Douglas as a tool of the slave power conspiracy. Republicans pointedly noted that, in *Dred Scott*, Taney had asserted that territorial legislatures lacked authority to ban slavery. Similarly, on December 17, 1859, in his third annual message, President Buchanan declared that the Court had held that slaveowners had the right to bring slaves into the territories, and that "neither Congress *nor a Territorial legislature* has any authority to annul or impair this sacred right [emphasis added]." Thus, Republicans argued, by pledging fealty to a decision of the Supreme Court on the question of the power of territorial legislatures, Douglas had effectively abandoned the Freeport Doctrine and embraced a view that was functionally no different than that of the most proslavery elements of the Democratic party.[3]

Ultimately, the election was dominated by sectionalists from both camps. The accommodationist candidates were successful in the upper South, as Bell carried Virginia, Kentucky, and Tennessee and Douglas was victorious in Missouri. But Breckenridge swept the Deep South, and Lincoln carried every non-slave state except New Jersey, winning the election outright with 180 out of a possible 303 electoral votes.

The ascension of a Northern sectionalist to the Presidency dramatically changed the dynamic of the dispute over slavery. The Court's treatment of *Kentucky v. Dennison* reflected the import of this change.

CHAPTER 27

Kentucky v. Dennison and
the Problem of Extradition

The Supreme Court's final encounter with the conflict over fugitive slaves came in *Kentucky v. Dennison*.[1] *Dennison* did not call upon the Court to revisit its interpretation of the Fugitive Slave Clause itself. Instead, the case arose from the efforts of a Southern state to obtain the extradition of a man accused of helping a slave to escape.

Prior to the Civil War, extradition issues intersected with the sectional struggle in a variety of different contexts. As we have seen, at the Constitutional Convention, Southerners viewed the return of escaped slaves as analogous to the extradition of fugitives from justice, and the language of the Fugitive Slave Clause was quite clearly derived from that of the Extradition Clause. Similarly, in 1793, it was a dispute over the extradition of a Virginian for allegedly violating the Pennsylvania Antikidnapping Law that created the impetus for the passage of the federal extradition statute, which in turn provided the occasion for the passage of the Fugitive Slave Act of 1793. A similar dispute over the extradition of a slave hunter from Maryland figured prominently in the background of *Prigg v. Pennsylvania*.[2]

Sectional tensions were heightened even more sharply in cases where Southern states sought the extradition of Northerners accused of enticing slaves to escape. The issue first gained prominence in 1839 in connection with a case involving a Virginia slave who had stowed away in Norfolk on a schooner bound for New York.[3] Although the slave was recaptured, three black seamen who had served on the schooner were charged in Virginia with participating in the escape because they had allegedly told the slave—a carpenter who had worked on the schooner in Norfolk—that he was foolish to remain in Virginia when he could earn good wages in the North, and that he should run away. The acting governor of Virginia then formally requested that the seamen be extradited from New York to stand trial.

In 1832, speaking through future Justice Samuel Nelson, in *In the Matter of Clark*, the New York Court of Appeals had concluded that "the word crime [in the Extradition Clause] is synonomous [*sic*] with misdemeanor ... and includes every offense below felony punished by indictment as an offense against the public." Nonetheless, Governor William Seward rejected the extradition request, asserting that "I believe the right to demand and the reciprocal obligation to surrender fugitives ... include only those cases in which the acts constituting the offence charged are recognized as crimes by the universal laws of all civilized countries." The lieutenant governor of Virginia responded sharply that the seamen were essentially charged with stealing a form of property, and that "I understand *stealing* to be recognized as *crime* by all laws human and Divine," but Seward retorted that "the general principle of civilized communities is in harmony with that which prevails in [New York], that men are not the subjects of property, and of course no crime can exist in countries where that principle prevails as the felonious stealing of a human being considered as property." Despite repeated appeals from the Virginia authorities and threats of retaliation, Seward remained steadfast in his refusal to extradite the seamen, and also took a similar view when Georgia requested extradition of a seaman under analogous circumstances. Governor Robert P. Dunlap of Maine also refused to extradite a citizen of Maine charged with enticing a slave to escape.[4]

The sequence of events that ultimately gave rise to *Kentucky v. Dennison* began more than twenty years later, when a slave named Charlotte, who resided in Louisville, Kentucky, was given permission by her master, one Nichols, to go with him to visit her mother in Wheeling, Virginia. In order to reach Wheeling by railroad, the pair first had to travel to Cincinnati, Ohio. While in Ohio, Charlotte was taken from Nichols by a group of abolitionists. She was then brought before a state judge, who declared her free under the laws of that state.[5]

This incident triggered two separate legal proceedings. Nichols was sued in Ohio for depriving Charlotte of her liberty in contravention of Ohio state law. In Kentucky, by contrast, a grand jury in Woodford County indicted Willis Lago, described as a "free man of color," charging that, on October 4, 1859, Lago "did seduce and entice Charlotte" to escape and did "aid and assist said slave in an attempt to escape."[6] While the indictment did not elaborate on the precise details of Lago's alleged wrongdoing, the indictment must have been based on the theory that, although Lago was a resident of Ohio, he had had some contact with Charlotte in Kentucky.

On February 10, 1860, following the procedures outlined in the Extradition Act of 1793, Governor Beriah Magoffin of Kentucky formally requested that Governor William Dennison of Ohio extradite Lago to Kentucky for trial. The staunchly antislavery Dennison referred the request to Christopher P. Wolcott, the state attorney general. Wolcott, taking a position similar to that which had been enunciated by Seward, concluded that Dennison need not honor the request for extradition. Magoffin responded provocatively by not only challenging Wolcott's legal analysis but also reminding Dennison that "the Constitution was the work of slaveholders" and that, in 1789, "non-slaveholding states were the exception, not the rule."[7] Not surprisingly, Magoffin's missive failed to move Dennison.

However, Kentucky refused to give up. Unlike the other Southern governments whose requests had been rebuffed, the state of Kentucky chose to seek legal redress for the refusal of Governor Dennison to grant extradition. Invoking the original jurisdiction of the Supreme Court on the ground that Kentucky was a party, the state petitioned the Court for a writ of mandamus compelling Dennison to issue an extradition order for Lagos.

The case was argued on February 20 and 21 in 1861, with Wolcott speaking for Dennison and the state of Kentucky represented by a team including John J. Crittenden, Thomas B. Monroe Jr., John W. Stevenson, and a fourth attorney identified only as Cooper. The arguments of counsel for both sides covered a wide range of both procedural and substantive issues.

Throughout, Wolcott's argument focused on the concept of enumerated powers. He emphasized not only the limitations on the powers of the federal government generally but also the idea that the federal judiciary in particular "is . . . one of limited and specific powers. . . . confined to the discharge of functions purely judicial in nature [and] only in the precise cases enumerated by the Constitution as subject to the judicial authority." Wolcott also contended that, while the Constitution described the classes of cases over which the Court might have power, "the existence in the court of the power [to decide cases] itself, and the methods and instruments of its exercise, depend on the affirmative legislative action of Congress."[8] Virtually all of Wolcott's arguments rested on elaborations of these principles.

Some of these arguments raised procedural objections to the petition for a writ of mandamus. Wolcott asserted that the dispute presented a political question that was not justiciable in *any* court, state or federal. He also insisted that, even if the issue was cognizable in some court, the Supreme Court was not the appropriate forum to hear the claim.

In defending this position, Wolcott challenged the constitutional basis for the invocation of the Court's original jurisdiction in *Dennison,* contending that the Constitution vested the right to demand extradition in the governor personally, rather than in the state of Kentucky as a corporate entity. In addition, he asserted that the action was not a "controversy of a civil nature" and was thus outside the scope of the Court's original jurisdiction as delineated in the Judiciary Act of 1789. Finally, Wolcott argued that the writ of mandamus could not be issued because *Dennison* did not fall into one of the categories in which the Judiciary Act authorized the use of the writ, and that in any event the

Constitution allowed the Court to issue the writ only to inferior courts in the federal system.[9]

Not surprisingly, the attorneys for the state of Kentucky disputed all of these contentions. They began by asserting that Kentucky was a proper plaintiff in the case because the suit was for the benefit of the state, and that Dennison was the appropriate defendant because he was the person who would be required to issue the extradition order. They further insisted that, because the case was one of original jurisdiction, the Court needed no authority from Congress to issue the writ and that Kentucky had no other adequate legal remedy.[10]

The attorneys also had starkly different visions of the merits. Wolcott reiterated his view that the Extradition Clause applied only to actions made criminal by the law of the rendering state or the "general usage of civilized nations." Drawing on his vision of federalism, he also challenged the constitutionality of the Extradition Act of 1793 on two grounds. First, reasserting the basic claim that had been rejected in *Prigg,* Wolcott contended that, given the absence of an explicit grant of enforcement authority in the Constitution, Congress lacked the power to pass any legislation designed to implement the Extradition Clause. Second, relying on *Prigg,* he asserted that Congress could not constitutionally impose duties on the officials of the state governments.[11]

Crittenden and his compatriots addressed each of these contentions in turn. Taking the position that the Extradition Clause applied to all conduct made criminal by the requesting state, they first briefly reviewed the status of extradition requests under international law and noted that the original draft of the clause referred to "high misdemeanors," but that the phrase "other crimes" had been substituted because the former might have been seen as too limited in scope. They bolstered their argument with an appeal to the principle of horizontal federalism, contending that to adopt the position taken by Wolcott "would, in effect, destroy the force of this clause of the Constitution at its inception, and, instead of placing the states in bonds of mutual obligation to vindicate the jurisdiction of each other . . . would make each a supervisor of the police power of the others, and, by reason of conflicting policies in their progress, would inevitably lead to alienation, confusion, and ultimate discord."[12]

They then observed that the Extradition Clause had expanded the obligations of the states to one another in this regard "by dispensing with comity and the rule of publicists, and making the obligation to render criminals to the jurisdiction they have offended a perfect obligation, in express constitutional compact," and that the clause "expresses plainly what is to be done, upon whose demand it is to be done, the circumstances under which it is to be done, and the purpose for which it is to be done." While conceding that the responsible state official retained authority to prescribe the mode by which the fugitive was to be delivered, the petitioners contended that "beyond this simple and single ministerial performance, the Constitution and the law have left [the governor] with no discretion whatsoever." Given this view, they contended that the federal judiciary must have authority to require the governor to respect this obligation, relying on *Prigg* for the propositions that "the General Government is bound, through its own departments, Legislative, Judicial, or Executive, as the case may be, to carry into effect all the rights and duties imposed upon it by the Constitution."[13]

At the same time, the attorneys for the state of Kentucky recognized that in some respects, Justice Story's opinion in *Prigg* was an important obstacle to the success of their petition—particularly Story's conclusion that Congress could not require state officials to participate in the rendition of fugitive slaves. The Kentucky attorneys had two responses to the assertion that their claim was barred by *Prigg*. First, they asserted that Story's conclusion on this point was dictum and that McLean, who had taken issue with Story's analysis, had the better of the argument. In addition, the attorneys sought to distinguish the rendition process for putative fugitive slaves from the rendition process for fugitives from justice.

Relying on an argument much like that made by William Seward in *Jones v. Van Zandt,* they reasoned that the effectuation of the Fugitive Slave Clause required the responsible officials to make a preliminary judgment on the status of the alleged escapee prior to vindicating the claim of the putative master. By contrast, in an extradition case, the attorneys argued, the duties of the governor of the rendering state were entirely ministerial—he was to do nothing more than examine the relevant documents for regularity and arrange for delivery of the fugitive from justice if the formal prerequisites were met. In effect, Kentucky argued, they were doing nothing more than asking the Court to require the governor of Ohio to obey the formal commands of the Constitution.[14]

Against the background of these arguments, on March 14, 1861—the last day of the term—Chief Justice Taney delivered the opinion for a unanimous Court in *Dennison.* Taney began by brushing aside the jurisdictional objections to the petition, declaring that, since the passage of the Judiciary Act, "in all cases where original jurisdiction is given by the Constitution, this court has authority to exercise it without any further act of Congress to regulate its process or confer jurisdiction, and that the court may regulate and mould [*sic*] the process it uses in such manner as in its judgment will best promote the purposes of justice." He also averred that there were no special limitations on the authority of the Court to issue a writ of mandamus, describing the writ as "nothing more than the ordinary process of a court of justice, to which everyone is entitled, where it is the appropriate process for asserting the right he claims" and that "it is very clear that, if the right claimed by Kentucky can be enforced by judicial process, the proceeding by mandamus is the only mode in which the object can be accomplished."[15]

Turning to the merits, Taney once again rejected the view advanced by the state of Ohio. Instead, he took the position that the mandate of the Extradition Clause "embrace[s] every act forbidden or made punishable by a law of [a] State." To hold otherwise, he reasoned, would engender great uncertainty about the applicability of the clause in many cases, creating a situation in which "the article would not be a bond of peace and union, but a constant source of controversy and irritating discussion."[16] Taney then described the scope of the Extradition Clause in the broadest possible terms, asserting that the officials of the extraditing state were constitutionally bound to deliver persons charged with any action made criminal by the law of the state requesting extradition:

The conclusion is irresistible that this compact engrafted in the Constitution included, and was intended to include, every offence made punishable by the law of the State in which it was committed, and that it gives the right to the Executive authority of the State to demand the fugitive from the Executive authority of the State in which he is found; that the right given to "demand" implies that it is an absolute right; and it follows that there must be a correlative obligation to deliver, without any reference to the character of the crime charged, or to the policy or laws of the State to which the fugitive has fled.[17]

Taney was equally emphatic in affirming both the constitutionality of the Extradition Act and the duty of state governors to arrest and deliver fugitives whose extradition was demanded according to its terms. He asserted that

th[e] duty of providing by law the regulations necessary to carry this compact into execution, from the nature of the duty and the object in view, was manifestly devolved upon Congress, for if it was left to the States, each State might require different proof to authenticate the judicial proceeding upon which the demand was founded, and as the duty of the Governor of the State where the fugitive was found is, in such cases, merely ministerial, without the right to exercise either executive or judicial discretion, he could not lawfully issue a warrant to arrest an individual without a law of the State or of Congress to authorize it.[18]

In addition, Taney also averred that the officials of the extraditing state were not allowed to make an independent inquiry into the grounds for extradition, but were instead required to accept the allegations in the petition for extradition at face value. He proclaimed that it will be observed that the judicial acts which are necessary to authorize the demand are plainly specified in the act of Congress, and the certificate of the Executive authority is made conclusive as to their verity when presented to the Executive of the State where the fugitive is found. He has no right to look behind them, or to question them, or to look into the character of the crime specified in this judicial proceeding. The duty which he is to perform is, as we have already said, merely ministerial—that is, to cause the party to be arrested and delivered to the agent or authority of the State where the crime was committed. It is said in the argument that the Executive officer upon whom this demand is made must have a discretionary executive power, because he must inquire and decide who is the person demanded. But this certainly is not a discretionary duty upon which he is to exercise any judgment, but is a mere ministerial duty—that is, to do the act required to be done by him, and such as every marshal and sheriff must perform when process, either criminal or civil, is placed in his hands to be served on the person named in it.[19]

But despite this characterization of the import of the Extradition Clause and the statute, the Court refused to issue the writ of mandamus. Although Taney observed that the statute used language "ordinarily employed when an undoubted obligation is to be performed," he also averred "that the performance of this duty . . . is left to depend on the fidelity of the State Executive to the compact entered into with the other States when it adopted the Constitution of the United States, and became a member of the Union." He concluded that "if the Governor of Ohio refuses to discharge this duty, there is no power delegated to the General Government, either through the Judicial Department or any other department, to use any coercive means to compel him."[20]

In the abstract, the refusal to issue the writ of mandamus might be seen as a decision to avoid undue involvement in the sectional crisis that came to a head with Lincoln's election. But if Taney had truly wished to stand aloof from the conflict, he could have disposed of *Dennison* solely on the basis of the mandamus issue, eschewing discussion of the substance of the Extradition Clause altogether. Instead, he issued an opinion that, taken as a whole, was in essence a microcosm of secessionist constitutional theory in early 1861. On one hand, his implicit condemnation of Governor Dennison's lack of "fidelity to a compact" that Taney described as "absolutely essential to [the states'] well being in their internal concerns, as well as members of the Union"[21] echoed the more general Southern complaint that the Northern states had failed to honor their constitutional commitments to the South, particularly with respect to the return of fugitive slaves. On the other, the conclusion that the Court lacked the power to enforce compliance with the Extradition Clause fit well with the Southern claim that the federal government could not constitutionally use force against the secessionist states, even if secession was not constitutionally permitted in the abstract.

In any event, even if the Court had issued the writ of mandamus, there was no realistic possibility that it would have ultimately been enforced. One cannot imagine Governor Dennison complying voluntarily with such an order, and a Republican president—particularly one preoccupied with the secession crisis—was unlikely to have moved against a political ally to vindicate the Southern position on an issue that was related indirectly to the dispute over fugitive slaves. By structuring the opinion as he did, Taney was able to strike a rhetorical blow at his political adversaries, while at the same time avoiding an embarrassing confrontation that would have revealed the Court's inability to enforce its own decrees. From this perspective, Taney's strategy was much like that of John Marshall in *Marbury v. Madison*.[22]

Although the nation's attention was riveted on the secession crisis, Taney's resolution of *Dennison* did attract some attention. Characterizing the opinion as "Judicial Twaddle," the New York *Evening Post* attacked Taney for discussing the scope of the Extradition Clause rather than contenting himself with the simple conclusion that the Court lacked the authority to issue writ of mandamus in any event. On the other hand, whether naively or with tongue in cheek, the *Nashville Republican Banner* predicted that Governor Dennison would surrender Lago to the Kentucky authorities.[23] In any event, there is no record of Dennison complying with the request for extradition.

Dennison was the Court's last important encounter with the questions raised by the dispute over slavery. It soon became clear that the fate of slavery in the Southern states would be decided not in the courts, but on the battlefield. The Northern victory and the adoption of the Thirteenth Amendment forever ended slavery in the United States, and at the same time created an entire new set of constitutional issues that continue to bedevil the Court today.

Conclusion
The Lessons of the Slavery Cases

In addition to embodying the views of the justices on the specific issues that came before the Supreme Court, when considered together the slavery cases provide an excellent illustration of the relationship between judicial decision-making and the political culture of the nation more generally. On one hand, the progression of the Court's decisions over time clearly reflects the impact of the change in the tenor of the conflict over slavery from the early 1840s through the late 1850s. On the other, the aftermath of the major decisions illustrates the limits of the Court's ability to change the dynamic that ultimately determines the outcome of political struggles over controversial issues.

The pattern of the decisions in the trilogy of cases decided in the early 1840s were the byproduct of a complicated interaction between "neutral" legal principles and political ideology. In *The Amistad,* conditions were ripe for the dominance of distinctively legal analysis. Although the case had important political overtones and public opinion was at least somewhat divided along sectional lines, the issues confronting the Court did not implicate the core interests of either the free states or the slave states and did not have long-term significance for the North-South conflict. Thus, despite the provocative rhetoric of both Roger Baldwin and John Quincy Adams, the Southern justices were willing to follow the dictates of legal ideology and join in the near-unanimous antislavery decision.

By contrast, *Groves v. Slaughter* and *Prigg v. Pennsylvania* stood on a quite different footing. Unlike *The Amistad,* each of these cases raised important questions about the basic structure of federalism, which clearly influenced the approach of some of the justices. Even more importantly, *Groves* and *Prigg* involved issues of profound significance to the relationship between North and South and, although the arguments were generally couched in legal terms, political considerations were clearly a dominant force in the treatment of those issues. As one might expect in a political culture dominated by two bisectional coalitions that were committed to the maintenance of sectional peace, the advocates for both sides generally struck a moderate tone and at times sought to portray their adversaries as sectional extremists. The justices themselves typically struck a similar chord, as they made a strong effort to avoid exacerbating tensions between North and South in *Groves,* and a majority also sought to create a workable compromise on the issue of fugitive slaves in *Prigg.*

The intensification of the sectional conflict brought with it a number of important changes to the cases that were decided by the Court. First, the subject matter of the cases themselves at times reflected the radicalization of attitudes in both the North and South. Both *Strader v. Graham* and *Dred Scott v. Sandford* came to the Court only because Southern state courts had become increasingly unwilling to recognize the freedom of putative slaves based upon their temporary residence in jurisdictions in which slavery was forbidden by law, while *Ableman v. Booth* arose from outright resistance to the Fugitive Slave Act by both private citizens in the North and the government of the free state of Wisconsin. As early as 1847, the arguments of the antislavery attorneys in *Jones v. Van Zandt* had reflected a similar attitude, as both Salmon P. Chase and William Seward eschewed the accommodationist language of the Northern arguments in *Prigg* in favor of a forthrightly confrontational attack on the constitutionality of the Fugitive Slave Act of 1793.

Nonetheless, as late as early 1856, most of the justices apparently were unwilling to commit themselves to outright sectional combat. Squarely presented with the opportunity to address the issue of slavery in the territories in *Dred Scott,* a majority initially decided to avoid the question. But a disagreement over a technical legal issue led to a postponement of the decision, and in the interim the strong showing of the Republican Party in the presidential election of November 1856 convinced a majority of the Southern justices of the desirability of constitutionalizing the proslavery position on the contentious territorial issue. Considerations of federalism faded into the background, as the actions of all of the justices in that case reflected Carl Schurz's observation that "in the North as well as the South, men's sympathies with regard to slavery shaped and changed their . . . constitutional theories."[1]

But even in *Dred Scott* itself, the commitment to legal reasoning retained considerable influence on the Court. This influence was particularly apparent in the refusal of Justices John Catron, Samuel Nelson, and John Campbell to consider the merits of the claim that Dred Scott could not be a citizen of the United States, thereby denying the chief justice a majority on this point. In short, taken together, the slavery cases demonstrate that, even under the most trying circumstances, the actions of each justice were determined by a complex interaction between political and doctrinal considerations.

Conversely, the reaction to the slavery-related decisions exemplifies the limitations on the Court's ability to finally resolve hotly contested, controversial political issues for the society as a whole. *Dred Scott* provides one of the most spectacular examples of those limitations. In reaching out to decide the question of whether the Constitution required that slavery be recognized as legal in the territories, the majority hoped to permanently resolve the issue in favor of the South and to remove an irritant from national politics. From this perspective the decision was totally ineffectual, as antislavery Northerners simply denied that they were bound to follow the decision and continued to press for the principles that had been embodied in the Wilmot Proviso.

Assessing the impact of *Prigg v. Pennsylvania* and its progeny is more complex. The *Prigg* Court did not and could not aspire to remove the issue of fugitive slaves from national politics. Instead, the majority of the justices sought to craft a set of formal legal principles that governed the obligations of the Northern states and hoped that adherence to these principles would help to reduce the sectional tensions created by this issue. In one narrow but important sense, the political impact of the decision became apparent almost immediately. From a purely legal perspective, those who opposed slavery understood that only statutes that conformed to the rules enunciated by Justice Story could be deployed effectively against efforts by Southerners to recover erstwhile slaves who had escaped to the North. Thus, antislavery state legislators acted quickly to adopt measures that were consistent with the standards laid down by the *Prigg* majority.

But from a broader perspective, the Court failed in its apparent effort to reduce sectional tensions over the issue of fugitive slaves. For a time, the principles established by the Court were generally respected by the state governments of the North. Nonetheless—not because of these principles but in spite of them—the dispute over fugitive slaves continued to be a major source of friction between North and South in the 1840s and 1850s.

Moreover, as the sectional conflict became more intense, the very power of the Court to establish binding rules came under attack from some quarters. In *Ableman v. Booth,* the Court faced open resistance from the Wisconsin state government. Only the strong support of the executive branch ultimately ensured that the Court's authority would be respected. The election of Lincoln in 1860 made it clear that such support would not continue to be forthcoming on issues related to slavery. Thus, in *Kentucky v. Dennison,* the Court declined to risk its standing by issuing a binding decree.

The foregoing should not be taken to suggest that the actions of the Court were completely irrelevant to the evolution of the sectional conflict. Even where decisions ultimately have little practical effect, the symbolism of the decisions can have a profound effect on the political dynamic. The reaction to *Dred Scott* exemplifies this phenomenon; although the decision did not ultimately change the course of the debate over slavery in the territories, Republicans were able to effectively use the case as evidence to support their claim that the federal government was controlled by a slave power conspiracy.

Nonetheless, one point emerges clearly from the Supreme Court's experience with the conflict over slavery. The Court was only a junior partner in the struggle to resolve this conflict. To be sure, in the short term the decisions of the justices played an important role in framing the terms of the national debate over a variety of slavery-related issues. But ultimately, the Court proved unable to definitively resolve those issues. Instead, the long-term impact of the Court's decisions, like the resolution of the larger issues raised by the sectional conflict, was ultimately determined by the actions taken by other political institutions.[2] As the justices are confronted with other controversial issues in the future, they forget this lesson only at their peril.

Notes

FOREWORD: THE BANALITY OF CONSTITUTIONAL EVIL

1. Hannah Arendt, *Eichmann in Jerusalem: A Report on the Banality of Evil,* rev. ed. (New York: Viking Press, 1964), 25–26.

2. 41 U.S. 539 (1842).

3. U.S. 393 (1856).

4. *The Collected Works of Abraham Lincoln,* ed. Roy P. Basler, vol. 2, *1848–1858* (New Brunswick, N.J.: Rutgers University Press, 1953), 461.

5. The Case of James Somersett (1772) 20 State Trials 1, 82 (K.B.).

6. Oliver v. Kauffmann, 18 F. Cas. 657, 660 (C.C.D. Pa. 1850).

7. For the attitudinal model, see Jeffrey A. Segal and Harold J. Spaeth, *The Supreme Court and the Attitudinal Model Revisited* (New York: Cambridge University Press, 2002). For the strategic model, see Lee Epstein and Jack Knight, *The Choices Justices Make* (Washington, D.C.: CQ Press, 1998). For one version of the legal model, see Mark A. Graber, "Constitutional Law and American Politics," in *The Oxford Handbook of Law and Politics,* ed. Keith E. Whittington, R. Daniel Kelemen, and Gregory A. Caldeira (New York: Oxford University Press, 2008).

8. See Lawrence Baum, *The Puzzle of Judicial Behavior* (Ann Arbor: University of Michigan Press, 1998).

9. See Miln v. Mayor of New York, 34 U.S. 85 (1835); The Passenger Cases, 48 U.S. 283 (1849).

10. Helen Tunnicliff Catterall, *Judicial Cases concerning American Slavery and the Negro,* 5 vols. (New York: Octagon Books, 1968).

11. Julie Novkov, *Racial Union: Law, Intimacy, and the White State in Alabama, 1865–1954* (Ann Arbor: University of Michigan Press, 2008).

12. Robert M. Cover, *Justice Accused: Antislavery and the Judicial Process* (New Haven, Conn.: Yale University Press, 1975).

13. See, e.g., Trop v. Dulles, 356 U.S. 86, 120 (1958) (Frankfurter, J., dissenting); West Virginia State Board of Education v. Barnette, 319 U.S. 624, 647 (1943) (Frankfurter, J., dissenting).

14. Yosal Rogat, "The Judge as Spectator," *University of Chicago Law Review* 31 (1964): 213; quote at 255.

15. Benjamin N. Cardozo, *The Nature of the Judicial Process* (New Haven, Conn.: Yale University Press, 1921), 114.

16. James G. Blaine, *Twenty Years of Congress from Lincoln to Garfield* (Norwich, Conn.: Henry Bill Publishing Co., 1884), 1:272.

PREFACE

1. 60 U.S. (19 How.) 393 (1857).

2. The classic study is Don E. Fehrenbacher, *The Dred Scott Case: Its Significance in American Law and Politics* (New York: Oxford University Press, 1978). In addition, see Austin Allen, *Origins of the Dred Scott Case: Jacksonian Jurisprudence and the Supreme Court, 1837–1857* (Athens: University of Georgia Press, 2006); Walter Ehrlich, *They Have No Rights: Dred Scott's Struggle for Freedom* (Westport, Conn.: Greenwood Press, 1979); Mark A. Graber, *Dred Scott and the Problem of Constitutional Evil* (New York: Cambridge University Press, 2006).

3. 23 U.S. (10 Wheat.) 66 (1825).

4. 40 U.S. (15 Pet.) 518 (1841).

5. 62 U.S. (21 How.) 506 (1859).

6. John T. Noonan, *The Antelope: The Ordeal of the Recaptured Africans in the Administrations of James Monroe and John Quincy Adams* (Berkeley: University of California Press, 1977); Howard Jones, *Mutiny on the Amistad: The Saga of a Slave Revolt and Its Impact on American Abolition, Law and Diplomacy* (New York: Oxford University Press, 1988); H. Robert Baker, *The Rescue of Joshua Glover: A Fugitive Slave, the Constitution, and the Coming of the Civil War* (Athens: University of Ohio Press, 2006).

7. 41 U.S. (16 Pet.) 539 (1842).

8. On *Prigg*, see, for example, Thomas D. Morris, *Free Men All: The Personal Liberty Laws of the North, 1780–1861* (Baltimore: Johns Hopkins University Press, 1974), 94–107; R. Kent Newmyer, *Supreme Court Justice Joseph Story: Statesman of the Old Republic* (Chapel Hill: University of North Carolina Press, 1985), 370–378; Paul Finkelman, "Storytelling on the Supreme Court: *Prigg v. Pennsylvania* and Justice Joseph Story's Judicial Nationalism," *Supreme Court Review* (1994): 247–273. Most of the major slavery-related cases are discussed in Carl B. Swisher, *History of the Supreme Court, Volume 5: The Taney Period, 1836–64* (New York: Macmillan, 1974); and Charles Warren, *The Supreme Court in United States History* (Littleton, Colo.: Fred B. Rothman, 1987). In addition, see William M. Wiecek, "Slavery and Abolition before the United States Supreme Court, 1820–1860," *Journal of American History* 65 (1978): 34–59.

9. Warren, *The Supreme Court in United States History*, vol. 2; Robert G. McCloskey, *The American Supreme Court* (Chicago: University of Chicago Press, 1961), 90–93.

10. The classic discussion of the concept of neutral principles is Herbert Wechsler, "Toward Neutral Principles of Constitutional Law," *Harvard Law Review* 73 (1959): 1–35.

11. Fehrenbacher, *The Dred Scott Case*; Finkelman, "Storytelling." In addition, see Leonard L. Richards, *The Slave Power: The Free North and Southern Domination* (Baton Rouge: Louisiana State University Press, 2000), 94–96.

12. The implications of this insight are elaborated in detail in Mark A. Graber, *Dred Scott and the Problem of Constitutional Evil* (New York: Cambridge University Press, 2006).

13. 46 U.S. (5 How.) 215 (1847).

14. 51 U.S. (10 How.) 82 (1851).

CHAPTER 1. PRELUDE TO CONFLICT: THE MARSHALL
COURT AND *THE ANTELOPE*

1. These debates are chronicled in detail in Matthew Mason, *Slavery and Politics in the Early American Republic* (Chapel Hill: University of North Carolina Press, 2006); and Donald L. Robinson, *Slavery in the Structure of American Politics, 1765–1820* (New York: Harcourt Brace Jovanovich, 1971).

2. Sean Wilentz, *The Rise of American Democracy: Jefferson to Lincoln* (New York: W. W. Norton, 2005), 163–164, 219–221.

3. 23 U.S. (10 Wheat.) 66 (1825).

4. Robinson, *Slavery in the Structure of American Politics*, 82–83.

5. Max Farrand, ed., *The Records of the Federal Convention of 1787* (New Haven: Yale University Press, 1937), 4 vols., 2:169, 371–375, 416.

6. The evolution of the federal legislation dealing with the slave trade is described in detail in Robinson, *Slavery in the Structure of American Politics*, chap. 8.

7. United States v. La Jeune Eugenie, 26 F. Cas. 832 (No. 15,551) (C.C.D. Mass. 1822); The Amedie, 1 Acton's Rep. 240 (1808); *La Jeune Eugenie* at 836–837; The Louis, 2 Dodson 238 (1817).

8. *La Jeune Eugenie* at 845–847.

9. Ibid., 845, 846.

10. Ibid., 846, 851.

11. The classic study of *The Antelope* is John T. Noonan, *The Antelope: The Ordeal of the Recaptured Africans in the Administrations of James Monroe and John Quincy Adams* (Berkeley: University of California Press, 1977). In addition, see G. Edward White, *History of the Supreme Court of the United States, Volumes 3–4: The Marshall Court and Cultural Change, 1815–1835* (New York: Macmillan, 1988), 691–703.

12. Quoted in G. Edward White, *The Marshall Court and Cultural Change*, 694.

13. *The Antelope*, 23 U.S. at 71.

14. Ibid. at 73.

15. Ibid. at 73, 74.

16. Ibid. at 76, 79, 80.

17. Ibid. at 85, 99, 98.

18. Ibid. at 86.

19. Ibid. at 90.

20. Ibid. at 96–97, 90, 104.

21. Ibid. at 107–108.

22. Ibid. at 111–112.

23. Ibid. at 115, 121, 122.

24. Ibid. at 126–127.

25. White, *The Marshall Court and Cultural Change*, 699.

26. This aspect of *The Antelope* is emphasized in ibid., 703.

CHAPTER 2. THE MARSHALL COURT AND FEDERALISM

G. Edward White, *History of the Supreme Court, Volumes 3–4: The Marshall Court and Cultural Change, 1815–35* (New York: Macmillan, 1988), chap. 7, provides a detailed account of the Marshall Court's treatment of issues related to federalism.

1. "Kentucky and Virginia Resolutions," in Herman V. Ames, ed., *State Documents on Federal Relations: The States and the United States* (Philadelphia: University of Pennsylvania, 1911); "Resolutions of the Hartford Convention," ibid. at 83.

2. Martin v. Hunter's Lessee, 14 U.S. (1 Wheat.) 304 (1816).

3. Hunter v. Fairfax's Devisee, 1 Munf. 218 (Va., 1810); Fairfax's Devisee v. Hunter's Lessee, 11 U.S. (7 Cranch) 603 (1813).

4. Hunter v. Martin, 4 Munf. 1, 8, 19 (1815).

5. Martin v. Hunter's Lessee, 14 U.S. at 325, 324.

6. Ibid. at 343–344.

7. Thomas Jefferson, "Opinion on the Constitutionality of a National Bank, 15 February 1791," in Merrill D. Peterson, ed., *The Portable Thomas Jefferson* (New York: Penguin, 1975), 262.

8. Hamilton to Washington, February 23, 1791, in Harold Syrett, ed., *Papers of Alexander Hamilton* (New York: Columbia University Press, 1961), 8:98.

9. 17 U.S. (4 Wheat.) 316 (1819).

10. Ibid., 421.

11. 17 U.S. (4 Wheat.) 122 (1819).

12. 18 U.S. (5 Wheat.) 1 (1820).

13. *Sturges,* 17 U.S. at 193.

14. *Houston,* 18 U.S. at 23.

15. 22 U.S. (9 Wheat.) 1 (1824).

16. Ibid. at 209.

17. 25 U.S. (12 Wheat.) 419, 447 (1827).

18. *Gibbons,* 22 U.S. at 203.

19. 27 U.S. (2 Pet.) 245 (1829).

20. Ibid., 252.

CHAPTER 3. SECTIONALISM AND THE RISE OF THE SECOND-PARTY SYSTEM

1. For discussions of divisions among the Democratic-Republicans, see Glover Moore, *The Missouri Controversy 1819–1821* (Lexington, Ky.: University of Kentucky Press, 1953), 16–17; and Sean Wilentz, *The Rise of American Democracy: Jefferson to Lincoln* (New York: W. W. Norton, 2005), chap. 6.

2. *Annals of Congress,* 15th Cong., 2d Sess. (1819).

3. Robert Pierce Forbes, *The Missouri Compromise and Its Aftermath: Slavery and the Meaning of America* (Chapel Hill: University of North Carolina Press, 2007); and Moore, *The Missouri Controversy,* are the standard treatments of the dispute over the

admission of Missouri. Other useful treatments of the controversy include William W. Freehling, *The Road to Disunion, Volume 1: Secessionists at Bay 1776–1854* (New York: Oxford University Press, 1990), chap. 8; Mark Graber, *Dred Scott and the Problem of Constitutional Evil* (New York: Cambridge University Press, 2006), 120–126; Michael A. Morrison, *Slavery and the American West: The Eclipse of Manifest Destiny and the Coming of the Civil War* (Chapel Hill: University of North Carolina Press, 1997), chap. 2; Leonard Richards, *The Slave Power: The Free North and Southern Domination, 1780–1860* (Baton Rouge: Louisiana State University Press, 2000), chap. 3; Donald Robinson, *Slavery and the Structure of American Politics, 1765–1820* (New York: Harcourt Brace Jovanovich, 1971), chap. 10; and Wilentz, *The Rise of American Democracy,* chap. 7.

4. Wilentz, *The Rise of American Democracy,* 240–257 gives a detailed account of the election of 1824.

5. Van Buren's motives are discussed in Robert V. Remini, *Martin Van Buren and the Making of the Republican Party* (New York: W. W. Norton, 1970); and Wilentz, *The Rise of American Democracy,* 294–297.

6. Michael F. Holt, *The Rise and Fall of the American Whig Party: Jacksonian Politics and the Coming of the Civil War* (New York: Oxford University Press, 1999), 8–10; Wilentz, *The Rise of American Democracy,* 301–309.

7. Holt, *The Rise and Fall of the American Whig Party,* 10–15.

8. Wilentz, *The Rise of American Democracy,* 299–300.

9. The draft and final text of the *Exposition and Protest* can be found in Robert L. Meriweather et al., eds., *The Papers of John C. Calhoun* (Columbia: University of South Carolina Press, 1959–2003), 10:442–539.

10. Freehling, *The Road to Disunion,* 270.

11. Ibid., 271–277.

12. James D. Richardson, comp., *A Compilation of the Messages and Papers of the Presidents, 1789–1902* (Washington, D.C.: Bureau of National Literature and Art, 1904), 2:640–656. For thorough accounts of the nullification crisis, see William W. Freehling, *Prelude to Civil War: The Nullification Crisis in South Carolina, 1816–1836* (New York: Oxford University Press, 1966); and Richard E. Ellis, *Union at Risk: Jacksonian Democracy, States Rights, and the Nullification Crisis* (New York: Oxford University Press, 1989).

13. Wilentz, *The Rise of American Democracy,* 386.

14. For a complete account of the dispute over the Bank of the United States and its consequences, see Robert V. Remini, *Andrew Jackson and the Bank War* (New York: W. W. Norton, 1967). In addition, see Wilentz, *The Rise of American Democracy,* 392–401.

15. Michael F. Holt, *The Rise and Fall of the American Whig Party: Jacksonian Politics and the Onset of the Civil War* (New York: Oxford University Press, 1999), 24.

16. Freehling, *The Road to Disunion,* 289–295; Wilentz, *The Rise of American Democracy,* 330–341.

17. The best account of the controversy over the gag rule is Freehling, *The Road to Disunion,* 287–352. In addition, see William Lee Miller, *Arguing about Slavery: The Great Battle in the United States Congress* (New York: A. A. Knopf, 1996).

18. *Congressional Globe,* 24th Cong., 1st Sess. 506 (1836).

19. On the election of 1836, see Holt, *The Rise and Fall of the American Whig Party,*

38–49; and Wilentz, *The Rise of American Democracy,* 446–454. For a detailed analysis of the presidential campaign in the South, see William J. Cooper, *The South and the Politics of Slavery, 1828–1856* (Baton Rouge: Louisiana State University Press, 1978), 74–97.

20. Andrew Jackson, "Farewell Address," in Richardson, *A Compilation of the Messages and Papers of the Presidents,* 3:292.

21. Wilentz, *The Rise of American Democracy,* 454; Holt, *The Rise and Fall of the American Whig Party,* 91–92; Freehling, *The Road to Disunion,* 337–352.

22. Wilentz, *The Rise of American Democracy,* 502.

23. Ibid., 501.

CHAPTER 4. THE SUPREME COURT IN THE EARLY 1840S

1. Biographical sketches of the justices can be found in Carl B. Swisher, *History of the Supreme Court, Volume 5: The Taney Period, 1836–64* (New York: Macmillan, 1974), 39–70; and Leon Friedman and Fred L. Israel, eds., *The Justices of the Supreme Court: Their Lives and Major Opinions,* 5 vols. (New York: Chelsea House, 1997).

2. Taney is the subject of a number of full biographies, including H. H. Walker Lewis, *Without Fear or Favor: A Biography of Chief Justice Roger Brooke Taney* (Boston: Houghton Mifflin, 1965); and Carl B. Swisher, *Roger B. Taney* (New York: Macmillan, 1935).

3. Taney's role in Jackson's struggle with the bank is described in detail in Swisher, *Roger B. Taney,* 160–306.

4. Ibid., 312–314.

5. Ibid., 94–96.

6. Ibid., 154.

7. Biographies of Justice Story include Gerald T. Dunne, *Justice Joseph Story and the Rise of the Supreme Court* (New York: Simon and Schuster, 1970); and R. Kent Newmyer, *Supreme Court Justice Joseph Story: Statesman of the Old Republic* (Chapel Hill: University of North Carolina Press, 1985).

8. Newmyer, *Supreme Court Justice Joseph Story,* 59.

9. Joseph Story, *Commentaries on the Constitution of the United States: With a Preliminary View of the Constitutional History of the Colonies and States, before the Adoption of the Constitution,* 2 vols. (Boston: Little Brown, 1858).

10. 14 U.S. (1 Wheat.) 304 (1816).

11. William W. Story, ed., *Life and Letters of Joseph Story* (London: Little Brown, 1851), 1:336, 340–341.

12. Newmyer, *Supreme Court Justice Joseph Story,* 166; Commonwealth v. Aves, 35 U.S. 193 (1836); Newmyer, *Supreme Court Justice Joseph Story,* 351.

13. Ibid., 356.

14. Story, *Commentaries on the Constitution,* 2:211.

15. Newmyer, *Supreme Court Justice Joseph Story,* 377.

16. Thompson's life and career are described in David M. Roper, *Mr. Justice Thompson and the Constitution* (New York: Garland, 1987). In addition, see G. Edward White, *History of the Supreme Court of the United States Volumes 3–4: The Marshall Court and Cultural Change, 1815–1835* (New York: Macmillan, 1988), 307–318.

17. Ibid., 690.

18. See, for example, Ogden v. Saunders, 25 U.S. (12 Wheat.) 213 (1827).

19. For a complete account of McLean's life and career, see Francis P. Weisenburger, *The Life of John McLean: A Politician on the United States Supreme Court* (Columbus: Ohio State University Press, 1937).

20. Weisenburger, *The Life of John McLean,* 27; William E. Gienapp, *The Origins of the Republican Party, 1852–1856* (New York: Oxford University Press, 1987), 314.

21. Quoted in Thomas E. Carney, "The Political Judge: Justice John McLean's Pursuit of the Presidency," *Ohio History* 111 (2002): 121–144, 135–136. McLean's approach to slavery-related issues is discussed in detail in Robert M. Cover, *Justice Accused: Antislavery and the Judicial Process* (New Haven: Yale University Press, 1984).

22. Swisher, *The Taney Period,* 51.

23. Ibid., 49.

24. Henry Baldwin, *General View of the Origin and Nature of the Constitution and Government of the United States* (New York: Da Capo Press, 1970); White, *The Marshall Court and Cultural Change,* 300.

25. Baldwin, *General View,* 11 (emphasis in original).

26. Glover Moore, *The Missouri Controversy, 1819–1821* (Lexington: University of Kentucky Press, 1953), 104–105; Johnson v. Tompkins, 13 Fed. Cas. 810 C.C.E.D. Pa. (No. 7,416) (1833).

27. Ibid., 843, 843–844.

28. Ibid.

29. Ibid.

30. Alexander A. Lawrence, *James Moore Wayne, Southern Unionist* (Chapel Hill: University of North Carolina Press, 1934), provides a detailed account of Wayne's life and career.

31. Ibid., 38–40.

32. Ibid., 55, 72, 82.

33. Ibid., 79.

34. William W. Freehling, *The Road to Disunion, Volume 2: Secessionists Triumphant 1854–1861* (New York: Oxford University Press, 2007), 112–113; Benjamin R. Curtis Jr., ed., *A Memoir of Benjamin Robbins Curtis with Some of His Professional and Miscellaneous Writings* (New York: Da Capo Press, 1970), 1:168.

35. Catron's own account of his early life can be found in John Catron, "Biographical Letter from Judge Catron," *U.S. Monthly Law Magazine* 5 (1852): 145.

36. 14 Tenn. 119, 126 (1834).

37. 16 Tenn. 256 (1835).

38. 31 U.S. (6 Pet.) 515 (1832).

39. Curtis Nettels, "The Mississippi Valley and the Federal Judiciary, 1807–1837," *Mississippi Valley Historical Review* 12 (1925): 202–226.

40. McKinley's life is discussed in Herbert U. Feibelman, "John McKinley of Alabama," *Alabama Lawyer* 22 (1961): 424.

41. The events leading to McKinley's ascension to the Court are described in Swisher, *The Taney Court,* 65–66.

42. Newmyer, *Supreme Court Justice Joseph Story,* 310; Swisher, *The Taney Period,* 67.

43. Daniel's life and ideology are described in detail in John P. Frank, *Justice Daniel Dissenting: A Biography of Peter V. Daniel, 1784–1860* (Cambridge, Mass.: Harvard University Press, 1964).

44. Frank, *Justice Daniel Dissenting,* 51.

45. The struggle over Daniel's confirmation is described in Frank, *Justice Daniel Dissenting,* 155–160.

46. Ibid., 160–161, 88, 87, 88, 166.

47. 40 U.S. (15 Pet.) 449 (1841).

48. 41 U.S. (16 Pet.) 539 (1842).

49. 40 U.S. (15 Pet.) 518 (1841).

CHAPTER 5. *UNITED STATES V. THE AMISTAD*

1. 40 U.S. (15 Pet.) 518 (1841).

2. The account of the facts of the case that follows is taken from Howard Jones, *Mutiny on the Amistad: The Saga of a Slave Revolt and Its Impact on American Abolition, Law, and Diplomacy* (New York: Oxford University Press, 1987), chap. 1; and Carl B. Swisher, *History of the Supreme Court of the United States, Volume 5: The Taney Period 1836–1864* (New York: Macmillan, 1974), 189–194. In addition, see William A. Owen, *Black Mutiny: The Revolt on the Schooner Amistad* (Cleveland: Pilgrim Press, 1997); William M. Wiecek, "Slavery and Abolition before the United States Supreme Court, 1820–1860," *Journal of American History* 65 (1978): 34–59.

3. Jones, *Mutiny on the Amistad,* 50–51.

4. Ibid., 57, 45.

5. "The African Captives: Trial of the Prisoners of the Amistad on the Writ of Habeas Corpus before the Circuit Court of the United States for the District of Connecticut, at Hartford," in *The African Slave Trade and American Courts,* ed. Paul Finkelman (New York: Garland, 1988), 1:145–192, at 158, 165–166.

6. Ibid., 186–187.

7. Ibid., 189 (emphasis in original), 188–191.

8. Jones, *Mutiny on the Amistad,* 86.

9. Ibid., 87–89.

10. Ibid., 89–91.

11. Ibid., 91.

12. "Case of the Amistad—Surrender under Treaty with Spain," *Official Opinions of the Attorneys General of the United States,* 3:484–92 (1839): 485, 486.

13. Ibid., 487.

14. Ibid.

15. Ibid., 487, 489, 489, 489.

16. Ibid., 490–494.

17. *New York Morning Herald,* November 21, 1839.

18. Jones, *Mutiny on the Amistad,* 104.

19. Ibid., 111–112, 113–114.

20. "A History of the Amistad Captives: Being a Circumstantial Account of the Cap-

ture of the Spanish Schooner Amistad, by the Africans on Board," in Finkelman, *The African Slave Trade in American Courts,* 1:193–224, at 215–216.

21. *The Liberator,* May 12, 1840; *New York Express,* June 12, 1840, quoted in Jones, *Mutiny on the Amistad,* 145.

22. Jones, *Mutiny on the Amistad,* 155–156.

23. Ibid., 152–153, 153.

24. Quoted in ibid., 247, n. 43; *Congressional Globe,* 26th Cong., 1st Sess. 281 (1840).

25. Jones, *Mutiny on the Amistad,* 146; *Congressional Globe,* 26th Cong., 2nd Sess. 13 (1840).

26. Ibid., 148.

27. United States v. The Amistad, 40 U.S. at 541, 542, 542.

28. Ibid., 545–546, 546–547, 547–549.

29. "Argument of Roger S. Baldwin of New Haven before the Supreme Court of the United States, in the Case of the United States, Appellants, vs. Cinque, and Others," in Finkelman, *The African Slave Trade and American Courts,* 1:377–408, at 380.

30. Ibid., 384, 390, 390–391, 393.

31. The evolution of radical antislavery theory in the United States is described in detail in William M. Wiecek, *The Sources of Antislavery Constitutionalism in America, 1760–1848* (Ithaca, N.Y.: Cornell University Press, 1977).

32. "Argument of Roger S. Baldwin," 396–397, 399, 397, 396.

33. Ibid., 401–408.

34. "Argument of John Quincy Adams, before the Supreme Court of the United States in the Case of the United States, Appellants, vs. Cinque, and Others, Africans, Captured in the Schooner Amistad," in Finkelman, *The African Slave Trade in American Courts,* 1:241–376; Jones, *The Amistad Affair,* 182.

35. "Argument of John Quincy Adams," at 248–249.

36. Ibid., 245, 270, 256, 275, 315.

37. United States v. The Amistad, 40 U.S. at 567–580, 583–587.

38. Ibid. at 596, 593, 594, 593.

39. Ibid. at 595–596.

40. Quoted in Jones, *Mutiny on the Amistad,* 195; Report from Committee on Foreign Affairs, *House Reports,* 426, 28th Cong., 1st Sess. (1844).

41. See, for example, "The Case of the Amistad," *The American Farmer, and Spirit of the Agricultural Journals of the Day,* March 24, 1841, in which a Baltimore periodical praised the Supreme Court's decision, while at the same time condemning the abolitionist supporters of the captured Africans.

CHAPTER 6. SLAVERY, THE COMMERCE POWER,
AND *GROVES V. SLAUGHTER*

1. 40 U.S. (15 Pet.) 449 (1841). For other useful discussions of *Groves,* see Austin Allen, *Origins of the Dred Scott Case: Jacksonian Jurisprudence and the Supreme Court, 1837–1857* (Athens: University of Georgia Press, 2006), 65–67; Robert D. Gudmestad, *A Troublesome Commerce: The Transformation of the Interstate Trade* (Baton Rouge: Louisiana

State University Press, 2003), 193–200; David Lightner, *Slavery and the Commerce Power: How the Struggle against the Interstate Slave Trade Led to the Civil War* (New Haven: Yale University Press, 2006), 71–78; and Carl B. Swisher, *History of the Supreme Court of the United States, Volume 5: The Taney Court* (New York: Macmillan, 1974), 364–370.

2. Lightner, *Slavery and the Commerce Power,* chap. 2, argues persuasively that the framers of the Constitution did not intend to vest Congress with the authority to regulate the interstate slave trade. For the contrary view, see Walter Berns, "The Constitution and the Migration of Slaves," *Yale Law Journal* 78 (1968): 198–228.

3. The attitudes of white Southerners toward the interstate slave trade are discussed in detail in Steven Doyle, *Carry Me Back: The Domestic Slave Trade in American Life* (New York: Oxford University Press, 2005); and Gudmestad, *A Troublesome Commerce.*

4. *Annals of Congress,* 9th Cong., 2d Sess. 484 (1807). The debates over the slave trade bill are discussed in detail in Donald L. Robinson, *Slavery in the Structure of American Politics, 1765–1820* (New York: Harcourt Brace Jovanovich, 1971), 325–337.

5. *Annals of Congress,* 9th Cong., 2d Sess. 626 (1807).

6. Lightner, *Slavery and the Commerce Power,* 59–64, 57.

7. Ibid., 101, 108.

8. 36 U.S. (11 Pet.) 102 (1837).

9. Ibid., 136–137, 142, 132–133.

10. The description of the efforts to regulate the slave trade in Mississippi is taken from Charles Sydnor, *Slavery in Mississippi* (Baton Rouge: Louisiana State University Press, 1966).

11. 6 Miss. 80 (1841).

12. Ibid., 100, 101.

13. 6 Miss. 140, 148 (1841).

14. *Groves v. Slaughter,* 40 U.S. at 461–462; "Argument of Robert J. Walker, Esq., before the Supreme Court of the United States, on the Mississippi Slave Question, at January Term, 1841, Involving the Power of Congress and of the States to Prohibit the Interstate Slave Trade," in *Southern Slaves in Free State Courts: The Pamphlet Literature,* ed. Paul Finkelman (New York: Garland, 1988), 2:73–162, at 81–82.

15. *Groves,* 448, 448–449; "Argument of Robert J. Walker," 75, 79.

16. "Argument of Robert J. Walker," 123.

17. Ibid., 162.

18. *Groves,* 448–449; "Argument of Robert J. Walker," 137, 145–162.

19. "Argument of Robert J. Walker," 130–131, 136–137.

20. Ibid., 129, 131, 128, 138–139, 144–145; *Groves,* 465–467, 468–469.

21. *Groves,* 480, 485, 489, 480, 489, 486.

22. Ibid., 485.

23. Ibid., 486.

24. Ibid., 48.

25. Ibid., 483, 481, 492.

26. Ibid., 484, 487.

27. Ibid., 489, 494–495.

28. Lightner, *Slavery and the Commerce Power,* 51–52; *Congressional Globe,* 25th Cong., 3d Sess. App. 357 (1839); *Groves,* 488, 488–489.

29. *Groves,* 499–500.

30. Ibid., 501.

31. Ibid., 504.

32. Ibid., 510.

33. Ibid., 512–513, 515–516.

34. Ibid., 508, 509–510, 510.

35. *Columbus Democrat,* May 8, 1841, quoted in Charles Warren, *The Supreme Court in United States History* (Littleton, Colo.: Fred Rothman, 1987), 2:72.

CHAPTER 7. THE PROBLEM OF FUGITIVE SLAVES

1. The problem of kidnapping is emphasized in Carol Wilson, *Freedom at Risk: The Kidnapping of Free Blacks in America, 1780–1865* (Lexington: University of Kentucky Press, 1994). The Northern response is discussed in detail in Thomas D. Morris, *Free Men All: The Personal Liberty Laws of the North, 1780–1861* (Baltimore: Johns Hopkins University Press, 1974).

2. The principals in *Somerset v. Stewart* were James Somersett and Charles Steuart. The case is commonly cited by the variant spellings of their names. Max Farrand, ed., *The Records of the Federal Convention of 1787* (New Haven: Yale University Press, 1937), 2:443; Somerset v. Stewart, 1 Lofft's Rep.1, 82 (1772).

3. Notable discussions of *Somerset* include Daniel J. Hulsebosch, "Nothing but Liberty: Somerset's Case and the British Empire," *Law and History Review* 24 (2006): 647–658; Ruth Paley, "Imperial Politics and English Law: The Many Contexts of Somerset," *Law and History Review* 24 (2006): 659–664; George Van Cleve, "Somerset's Case and Its Antecedents in Imperial Perspective," *Law and History Review* 24 (2006): 601–646; George Van Cleve, "Mansfield's Decision: Toward Human Freedom," *Law and History Review* 24 (2006): 665–671; and William M. Wiecek, "*Somerset:* Lord Mansfield and the Legitimacy of Slavery in the Anglo-American World," *University of Chicago Law Review* 42 (1976): 86–146.

4. Farrand, *The Records of the Federal Convention of 1787,* 2:443, 453–454, 601–602.

5. See, for example, "George Mason and James Madison Debate the Slave-Trade Clause," in Bernard Bailyn, ed., *The Debate on the Constitution: Federalist and Antifederalist Speeches, Articles and Letters during the Struggle over Ratification, Part Two* (New York: Library of America, 1993), 707.

6. The background and evolution of the Fugitive Slave Act of 1793 are described in detail in Paul Finkelman, "The Kidnapping of John Davis and the Adoption of the Fugitive Slave Law of 1793," *Journal of Southern History* 56 (1990): 397–422; and William R. Leslie, "A Study in the Origins of Interstate Rendition: The Big Beaver Creek Murders," *American Historical Review* 57 (1951): 63–76.

7. The Sedgwick bill is described in Finkelman, "The Kidnapping of John Davis," 408–410.

8. The evolution of the language in the Senate is discussed in Finkelman, "The Kidnapping of John Davis," 411–417; and Morris, *Free Men All,* 19–22.

9. *Annals of Congress,* 2d Cong., 1st Sess., 630, 640 (1793).

10. *Annals of Congress,* 7th Cong., 1st Sess. 336, 423, 426 (1801–02).

11. Ibid., 15th Cong., 1st Sess., 446–47, 813, 819 (1817–18).

12. Ibid. at 826, 231, 826, 245–246, 232, 827–828.

13. Ibid. at 838.

14. Ibid. at 840, 262.

15. Commonwealth v. Griffith, 14 Mass. (2 Pick.) 11 (1823); Wright v. Deacon, 5 Serg. & Rawle 63 (Pa. 1819).

16. 12 Wendell 311 (N.Y., 1834), 14 Wendell 507 (N.Y., 1835).

17. 14 Wendell 318, 319, 320.

18. 14 Wend. at 528.

19. Ibid.

20. Reprinted in Paul Finkelman, ed., *Slavery, Race and the American Legal System, 1700–1872: Fugitive Slaves and American Courts* (New York: Garland, 1988), 1:97–104.

21. Ibid. at 99, 100–101, 101.

22. Ibid. at 102.

23. 41 (16 Pet.) 539 (1842).

24. Morris, *Free Men All,* 42–53 provides a detailed account of the evolution of the Pennsylvania statute.

25. Ibid., 52–53. The facts of *Prigg* are described in detail in Paul Finkelman, "Storytelling on the Supreme Court: *Prigg v. Pennsylvania* and Justice Joseph Story's Judicial Nationalism," *Supreme Court Review* (1994): 247–294. In addition, see Carl B. Swisher, *History of the Supreme Court, Volume 5: The Taney Period* (New York: Macmillan, 1974), 535–537.

26. Finkelman, "Storytelling," at 275 and n. 12.

27. *Prigg,* 41 U.S. at 556–557.

28. Finkelman, "Storytelling," 278, n. 123

29. "Argument of Mr. Hambly of York, (Pa.) in the case of Edward Prigg v. The Commonwealth of Pennsylvania," in Paul Finkelman, ed., *Fugitive Slaves and American Courts: The Pamphlet Literature* (New York: Garland, 1988), 1:121–156, at 129.

30. *Prigg,* 41 U.S. at 559, 572.

31. Ibid. at 559.

32. Ibid. at 560–562.

33. Ibid. at 564–565.

34. Ibid. at 568–569.

35. Ibid. at 569, 570.

36. Ibid. at 582, 598–599, 576, 590.

37. Ibid. at 595, 579–588, 596.

38. Ibid. at 600.

39. Ibid. at 610.

40. Ibid. at 610–611.

41. 1 Lofft's Rep. 1 (1772). For detailed analyses of *Somerset* and its implications, see George Van Cleve, "Somerset's Case and Its Antecedents in Imperial Perspective," *Law and History Review* 24 (2006): 601–646; and Wiecek, "*Somerset:* Lord Mansfield and the Legitimacy of Slavery," 86–146.

42. *Prigg,* 41 U.S. at 611.

43. Ibid., 611, 612, 612–613. Paul Finkelman takes strong issue with Story's claim that the inclusion of the Fugitive Slave Clause was central to the constitutional bargain between North and South. Finkelman, "Storytelling," 256–257.

44. *Prigg,* 41 U.S. at 613.

45. Ibid., 614–615.

46. McCulloch v. Maryland, 17 U.S. (4 Wheat.) 316, 421 (1819); *Prigg,* 615, 618–619, 621–622.

47. *Prigg,* 618.

48. Ibid. at 622, 623, 624.

49. Ibid. at 615–616, 625.

50. The opinions of the different justices in *Prigg* are discussed in detail in Earl M. Maltz, "Majority, Concurrence and Dissent: *Prigg v. Pennsylvania* and the Structure of Supreme Court Decisionmaking," *Rutgers Law Journal* 31 (2000): 345–398.

51. Joseph C. Burke, "What Did the Prigg Decision Really Decide," *Pennsylvania Magazine of History and Biography* 93 (1969): 75–83; R. Kent Newmyer, *Supreme Court Justice Joseph Story: Statesman of the Old Republic* (Chapel Hill: University of North Carolina Press, 1985), 374–375; Paul Finkelman, "Sorting Out *Prigg v. Pennsylvania,*" *Rutgers Law Journal* 24 (1993): 605–665 at 607.

52. 38 U.S. (13 Pet.) 519 (1839).

53. Ibid. at 643, 648, 645, 643–644.

54. Ibid. at 641–642, 649, 650.

55. 16 Fed. Cas. 881 (No. 9154) (S.D.N.Y. 1835).

56. Ibid. at 883.

57. Ibid. at 884.

58. See, for example, City of New York v. Miln, 36 U.S. (11 Pet.) 102 (1837) (dormant commerce clause); Brown v. Maryland, 25 U.S. (12 Wheat.) 419 (1827) (original package doctrine); Ogden v. Saunders, 25 U.S. (12 Wheat.) 213 (1827) (insolvency laws).

59. *Prigg,* 41 U.S. at 634, 634, 635.

60. Henry Baldwin, *A General View of the Origin and Nature of the Constitution and Government of the United States* (New York: Da Capo Press, 1970).

61. *Prigg,* 41 U.S. at 635, 637.

62. Ibid., 660, 660–661, 661–663, 664–666.

63. Ibid., 667, 669, 672, 673.

64. Ibid., 654–655.

65. *Prigg,* 41 U.S. at 656–657, 656, 657.

66. Ibid. at 626–633, 628, 629.

67. Morris, *Free Men All,* 103; Newmyer, *Justice Joseph Story,* 370; Don E. Fehrenbacher and Ward M. McAfee, *The Slaveholding Republic: An Account of the United States Government's Relation to Slavery* (New York: Oxford University Press, 2001), 221; Paul Finkelman, "The Taney Court (1836–1864): The Jurisprudence of Slavery and the Crisis of the Union," in Christopher L. Tomlin, ed., *The United States Supreme Court: The Pursuit of Justice* (New York: Houghton Mifflin, 2005), 73–104, at 87. Christopher L. M. Eisgruber, "Justice Story, Slavery, and the Natural Law Foundations of American Constitutionalism," *University of Chicago* 55 (1988): 273–327, disputes such characterizations based on an argument quite different from mine.

68. Finkelman, "Storytelling," 253; Morris, *Free Men All*, 104; Akhil Reed Amar, *America's Constitution: A Biography* (New York: Random House, 2005), 243.

69. *Prigg*, 41 U.S. at 650; Johnson v. Tompkins, 13 F. Cas. 840 (C.C.E.D. Pa. 1833).

70. See, for example, Morris, *Free Men All*, 104; Salmon P. Chase, "Reclamation of Fugitives from Service: An Argument for the Defendant in *Jones v. Van Zandt*," in *Fugitive Slaves and American Courts: The Pamphlet Literature*, ed. Paul Finkelman (New York: Garland, 1988), 341–448, 388–389.

71. Barbara Holden Smith, "Lords of Lash, Loom, and Law: Justice Story, Slavery, and Prigg v. Pennsylvania," *Cornell Law Review* 78 (1993): 1086–1151, 1131; Chase, "Reclamation of Fugitives from Service," 438–441.

CHAPTER 9. SLAVERY AND TERRITORIAL EXPANSION

1. The development of the schism between Tyler and mainstream Whigs is chronicled in Michael F. Holt, *The Rise and Fall of the American Whig Party: Jacksonian Politics and the Onset of the Civil War* (New York: Oxford University Press, 1999), 127–150.

2. Virtually all of the studies of the politics of the Jacksonian era devote considerable time to the dispute over the annexation of Texas. Valuable specialized studies include Thomas R. Hietala, *Manifest Design: Anxious Aggrandizement in Late Jacksonian America* (Ithaca, N.Y.: Cornell University Press, 1985), chaps. 2 and 3; Frederick Merk, *Slavery and the Annexation of Texas* (New York: Alfred A. Knopf, 1972); David M. Pletcher, *The Diplomacy of Annexation: Texas, Oregon, and the Mexican War* (Columbia: University of Missouri Press, 1973); Charles G. Sellers, *James K. Polk, Continentalist 1843–1846* (Princeton: Princeton University Press, 1966); Joel H. Silbey, *Storm over Texas: The Annexation Controversy and the Road to Civil War* (New York: Oxford University Press, 2005); and Justin H. Smith, *The Annexation of Texas* (New York: AMS Press, 1971).

3. Smith, *The Annexation of Texas*, 67–68.

4. On Upshur's role, see William W. Freehling, *The Road to Disunion: Secessionists at Bay, 1776–1854* (New York: Oxford University Press, 1990), 389–393; and Sean Wilentz, *The Rise of American Democracy: Jefferson to Lincoln* (New York: W. W. Norton, 2005), 559–561, 565–566.

5. See, for example, Freehling, *The Road to Disunion*, 408–410; Wilentz, *The Rise of American Democracy*, 567–568.

6. Smith, *The Annexation of Texas*, 240–242.

7. Ibid., 242–244.

8. *Congressional Globe*, 28th Cong., 1st Sess. 652 (1844).

9. See, for example, Michael A. Morrison, *Slavery and the American West: The Eclipse of Manifest Destiny and the Coming of the Civil War* (Chapel Hill: University of North Carolina Press, 1997), 35–36. For a detailed analysis of the election results, see Holt, *The Rise and Fall of the American Whig Party*, 194–206.

10. *Congressional Globe*, 28th Cong., 2d Sess. 87, 171 (1844–45).

11. Smith, *The Annexation of Texas*, 327–355 provides a detailed account of the complex maneuvering that ultimately resulted in the passage of the bill. In addition, see Freehling, *The Road to Disunion*, 440–447; Holt, *The Rise and Fall of the Whig Party*, 218–222.

12. Smith, *The Annexation of Texas,* 338.

13. Frederick Merk, *The Oregon Question: Essays in Anglo-American Diplomacy and Politics* (Cambridge, Mass.: Belknap Press, 1967) provides a detailed account of the long-running controversy.

14. *Congressional Globe,* 28th Cong., 2d Sess. 236–237 (1845).

15. The most complete account of the political maneuvering surrounding the Oregon issue is Sellers, *James K. Polk, Continentalist,* 338–415.

16. David M. Potter, *The Impending Crisis, 1848–1861* (New York: Harper & Row, 1976), 25.

17. *Congressional Globe,* 29th Cong., 1st Sess. 110 (1846).

18. Holt, *Origins of the Whig Party,* 248–255; Morrison, *Slavery and the American West,* 40–41.

19. *Congressional Globe,* 29th cong., 1st Sess. 1217 (1846).

20. The Wilmot Proviso is treated extensively in the book-length treatments of the sectional conflict cited elsewhere in this chapter. The Proviso is the focus of Chaplain W. Morrison, *Democratic Politics and Sectionalism: The Wilmot Proviso Controversy* (Chapel Hill: University of North Carolina Press, 1967); and Eric Foner, "The Wilmot Proviso Revisited," *Journal of American History* 46 (1969): 262–279. The Southern reaction is chronicled in William J. Cooper, *The South and the Politics of Slavery, 1828–1856* (Baton Rouge: Louisiana State University Press, 1978), 232–244.

21. *Congressional Globe,* 29th Cong., 1st Sess. 1217–18, 1220–21 (1846).

22. *Congressional Globe,* 29th Cong., 2d Sess. 105 (1847).

23. Ibid., 455.

24. Ibid., App. 154; Freehling, *The Road to Disunion,* 461.

25. *Congressional Globe,* 29th Cong., 2d Sess. App. 345, 334, 318 (1847).

26. Ibid., 425, 555, 573, 573.

27. The rise and fall of the Free Soil Party is described in detail in Frederick J. Blue, *The Free Soilers: Third Party Politics, 1848–54* (Urbana: University of Illinois Press, 1973); John Mayfield, *Rehearsal for Republicanism: Free Soil and the Politics of Anti-Slavery* (Port Washington, N.Y.: Kennikat Press, 1980): Joseph G. Rayback, *Free Soil: The Election of 1848* (Lexington: University of Kentucky Press, 1970); and Richard H. Sewell, *Ballots for Freedom: Antislavery Politics in the United States, 1837–1860* (New York: Oxford University Press, 1976).

28. Potter, *The Impending Crisis,* 77–78.

29. For a detailed description of the maneuvering that ultimately led to Taylor's nomination, see Holt, *Rise and Fall of the Whig Party,* 260–330.

30. *Congressional Globe,* 29th Cong., 1st Sess. 1200 (1846).

31. *Congressional Globe,* 29th Cong., 2d Sess. 178 (1847).

32. Ibid., 187–188, 198.

33. Holt, *Rise and Fall of the Whig Party,* 310–311; Potter, *The Impending Crisis,* 5–6.

34. *Congressional Globe,* 30th Cong., 1st Sess. 875, 876, 879, 988–989.

35. Ibid., 1031 (1848).

36. Ibid., 1002, 1007.

37. Holt, *Rise and Fall of the Whig Party,* 337.

38. Ibid., 334–338; Potter, *The Impending Crisis,* 72–76.

39. Holt, *The Impending Crisis,* 376–381; Wilentz, *The Rise of American Democracy,* 628–630.

40. Charles M. Wiltse, *John C. Calhoun, Sectionalist* (Indianapolis: Bobbs Merrill, 1951), 378–388. The text of the "Southern Address" can be found in Clyde N. Wilson and Shirley B. Cook, eds., *The Papers of John C. Calhoun* (Columbia: University of South Carolina Press, 2001), 26:225–244.

41. Holt, *Rise and Fall of the Whig Party,* 470–472.

42. The dispute over California and its impact on the sectional conflict is described in detail in Leonard L. Richards, *The California Gold Rush and the Coming of the Civil War* (New York: Knopf, 2007).

43. *Congressional Globe,* 30th Cong., 2d Sess. 21, 477 (1849).

44. Ibid., App. 121; Morrison, *Slavery and the American West,* 100–103.

45. The book-length studies of the sectional conflict provide detailed analyses of the complex struggle that began with the unfolding events in California and ultimately led to the adoption of the Compromise of 1850. Holden Hamilton, *Prologue to Conflict: The Crisis and Compromise of 1850* (Lexington: University of Kentucky Press, 1964); and John C. Waugh, *On the Brink of Civil War: The Compromise of 1850 and How It Changed the Course of American History* (Wilmington, Del.: Scholarly Resources, 2003) focus specifically on this struggle. In addition, see Mark J. Stegmaier, *Texas, New Mexico, and the Compromise of 1850: Boundary Dispute and Sectional Crisis* (Kent, Ohio: Kent State University Press, 1996).

46. Holt, *Rise and Fall of the Whig Party,* 474–475.

47. *Congressional Globe,* 31st Cong., 1st Sess. 1491, app. 1470–1488 (1850). The political maneuvering that surrounded the creation and defeat of the omnibus bill are discussed in detail in Holt, *Rise and Fall of the Whig Party,* 482–504. Hamilton, *Prologue to Conflict,* 109–117 provides a complete analysis of the relevant roll call votes.

48. *Congressional Globe,* 31st Cong., 1st Sess. 1502–1837 (1850) passim. Hamilton, *Prologue to Conflict,* chronicles the battle over Douglas's proposals and analyzes the voting patterns on the different bills.

CHAPTER 10. THE CONTROVERSY OVER FUGITIVE SLAVES, 1843–1853

1. Quoted in Charles Warren, *The Supreme Court in United States History* (Littleton, Colo.: Fred B. Rothman, 1987), 2:86; "House No. 41, Commonwealth of Massachusetts Report," in *Fugitive Slaves and American Courts: The Pamphlet Literature,* ed. Paul Finkelman (New York: Garland, 1988), 1:190, 194; Carl B. Swisher, *History of the Supreme Court, Volume 5: The Taney Period, 1836–64* (New York: Macmillan, 1974), 544, 545.

2. The Latimer affair is described in detail in Thomas D. Morris, *Free Men All: The Personal Liberty Laws of the North, 1780–1861* (Baltimore: Johns Hopkins University Press, 1974), 109–111.

3. "Proceedings of the Borough of Norfolk, on the Boston Outrage, in the Case of the Runaway Slave George Latimer," in Paul Finkelman, ed., *Fugitive Slaves and American Courts: The Pamphlet Literature* (New York: Garland, 1988), 1:211–230; Morris, *Free*

Men All, 111–114; Paul Finkelman, "*Prigg v. Pennsylvania* and Northern State Courts: Anti-Slavery Use of a Pro-Slavery Decision," *Civil War History* 25 (1979): 5–35; Stanley W. Campbell, *The Slave Catchers: Enforcement of the Fugitive Slave Law, 1850–1860* (Chapel Hill: University of North Carolina Press, 1968); "The McClintock Riots: June 2, 1847," http://chronicles.dickinson.edu/encyclo/m/ed_mcClintockriot.htm, accessed January 15, 2009.

4. Campbell, *The Slave Catchers,* 14; John C. Calhoun, "The Southern Address," in *The Works of John C. Calhoun,* ed. Richard K. Crallé (Columbia, S.C.: A. S. Johnston, 1851), 4:290–313; "The Slavery Question, or the Rights and the Union of the States," *American Law Journal* (April 1850): 9–21 at 10.

5. The legislative history of the Fugitive Slave Act of 1850 is reviewed in Stanley W. Campbell, *The Slave Catchers: Enforcement of the Fugitive Slave Law, 1850–1860* (Chapel Hill: University of North Carolina Press, 1968), 15–25; William W. Freehling, *The Road to Disunion, Volume 1: Secessionists at Bay* (New York: Oxford University Press, 1990), 501–505; Morris, *Free Men All,* 132–145.

6. *Congressional Globe,* 31st Cong., 1st Sess. App. 79 (1850).

7. Ibid., 231, 525, 481, 1111 (1850).

8. Ibid., 231.

9. Ibid., 946.

10. Ibid., 964.

11. Ibid., App. 640–641, 816–817, 1583.

12. *Congressional Globe,* 31st Cong., 1st Sess. 1660, 1806–07 (1850).

13. Herman V. Ames, ed., *State Documents on Federal Relations: The States and the United States* (Philadelphia: University of Pennsylvania, 1911), 271; Sean Wilentz, *The Rise of American Democracy: Jefferson to Lincoln* (New York: W. W. Norton, 2005), 650.

14. Quoted in Campbell, *The Slave Catchers,* 52.

15. Potter, *The Impending Crisis, 1848–1861,* 141–142.

16. The campaign for the Whig nomination in 1852 is described in detail in Holt, *The Rise and Fall of the American Whig Party,* 674–724.

17. Potter, *The Impending Crisis,* 142–143.

18. *The Road to Disunion: Secessionists at Bay,* 554.

CHAPTER 11. THE SUPREME COURT IN 1846

1. The process by which Nelson was chosen is described in Carl B. Swisher, *History of the Supreme Court, Volume 5: The Taney Period, 1836–64* (New York: Macmillan, 1974), 220–221.

2. The process by which Woodbury was chosen is described in Swisher, *The Taney Period,* 234–236.

3. Ibid., 235–236.

4. The complex maneuvering that followed Baldwin's death is described in ibid., 215–219, 229–232.

5. Ibid., 232.

6. 18 Fed. Cas. 657 (No. 10,497) (C.C.E.D. Pa. 1850).

7. Ibid., 659, 658, 658.

8. Ibid., 658, 659.

9. 26 Fed. Cas. 105 (No. 15229) (C.C.E.D. Pa. 1851).

10. The Christiana incident is described in Stanley W. Campbell, *The Slave Catchers: Enforcement of the Fugitive Slave Law, 1850–1860* (Chapel Hill: University of North Carolina Press, 1968), 151–153.

11. Ibid., 152, 152–153.

12. Hanaway, 26 Fed. Cas. at 123.

13. Ibid. at 123, 124.

14. Ibid. at 122–123.

15. Ibid. at 122, 129.

CHAPTER 12. REVISITING THE COMMERCE POWER

1. 46 U.S. (5 How) 134 (1847).

2. 41 U.S. (16 Pet.) 1 (1841).

3. Ibid., 18, 19.

4. 48 U.S. (7 How.) 283 (1849). The *Passenger Cases* are discussed in detail in Carl B. Swisher, *History of the Supreme Court of the United States, Volume 5: The Taney Period, 1836–64* (New York: Macmillan, 1974), 382–391; and Charles Warren, *The Supreme Court in United States History* (Littleton, Colo.: Fred B. Rothman, 1987), 2:174–182.

5. Elkison v. Deliesseline, 8 F. Cas. 493 (C.D.S.C. 1823) (No. 4,366); "Validity of the South Carolina Police Bill," *Official Opinions of the Attorneys General of the United States*, 1:659–660 (1824); "Validity of the South Carolina Police Bill," *Official Opinions of the Attorneys General of the United States*, 2:426–241 (1831). The ongoing controversy over the Negro Seamen's Acts is discussed in detail in Robert Pierce Holmes, *The Missouri Compromise and Its Aftermath: Slavery and the Meaning of* America (Chapel Hill: University of North Carolina Press, 2007), 155–162; and Philip M. Hamer, "Great Britain, the United States, and the Negro Seamen's Acts, 1822–1848," *Journal of Southern History* 1 (1935): 3–28.

6. *House of Representatives Report No. 80*, 27th Cong., 3d Sess. (1843); *Congressional Globe*, 27th Cong., 3d Sess. 384 (1843).

7. Hamer, "Great Britain, the United States, and the Negro Seamen's Acts," 22–23.

8. Ibid., 382, 349–350, 357–358, 356, 306, 373–374.

9. Ibid., 331, 357, 374.

10. Ibid., 428.

11. Ibid., 550; Swisher, *The Taney Period*, 393.

CHAPTER 13. THE ONGOING STRUGGLE OVER FUGITIVE SLAVES

1. 46 U.S. (5 How.) 215 (1847). *Van Zandt* is discussed in detail in Carl B. Swisher, *History of the Supreme Court, Volume 5: The Taney Period 1836–64* (New York: Macmillan,

1974), 547–554. Chase's life and ideology are examined in John Niven, *Salmon P. Chase: A Biography* (New York: Oxford University Press, 1995).

2. Jones v. Van Zandt, 13 Fed. Cas. 1040 (No. 7501), 1047 (No. 7502) (C.C.D. Ohio 1843).

3. Salmon P. Chase, "Reclamation of Fugitives from Service: An Argument for the Defendant in Jones v. Van Zandt," in *Fugitive Slaves in American Courts: The Pamphlet Literature,* ed. Paul Finkelman (New York: Garland, 1988), 1:341–448, at 353–361, 363–368, 368–386, 386–398.

4. Ibid. at 401–411 (quotations at 403); "Argument of William H. Seward on the Law of Congress Concerning the Recapture of Fugitive Slaves. In the Supreme Court of the United States. John Van Zandt as Sectum Wharton Jones. Argument for the Defendant," in Finkelman, *Fugitive Slaves in American Courts,* 2:449–486, 471; Chase, "Reclamation of Fugitives from Service," 406–407.

5. Chase, "Reclamation of Fugitives from Service," 411–412, 413–414, 414.

6. Ibid., 427–428, 428–431; "Argument of William H. Seward," 477.

7. "Argument of William H. Seward," 484–485; Chase, "Reclamation of Slaves from Service," 88–89, 91, 92, 86.

8. "Argument of William H. Seward," 486; Chase, "Reclamation of Slaves from Service," 83, 93, 94.

9. "Argument of William H. Seward," 486.

10. *Van Zandt,* 46 U.S. at 230–231 (citation omitted).

11. Ibid., 231.

12. Quoted in Frederick J. Blue, *Salmon P. Chase: A Life in Politics* (Kent, Ohio: Kent State University Press, 1987), 38.

13. 55 U.S. (19 How.) 13 (1852).

14. Eells v. Illinois, 5 Ill. (4 Scammon) 498, 499, 499, 501 (1843).

15. Ibid., 499–500, 500, 503.

16. Ibid., 509–510, 514.

17. Ibid., 510, 511, 512–514.

18. 5 Ill. (4 Scam.) 461.

19. *Eells,* 514–515, 518–519, 518, 518, 517.

20. Swisher, *The Taney Period,* 588.

21. *Moore,* 55 U.S. at 13–15, 15.

22. *New York Times,* December 11, 1852.

23. *Moore,* 55 U.S. at 21–22, 21, 21.

24. *Prigg,* 41 U.S. at 623.

25. Ibid., 625.

26. 51 U.S. (10 How.) 82 (1851).

CHAPTER 14. PRELUDE TO *DRED SCOTT: STRADER V. GRAHAM* AND THE DOCTRINE OF REATTACHMENT

1. The political and legal issues raised by these cases are comprehensively discussed in Paul Finkelman, *An Imperfect Union: Slavery, Comity and Federalism* (Chapel Hill: University of North Carolina Press, 1981).

2. Max Farrand, ed., *The Records of the Federal Convention of 1787* (New Haven: Yale University Press, 1937), 2:443; Somerset v. Stewart, 1 Lofft 1, 82 (1772).

3. Finkelman, *An Imperfect Union,* 15; Commonwealth v. Aves, 35 Mass. (18 Pick.) 193 (1836); Willard v. The People, 4 Scam. 461 (Ill. 1843).

4. The facts that gave rise to the Lemmon controversy are described in greater detail in Finkelman, *An Imperfect Union,* 296–297.

5. Lemmon v. The People *ex rel.* Napoleon, 5 Sand. 681 (New York, 1852).

6. *New York Times,* November 15, 1852; *New York Evangelist,* November 18, 1852.

7. *Washington Union,* quoted in *National Era,* November 25, 1852; Finkelman, *An Imperfect Union,* 299, 300.

8. The subsequent proceedings in *Lemmon* are described in detail in Finkelman, *An Imperfect Union,* 297–300.

9. Barron v. City of Baltimore, 32 U.S. (7 Pet.) 243 (1833).

10. The Slave, Grace, 2 Hagg. Adm. 94, 94, 124 (1827).

11. Finkelman, *An Imperfect Union,* 188.

12. Strader et al. v. Graham, 5 B. Mon. 173 (Ky. 1844).

13. Ibid., 179, 181, 183, 182.

14. Strader v. Graham, 7 B. Mon. 633, 635 (Ky. 1847).

15. Strader v. Graham, 51 U.S. (10 How.) 82, 87, 88, 85–87 (1851).

16. Ibid., 85, 84, 92.

17. Ibid., 84.

18. Ibid., 89, 89, 91.

19. Ibid., 93–94.

20. Ibid., 94, 94–95, 95–96.

21. Ibid., 97.

22. *National Era,* June 16, 1851; Charles Warren, *The Supreme Court in United States History* (Littleton, Colo.: Fred B. Rothman, 1987), 2:225.

CHAPTER 16. THE KANSAS-NEBRASKA ACT,
THE ANTHONY BURNS AFFAIR, AND THE DEMISE
OF THE SECOND-PARTY SYSTEM

1. David M. Potter, *The Impending Crisis, 1848–1861* (New York: Harper & Row, 1976), 116; Michael A. Morrison, *Slavery and the American West: The Eclipse of Manifest Destiny and the Coming of the Civil War* (Chapel Hill: University of North Carolina Press, 1997), 130.

2. See, for example, *Congressional Globe,* 33rd Cong., 1st Sess. 277 (1854).

3. *Congressional Globe,* 32nd Cong., 2nd Sess. 565, 1117 (1853).

4. *Congressional Globe,* 33rd Cong., 1st Sess. 115 (1854).

5. William W. Freehling, *The Road to Disunion, Volume 1: Secessionists at Bay 1776–1854* (New York: Oxford University Press, 1990), 552.

6. *Congressional Globe,* 33rd Cong., 1st Sess. 115 (1854); Potter, *The Impending Crisis,* 159–161; *Congressional Globe, supra,* 175, 221.

7. Notable accounts of the struggle over the Kansas-Nebraska Act include Michael F.

Holt, *The Rise and Fall of the Whig Party: Jacksonian Politics and the Onset of the Civil War* (New York: Oxford University Press, 1999), 806–821; Morrison, *Slavery and the American West*, 142–154; Allan Nevins, *Ordeal of the Union* (New York: Charles Scribner's Sons, 1947), 2:88–121; Potter, *The Impending Crisis*, 160–177; Sean Wilentz, *The Rise of American Democracy: Jefferson to Lincoln* (New York: W. W. Norton, 2005), 668–675; and Gerald W. Wolff, *The Kansas-Nebraska Bill: Party, Section, and the Coming of the Civil War* (New York: Revisionist Press, 1977).

8. *Congressional Globe,* 33rd Cong., App. 143, 514; Morrison, *Slavery in the American West,* 148.

9. *Congressional Globe,* 33rd Cong., 1st Sess. App. 1002 (1854); Potter, *The Impending Crisis,* 163.

10. *Congressional Globe,* 33rd Cong., 1st Sess. 532 (1854); Holt, *The Rise and Fall of the Whig Party,* 815–821; *Congressional Globe, supra,* 1254.

11. The struggle for control of Kansas is discussed in detail in Nicole Etcheson, *Bleeding Kansas: Contested Liberty in the Civil War Era* (Lawrence: University Press of Kansas, 2003).

12. Thomas D. Morris, *Free Men All: The Personal Liberty Laws of the North 1780–1861* (Baltimore: Johns Hopkins University Press, 1974), 167.

13. Albert J. Von Frank, *The Trials of Anthony Burns: Freedom and Slavery in Emerson's Boston* (Cambridge, Mass.: Harvard University Press, 1998), provides a detailed but somewhat idiosyncratic account of the Burns affair. For a more straightforward description of the relevant events, see Stanley W. Campbell, *The Slave Catchers: Enforcement of the Fugitive Slave Law, 1850–1860* (Chapel Hill: University of North Carolina Press), 124–132.

14. Quoted in William E. Gienapp, *The Origins of the Republican Party, 1852–1856* (New York: Oxford University Press, 1987), 354.

15. The rise of the Republican Party and the principles of the party's ideology are chronicled in Eric Foner, *Free Soil, Free Labor, Free Men: The Ideology of the Republican Party before the Civil War* (New York: Oxford University Press, 1970); Gienapp, *Origins of the Republican Party;* and Michael F. Holt, *The Political Crisis of the 1850s* (New York: Wiley, 1978).

CHAPTER 17. THE SUPREME COURT IN THE MID-1850S

1. The most complete account of Curtis's life and jurisprudence is Stuart Streichler, *Justice Curtis in the Civil War Era: At the Crossroads of American Constitutionalism* (Charlottesville: University of Virginia Press, 2005).

2. 35 Mass. (18 Pick.) 193 (1836).

3. Benjamin R. Curtis Jr., ed., *A Memoir of Benjamin Robbins Curtis with Some of His Professional and Miscellaneous Writings* (New York: Da Capo Press, 1970), 1:136, 134.

4. Ibid., 155.

5. Ibid., 1:161, 2:172, 1:163.

6. Ibid., 2:174, 175.

7. Curtis, *A Memoir of Benjamin Robbins Curtis,* 2:211.

324 Notes to Pages 187–196

8. Ibid., 1:177–178.

9. *New York Times,* April 14, 1855; *The Liberator,* June 8, 1855.

10. Robert Saunders Jr., *John Archibald Campbell, Southern Moderate, 1811–1889* (Tuscaloosa: University of Alabama Press, 1997) provides a detailed, sympathetic account of Campbell's life and career. In addition, see Henry Groves Connor, *John Archibald Campbell, Associate Justice of the United States Supreme Court, 1854–1861* (Boston: Houghton Mifflin, 1920).

11. The struggle over the selection of McKinley's successor is described in detail in Charles Warren, *The Supreme Court in United States History* (Littleton, Colo.: Fred Rothman, 1987), 2:242–247.

12. *New York Times,* March 23, 1853; *New York Tribune,* March 24, 1853.

13. Saunders, *John Archibald Campbell,* 74–75.

14. Ibid., 73; Connor, *John Archibald Campbell,* 118; Carl B. Swisher, *History of the Supreme Court of the United States, Volume 5: The Taney Period, 1836–1864* (New York: Macmillan, 1974), 565–566.

15. Saunders, *John Archibald Campbell,* 88–89.

16. John A. Campbell, "The Rights of the Slave State," *Southern Quarterly Review* 3 (1851): 101–145, 140, 138, 142, 141.

17. Warren, *The Supreme Court in United States History,* 2:247.

18. Swisher, *The Taney Court,* 708.

19. Ibid.

20. John P. Frank, *Mr. Justice Daniel, Dissenting: A Biography of Peter V. Daniel, 1784–1860* (Cambridge, Mass.: Harvard University Press, 1964), 245–246.

21. Swisher, *The Taney Period,* 69–70; Don E. Fehrenbacher, *The Dred Scott Case: Its Significance in American Law and Politics* (New York: Oxford University Press, 1978), 234.

22. Ibid., 311.

23. Michael F. Holt, *The Rise and Fall of the American Whig Party: Jacksonian Politics and the Onset of the Civil War* (New York: Oxford University Press, 1999), 261–272, 280–284, 290–297, explores McLean's efforts to gain the nomination of the Whig Party in 1848.

24. William E. Gienapp, *The Origins of the Republican Party, 1852–1856* (New York: Oxford University Press, 1987), 312.

25. Thomas E. Carney, "The Political Judge: Justice John McLean's Pursuit of the Presidency," *Ohio History* 111 (2002): 121–144; and William E. Gienapp, *The Origins of the Republican Party, 1852–1856* (New York: Oxford University Press, 1987), 311–316, 338–342, describe McLean's campaign for the Republican nomination in 1856.

26. Gienapp, *Origins of the Republican Party,* 313, 312.

27. Ibid., 312.

28. Ibid., 315.

CHAPTER 18. *ABLEMAN V. BOOTH,* PART 1: NORTHERN NULLIFICATION

1. This account of the facts is taken from H. Robert Baker, *The Rescue of Joshua Glover: A Fugitive Slave, the Constitution, and the Coming of the Civil War* (Athens: Uni-

versity of Ohio Press, 2006). A. J. Beitzinger, "Federal Law Enforcement and the Booth Cases," *Marquette Law Review* 41 (1957–58): 7–32 also provides useful information on many aspects of the dispute. In addition, see "Slavery, Federalism and the Constitution: *Ableman v. Booth* and the Struggle over Fugitive Slaves," *Cleveland State Law Review* 56 (2007): 83–110.

2. Baker, *The Rescue of Joshua Glover*, 7.

3. Beitzinger, "Federal Law Enforcement and the Booth Cases," 10.

4. United States *ex rel.* Garland v. Morris, 26 Fed. Cas. 1318, 1319 (No. 15811) (D.C.D. Wis. 1854).

5. "Argument of Byron Paine, Esq., and Opinion of A. D. Smith, Associate Justice of the Supreme Court of the State of Wisconsin, Habeas Corpus Trial. Before Judge Smith. In the Matter of the Petition of Sherman M. Booth for a Writ of Habeas Corpus and to be Discharged from Imprisonment," in *Fugitive Slaves and American Courts: The Pamphlet Literature*, ed. Paul Finkelman (New York: Garland, 1988), 3:347–382, at 349.

6. Ibid., 355, 357.

7. *In re* Sherman M. Booth, 3 Wis. 13, 21, 24 (1854).

8. Ibid., 31, 32.

9. Ibid., 33, 41, 40.

10. Ibid., 45, 44.

11. Ibid. at 52.

12. *National Era*, June 22, 1854. See also, for example, *New York Times*, June 14, 1854.

13. 3 Wis. 54, 86–134, 57–58, 72–73, 61–62, 85–86 (1854).

14. Ibid., 66–71, 66.

15. Ibid., 82, 74, 80.

16. *New York Evangelist*, July 27, 1854; Boston *Commonwealth*, quoted in *The Liberator*, August 10, 1854.

17. "Constitutionality of the Law for the Extradition of Fugitives," *Official Opinions of the Attorney General of the United States*, 6:713 (1854); Carl B. Swisher, *History of the Supreme Court of the United States, Volume 5: The Taney Court* (New York: Macmillan, 1974), 659; Beitzinger, "Federal Law Enforcement and the Booth Cases," 14.

18. 3 Wis. 134, 141 (1854).

19. *Washington Union*, August 6, 1854; *Milwaukee News*, quoted in *The Liberator*, August 4, 1854.

20. Baker, *The Rescue of Joshua Glover*, 97, 98.

21. United States v. Rycraft, 27 Fed. Cas. 918, 920, 921 (No. 16,211) (D.C.D. Wis. 1854).

22. Ibid., 923, 922.

23. Ibid., 923.

24. Beitzinger, "Federal Law Enforcement and the Booth Cases," 14.

25. Baker, *The Rescue of Joshua Glover*, 104, 107.

26. Swisher, *The Taney Court*, 659.

27. *New York Times*, February 2, 1855.

28. Quoted in *New York Independent*, February 1, 1855.

29. Ibid.; *New York Times*, February 2, 1855.

30. *In re* Booth and Rycraft, 3 Wis. 157, 158–59 (1855); Beitzinger, "Federal Law Enforcement and the Booth Cases," 16.

31. *In re* Booth and Rycraft, at 159.

32. 3 Wis. 157 (1855).

33. Ibid., 161, 175.

34. Ibid., 163, 163–164.

35. Ibid., 165–166, 166–170.

36. 28 U.S. (3 Pet.) 197 (1829).

37. Ibid., 207.

38. Beitzinger, "Federal Law Enforcement and the Booth Cases," 18, 17. *New York Tribune* quoted in Charles Warren, *The Supreme Court in United States History* (Boston: Little Brown, 1926), 5:260–261.

39. Beitzinger, "Federal Law Enforcement and the Booth Cases," 17–18.

40. 14 U.S. (1 Wheat.) 304 (1816).

41. Ibid., 18; 14 U.S. (1 Wheat.) 304 (1816); *Chicago Tribune,* quoted in *The Liberator,* November 23, 1855.

42. Beitzinger, "Federal Law Enforcement and the Booth Cases," 18.

43. Ableman v. Booth, 59 U.S. (19 How.) 459 (1856).

CHAPTER 19. *DRED SCOTT,* PART 1: THE ROAD TO
THE SUPREME COURT

1. The facts of *Dred Scott* are described in detail in Walter Ehrlich, *They Have No Rights: Dred Scott's Struggle for Freedom* (Westport, Conn.: Greenwood Press, 1979), 9–29; and Don E. Fehrenbacher, *The Dred Scott Case: Its Significance in American Law and Politics* (New York: Oxford University Press, 1979), 239–249. Other notable book-length treatments of the case include Austin Allen, *Origins of the Dred Scott Case: Jacksonian Jurisprudence and the Supreme Court, 1837–1857* (Athens: University of Georgia Press, 2006); and Mark A. Graber, *Dred Scott and the Problem of Constitutional Evil* (New York: Cambridge University Press, 2006).

2. Lea Vandervelde and Sandhya Subramanian, "Mrs. Dred Scott," *Yale Law Journal* 106 (1997): 1033–1122 examines the life of Harriet Scott in detail.

3. The progress of the Scotts' lawsuit in the lower state court is traced in Ehrlich, *They Have No Rights,* 41–54; Fehrenbacher, *The Dred Scott Case,* 250–254; and Earl M. Maltz, *Dred Scott and the Politics of Slavery* (Lawrence: University Press of Kansas, 2007), 63–64, 66–67.

4. 4 Mo. 350 (1836).

5. Ehrlich, *They Have No Rights,* 58–60; Fehrenbacher, *The Dred Scott Case,* 258–259.

6. Ehrlich, *They Have No Rights,* 60–61; Fehrenbacher, *The Dred Scott Case,* 259.

7. Scott v. Emerson, 15 Mo. 582 (1852).

8. Ibid., 595–596.

9. Ibid., 583–584.

10. Fehrenbacher, *The Dred Scott Case,* 267.

11. Ehrlich, *They Have No Rights,* 79–80.

12. 41 U.S. (16 Pet.) 1 (1842).

13. Fehrenbacher, *The Dred Scott Case,* 271–275.

14. Ibid., 276; Ehrlich, *They Have No Rights*, 82.

15. The discussion that follows is taken from Earl M. Maltz, *The Fourteenth Amendment and the Law of the Constitution* (Durham, N.C.: Carolina Academic Press, 2003), 40–42.

16. Amy v. Smith, 1 Littell 326 (Kentucky 1822); *Congressional Globe*, 31st Cong., 1st Sess. App. 288 (1850).

17. State v. Manuel, 20 N.C. (4 Dev. And Bat.) 144 (1838); Fisher's Negroes v. Dabbs, 14 Tenn. (6 Yerg.) 119 (1834); James H. Kettner, *The Development of American Citizenship, 1608–1870* (Chapel Hill: University of North Carolina Press, 1978), 320. In addition, see Rogers M. Smith, *Civic Ideals: Conflicting Visions of Citizenship in U.S. History* (New Haven: Yale University Press, 1997), 255–260.

18. Fehrenbacher, *The Dred Scott Case*, 276–278.

19. Ehrlich, *They Have No Rights*, 83.

20. Ibid., 83–84; Fehrenbacher, *The Dred Scott Case*, 277.

21. Ehrlich, *They Have No Rights*, 85–86; Fehrenbacher, *The Dred Scott Case*, 279.

22. Fehrenbacher, *The Dred Scott Case*, 281–282.

23. "Brief of Plaintiff. In the Supreme Court of the United States, Dred Scott v. John F. A. Sandford," in *Southern Slaves in Free State Courts: The Pamphlet Literature*, ed. Paul Finkelman (New York: Garland, 1988), 3:17–28 at 18–21.

24. Paul Finkelman, *An Imperfect Union: Slavery, Federalism and Comity* (Chapel Hill: University of North Carolina Press, 1981), 276–277.

25. Roswell Field to Montgomery Blair, January 7, 1855.

26. "Brief of Plaintiff," 21–27.

27. Roswell Field to Montgomery Blair, January 7, 1855.

28. Fehrenbacher, *The Dred Scott Case*, 287; Ehrlich, *They Have No Rights*, 91–92.

29. Ibid., quotations on 21.

30. Ehrlich, *They Have No Rights*, 95; Fehrenbacher, *The Dred Scott Case*, 288.

31. Fehrenbacher, *The Dred Scott Case*, 289; Benjamin R. Curtis Jr., ed., *Memoir and Writings of Benjamin Robbins Curtis* (New York: Da Capo Press, 1970), 1:180.

32. Ehrlich, *They Have No Rights*, 101–104; Fehrenbacher, *The Dred Scott Case*, 289–290.

CHAPTER 20. THE COURT ON THE BRINK

1. *New York Tribune*, May 15, 1856; Walter Ehrlich, *They Have No Rights: Dred Scott's Struggle for Freedom* (Westport, Conn.: Greenwood Press, 1979), 104; Don E. Fehrenbacher, *The Dred Scott Case: Its Significance in American Law and Politics* (New York: Oxford University Press, 1978), 290.

CHAPTER 21. SECTIONALISM ON THE MARCH

1. 59 U.S. (18 How.) 595 (1856).

2. Benjamin R. Curtis Jr., ed., *Memoir and Writings of Benjamin Robbins Curtis* (New York: Da Capo Press, 1970), 1:210.

3. William Gienapp, *The Origins of the Republican Party, 1852–1856* (New York: Oxford University Press, 1987), 240–246, 273.

4. The impact of these events is chronicled in ibid., 273–303; William E. Gienapp, "The Crime against Sumner: The Caning of Charles Sumner and the Rise of the Republican Party," *Civil War History* 25 (1979): 218–245; and Michael F. Holt, *The Political Crisis of the 1850s* (New York: John Wiley and Sons, 1978), 192–196.

5. Gienapp, *The Origins of the Republican Party,* 259–264; David M. Potter, *The Impending Crisis, 1848–1861* (New York: Harper & Row, 1976), 254–255.

6. Gienapp, *The Origins of the Republican Party,* 329–334.

7. Ibid., 315; "Republican Party Platform of 1856," in *Political Party Platforms: Parties Receiving Electoral Votes: 1840–2008* http://www.presidency.ucsb.edu/ws/index.php?pid=29619, accessed January 28, 2009.

8. Potter, *The Impending Crisis,* 259–260; "Democratic Party Platform of 1856," in *Political Party Platforms: Parties Receiving Electoral Votes: 1840–2008,* http://www.presidency.ucsb.edu/ws/index.php?pid=29576, accessed January 28, 2009.

9. Svend Petersen, *A Statistical History of American Presidential Elections* (New York: Ungar, 1963), 33–35.

10. Ibid.

11. Gienapp, *The Origins of the Republican Party,* 442.

12. James D. Richardson, ed., *A Compilation of the Messages and Papers of the Presidents, 1789–1902* (New York: Bureau of National Literature and Art, 1907), 4:2930–2933; *Congressional Globe,* 34th Cong., 3d Sess. 10–11, 15–16, 71–74, 85–87 (1856).

CHAPTER 22. *DRED SCOTT,* PART 2: REARGUMENT AND
RECONSIDERATION

1. Don E. Fehrenbacher, *The Dred Scott Case: Its Significance in American Law and Politics* (New York: Oxford University Press, 1979), 293.

2. "Argument of Mr. Curtis on Behalf of Plaintiff. In the Supreme Court of the United States, Dred Scott vs. John F. A. Sandford," in *Southern Slaves in Free State Courts: The Pamphlet Literature,* ed. Paul Finkelman (New York: Garland, 1988), 3:83–128; "Argument of Montgomery Blair of Counsel for the Plaintiff in Error. In the Supreme Court of the United States, Dred Scott vs. John F. A. Sandford," in *Southern Slaves in Free State Courts, supra,* 3:29–68, at 55–56.

3. *New York Daily Tribune,* December 17, 18, 1856.

4. "Argument of Montgomery Blair," 32–33; "Brief for Defendant in Error. In the Supreme Court of the United States Dred Scott v. Sandford," in *Southern Slaves in Free State Courts: The Pamphlet Literature,* ed. Paul Finkelman (New York: Garland, 1988), 3:69–82, at 74–75.

5. "Argument of Montgomery Blair," 33–44; "Brief for Defendant in Error," 75–76.

6. "Brief for Defendant in Error," 79; "Argument of Montgomery Blair," 45–46.

7. "Argument of Montgomery Blair," 44.

8. Ibid., 46–47.

9. Ibid., 47–49.

10. "Brief for Defendant in Error," 76–79.

11. "Argument of Mr. Curtis," 92–121; "Argument of Montgomery Blair," 66–67.

12. "Brief for Defendant in Error," 80–82.

13. See Walter Ehrlich, *They Have No Rights: Dred Scott's Struggle for Freedom* (Westport, Conn.: Greenwood Press, 1979), 122–124.

14. Fehrenbacher, *The Dred Scott Case,* 307.

15. Ibid.; Ehrlich, *They Have No Rights,* 126–127.

16. Ehrlich, *They Have No Rights,* 130.

17. Holt, *Rise and Fall of the Whig Party,* 337; Ehrlich, *They Have No Rights,* 128; Fehrenbacher, *The Dred Scott Case,* 306–307.

18. 67 U.S. (2 Black) 635 (1863).

19. 71 U.S. 2 (1866).

20. William Freehling, *The Road to Disunion, Volume 2: Secessionists Triumphant 1854–1861* (New York: Oxford University Press, 2007), 110–118.

21. Fehrenbacher, *The Dred Scott Case,* 309; Potter, *The Impending Crisis,* 273; Curtis, *Memoir of Benjamin Robbins Curtis,* 1:234–235; Ehrlich, *They Have No Rights,* 129. Fehrenbacher dismisses the Catron and Grier letters as "second-hand information that is unsupported by any contemporary testimony from [the other justices]." Fehrenbacher, *The Dred Scott Case,* 309. He ignores the fact that both justices were actually present at the crucial conferences, and that they would have had no motive to mislead Buchanan (a Southern ally) in letters that they had no reason to believe would ever be published.

22. Ehrlich, *They Have No Rights,* 128.

23. Ibid., 131–132; Fehrenbacher, *The Dred Scott Case,* 311–312.

24. Fehrenbacher, *The Dred Scott Case,* 313.

CHAPTER 23. *DRED SCOTT,* PART 3: THE OPINIONS
OF THE JUSTICES

1. *Dred Scott v. Sandford,* 60 U.S. (19 How.) 393, 400–03 (1857). Rogers M. Smith, *Civic Ideals: Conflicting Visions of Citizenship in U.S. History* (New Haven: Yale University Press, 1997), 263–272, analyzes the differing approaches of the justices to the citizenship issue.

2. Ibid., 403.

3. Ibid., 403–407, quotations at 403, 406, 406.

4. Ibid., 407.

5. Ibid., 407–423, quotation at 411.

6. Ibid., 417.

7. Ibid., 423.

8. Ibid., 427–430, quotation at 429.

9. Ibid., 432–446.

10. 26 U.S. (1 Pet.) 511, 542 (1828).

11. *Dred Scott,* 60 U.S. at 442–446.

12. Ibid., 447–449, quotation at 448.

13. Ibid., 450.

14. Ibid., 452, 448.

15. Ibid., 453–454.

16. Ibid., 458, 464, 462.

17. Ibid., 460, 460, 464, 464.

18. Ibid., 465–469.

19. Ibid., 469, 454–456.

20. Ibid., 469–493.

21. Ibid., 475.

22. Ibid., 477, 482.

23. Ibid., 485.

24. Ibid., 490.

25. Ibid., 493–518.

26. Ibid., 493–500.

27. Ibid., 514, 515–516.

28. Ibid., 514–515.

29. Carl B. Swisher, *History of the Supreme Court, Volume 5: The Taney Period, 1836–64* (New York: Macmillan, 1974), 564.

30. *Dred Scott,* 60 U.S. at 518–519, 519–524.

31. Ibid., 524–526.

32. Ibid., 527.

33. William E. Gienapp, *The Origins of the Republican Party, 1852–1856* (New York: Oxford University Press, 1987), 314–315.

34. *Dred Scott,* 529–564.

35. Ibid., 530–531, 531.

36. Ibid., 538, 534–535, 538, 542.

37. Ibid., 540–542, 547.

38. Ibid., 558, 561.

39. Ibid., 550–555, 557, 563.

40. Ibid., 558, 559.

41. Ibid., 537, 543, 550.

42. Ibid., 564–577, quotation at 577.

43. Ibid., 577–579 (my emphasis).

44. Ibid., 579–582 (my emphasis).

45. Ibid., 583–584.

46. Ibid., 589–590, quotations at 590.

47. Ibid., 613, 615.

48. Ibid., 624–628.

49. Ibid., 624, 625.

50. Ibid., 625–626, quotation at 626.

51. Ibid., 626.

52. Ibid., 599–601, quotation at 600.

53. Ibid., 600, 603–604.

54. Ibid., 596–597.

55. Ibid., 594.

56. Fairman, *The Taney Period,* 630; Fehrenbacher, *The Dred Scott Case,* 414. For

quite different assessments of the legal arguments, see Austin Allen, *Origins of the Dred Scott Case: Jacksonian Jurisprudence and the Supreme Court, 1837–1857* (Athens: University of Georgia Press, 2006); and Mark A. Graber, *Dred Scott and the Problem of Constitutional Evil* (New York: Cambridge University Press, 2006).

57. Much of the analysis which follows is taken from Earl M. Maltz, "The Last Angry Man: Benjamin Robbins Curtis and the *Dred Scott* Case," *Chicago-Kent Law Review* 82 (2007): 265–276.

58. *Dred Scott,* 60 U.S. at 590 (Curtis, J., dissenting) (emphasis added).

59. *Dred Scott,* 60 U.S. at 493 (Campbell, J., concurring), 458 (opinion of Nelson, J.). While Campbell himself later took a similar view of the legal import of Taney's conclusions on the citizenship issue, Fehrenbacher disagrees. Fehrenbacher, *The Dred Scott Case,* 328–330.

CHAPTER 24. *DRED SCOTT,* PART 4: THE REACTION
TO THE COURT'S DECISION

1. The reaction to *Dred Scott* is discussed in Kenneth M. Stampp, *America in 1857: A Nation on the Brink* (New York: Oxford University Press, 1992).

2. The dispute between Chief Justice Taney and Justice Curtis is chronicled in Benjamin R. Curtis Jr., ed., *A Memoir of Benjamin Robbins Curtis, with Some of His Professional and Miscellaneous Writings* (New York: Da Capo Press, 1970), 1:211–229; Don E. Fehrenbacher, *The Dred Scott Case: Its Significance in American Law and Politics* (New York: Oxford University Press, 1978), 316–319; and Carl B. Swisher, *History of the Supreme Court of the United States, Volume 5: The Taney Period, 1836–64* (New York: Macmillan, 1974), 633–636.

3. Curtis, *Memoir and Writings of Benjamin Robbins Curtis,* 1:221, 222, 229, 219.

4. Ibid., 1:216, 212, 212, 213.

5. Ibid., 1:224, 214–215.

6. The responses to *Dred Scott* are collected in Fehrenbacher, *The Dred Scott Case,* 417–443; Michael A. Morrison, *Slavery and the American West: The Eclipse of Manifest Destiny and the Coming of the Civil War* (Chapel Hill: University of North Carolina Press, 1997), 189–196; and Charles Warren, *The Supreme Court in United States History* (Littleton, Colo.: Fred Rothman, 1987), 2:303–319.

7. Fehrenbacher, *The Dred Scott Case,* 417, 423; Morrison, *Slavery and the American West,* 191–192; Fehrenbacher, *The Dred Scott Case,* 417; Morrison, *Slavery and the American West,* 191.

8. Morrison, *Slavery and the American West,* 195; Fehrenbacher, *The Dred Scott Case,* 419.

9. Morrison, *Slavery and the American West,* 194, 195; Fehrenbacher, *The Dred Scott Case,* 419.

10. Earl M. Maltz, *Dred Scott and the Politics of Slavery* (Lawrence: University Press of Kansas, 2007).

11. Fehrenbacher, *The Dred Scott Case,* 509; Morrison, *Slavery and the American West,* 195.

12. For detailed accounts of the struggle over the admission of Kansas, see Fehren-bacher, *The Dred Scott Case,* 458–482; Morrison, *Slavery and the American West,* 196–206; and David M. Potter, *The Impending Crisis, 1848–1861* (New York: Harper & Row, 1976), 297–327.

13. Morrison, *Slavery and the American West,* 196.

14. *Congressional Globe,* 35th Cong., 1st Sess. 18 (1857).

15. Ibid., 345, 617

16. Ibid., 617, 1065–1071.

17. Ibid., 1589.

18. Ibid., 1590.

19. Fehrenbacher, *The Dred Scott Case,* 503–504.

20. *New York Times,* June 23, 1857.

21. "Mr. Douglas's Opening Speech," http://lincoln.lib.niu.edu/cgi-bin/philologic/getobject.pl?c.2221:1.lincoln, at 215, accessed January 28, 2009.

22. "Lincoln's Rejoinder in the Charleston Joint Debate," http://lincoln.lib.niu.edu/cgi-bin/philologic/getobject.pl?c.2222:3.lincoln, at 185, accessed January 28, 2009.

23. "Mr. Lincoln's Reply in the Ottawa Joint Debate," http://lincoln.lib.niu.edu/cgi-bin/philologic/getobject.pl?c.2221:2.lincoln, 237–234, accessed January 28, 2009.

24. Ibid., 247–249; *Washington Union,* April 17, 1857.

25. "Mr. Lincoln's Opening Speech," http://lincoln.lib.niu.edu/cgi-bin/philologic/getobject.pl?c.2224:1.lincoln, 273, accessed January 28, 2009; "Mr. Douglas's Reply in the Freeport Joint Debate," http://lincoln.lib.niu.edu/cgi-bin/philologic/getobject.pl?c.2224:2.lincoln, 297–298, 300–302, accessed January 28, 2009.

CHAPTER 25. *ABLEMAN V. BOOTH,* PART 2: THE COURT DECIDES

1. 62 U.S. (21 How.) 506 (1859).

2. Passmore Williamson's Case, 26 Penn State 9 (1859); Carl B. Swisher, *History of the Supreme Court, Volume 5: The Taney Period, 1836–1865* (New York: Macmillan, 1974), 662.

3. 20 Fed. Cas. 973 (No. 11935) (C.C.S.D. Ohio 1855).

4. Ableman, 62 U.S. at 514, 515.

5. Ibid., 516.

6. Ibid., 523, 524.

7. Ibid., 518, 518–519, 519–520, 526.

8. Ibid., 525.

9. Ibid., 520.

10. Charles Warren, *The Supreme Court in United States History* (Littleton, Colo.: Fred B. Rothman, 1987), 2:336; Swisher, *The Taney Period,* 662.

11. Ibid., 526.

12. Ibid., 339, 338; *Congressional Globe,* 36th Cong., 1st Sess. 892 (1860).

13. Warren, *The Supreme Court in United States History,* 2:339, 340, 341.

14. *Congressional Globe,* 36th Cong., 1st Sess. App. 125 (1860).

15. Swisher, *The Taney Period,* 665.

16. Ableman v. Booth, 11 Wis. 498 (1859).

17. Ibid.

18. *The Liberator,* May 11, August 3, 1860.

19. *New York Times,* August 8, 13 (1860); A. J. Beitzinger, "Federal Law Enforcement and the Booth Cases," *Marquette Law Review* 41 (1957–58): 7–32, 31–32.

20. *New York Times,* April 9, March 4, 1859.

CHAPTER 26. THE ELECTION OF 1860

1. The maneuvering that ultimately led to the division of the Democratic Party is described in Michael A. Morrison, *Slavery and the American West: The Eclipse of Manifest Destiny and the Coming of the Civil War* (Chapel Hill: University of North Carolina Press, 1997), 219–228; and David M. Potter, *The Impending Crisis, 1848–61* (New York: Harper & Row, 1976), 407–416.

2. The course of the presidential campaign is described in Morrison, *Slavery in the American West,* 233–251; and Potter, *The Impending Crisis,* 430–447.

3. Campaign literature from the presidential election of 1860 is collected in Joel H. Silbey, ed., *American Party Battle: Election Campaign Pamphlets, 1828–1876,* 2 vols. (Cambridge, Mass.: Harvard University Press, 1999), 2:1854–1876.

CHAPTER 27. *KENTUCKY V. DENNISON* AND THE
PROBLEM OF EXTRADITION

1. 65 U.S. (24 How.) 66 (1861).

2. See the discussions in chapter 7, above.

3. The description of this incident is taken from Carl B. Swisher, *History of the Supreme Court, Volume 5: The Taney Period, 1836–64* (New York: Macmillan, 1974), 677–682.

4. In the Matter of Clark, 9 Wend. 212, 222 (New York, 1832); Swisher, *The Taney Period,* 679, 679, 683–684.

5. Swisher, *The Taney Period,* 686.

6. Ibid.; *Dennison,* 65 U.S. at 66.

7. Swisher, *The Taney Period,* 687.

8. *Dennison,* 86, 88.

9. Ibid., 90, 92, 88–89, 93–94.

10. Ibid., 72, 74–75, 75–76.

11. Ibid., 102, 90–91, 93.

12. Ibid., 76, 76, 84.

13. Ibid., 77, 77–78, 78, 79.

14. Ibid., 79, 79, 80–82, 80.

15. Ibid., 98.

16. Ibid., 99, 102.

17. Ibid., 103.

18. Ibid., 104.
19. Ibid., 106–107.
20. Ibid., 109, 110.
21. Ibid., 109.
22. 5 U.S. (1 Cranch.) 137 (1803).
23. Swisher, *The Taney Period,* 690.

CONCLUSION: THE LESSONS OF THE SLAVERY CASES

1. Charles Warren, *The Supreme Court in United States History* (Littleton, Colo.: Fred B. Rothman, 1987), 2:343–344.
2. This point is developed in far greater detail in Gerald N. Rosenberg, *The Hollow Hope: Can Courts Bring about Social Change?* (Chicago: University of Chicago Press, 1993).

Bibliography

CASES

Ableman v. Booth, 59 U.S. (19 How.) 459 (1856), 62 U.S. (21 How.) 506 (1859).

Ableman v. Booth, 11 Wis. 498 (1859).

The Amedie, 1 Acton's Rep. 240 (1808).

American Ocean Insurance Co. v. Canter, 26 U.S. (1 Pet.) 511 (1828).

Amy v. Smith, 1 Littell 326 (Kentucky 1822).

The Antelope, 23 U.S. (10 Wheat.) 66 (1825).

Bank of Augusta v. Earle, 38 U.S. (13 Pet.) 519 (1839).

Barron v. City of Baltimore, 32 U.S. (7 Pet.) 243 (1833).

Brown v. Maryland, 25 U.S. (12 Wheat.) 419 (1827).

Commonwealth v. Aves, 35 Mass. (18 Pick.) 193 (1836).

Commonwealth v. Griffith, 14 Mass. (2 Pick.) 11 (1823).

Dred Scott v. Sandford, 60 U.S. (19 How.) 393 (1857).

Eells v. Illinois, 5 Ill. (4 Scammon) 498 (1843).

Elkison v. Deliesseline, 8 F. Cas. 493 (C.D.S.C. 1823) (No. 4,366).

Ex Parte Milligan, 71 U.S. 2 (1866).

Ex Parte Robinson, 20 Fed. Cas. 973 (No. 11935) (C.C.S.D. Ohio 1855).

Ex Parte Sherman M. Booth, 3 Wis. 134 (1854).

Fairfax's Devisee v. Hunter's Lessee, 11 U.S. (7 Cranch) 603 (1813).

Fisher's Negroes v. Dobbs, 14 Tenn. (6 Yerg.) 119 (1834).

Gibbons v. Ogden, 22 U.S. (9 Wheat.) 1 (1824).

Glidewell v. Hite, 6 Miss. 140, 148 (1841).

Green v. Robinson, 6 Miss. 80 (1841).

Groves v. Slaughter, 40 U.S. (15 Pet.) 449 (1841).

Houston v. Moore, 18 U.S. (5 Wheat.) 1 (1820).

Hunter v. Fairfax's Devisee, 1 Munf. 218 (Va. 1810).

Hunter v. Martin, 4 Munf. 1 (1815).

In re Booth and Rycraft, 3 Wis. 157 (1855).

In re Martin, 16 Fed. Cas. 881 (No. 9154) (S.D.N.Y. 1835).

In re Sherman M. Booth, 3 Wis. 13, 3 Wis. 54 (1854).

In the Matter of Clark, 9 Wend. 212 (New York, 1832).

Jack v. Martin, 12 Wendell 311 (N.Y., 1834), 14 Wendell 507 (N.Y., 1835).

Johnson v. Tompkins, 13 Fed. Cas. 810 C.C.E.D. Pa. (No. 7,416) (1833).

Jones v. Van Zandt, 46 U.S. (5 How.) 215 (1847).

Jones v. Van Zandt, 13 Fed. Cas. 1040 (No. 7501), 1047 (No. 7502) (C.C.D. Ohio 1843).

Kentucky v. Dennison, 65 U.S. (24 How.) 66 (1861).

La Jeune Eugenie, 26 F. Cas. 832 (1822).

Lemmon v. The People ex rel. Napoleon, 5 Sand. 681 (New York, 1852).

The Louis, 2 Dodson 238 (1817).

Martin v. Hunter's Lessee, 14 U.S. (1 Wheat.) 304 (1816).

McCulloch v. Maryland, 17 U.S. (4 Wheat.) 316 (1819).

Moore v. Illinois, 55 U.S. (19 How.) 13 (1852).

New York v. Miln, 36 U.S. ((11 Pet.) 102 (1837).

Ogden v. Saunders, 25 U.S. (12 Wheat.) 213 (1827).

The Passenger Cases, 48 U.S. (7 How.) 283 (1849).

Passmore Williamson's Case, 26 Penn State 9 (1859).

Pease v. Peck, 59 U.S. (18 How.) 595 (1856).

Prigg v. Pennsylvania, 41 U.S. (16 Pet.) 539 (1842).

The Prize Cases, 67 U.S. (2 Black) 635 (1863).

Rachel v. Walker, 4 Mo. 350 (1836).

Rowan v. Runnels, 46 U.S. (5 How) 134 (1847).

Scott v. Emerson, 15 Mo. 582 (1852).

The Slave, Grace, 2 Hagg. Adm. 94 (1827).

Somerset v. Stewart, 1 Lofft's Rep.1 (1772).

State v. Foreman, 15 Tenn. 256 (1835).

State v. Manuel, 20 N.C. (4 Dev. And Bat.) 144 (1838).

Strader v. Graham, 51 U.S. (10 How.) 82 (1851).

Strader et al. v. Graham, 5 B. Mon. 173 (Ky. 1844), 7 B. Mon. 633, 635 (Ky. 1847).

Sturges v. Crowninshield, 17 U.S. (4 Wheat.) 122 (1819).

Swift v. Tyson, 41 U.S. (16 Pet.) 1 (1841).

United States ex rel. Garland v. Morris, 26 Fed. Cas. 1318 (No. 15811) (D.C.D. Wis. 1854).

United States v. The Amistad, 40 U.S. (15 Pet.) 518 (1841).

United States v. Hanaway, 26 Fed. Cas. 105 (No. 15229) (C.C.E.D. Pa. 1851).

United States v. La Jeune Eugenie, 26 Fed. Cas. 832 (No. 15551) (C.C.D. Mass. 1822).

United States v. Palmer, 16 U.S. (4 Wheat.) 610 (1818).

United States v. Rycraft, 27 Fed. Cas. 918 (No. 16,211) (D.C.D. Wis. 1854).

United States v. Smith, 18 U.S. (5 Wheat.) 153 (1820).

Willard v. The People, 5 Ill. (4 Scammon) 461.

Willson v. Black-Bird Creek Marsh Co., 27 U.S. (2 Pet.) 245 (1829).

Worcester v. Georgia, 31 U.S. (6 Pet.) 515 (1832).

Wright v. Deacon, 5 Serg. & Rawle 63 (Pa. 1819).

OTHER OFFICIAL FEDERAL GOVERNMENT DOCUMENTS

Annals of Congress

"Case of *The Amistad*—Surrender under Treaty with Spain." *Official Opinions of the Attorney General of the United States,* 3:484–492 (1839).

Congressional Globe

"Constitutionality of the Law for the Extradition of Fugitives." *Official Opinions of the Attorney General of the United States,* 6:713 (1854).

Report from Committee on Foreign Affairs. *House Reports,* 426, 28th Cong., 1st Sess. (1844).

"Validity of the South Carolina Police Bill." *Official Opinions of the Attorneys General of the United States,* 1:659–660 (1824).

"Validity of the South Carolina Police Bill." *Official Opinions of the Attorneys General of the United States,* 2:426–441 (1831).

NEWSPAPERS

The American Farmer, and Spirit of the Agricultural Journals of the Day
The Liberator
The National Era
New York Evangelist
New York Independent
New York Morning Herald
New York Times
New York Tribune
Washington Union

BOOKS, ARTICLES, AND WEB SITES

"The African Captives: Trial of the Prisoners of the Amistad on the Writ of Habeas Corpus before the Circuit Court of the United States for the District of Connecticut, at Hartford." In *The African Slave Trade and American Courts,* ed. Paul Finkelman. 2 vols. New York: Garland, 1988, 1:145–192.

Allen, Austin. *Origins of the Dred Scott Case: Jacksonian Jurisprudence and the Supreme Court, 1837–1857.* Athens: University of Georgia Press, 2006.

Amar, Akhil Reed. *America's Constitution: A Biography.* New York: Random House, 2005.

Ames, Herman V., ed. *State Documents on Federal Relations: The States and the United States.* Philadelphia: University of Pennsylvania, 1911.

"Argument of Byron Paine, Esq., and Opinion of A. D. Smith, Associate Justice of the Supreme Court of the State of Wisconsin, Habeas Corpus Trial. Before Judge Smith. In the Matter of the Petition of Sherman M. Booth for a Writ of Habeas Corpus and to be Discharged from Imprisonment." In *Fugitive Slaves and American Courts: The Pamphlet Literature,* ed. Paul Finkelman. 4 vols. New York: Garland, 1988, 3:347–382.

"Argument of John Quincy Adams, before the Supreme Court of the United States in the Case of the United States, Appellants, vs. Cinque, and Others, Africans, Captured in the Schooner Amistad." In *The African Slave Trade in American Courts,* ed. Paul Finkelman. 2 vols. New York: Garland, 1988, 1:241–376.

"Argument of Montgomery Blair of Counsel for the Plaintiff in Error. In the Supreme Court of the United States, Dred Scott vs. John F. A. Sandford." In *Southern Slaves in Free State Courts: The Pamphlet Literature,* ed. Paul Finkelman. 3 vols. New York: Garland, 1988, 3:29–68.

"Argument of Mr. Curtis on Behalf of Plaintiff. In the Supreme Court of the United States, Dred Scott vs. John F. A. Sandford." In *Southern Slaves in Free State Courts: The Pamphlet Literature,* ed. Paul Finkelman. 3 vols. New York: Garland, 1988, 3:83–128.

"Argument of Mr. Hambly of York (Pa.) in the case of Edward Prigg v. the Commonwealth of Pennsylvania." In *Fugitive Slaves and American Courts: The Pamphlet Literature,* ed. Paul Finkelman. 4 vols. New York: Garland, 1988, 1:121–156.

"Argument of Robert J. Walker, Esq., before the Supreme Court of the United States, on the Mississippi Slave Question, at January Term, 1841, Involving the Power of Congress and of the States to Prohibit the Interstate Slave Trade." In *Southern Slaves in Free State Courts: The Pamphlet Literature,* ed. Paul Finkelman. 3 vols. New York: Garland, 1988, 2:73–162.

"Argument of Roger S. Baldwin of New Haven before the Supreme Court of the United States, in the Case of the United States, Appellants, vs. Cinque, and Others." In *The African Slave Trade and American Courts: The Pamphlet Literature,* ed. Paul Finkelman. 2 vols. New York: Garland, 1988, 1:377–408.

"Argument of William H. Seward on the Law of Congress Concerning the Recapture of Fugitive Slaves. In the Supreme Court of the United States. John Van Zandt as Sectum Wharton Jones. Argument for the Defendant." In *Fugitive Slaves in American Courts: The Pamphlet Literature,* ed. Paul Finkelman. 4 vols. New York: Garland, 1988, 2:449–486.

Baker, H. Robert. *The Rescue of Joshua Glover: A Fugitive Slave, the Constitution, and the Coming of the Civil War.* Athens: University of Ohio Press, 2006.

Baldwin, Henry. *General View of the Origin and Nature of the Constitution and Government of the United States.* New York: Da Capo Press, 1970.

Basler, Roy J., ed. *The Collected Works of Abraham Lincoln.* New Brunswick, N.J.: Rutgers University Press, 1953, 2:465–467.

Beitzinger, A. J. "Federal Law Enforcement and the Booth Cases." *Marquette Law Review* 41 (1957–58): 7–32.

Berns, Walter. "The Constitution and the Migration of Slaves." *Yale Law Journal* 78 (1968): 198–228.

Blue, Frederick J. *The Free Soilers: Third Party Politics, 1848–54.* Urbana: University of Illinois Press, 1973.

———. *Salmon P. Chase: A Life in Politics.* Kent, Ohio: Kent State University Press, 1987.

"Brief for Defendant in Error. In the Supreme Court of the United States Dred Scott v. Sandford." In *Southern Slaves in Free State Courts: The Pamphlet Literature,* ed. Paul Finkelman. 3 vols. New York: Garland, 1988, 3:69–82.

"Brief of Plaintiff. In the Supreme Court of the United States, Dred Scott v. John F. A. Sandford." In *Southern Slaves in Free State Courts: The Pamphlet Literature,* ed. Paul Finkelman. 3 vols. New York: Garland, 1988, 3:17–28.

Burke, Joseph C. "What Did the Prigg Decision Really Decide." *Pennsylvania Magazine of History and Biography* 93 (1969): 75–83.

Calhoun, John C. "The Southern Address." In *The Works of John C. Calhoun,* ed. Richard K. Crallé. Columbia, S.C.: A. S. Johnston, 1851, 4:290–313.

Campbell, John A. "The Rights of the Slave State." *Southern Quarterly Review* 3 (1851): 101–145.

Campbell, Stanley W. *The Slave Catchers: Enforcement of the Fugitive Slave Law, 1850–1860.* Chapel Hill: University of North Carolina Press, 1968.

Carney, Thomas E. "The Political Judge: Justice John McLean's Pursuit of the Presidency." *Ohio History* 111 (2002): 121–144.

Catron, John. "Biographical Letter from Judge Catron." *U.S. Monthly Law Magazine* 5 (1852): 145.

Chase, Salmon P. "Reclamation of Fugitives from Service: An Argument for the Defendant in *Jones v. Van Zandt*." In *Fugitive Slaves and American Courts: The Pamphlet Literature*, ed. Paul Finkelman. 4 vols. New York: Garland, 1988, 1:341–448.

Connor, Henry Groves. *John Archibald Campbell, Associate Justice of the United States Supreme Court, 1854–1861.* Boston: Houghton Mifflin, 1920.

Cooper, William J. *The South and the Politics of Slavery, 1828–1856.* Baton Rouge: Louisiana State University Press, 1978.

Cover, Robert M. *Justice Accused: Antislavery and the Judicial Process.* New Haven: Yale University Press, 1984.

Curtis, Benjamin R., Jr., ed. *A Memoir of Benjamin Robbins Curtis with Some of His Professional and Miscellaneous Writings.* 2 vols. New York: Da Capo Press, 1970.

Doyle, Steven. *Carry Me Back: The Domestic Slave Trade in American Life.* New York: Oxford University Press, 2005.

Dunne, Gerald T. *Justice Joseph Story and the Rise of the Supreme Court.* New York: Simon and Schuster, 1970.

Ehrlich, Walter. *They Have No Rights: Dred Scott's Struggle for Freedom.* Westport, Conn.: Greenwood Press, 1979.

Eisgruber, Christopher L. M. "Justice Story, Slavery, and the Natural Law Foundations of American Constitutionalism." *University of Chicago Law Review* 55 (Winter 1988): 273–327.

Ellis, Richard E. *Union at Risk: Jacksonian Democracy, States Rights, and the Nullification Crisis.* New York: Oxford University Press, 1989.

Etcheson, Nicole. *Bleeding Kansas: Contested Liberty in the Civil War Era.* Lawrence: University Press of Kansas, 2003.

Farrand, Max, ed. *The Records of the Federal Convention of 1787.* 4 vols. New Haven: Yale University Press, 1937.

Fehrenbacher, Don E. *The Dred Scott Case: Its Significance in American Law and Politics.* New York: Oxford University Press, 1978.

———, and Ward M. McAfee. *The Slaveholding Republic: An Account of the United States Government's Relation to Slavery.* New York: Oxford University Press, 2001.

Feibelman, Herbert U. "John McKinley of Alabama." *Alabama Lawyer* 22 (1961): 424–428.

Finkelman, Paul. *An Imperfect Union: Slavery, Comity and Federalism.* Chapel Hill: University of North Carolina Press, 1981.

———. "The Kidnapping of John Davis and the Adoption of the Fugitive Slave Law of 1793." *Journal of Southern History* 56 (1990): 397–422.

———. "*Prigg v. Pennsylvania* and Northern State Courts: Anti-Slavery Use of a Pro-Slavery Decision." *Civil War History* 25 (1979): 5–35.

———. "Sorting Out *Prigg v. Pennsylvania*." *Rutgers Law Journal* 24 (1993): 605–665.

———. "Storytelling on the Supreme Court: *Prigg v. Pennsylvania* and Justice Joseph Story's Judicial Nationalism." *Supreme Court Review* 1994: 247–273.

———. "The Taney Court (1836–1864): The Jurisprudence of Slavery and the Crisis of the Union." In *The United States Supreme Court: The Pursuit of Justice,* ed. Christopher L. Tomlin. New York: Houghton Mifflin, 2005, 73–104.

———, ed. *Slavery, Race and the American Legal System, 1700–1872: Fugitive Slaves and American Courts.* 2 vols. New York: Garland, 1988.

Foner, Eric. *Free Soil, Free Labor, Free Men: The Ideology of the Republican Party before the Civil War.* New York: Oxford University Press, 1970.

———. "The Wilmot Proviso Revisited." *Journal of American History* 46 (1969): 262–279.

Forbes, Robert Pierce. *The Missouri Compromise and Its Aftermath: Slavery and the Meaning of America.* Chapel Hill: University of North Carolina Press, 2007.

Frank, John P. *Justice Daniel Dissenting: A Biography of Peter V. Daniel, 1784–1860.* Cambridge, Mass.: Harvard University Press, 1964.

Freehling, William W. *Prelude to Civil War: The Nullification Crisis in South Carolina, 1816–1836.* New York: Oxford University Press, 1966.

———. *The Road to Disunion, Volume 1: Secessionists at Bay 1776–1854.* New York: Oxford University Press, 1990.

———. *The Road to Disunion, Volume 2: Secessionists Triumphant 1854–1861.* New York: Oxford University Press, 2007.

Friedman, Leon, and Fred L. Israel, eds. *The Justices of the Supreme Court: Their Lives and Major Opinions.* 5 vols. New York: Chelsea House, 1997.

"George Mason and James Madison Debate the Slave-Trade Clause." In *The Debate on the Constitution: Federalist and Antifederalist Speeches, Articles and Letters during the Struggle over Ratification, Part Two,* ed. Bernard Bailyn. New York: Library of America, 1993, 707.

Gienapp, William E. "The Crime against Sumner: The Caning of Charles Sumner and the Rise of the Republican Party." *Civil War History* 25 (1979): 218–245.

———. *The Origins of the Republican Party, 1852–1856.* New York: Oxford University Press, 1987.

Graber, Mark A. *Dred Scott and the Problem of Constitutional Evil.* New York: Cambridge University Press, 2006.

Gudmestad, Robert D. *A Troublesome Commerce: The Transformation of the Interstate Trade.* Baton Rouge: Louisiana State University Press, 2003.

Hamer, Philip M. "Great Britain, the United States, and the Negro Seamen's Acts, 1822–1848." *Journal of Southern History* 1 (1935): 3–28.

Hamilton, Holden. *Prologue to Conflict: The Crisis and Compromise of 1850.* Lexington: University of Kentucky Press, 1964.

Hamilton to Washington, February 23, 1791. In *Papers of Alexander Hamilton,* ed. Harold Syrett. 27 vols. New York: Columbia University Press, 1961, 8:98.

Hietala, Thomas R. *Manifest Design: Anxious Aggrandizement in Late Jacksonian America.* Ithaca, N.Y.: Cornell University Press, 1985.

"A History of the Amistad Captives: Being a Circumstantial Account of the Capture of the Spanish Schooner Amistad, by the Africans on Board." In *The African Slave Trade in American Courts,* ed. Paul Finkelman. 2 vols. New York: Garland, 1988, 1:193–224.

Holt, Michael F. *The Political Crisis of the 1850s.* New York: Wiley, 1978.

————. *The Rise and Fall of the American Whig Party: Jacksonian Politics and the Onset of the Civil War.* New York: Oxford University Press, 1999.

"House No. 41, Commonwealth of Massachusetts Report." In *Fugitive Slaves and American Courts: The Pamphlet Literature,* ed. Paul Finkelman. 4 vols. New York: Garland, 1988, 1:190–194.

Hulsebosch, Daniel J. "Nothing but Liberty: Somerset's Case and the British Empire." *Law and History Review* 24 (2006): 647–658.

Jefferson, Thomas. "Opinion on the Constitutionality of a National Bank, 15 February 1791." In *The Portable Thomas Jefferson,* ed. Merrill D. Peterson. New York: Penguin, 1975, 262.

Jones, Howard. *Mutiny on the Amistad: The Saga of a Slave Revolt and Its Impact on American Abolition, Law and Diplomacy.* New York: Oxford University Press, 1988.

Kettner, James H. *The Development of American Citizenship, 1608–1870.* Chapel Hill: University of North Carolina Press, 1978.

Lawrence, Alexander A. *James Moore Wayne, Southern Unionist.* Chapel Hill: University of North Carolina Press, 1934.

Leslie, William R. "A Study in the Origins of Interstate Rendition: The Big Beaver Creek Murders." *American Historical Review* 57 (1951): 63–76.

Lewis, H. H. Walker. *Without Fear or Favor: A Biography of Chief Justice Roger Brooke Taney.* Boston: Houghton Mifflin, 1965.

Lightner, David. *Slavery and the Commerce Power: How the Struggle against the Interstate Slave Trade Led to the Civil War.* New Haven: Yale University Press, 2006.

"Lincoln's Rejoinder in the Charleston Joint Debate." http://lincoln.lib.niu.edu/cgi-bin/philologic/getobject.pl?c.2222:3.lincoln. Accessed April 27, 2009.

Maltz, Earl M. *Dred Scott and the Politics of Slavery.* Lawrence: University Press of Kansas, 2007.

————. *The Fourteenth Amendment and the Law of the Constitution.* Durham, N.C.: Carolina Academic Press, 2003.

————. "The Last Angry Man: Benjamin Robbins Curtis and the *Dred Scott* Case." *Chicago-Kent Law Review* 82 (2007): 265–276.

————. "Majority, Concurrence and Dissent: *Prigg v. Pennsylvania* and the Structure of Supreme Court Decisionmaking." *Rutgers Law Journal* 31 (2000): 345–398.

————. "Slavery, Federalism and the Constitution: *Ableman v. Booth* and the Struggle over Fugitive Slaves." *Cleveland State Law Review* 56 (2007): 83–110.

Mason, Matthew. *Slavery and Politics in the Early American Republic.* Chapel Hill: University of North Carolina Press, 2006.

Mayfield, John. *Rehearsal for Republicanism: Free Soil and the Politics of Anti-Slavery.* Port Washington, N.Y.: Kennikat Press, 1980.

"The McClintock Riots: June 2, 1847." http://chronicles.dickinson.edu/encyclo/m/ed_mcClintockriot.htm, Accessed April 27, 2009.

McCloskey, Robert G. *The American Supreme Court.* Chicago: University of Chicago Press, 1961.

Meriweather, Robert L., et al., eds. *The Papers of John C. Calhoun.* Columbia: University of South Carolina Press, 1959–2003.

Merk, Frederick. *The Oregon Question: Essays in Anglo-American Diplomacy and Politics.* Cambridge, Mass.: Belknap Press, 1967.

―――. *Slavery and the Annexation of Texas.* New York: Alfred A. Knopf, 1972.

Miller, William Lee. *Arguing about Slavery: The Great Battle in the United States Congress.* New York: A. A. Knopf, 1996.

Moore, Glover. *The Missouri Controversy, 1819–1821.* Lexington: University of Kentucky Press, 1953.

Morris, Thomas D. *Free Men All: The Personal Liberty Laws of the North, 1780–1861.* Baltimore: Johns Hopkins University Press, 1974.

Morrison, Chaplain W. *Democratic Politics and Sectionalism: The Wilmot Proviso Controversy.* Chapel Hill: University of North Carolina Press, 1967.

Morrison, Michael A. *Slavery and the American West: The Eclipse of Manifest Destiny and the Coming of the Civil War.* Chapel Hill: University of North Carolina Press, 1997.

"Mr. Douglas's Opening Speech." http://lincoln.lib.niu.edu/cgi-bin/philologic/getobject.pl?c.2221:1.lincoln. Accessed April 27, 2009.

"Mr. Douglas's Reply in the Freeport Joint Debate." http://lincoln.lib.niu.edu/cgi-bin/philologic/getobject.pl?c.2224:2.lincoln. Accessed April 27, 2009.

"Mr. Lincoln's Opening Speech." http://lincoln.lib.niu.edu/cgi-bin/philologic/getobject.pl?c.2224:1.lincoln. Accessed April 27, 2009.

"Mr. Lincoln's Reply in the Ottawa Joint Debate." http://lincoln.lib.niu.edu/cgi-bin/philologic/getobject.pl?c.2221:2.lincoln. Accessed April 27, 2009.

Nettels, Curtis. "The Mississippi Valley and the Federal Judiciary, 1807–1837." *Mississippi Valley Historical Review* 12 (1925): 202–226.

Newmyer, R. Kent. *Supreme Court Justice Joseph Story: Statesman of the Old Republic.* Chapel Hill: University of North Carolina Press, 1985.

Niven, John. *Salmon P. Chase: A Biography.* New York: Oxford University Press, 1995.

Noonan, John T. *The Antelope: The Ordeal of the Recaptured Africans in the Administrations of James Monroe and John Quincy Adams.* Berkeley: University of California Press, 1977.

Owen, William A. *Black Mutiny: The Revolt on the Schooner Amistad.* Cleveland: Pilgrim Press, 1997.

Paley, Ruth. "Imperial Politics and English Law: The Many Contexts of Somerset." *Law and History Review* 24 (2006): 659–664.

Petersen, Svend. *A Statistical History of American Presidential Elections.* New York: Ungar, 1963.

Pletcher, David M. *The Diplomacy of Annexation: Texas, Oregon, and the Mexican War.* Columbia: University of Missouri Press, 1973.

Porter, Kirk H., and Donald Bruce Johnson, comp. *National Party Platforms, 1840–1964.* Urbana: University of Illinois Press, 1966.

Potter, David M. *The Impending Crisis, 1848–1861.* New York: Harper & Row, 1976.

"Proceedings of the Borough of Norfolk, on the Boston Outrage, in the Case of the Runaway Slave George Latimer." In *Fugitive Slaves and American Courts: The Pamphlet Literature,* ed. Paul Finkelman. 4 vols. New York: Garland, 1988, 1:211–230.

Rayback, Joseph G. *Free Soil: The Election of 1848.* Lexington: University of Kentucky Press, 1970.

Remini, Robert V. *Andrew Jackson and the Bank War.* New York: W. W. Norton, 1967.

———. *Martin Van Buren and the Making of the Republican Party.* New York: W. W. Norton, 1970.

"A Report of the Case of the Jeune Eugenie, Determined in the Circuit of the United States, for the First Circuit, at Boston, December, 1821." In *The African Slave Trade and American Courts: The Pamphlet Literature,* ed. Paul Finkelman. 2 vols. New York: Garland, 1988, 1:31–144.

Richards, Leonard L. *The California Gold Rush and the Coming of the Civil War.* New York: Knopf, 2007.

———. The *Slave Power: The Free North and Southern Domination, 1780–1860.* Baton Rouge: Louisiana State University Press, 2000.

Richardson, James D., comp. *A Compilation of the Messages and Papers of the Presidents, 1789–1902.* Washington, D.C.: Bureau of National Literature and Art, 1904.

Robinson, Donald L. *Slavery in the Structure of American Politics, 1765–1820.* New York: Harcourt Brace Jovanovich, 1971.

Roper, David M. *Mr. Justice Thompson and the Constitution.* New York: Garland, 1987.

Rosenberg, Gerald N. *The Hollow Hope: Can Courts Bring about Social Change?* Chicago: University of Chicago Press, 1993.

Saunders, Robert, Jr. *John Archibald Campbell, Southern Moderate, 1811–1889.* Tuscaloosa: University of Alabama Press, 1997.

Sellers, Charles G. *James K. Polk, Continentalist 1843–1846.* Princeton: Princeton University Press, 1966.

Sewell, Richard H. *Ballots for Freedom: Antislavery Politics in the United States, 1837–1860.* New York: Oxford University Press, 1976.

Silbey, Joel H., ed. *American Party Battle: Election Campaign Pamphlets, 1828–1876.* 2 vols. Cambridge, Mass.: Harvard University Press, 1999.

———. *Storm over Texas: The Annexation Controversy and the Road to Civil War.* New York: Oxford University Press, 2005.

"The Slavery Question, or the Rights and the Union of the States." *American Law Journal* (April 1850): 9–21.

Smith, Barbara Holden. "Lords of Lash, Loom, and Law: Justice Story, Slavery, and *Prigg v. Pennsylvania.*" *Cornell Law Review* 78 (1993): 1086–1151.

Smith, Justin H. *The Annexation of Texas.* New York: AMS Press, 1971.

Smith, Rogers M. *Civic Ideals: Conflicting Visions of Citizenship in U.S. History.* New Haven: Yale University Press, 1997.

Stampp, Kenneth M. *America in 1857: A Nation on the Brink.* New York: Oxford University Press, 1992.

Stegmaier, Mark J. *Texas, New Mexico, and the Compromise of 1850: Boundary Dispute and Sectional Crisis.* Kent, Ohio: Kent State University Press, 1996.

Story, Joseph. *Commentaries on the Constitution of the United States: With a Preliminary View of the Constitutional History of the Colonies and States, before the Adoption of the Constitution.* 2 vols. Boston: Little Brown, 1858.

Story, William W., ed. *Life and Letters of Joseph Story.* 2 vols. London: Little Brown, 1851.

Streichler, Stuart. *Justice Curtis in the Civil War Era: At the Crossroads of American Constitutionalism.* Charlottesville: University of Virginia Press, 2005.

Swisher, Carl B. *History of the Supreme Court, Volume 5: The Taney Period, 1836–64.* New York: Macmillan, 1974.

———. *Roger B. Taney.* New York: Macmillan, 1935.

Sydnor, Charles. *Slavery in Mississippi.* Baton Rouge: Louisiana State University Press, 1966.

Van Cleve, George. "Mansfield's Decision: Toward Human Freedom." *Law and History Review* 24 (2006): 665–671.

———. "Somerset's Case and Its Antecedents in Imperial Perspective." *Law and History Review* 24 (2006): 601–646.

Vandervelde, Lea, and Sandhya Subramanian. "Mrs. Dred Scott." *Yale Law Journal* 106 (1997): 1033–1122.

Von Frank, Albert J. *The Trials of Anthony Burns: Freedom and Slavery in Emerson's Boston.* Cambridge, Mass.: Harvard University Press, 1998.

Warren, Charles. *The Supreme Court in United States History.* Littleton, Colo.: Fred B. Rothman, 1987.

Waugh, John C. *On the Brink of Civil War: The Compromise of 1850 and How It Changed the Course of American History.* Wilmington, Del.: Scholarly Resources, 2003.

Wechsler, Herbert. "Toward Neutral Principles of Constitutional Law." *Harvard Law Review* 73 (1959): 1–35.

Weisenburger, Francis P. *The Life of John McLean: A Politician on the United States Supreme Court.* Columbus: Ohio State University Press, 1937.

White, G. Edward. *History of the Supreme Court of the United States, Volumes 3–4: The Marshall Court and Cultural Change, 1815–1835.* New York: Macmillan, 1988.

Wiecek, William M. "Slavery and Abolition before the United States Supreme Court, 1820–1860." *Journal of American History* 65 (1978): 34–59.

———. "*Somerset:* Lord Mansfield and the Legitimacy of Slavery in the Anglo-American World." *University of Chicago Law Review* 42 (1976): 86–146.

———. *The Sources of Antislavery Constitutionalism in America, 1760–1848.* Ithaca, N.Y.: Cornell University Press, 1977.

Wilentz, Sean. *The Rise of American Democracy: Jefferson to Lincoln.* New York: W. W. Norton, 2005.

Wilson, Carol. *Freedom at Risk: The Kidnapping of Free Blacks in America, 1780–1865.* Lexington: University of Kentucky Press, 1994.

Wilson, Clyde N., and Shirley B. Cook, eds. *The Papers of John C. Calhoun.* Columbia: University of South Carolina Press, 2001.

Wiltse, Charles M. *John C. Calhoun, Sectionalist.* Indianapolis: Bobbs Merrill, 1951.

Wolff, Gerald W. *The Kansas-Nebraska Bill: Party, Section, and the Coming of the Civil War.* New York: Revisionist Press, 1977.

Index